Complexity and Healthcare Organization

A view from the street

Edited by

David Kernick

General Practitioner
Exeter

Foreword by

Helen Bevan

Director, Innovation & Knowledge Group
NHS Modernisation Agency

D1089588

Radcliffe Medical Press
Oxford • San Francisco

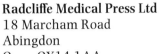

Radcliffe Medical Press Ltd
18 Marcham Road
Abingdon
Oxon OX14 1AA
United Kingdom

www.radcliffe-oxford.com
The Radcliffe Medical Press electronic catalogue and online ordering facility.
Direct sales to anywhere in the world.

British Library Cataloguing in Publication Data

A catalogue record for this book is available from the British Library.

ISBN 1 85775 814 5

Typeset by Aarontype Ltd, Easton, Bristol
Printed and bound by TJ International Ltd, Padstow, Cornwall

Contents

Foreword   vii

About this book   ix

List of contributors   xi

Prologue: a view from the street   xv

Section 1:   Getting to grips with the basics   1

Introduction   1

1   Models, metaphors and paradigms: making sense of the world
and the road to complexity   3
David Kernick

2   Chaos theory and its relationship to complexity   13
David Kernick

3   An introduction to complexity theory   23
David Kernick

Section 2:   The spectrum of how we think about
organizations   39

Introduction   39

4   An introduction to systems theory: from hard to soft systems
thinking in the management of complex organizations   43
John Powell

5   Organizations as learning systems   59
Huw Davies and Sandra Nutley

6 Making sense of organizational change in practice: change as   69
   complex responsive processes
   Jo Poole

**Section 3:   Complexity perspectives on healthcare   81
              organization**

Introduction   81

7 Complexity and the development of organizational theory   83
   David Kernick

8 The search for the correct organizational solution for the NHS   93
   David Kernick

9 Organizational culture and complexity   105
   David Kernick

10 Leadership and change   117
   David Kernick

**Section 4:   Facilitating emergence in healthcare   129
              organizations**

Introduction   129

11 Allocating limited healthcare resources   131
   David Kernick

12 Improving patient access in a large medical practice: a complex   143
   and complicated system problem
   Will Liddell and John Powell

13 Agent-based working: a device for systemic dialogue   159
   Sean Boyle and Julian Pratt

14 Using the visual arts to facilitate emergence in organizations   171
   Julian Burton

15 Using the performing arts to facilitate emergence in   181
   organizations
   Marian Naidoo and Shaun Naidoo

Section 5: Going on together in organizations: 189
perspectives on healthcare provision

Introduction   189

16 **Progressing clinical governance through complexity:**   191
     from managing to co-creating
     Kieran Sweeney

17 **Skill mix in the NHS: adaptability or efficiency?**   205
     David Kernick

18 **Adaptation in action: the NHS Modernisation Agency's Critical**   217
     Care Programme
     Ceri Brown

19 **Educating the healthcare professional for capability**   227
     Jim Price

Section 6:   Going on together in organizations: 241
perspectives on whole systems

Introduction   241

20 **Social networks in organizations: social capital and health**   245
     Tim Wilson

21 **Organization and communities of practice**   255
     Alasdair Honeyman

22 **Imagining complex partnerships**   265
     Will Medd

Section 7: From theory to action: personal perspectives   275

Introduction   275
Sarah Fraser

23 Community regeneration and complexity 279
Robin Durie, Katrina Wyatt and Hazel Stuteley

24 Running an organization along complexity lines 289
Peter Fryer

25 Whole-systems working in practice: this house is for real 299
Barbara Douglas, Pat Gordon and Julian Pratt

26 Complex adaptive systems: interesting theory or useful practice? 311
The Piedmont Hospital Bed Control Experiment
Leigh Hamby, Laura Day and Sarah Fraser

27 Applying complexity theory to primary healthcare organizations 323
Paul Thomas

28 Using complexity science in community health promotion: novel 335
perspectives and a tool for change
Vivian S Rambihar

Epilogue: being vaguely right rather than precisely wrong 347

Appendix 1: Some complexity metaphors 349

Appendix 2: Cynefin domains 351

Glossary of complexity terms 353

Useful resources 357

Index 359

Foreword

Problems cannot be solved at the level of thinking that produced them.
(Albert Einstein)

Within our healthcare system, a radical evaluation is taking place. This will have a profound effect on the way care is perceived, organised and delivered in the future.

We are moving from a world where care is primarily based on the decisions of professionals and organisations to a world where care is customised and tailored according to individual needs and patient decisions. In the old world, performance is improved by top-down management-driven changes. In the new world, frontline clinical teams will have the power, responsibility and freedom to constantly improve their own performance. In the old world, patients are seen in places and in ways that are organised around the needs of the service. In the new world, patient time is valued. Patients can gain access to healthcare through a variety of means, times and places that are convenient to them. In the old world, care is often episodic and isolated, delivered through separate organisational units. In the new world, care is continuing and integrated, focusing on the patient's journey through the whole system of health and social care. We are moving from a world where the safety of patients, carers and staff is an individual responsibility to one where safety is seen as the responsibility of the whole system of healthcare.

Underpinning this direction is a shift away from the rational models that have traditionally dominated the way that we think about health, healthcare, organisation and service delivery. Our prevalent performance improvement approach is to isolate a problem, diagnose it at the level of the smallest possible part and find a solution. The unfortunate side-effect of this approach is that we often amplify the problems and create more. Our traditional ways of thinking may even be the root cause of many of the problems currently facing healthcare.

The study of complexity gives us inspiration and understanding that we require for our brave new world. It encourages us to focus on deep patterns and relationship building between the parts of the system; on values and culture; and on truly engaging our workforce in decision making and change. Complexity provides radical new perspectives on the patient and clinician encounter, clinical teams, the organisation of care and the wider health and social care system.

As this book demonstrates, many healthcare practitioners, leaders and researchers, motivated by the insights that the complexity perspective can bring, are developing new perspectives on the complex world of healthcare and are introducing new ways of practicing healthcare.

The emerging field of complexity can help service users, healthcare practitioners and organisations progress and prosper, despite the uncertainty and complexity of their worlds. This book clearly advances the cause!

Helen Bevan
Director, Innovation & Knowledge Group
NHS Modernisation Agency
February 2004

About this book

Who is it directed at?

All those who are involved in the planning, management, commissioning and delivery of healthcare.

What are its aims?

- To describe new insights that arise from the study of chaos and complexity theory.
- To explore how these insights can help us understand organizations, with an emphasis on healthcare organizations.

Where is it coming from?

This book is orchestrated from the 'swampy lowlands' of healthcare where life is not always about cosy certainties like evidence-based healthcare, economic studies and rational policy making. The focus is on the patterns of relationships within an organization, how they are sustained, how they self-organize and how outcomes emerge.

Who is the editor?

David Kernick started life as a chemical engineer but has been a general practitioner for the past 20 years. He is lead research GP in a practice that receives funding from the NHS Research & Development Executive.

His interests are in three areas. Firstly, addressing the gap between health economic theory and the realities of healthcare resource allocation. Secondly, the application of complexity theory insights to problems in healthcare. Thirdly, as

Vice Chairman of the British Association for the Study of Headache, the development of headache services in primary care.

As Medical Officer to Exeter City Football Club, he has supported their struggle to stay in the Third Division of the Football League for a number of years, alas unsuccessful in 2003.

List of contributors

Sean Boyle
Senior Research Fellow
Health & Social Care
London School of Economics

Ceri Brown
Consultant in Intensive Care
On secondment to NHS Modernisation Agency
Critical Care Programme
Leicester

Julian Burton
Organizational Consultant
London

Huw Davies
Professor of Health Care Policy & Management
Director, Centre for Public Policy & Management
Department of Management
University of St Andrews

Laura Day
Bed Control Nurse
Piedmont Hospital
NW Atlanta, GA, USA

Barbara Douglas
A Better Life in Later Life
Newcastle Healthy City Project
Newcastle-upon-Tyne

Robin Durie
Health Complexity Group
Peninsula Medical School
Exeter

Sarah Fraser
Independent Consultant
Visiting Professor, Middlesex University
Aylesbury
Bucks

Peter Fryer
Management Consultant – trojanmice
Hull

Pat Gordon
Urban Partnerships Group
Department of Operational Research & Decision Science
London School of Economics

Leigh Hamby
Vice President of Systems Improvement
Piedmont Hospital
NW Atlanta, GA, USA

Alasdair Honeyman
General Practitioner, Organizational Consultant & Executive Coach
Lambeth Walk Group Practice
London

David Kernick
General Practitioner
St Thomas' Health Centre
Exeter

Will Liddell
General Practitioner
Frome Medical Practice
Somerset

Will Medd
Research Fellow
Centre for Sustainable Urban & Regional Futures
Institute for Public Health Research & Policy
University of Salford

Marian Naidoo
Complexity & Creativity R&D Leads
Naidoo Associates
Wiltshire

Shaun Naidoo
Complexity & Creativity R&D Leads
Naidoo Associates
Wiltshire

Sandra Nutley
Reader in Public Policy & Management
Department of Management
University of St Andrews

Jo Poole
Nurse Practitioner
PCT Board Nurse & Research Student
Centre for Research in Primary Health Care
University of Hertfordshire

John Powell
Chair of Strategy
School of Management
University of Bath

Julian Pratt
Urban Partnerships Group
Department of Operational Research & Decision Science
London School of Economics

Jim Price
General Practitioner
Senior Lecturer in Primary Care
Postgraduate Medical School
University of Brighton

Vivian S Rambihar
Founder, Fractal Heart Foundation
Consultant Cardiologist
The Scarborough Hospital
Toronto, Canada

Hazel Stuteley
Health Visitor & Research Fellow
Health Complexity Group
Peninsula Medical School
Exeter

Kieran Sweeney
General Practitioner
Health Complexity Group
Peninsula Medical School
Exeter

Paul Thomas
Professor of Primary Care Research, Education & Development
Thames Valley University

Tim Wilson
General Practitioner & Policy Advisor
Department of Health Strategy Unit

Katrina Wyatt
Research Fellow
Health Complexity Group
Peninsula Medical School
Exeter

Prologue:
a view from the street

The history of the National Health Service (NHS) has been a continual search for the right organizational solution and the failure to find one. In the sunny uplands, policy makers remain oblivious to the fact that organizations just don't do as they are told. That everything is connected to everything else and every action causes uncertain effects in unanticipated parts of the system. Academics develop organizational models that are recycled without convergence to any workable framework, accompanied by a burgeoning literature whose impact upon service provision is barely perceptible. Perhaps organizations would manage just as well without the plethora of organizational theory?

In the swampy lowlands, managers muddle through, not seeking a solution to their seemingly intractable problems but hoping for means of coping with the messes in which they find themselves. Against a background of policy ambiguity, mutually exclusive objectives, historical precedent and limited room for manoeuvre, relating ends to means is highly problematic. They find themselves in charge but not in control. In many cases, doing something is better than doing nothing and becomes an end in itself. Healthcare practitioners struggle to mediate between the potential of science and the predicament of the individual in a world that contains anything but cosy certainties like evidence-based medicine and health economics.

Traditional organization models have drawn upon the physical sciences, proceeding on the confident assumption that their laws are the same, always and everywhere. The metaphor is the machine – predictable, composed of the sum of its component parts, and engineered towards a defined objective by a controller outside the system.

Converging from a number of disciplines, complexity theory draws upon the fundamental organizing principles of nature. It sees the world as a system (a network of elements that interact with each other and their environment) that is non-linear (there is not a straightforward relationship between cause and effect) and dynamic (changing continually with time and influenced by what has gone before). Organizations are viewed as structures that not only bring people together to discharge specific functions but also places where people make sense of their lives. The metaphor changes from machine to an ecosystem of co-evolving parts. The focus is on the patterns of relationships within an organization, how they are sustained, how they self-organize and how outcomes emerge. It is a perspective that resonates with the experience of those who work in the healthcare system.

Like the majority of contributors to this book, I am a healthcare practitioner struggling to come to terms with the implications of complexity theory and the insights it offers organizational sense making and the management of change. This book is a personal perspective at one point in that evolving journey. A collection of contributions edited in a way that does not conform to any particular academic canon or claim to expertise, but in a way that seems to make sense to me.

David Kernick
February 2004

Section I

Getting to grips with
the basics

Introduction

We need to make sense of the world and act. Chapter 1 explores how we do this using models and metaphors; and how these are packaged into disciplinary frameworks known as paradigms that in turn can exert a hold on how we view the world.

The classical or Newtonian approach has been the dominant paradigm within Western thought and traces its origins to the time of the enlightenment. It proceeds on the confident assumption that there are physical laws based on simple relationships between cause and effect that govern the behaviour of all natural systems. Individual knowledge of all the parts of a system add up to an understanding of the system as a whole and given its initial conditions, any future state can be predicted. When this approach is not applicable, systems are seen as exhibiting unpredictable random behaviour that can be described by statistical methods. However, neither of these two ideals occurs in the natural world. Most systems have features of both randomness and order and it is here that the study of chaos and complexity sits.

Despite considerable effort, ideas derived from classical science have had limited success when applied to human organizations. Structures like the NHS do not behave predictably and seem reluctant to be engineered towards desired objectives. Neither do they behave in a random manner. In many ways, organizations seem to have a life of their own and theories derived from chaos and complexity may offer us some useful insights into aspects of organizational behaviour.

However, these new theories have been compared to 'theological concepts' – lots of people talk about them but no one knows what they really mean. A major difficulty is that complexity science draws upon developments across a diverse number of disciplines, each with their own interpretation. Academics jostle to champion their particular perspectives and, inevitably, definitions and, conceptual themes remain contested.

Of particular contention is the relationship between chaos and complexity theory. Most books on complexity do not include a discussion of chaos theory. It is seen either as unhelpful or a sub-discipline of complexity theory. I find it a useful starting point as it helps to understand the concept of non-linearity, which for me is the essential feature of complex systems. Although many experts would not agree, I find it helpful from an organizational perspective to see chaos theory as the quantitative study of dynamic non-linear systems (systems that change with time, are dependent on what has gone before and have an uncertain relationship between cause and effect). Complexity theory is the qualitative study, drawing upon metaphors derived from chaos theory.

Chapter 2 explores chaos theory and the concept of non-linearity. The faint-hearted can move straight to Chapter 3 where we explore the fundamental concepts of complexity theory that are applied throughout this book.

CHAPTER 1

Models, metaphors and paradigms: making sense of the world and the road to complexity

David Kernick

Those who take for their standard anyone but nature weary themselves in vain.
(Leonardo da Vinci)

This chapter explores how we use models and metaphors to make sense of the world and act. It sets complexity in the evolving story of scientific thinking, from modern science, that traces its origins to the time of the enlightenment, through post-modernism to complexity science.

Key points
- Models create reality around bundles of related assumptions that help us make sense of the world and act.
- The use of metaphor offers insights that can be lost when we construct models.
- Models and metaphors are consolidated into disciplinary frameworks known as paradigms. Paradigms can exert a deep hold on how we view the world.
- Despite many successes, the paradigm of modern science has been limited in its ability to predict and control the behaviour of human organizations.
- Complexity science is the study of dynamic, non-linear systems. The model is a network of co-evolving elements where changes in one element can change the context for all other elements. This has profound implications for how we view organizations.

- The metaphor for understanding organizations changes from machine to ecosystem.
- Complexity aims to complement modern science, not overturn it.

Making sense of the world using models

As humans we have a recollection of the past and an anticipation of the future. Sense making allows us to make the connection and act. To do so we simplify the world by constructing models, creating reality around 'bundles of related assumptions'. We look for patterns in our experience while classifying them into categories. We also look for patterns in the interactions between categories, searching for relationships and regularities.[1] Philosophers struggle to reconcile what's out there with our internal representations without agreement – models are always approximations of the real world.

Models help us to address two questions:

- the descriptive element – what is happening, what will happen?
- the prescriptive element – how can we make what we want happen?

Our models powerfully influence how evidence is collected, analysed and understood. At an individual level, we create tacit models or knowledge by reflecting on our experience and comparing it with our expectations, continually rethinking our ideas on causation and intervention. We operate according to these internal mental models that are often below the level of consciousness. They represent the rules for how we order and categorize information and how we respond to our environment. They form our knowledge – how we process and act upon information presented to us. For example, practitioners usually know more than they can say. They reveal a capacity for reflection on intuitive knowledge in the midst of action and use this tacit capacity to cope with the unique uncertain and conflicting situations of practice.[2] However, when models are implicit, their potential to confuse or obscure new insights can go unnoticed.

Models can also be explicit and shared. Knowledge management is currently an important concept in organizational theory and a recurring theme in this book within the context of 'learning organizations'. The contention is that individual knowledge is largely unknown to others and therefore wasted. The aim is to capture and share this knowledge for the benefit of the whole organization.

Table 1.1 shows some differences between tacit and explicit models or knowledge.

Table 1.1 Some characteristics of tacit and explicit models or knowledge

Tacit models or knowledge	*Explicit models or knowledge*
• Practical and subjective. Focuses on how to do it	• Theoretical and objective. States what to do
• Engrained in the analytical and conceptual understanding of individuals	• Codified in terms of facts, rules and policies
• Created by clinicians, patients and managers	• Created by researchers
• Often captured in narrative or stories	• Invariably quantified in mathematical models or diagrammatic frameworks
• Rarely published or described	• Published in scientific journals
• Locally relevant	• Generalizable
• Traditionally of low value	• Traditionally high value
• Resides within a network of socially constructed relationships and shared through respect and trust	• Constrained within a hierarchical structure and shared within a power differential

In organizations, our shared models are constructed and maintained in symbols that we offer each other. These symbols can be artifactual (for example, organization strategies, documents, uniforms) or communicative, mainly through the use of language. We also design spaces for the creation of our ideas. These symbols and the design of spaces for the creation and interchange of our symbols not only allow us to explore our organizational possibilities but also to place boundaries on them. However, we need to be aware that different organizational cultures may have differing symbolic interpretations. Within organizational contexts, we might also anticipate dysfunctional consequences when there is a dissonance between future expectations derived from our own sense-making models and expectations imposed upon us within a bureaucratic structure derived from different models.

Models need to have external consistency (i.e. they have predictive value) and internal consistency (i.e. they are compatible with other models). Studies in stroke victims suggest that model making is reflected in brain architecture. The left hemisphere creates a model that it maintains at all costs whereas the right hemisphere detects anomalies and forces the left hemisphere to revise it, maintaining internal consistency.[3]

One way we test and share our models is through the use of narrative or storytelling.* We create our realities with the same motives, themes and structure as fiction. Our culture binds us by a set of connecting stories.[4] Perhaps

---

* A useful introduction to the importance of narrative and in particular its application in clinical practice is given by Greenhalgh (Greenhalgh T and Hurwitz B (1998) *Narrative-based Medicine: dialogue and discourse in clinical practice*. BMJ Books, London).

through storytelling we modulate the creative tension between our right and left brains as our models are formed and reformed.

Making sense of the world using metaphor

Because models simplify reality they often lose intuitive insights and the use of metaphor helps to retain this information. Metaphor brings together two areas of experience, treating one as if it had the features of the other applied to it. Metaphor can organize our patterns of thinking as we both reflect and interact with each other, helping us to grasp reality in clearer terms. It offers a framework to think and act differently. Aristotle wrote: 'ordinary words convey what we know already; it is from metaphor that we can get hold of something fresh.'

For example, sense making has been described in terms of the metaphor of cartography.[5] There is no one best map of any particular terrain – the ground is not already mapped. What sort of map is made depends on where cartographers look, how they look and what tools they have for representation. Map making tends to be social – we construct our maps through our relationships with others through the use of symbolic communication.

How we understand and behave in our organizations is reflected in the metaphors we use to describe them. For example, Morgan[6] offers a range of metaphorical interpretations ranging from machines to organisms, from brains to psychic prisons. However, metaphor has the potential to mislead if applied inappropriately as the following example demonstrates.

In 1998, in response to disappointing waiting-list statistics, the Secretary of State for Health, Frank Dobson, stated: *'I said last year that the waiting lists were like a supertanker. It would take time to slow them down, longer to bring them to a stop, and even longer to turn them around.'*[7] The explicit use of the metaphor 'supertanker' for 'NHS waiting lists' suggests many associations. A vessel with a large amount of inertia trying to change direction against resistance; a system that can be engineered by a directive from a captain on the bridge steering the ship to a new course. It brings an easier understanding of the situation than a complex statement on the differential rate of change of the waiting-list figures. The prescription for action followed, in 'a firm hand at the wheel'.* We will see in Section 3 how the use of this metaphor is illuminating for being so precisely wrong and how waiting lists form a complex network of interacting parts where changes in one part of the system can have unintended consequences in another and no one can be in overall control.

---

* I am indebted to Ceri Brown for alerting me to this example.

Metaphor is a recurring theme throughout this book, but we must be alert for inappropriate transfer of attributes from one domain to another. There is always a trade-off between the generation of new insights and misappropriation. This is particularly relevant for healthcare organization.

The consolidation of models and metaphors within paradigms

Traditionally, model building was seen as the product of a collective human enterprise to which all scientists make co-operative contributions. The goal, to develop a consensus of rational opinion over a wide field with the aim of developing an increasingly accurate model of the real world out there. This approach has been called logical positivism.

In 1962, Thomas Kuhn challenged this perception in the most cited work of the twentieth century.[8] He argued that rather than moving forward on a broad front, scientific disciplines consolidate their world-views into rigid conceptual boxes of models and metaphors called paradigms. This results in a strenuous attempt to force nature into the accepted disciplinary framework of a 'normal science'. There is a cessation of critical debate amongst the community and the accepted models remain largely unquestioned. Kuhn argued that the time to rethink the appropriateness of a paradigm is when it becomes less able to answer the questions asked of it. Rarely, periods of revolutionary science occur in which existing paradigms are unable to accommodate new insights and a discontinuity or paradigm shift occurs.

We are all influenced by our own paradigms, consolidated by our professional associations and the language we use. Our paradigms are embedded within our interactions and mental models. They tell us what is important and legitimate and, to some extent, make action possible. However, they can restrict our capacity to accommodate new ideas.

In the remainder of this chapter we plot the evolution of three important paradigms from modern or normal science, through post-modernism to complexity or post-normal science.

The paradigm of modern or normal science

In the enlightenment that began in the late eighteenth century, a confident assumption developed that the application of reason would purge the residues

---

Box 1.1   Elements of the 'modern' approach

- Linear – there is a simple relationship between inputs and outputs. Small inputs have small effects, large inputs have large effects.
- Reductionist – systems can be understood by breaking them down into their component parts.
- Deterministic – the future of a system can be predicted with certainty.
- Analytical – as the future can be predicted, problems can be formulated as the making of a rational choice between alternative means of achieving a known end. More information leads to a more accurate analysis.
- Impartiality – an observer can stand outside the system without being influenced by it and engineer it towards defined objectives.

---

of religion and mysticism that had directed previous world-views. Human progress was to be achieved through a programme that extended scientific knowledge and technical control to all aspects of society. The metaphor for modern science was to be the machine, underpinned by Newtonian classical physics.

The essential characteristics of this approach are shown in Box 1.1.

In this model of a 'clockwork universe', the belief is that there is a single universal condition that can be validated and which accumulates with time, building on what has gone before. Areas of ignorance are seen merely as puzzles waiting to be solved. The analysis of complicated systems needs complicated rules and when these do not yield the required results, even more rules must be created. Approximations and statistical manipulations are used to adjust for discrepancies while predictive limitations are viewed as data or processing inadequacies, omissions, bias or randomness.

With the confident assumption that the methods of science would transcend the social and cultural forces that had previously shaped world-views, the modern era and with it 'the paradigm of certainty' had arrived.

The challenge to modern science from post-modernism

The Newtonian approach of modern or normal science demanded the directives of classical physics. However, in the 1920s quantum physics defined the fundamental limits of our ability to describe systems and predict events. Arising from these concerns, post-modernism emphasized the process of knowing and the importance of how our minds form an integral part of that process. To the post-modern eye, the truth is not out there waiting to be revealed but something constructed by people, always provisional and contingent on context and power. Any description of reality is an ever-changing approximation which, as we make it more real, slips from our grasp. There are no certainties, only multiple perspectives. Different today from yesterday, different again tomorrow.

The paradigm of post-normal or complexity science

Complexity thinking or the study of dynamic non-linear systems grew out of the observations that there are many phenomena that modern scientific analysis could not adequately describe or predict. In particular, dogmatic attempts to address social systems often characterized by ambiguity and indeterminacy had been found wanting. For example, despite numerous attempts at reorganization, the national health system has never seemed to want to do as it is told by its political paymasters. The system seems to be inherently non-linear. Small inputs in one part of the system invariably have unanticipated and disproportional effects elsewhere.

Challenging the linear formulation of modern science and the restricted vision of post-modernism, complexity science sees disciplines as disparate as business, meteorology, ecology and politics converging to similar themes.

The complexity model

This model views the world as a network of interacting systems where change in any one element can alter the context for all other elements.* A network model is not new. However, the analytical focus has always been within the modern scientific paradigm with an emphasis on description at the aggregate level.

The complexity model sees systems as dynamic – they change with time in a way that is dependent on what has gone before, and non-linear – there can be disproportionate and unanticipated relationships between cause and effect. These characteristics arise from a fundamentally different notion of feedback that we shall turn to next.

The approach of modern science is to set a defined target output for a system. Changes in output are fed back and compared with the desired set point, and adjustments made to the system to maintain the output at the desired level.

---

*One interpretation is that complexity science offers an overarching 'meta-model'. Modern science is a special case and the nihilism of post-modernity merely a limited gaze – it's all there but you can only see one subspace at any one time.

For example, national waiting-list targets are set at government level and fed down through a number of performance-managed, hierarchical sub-systems. Waiting-list data is fed back to the Department of Health, which applies manipulations in terms of incentives or punishments in an attempt to maintain the desired target.

A complexity perspective views the NHS as a network of interacting elements. Changes in each system element influences its surrounding environment which in turn feeds back and influence the individual element. Although sub-systems can be identified as areas where there is a greater strength of connections, boundaries are less distinct. Feedback is seen as a reiterative process (i.e the output of one interaction is fed back and forms the input of the next in an incremental manner), occurring predominately at a local level. As we shall see in the next chapter, this leads to very different system behaviour than we would predict using traditional scientific thinking. For example, when a patient presents to me with a problem, communicative gestures and responses are fed back between us in a reiterative process. A decision to refer to hospital and thus influence waiting times may or may not emerge and will be influenced by a number of other factors. Over a longer time-scale, other patterns of behaviour evolve between myself and my local consultant colleagues due to reiterative feedback between us. Similar reiterative gestures occur amongst local hospital consultants and these patterns will in turn influence the local health community and potentially my consultation. In this way, complex non-linear patterns of behaviour emerge on the basis of reiterative feedback, predominately at a local level, but which have the potential to influence the whole system. For this reason, the mechanistic measures introduced by the government to influence waiting-list targets have not had the desired effect and, as we shall see in later chapters, evidence is forthcoming to suggest that a complexity model is a more accurate description of waiting-list behaviour.

Table 1.2 Some insights drawing upon machine and ecosystem metaphors

Machine (modern science)	*Ecosystem (complexity science)*
• The focus is on the characteristics of the individual parts.	• The focus is on the relationship between the parts.
• The system can be understood by breaking it down into its component parts.	• The system can only be understood as a whole.
• The future is predictable and can be controlled.	• The future is unpredictable but boundable.
• A change of one element of the system only affects those immediately close to it.	• A change of one element can alter the context for all other elements.
• The intelligence of the system resides in the mind of the designer.	• The intelligence of the system is distributed throughout it.

The complexity metaphor

Although complexity science offers a number of metaphors that are discussed in Chapter 3, a useful introduction is to compare the machine metaphor of modern science with a complexity metaphor of an ecosystem of co-evolving elements. Some important comparisons are shown in Table 1.2.

Conclusion

Our paradigms and the models and metaphors they contain form conceptual lenses through which we view the world. The themes underpinning complexity thinking are not new and have been debated for as long as knowledge has been recorded. What is new is a recognition of the limitations of modern science in many areas and the development of more appropriate analytical frameworks within which to understand non-linear, reiterative interactions and the system properties they infer.

The complexity approach is not without its detractors who see it as little more than intuition already contained in popular wisdom.[9] A misapplied metaphor, handy for the healthcare manager on an inadequate budget. Indeed, if models are approximations of reality and metaphors have the potential for misappropriation (particularly in complexity theory where metaphors are derived from many quite different disciplines), we must guard against becoming trapped in any one paradigm.

However, complexity does not seek to overturn modern science but to complement it – certain properties can be described by linear rules if they prove to be useful. It cautions that in many areas, descriptive and predictive power can only be obtained from standing back rather than attempting to analyse systems in more detail.

In the next chapter we will explore the concepts of non-linearity and reiterative feedback, with a brief description of chaos theory, before looking at complexity in more detail.

References

1 Stacey R (1996) *Strategic Management and Organisational Dynamics*. Pitman Publishing, London.
2 Schön D (1983) *The Reflective Practitioner*. Basic Books, New York.
3 Hammond K (2000) Coherence and correspondence. In: Connelly T, Arkes S and Hammond K (eds) *Theories in Judgement and Decision Making*, p. 57. Cambridge University Press, Cambridge.
4 Burner J (1989) *Acts of Meaning*. Harvard University Press, Cambridge.

5   Weick K (2001) *Making Sense of the Organisation*. Blackwell, Oxford.
6   Morgan G (1997) *Images of Organisation*. Sage, London.
7   Dobson F. Quoted in Hansard (1998) 18 May, Column 1291. The Stationery Office, London.
8   Kuhn T (1962) *The Structure of Scientific Revolutions*. University of Chicago Press, Chicago.
9   Marshall T (1999) Chaos and complexity. *British Journal of General Practice*. **49**: 234.

CHAPTER 2

Chaos theory and its relationship to complexity

David Kernick

This chapter introduces chaos theory and the concept of non-linearity. It highlights the importance of reiteration and the system features that arise from it. Although the relationship between chaos and complexity remains contested, chaos theory offers a useful starting point to understand complex systems.

Key points
- Chaos theory is the quantitative study of dynamic non-linear systems.
- Non-linear systems change with time and can demonstrate complex relationships between inputs and outputs due to reiterative feedback loops within the system.
- Providing sufficient computational power is available, these systems are predictable, but their behaviour is exquisitely sensitive to their starting point.
- Due to the complex nature of social systems, the mathematical application of chaos theory is limited to all but the simplest of systems.
- The relationship between chaos and complexity is contested. A useful starting point from an organizational perspective is to see complexity theory as the qualitative study of non-linear systems, drawing its metaphors from chaos theory.
- Health systems are non-linear. This has profound implications for analysis, prediction and control.

Introduction

The relationship between chaos and complexity theories is contested, which is not a useful start. The range of opinion includes: chaos is a sub-discipline of complexity; chaos and complexity are interchangeable and the distinction is arbitrary; the two phenomena have different origins and should not be considered together; the 'zone of complexity' sits at 'the edge of chaos'; the study of chaos is unhelpful and should be ignored. From an organizational perspective, I find the following model a useful starting point and one that makes sense to me:

> *Chaos and complexity theories study dynamic non-linear systems, i.e. systems that change with time and demonstrate complex relationships between inputs and outputs due to reiterative feedback loops within the systems. The quantitative study of these systems is chaos theory. Complexity theory is the qualitative aspect, drawing upon insights and metaphors that are derived from chaos theory.*

This book adopts that approach and this chapter explores the insights that chaos theory offers on the behaviour of non-linear systems.

What is non-linearity?

A non-linear system is one in which there is no simple relationship between cause and effect.* The main characteristics of non-linearity are:

- small inputs can have large system effects
- large inputs can lead to small system changes

---

*A variable changing in time in a linear manner allows simple prediction by adding a weighed sum of previous observations. A non-linear time series violates this simple assumption by including squares, cubes, etc. of previous terms or some more complex transformation such as the exponential. Prediction is still possible but needs much greater computational power. In more formal terms:

> Let x_1 and y_1 be respectively the input and output of a linear system ℓ. Let x_2 and y_2 be another pair of input and output of the same system ℓ. The output y corresponding to the combined linear sum of both inputs is proportional to the linear sum of the outputs corresponding to each of the inputs separately. In other words, if $y_1 = \ell(x_1)$ and $y_2 = \ell(x_2)$, then $y = \ell(\alpha x_1 + \beta x_2) = \alpha y_1 + \beta y_2$ where α and β are constants. In the case of non-linear systems, this does not hold.

There is extreme sensitivity of behaviour to initial conditions. Small changes in a variable in the system at one point will make a very large difference in the behaviour of a system at some future point. When error is introduced into a linear system, the prediction error stays relatively constant over time. For non-linear systems, prediction error increases rapidly with time. Due to our inability to measure initial system conditions accurately and the extreme sensitivity of non-linear systems' behaviour to these initial conditions, in practical terms, most natural non-linear systems are unpredictable.

What is chaos?

Unfortunately, the term 'chaos' is a misnomer and confusion arises from the outset over the common and mathematical interpretations of the term.* Chaotic behaviour appears random but when studied in a particular way, ordered features and patterns are discernible. Chaos can be understood by comparing it with two other types of behaviours – randomness and periodicity. These are shown in Box 2.1.

Box 2.1   What is chaos?

Chaos can be understood by comparing it with two other types of behaviour – randomness and periodicity.

Random behaviour never repeats itself although we can predict the average behaviour of a system using statistics.

Periodic behaviour is highly predictable because it always repeats itself, for example the swinging of a pendulum. Such systems are deterministic, i.e. if we know the conditions at any one point we can predict those conditions at any other point in time.

Chaos has characteristics of both behaviours. Although it looks disorganized like random behaviour, it is deterministic like periodic behaviour. However, the smallest difference in any system variable can make a very large difference to the future state of the system.

Chaotic systems are characterized by three key properties: predictability, extreme sensitivity to initial conditions and presence of an attractor or pattern of

---

*In the technical sense, the term chaos is used to denote a form of time evolution in dynamic systems in which the difference between two states that are initially very close grows exponentially with time. The Lyapunov exponent is a measure of this divergence and can be used to quantify chaotic systems.

behaviour. Chaotic patterns form the signature of non-linear behaviour that arises from recursive feedback among a system's components, i.e. the output of one stage feeds back into the input of the next. (This recursive or reiterative feature is critical to complex systems as it sets the focus of attention at a local level.) There are a number of approaches, both graphical and numerical, beyond the scope of this text to decide whether a system is chaotic or not. It is important to note that non-linear systems are not necessarily chaotic but non-linearity is prerequisite to chaos.

Although chaotic behaviour was suspected over a hundred years ago, it has only been the availability of computational power that has enabled scientists to probe the complex mathematical interior of non-linear equations. Over the last decade, the suspicion that chaos may play an important role in the functioning of living systems has been confirmed.[1,2] It seems that chaos is the healthy signature of physiology and during abnormal conditions such as a heart attack, systems revert to non-chaotic behaviour. The publication of James Gleick, *Chaos: making a new science*,[3] alerted a wider audience to the importance of an area that has now found applications as widespread as the study of the weather to the behaviour of stock markets.

In the next section, the concept of non-linearity and the road to chaotic behaviour is explored in more detail.

Non-linearity and the road to chaos

We first explore a basic non-linear equation. To do so we use a model of the population of fish in a pool, year on year. Where n is the number of fish in the pool in a given year and B is the birth rate, equation 1 shows a linear model to describe and predict events. (Although this equation describes an exponential curve, it is linear. Linear does not mean a straight line!)

Equation 1:
$$n_{(next\ year)} = B \cdot n_{(this\ year)}$$

However, a more realistic model is shown by equation 2, where n_{max} is the maximum number of fish that the pond can accommodate. As the fish numbers increase, the food supply reduces and the term $(n_{max} - n_{(this\ year)})$ is introduced as a reiterative feedback term.

Equation 2:
$$n_{(next\ year)} = B \cdot n_{(this\ year)} \cdot (n_{max} - n_{(this\ year)})$$

This introduces a non-linear term into the equation. (This simple feedback equation could be a starting point to explain behaviour in health systems. For

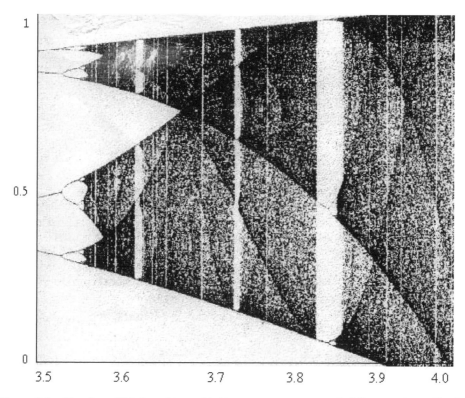

Figure 2.1   Number of fish found in pool 'n' in successive years with different values of birth rate B. x axis = birth rate; y axis = number of fish, $0 < n < 1$.

example, I refer patients to the physiotherapy department, but as the waiting list lengthens my referral rate is reduced. As patients are seen quicker, I refer more patients.)

We explore what happens year on year as we vary the birth rate B. To keep the sums simple, we take the maximum value of n as 1 and all values of n as proportions of 1. Figure 2.1 shows a record of the fish number that will be found in the pond for a given value of B.

For values of B under 3, the fish population converges or is attracted to a constant population (this is called a point attractor). However, when B reaches a value of 3, this attractor becomes unstable and splits or bifurcates into two – the population oscillates year on year around two stable values (a periodic attractor). (Bifurcation is the point in which there is an abrupt change in behaviour of a dynamic system that occurs when one of the parameters reaches a critical value.) As we increase the birth rate, these points split again until at a level of B of 3.57; plotting the fish in the pond year on year generates a huge number of values. We have arrived at chaotic behaviour. Although this pattern looks random, for each birth rate we look at, the values of population that we can get will generate a geometric pattern around what is known as a chaotic or strange attractor. We will explore this in a little more detail shortly. The pattern is also boundable. We can describe a 'possibility space' in which the solutions to the equation can be found.

Another interesting feature of this patterning is self-similarity at different levels of scale. If we examine a very small portion of the graph and amplify it, we will see the pattern repeating itself at smaller and smaller levels of scale. This is known as a fractal phenomenon.*

From our exploration, we can draw some important conclusions about non-linear behaviour:

- Complex behaviour can arise from the reiterative application of very simple equations or rules.
- Non-linear systems are predictable, providing we have adequate computational power to undertake the reiterative calculations and accurate starting conditions.
- Non-linear systems are exquisitely sensitive to where they start from (their initial conditions). For example, changing the value of B only very slightly can dramatically alter the output of the system. In practice, it is this feature that makes non-linear systems so unpredictable – we can never measure their initial conditions with absolute certainty.

If organizations demonstrate non-linear characteristics, we can make some interesting postulations:

- Our ability to predict events and engineer the system towards a defined objective may be limited. Any predictability will be short term due to the rapidly cumulative effects of feedback.
- Initial conditions are important. What happens in organizations will be influenced by what has gone before – you have to know where you have been to see where you might go.
- We can expect to see patterns reoccurring at different levels of system scale.
- The recursive application of a few simple rules may lead to complex organizational behaviour.
- Non-linear interaction between individuals will modulate their differences and create novelty that may not have been anticipated.

In the next section we explore two further concepts of chaos theory – phase space and attractors.

---

* The fractal dimension is defined as the slope of the function relating the numbers of points contained in a given 'magnification' to the magnification itself.

Phase space and attractors

One way of describing a dynamic system is by plotting its trajectory with time. If we describe an element in the system using n variables and for each variable allocate one dimension on a graph, we can plot the trajectory of that element in an n dimensional graph or phase space. This is the space that contains the range of values that can be found in a particular system.

Figure 2.2 shows a simple model to describe the motion of a particle in a fluid, across which there is a temperature gradient. It consists of three interrelated equations that form a non-linear system. The output can be drawn in three-dimensional phase space, as shown in Figure 2.3. We can see it forms a trajectory around a particular area of phase space – a chaotic attractor. The attractor is an area in phase space where the trajectories are more likely to be found. Although in theory we can calculate the exact position of the particle at any point in time, its trajectory will be extremely sensitive to its initial starting position. However, we can be more certain about the pattern that will be described.

We can use these concepts as metaphors when describing non-linear systems qualitatively. For example, in organizations we follow trajectories in phase space around attractors or system fundamentals. In the NHS, one important attractor could be equity. In the United States (US) health system, profit would play a more important role.

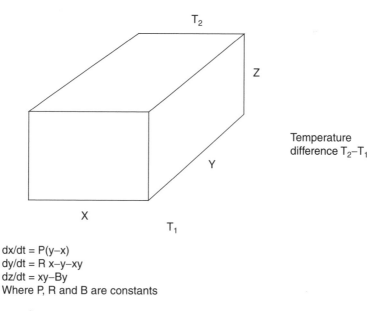

T_2

Z

Temperature difference $T_2 - T_1$

Y

X

T_1

$dx/dt = P(y{-}x)$
$dy/dt = R\,x{-}y{-}xy$
$dz/dt = xy{-}By$
Where P, R and B are constants

Figure 2.2 Non-linear equations to describe motion of a particle in a fluid across which there is a temperature difference.

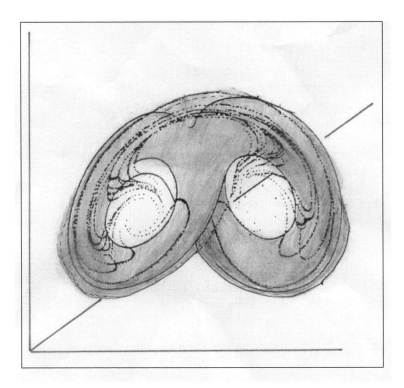

Figure 2.3   The path of a particle around an attractor in three-dimensional phase space calculated from the non-linear model shown in Figure 2.2.

Conclusion

Chaos theory studies non-linear systems mathematically. Although there have been advances in the prediction and control of the trajectories of chaotic systems,[4,5] these have been from a theoretical mathematical perspective and it is unlikely that these developments could be extrapolated to human systems. However, chaos can provide useful insights and metaphors for understanding social organizations that challenge much of current thinking.

From our own observations, we might deduce that the health system is non-linear. But more formal evidence is forthcoming. For example, Papadopoulos *et al.*[6] analysed surgical waiting lists in the NHS and confirmed chaotic properties. It was also suggested that waiting lists also demonstrate fractal properties, i.e. similar chaotic structure could be identified not only on waiting lists by speciality but on the waiting lists of individual consultants. The conclusion was that government measures to reduce waiting lists were destined to failure!

However, in most areas of organizational life mathematical analysis becomes restricted – the algorithms or equations that describe our interaction (our mental models that determine how we respond to the environment) are continually changing as we interact and learn. Nevertheless, we can gain some useful insights applying chaos principles to social organizations within the framework known as complexity theory. It is to this we turn in the next chapter.

References

1 Goldberger A (1996) Non-linear dynamics for clinicians: chaos theory, fractals and complexity at the bedside. *Lancet.* **347:** 312–14.
2 Sataloff R and Hawkshaw M (2001) *Chaos and Medicine: source readings.* Singular Press, San Diego, CA.
3 Gleick J (1987) *Chaos: making a new science.* Penguin Books, London.
4 Kantz H and Schreiber T (1997) *Non-linear Time Series Analysis.* Cambridge University Press, Cambridge.
5 Kapitaniak T (1996) *Controlling Chaos: theoretical and practical methods in non-linear dynamics.* Academic Press, London.
6 Papadopoulos M, Hadjitheodossiou M, Chrysostomu C *et al.* (2001) Is the National Health Service at the edge of chaos? *Journal of the Royal Society of Medicine.* **94 (12):** 613–16.

CHAPTER 3

An introduction to complexity theory

David Kernick

'*Complexus*' (Latin) – braided together

Complexity theory grew out of the observation that there are many phenomena that modern scientific analysis could not adequately describe or predict. Taking as its starting point a model of a non-linear network, it offers an alternative perspective on organizational life where we operate under the constraints of limited time, knowledge and processing power; where the bulk of our activity is to establish and modify relationships rather than seeking an endless series of goals, each of which disappear on attainment. This chapter describes some basic principles of this new paradigm.

Key points
- Complexity focuses on a perspective that sees systems undergoing continual transformation in a network of non-linear interactions.
- The emphasis moves away from prediction and control to an appreciation of the configuration of relationships amongst a system's components and an understanding of what creates patterns of order and behaviour among them.
- The important features are connectivity, feedback and the existence of self-ordering rules that give systems the capacity to emerge to new patterns of order.
- Different metaphors are derived from the study of complexity across different disciplines. We should be cautious when importing these insights into an understanding of healthcare organization.

From complicated to complex networks

A jumbo jet is a complicated network of interacting elements. Its action can be determined by an analysis of its component parts and its behaviour is linear and predictable. Each part of the system will behave in the same way, wherever it is installed. The intelligence of the designer resides in the system and it can be controlled from without.

A rose is a complex network of interacting elements. As it unfolds, its future shape has boundaries that can be described but cannot be predicted in detail. There is no pre-defined geometric plan or any one element in control. The pattern that emerges is the result of interaction between its elements as they respond to the information they are presented with at a local level, a response that is directed by the recursive application of a small number of simple rules.

Box 3.1   What is complexity?

A complex system is a network of elements (agents) that exchange information in such a way that change in the context of one element changes the context for all others. Complexity is the result of the interaction of elements that only respond to the limited information they are presented with.[1] Orderly patterns arise that could not have been predicted from the study of individual elements due to the presence of reiterative positive and negative feedback loops.

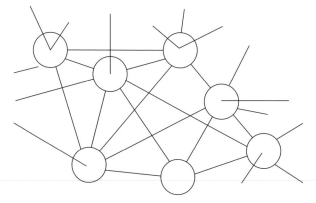

Figure 3.1

Approaches to complexity

The study of complex systems originated in the field of mathematics in the late 1980s and described how certain computer models of neural networks and artificial life behaved.[2,3] Other disciplines from the natural sciences adopted these concepts based on a model of multiple iterative interactions in a network of individual elements that produced orderly patterns of behaviour.

The study of complex systems can be divided depending on the focus of the investigation. Unfortunately, confusion often arises from insights from one perspective being imported into another. For example, humans in organizations behave very differently from mathematical equations in computers or animals in ecosystems. There is also a problem with a lack of consensus over complexity definitions and terminology – 45 definitions have been identified![4]

Some contrasting approaches to complexity are:

- *Simple complex systems* – the manner in which information is processed by individual elements does not change with time. For example, a biochemical reaction.
- *Complex adaptive systems* – the processing of information by elements changes with time as they learn and adapt in response to other elements or their environment. For example, evolutionary computer programs, biological systems. Complex adaptive systems need processes that both generate and prune variation to evolve.[5]
- *Complex cognitive systems* – this approaches complexity from a psychological perspective and offers a useful organizational definition of a complex system:
  – a highly flexible system with a large behavioural repertoire
  – one for which its future behaviour is difficult to predict with any certainty
  – that generates novel information-processing mechanisms resulting in interesting and unexpected emergent phenomena
  – in which behaviour evolves over time given appropriate resources.[6]
- *Complex social systems* – organizations are studied as complex social systems in their own right, not as metaphors or analogies of physical, chemical or biological systems.
- *Complex responsive processes* – the focus of study is on the interaction between individuals at the local level from which an unpredictable future emerges.

We next briefly look at the features of the individual elements in complex systems before describing how they interact to give the characteristics of complex adaptive systems and in particular the features of emergence and self-organization. Finally we discuss insights from some important metaphors, focusing on the metaphors derived from chaos theory and the concept of 'the edge of chaos'.

The behaviour of individual elements – mental models and local rules

Each system element (called an agent in complexity terminology) takes in information, processes it and forwards it to other elements as an output (*see* Figure 3.2). Complexity theory stresses the importance of the connections and relationships between the agents rather than the properties of the agents themselves.

Elements respond to their environment using internalized rules that direct action. In a simple complex system such as a biochemical system, the rules could be a series of chemical reactions. At a human level, as we saw in Chapter 1, these rules form the basis of our mental models or map of the world. They manifest in the way in which we respond to changes in our environment.

There are a number of important features of human agents:

- Our mental models change with time as we learn and adapt. Because of this, a rigorous mathematical analysis of human systems will be difficult. Complexity therefore focuses on the qualitative aspects of dynamic non-linear systems.
- We can have some awareness of the whole system and not just our local environment. Our technological artifacts such as television and the internet allow us to respond to global information, unlike simple complex systems that act only on local information.
- Our ability to hold mental images and project them into the future enables us to make sense of our environment. We can identify goals and purposes, develop strategies and choose amongst several alternatives. We are able to formulate values and social rules of behaviour.
- Our interactions take place within a network influenced by language and other symbolic forms. Through a shared context of meaning, we can acquire

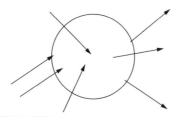

Figure 3.2   An element or agent in a complex system element takes in information, processes it and forwards it to other elements within a process of perception, decision making and action.

identities as members of social networks that generate the boundary of an organization. However, we are also capable of dysingenuity – what we say is not always how we intend to act.

Characteristics of complex adaptive systems

In this section we consider some basic characteristics of complex systems:

- Complex systems consist of a large number of elements that interact. Inter-actions are predominately short-range with information being received from near neighbours. However, the richness of network connections means that communications will pass across the system but will be modified on the way.
- There are reiterative feedback loops in network interactions. The effects of an agent's actions are fed back to the agent and this in turn affects the way the agent behaves in the future. Negative (damping/stable) and positive (amplify-ing/unstable) feedback give rise to non-linearity, which is the unique fea-ture that makes a complex system different from a complicated system. These non-linear instabilities lead to novelty and innovation and make the future behaviour of such systems unpredictable.

  Due to non-linear characteristics, small changes in one area can occa-sionally have large effects across the whole system. This has been called the 'butterfly effect'. (A butterfly in New York can flap its wings and cause a hurricane in Tokyo.) For example, the riding accident of the actor Chris-topher Reeve had a large but probably inappropriate impact on the redis-tribution of research funding into spinal injuries in the US.[7] Conversely, large influences may only have a negligible impact. The *Health of the Nation* was a major strategic UK government initiative designed to influ-ence the health of the public, but had little impact on the targets it sought to influence.[8]
- Systems are invariably nested within other systems. For example, my consul-tation sits within my health centre within my primary care organization within the health authority within the NHS. All these systems are nested complex adaptive systems – including myself, which in turn is a collection of nested systems.
- It is difficult to determine the boundaries of a complex system. The boundary is often based on the observer's needs and prejudices rather than any intrin-sic property of the system itself. For example, primary care practitioners find it dificult to define the boundaries between health and social care in their work, but these organizational demarcations are rigorously enforced.
- History is important in complex systems. The past influences present beha-viour. For example, it would be unwise to plan new primary care structures without a recognition of what has gone before.

- The system is different from the sum of the parts. In attempting to understand a system by reducing it into its component parts, the analytical method destroys what it seeks to understand. The corollary is that the parts cannot contain the whole and any one agent cannot 'know' what is happening in the system as a whole. If they could, all the complexity would have to be present in that element. Therefore, no one can stand outside the system and hope to understand and engineer it to a predetermined future, as approaches to organizational change in the NHS have repeatedly demonstrated.
- The behaviour of complex systems evolves from the interaction of agents at a local level without external direction or the presence of internal control. This property is known as emergence and gives systems the flexibility to adapt and self-organize in response to external challenge. Emergence is a pattern of system behaviour that could not have been predicted by an analysis of the component parts of that system.

Emergence and self-organization and central features of complex systems are considered in more detail in the next section.

Emergence and self-organization

Emergence in complex adaptive systems

The idea of emergence is used to indicate the development of unpredictable patterns that cannot be adequately explained by an understanding of the system's components at a lower level. Emergent behaviour is shown when a number of agents form more complex patterns of behaviour as a collective. Due to the presence of multiple feedback loops, properties of the system that shape both its identity and purpose emerge without the intervention of an external designer or the presence of any centralized form of control. The emergent behaviour is not a property of any single entity, nor can it easily be predicted or deduced from behaviour in the lower-level entities.

Emergent behaviour can be seen in areas ranging from traffic patterns, multicellular biological organism to organizational phenomena. For example, each individual brain cell functions in a simple manner, but the system of brain cells performs highly complex tasks that could not have been predicted by an analysis of the individual components. Complex behaviour emerges from the interaction between many simple elements that respond in a non-linear fashion to the local information that is presented to them. There is no central control. No one cell or group of cells is in charge. A health centre demonstrates similar properties. Although each individual employee has a defined role, the patterns of behaviour that emerge as staff interact with each other are very different from predictions derived from analysis of the individuals.

Emergence is a key feature of complex systems but, to date, no general laws or principles have been identified to explain this property.

Self-organization in complex adaptive systems

Closely aligned to the concept of emergence is the principle of self-organization. The evolution of all living systems has been underpinned by this principle whereby a dynamic system reorganizes its structure so that it can more effectively cope with environmental demands. When change is introduced from outside, the system self-organizes around the disturbance that is created. For example, Lipsky[9] studied the behaviour of public servants in New York. He identified that when top-down policy directives were issued, these 'street bureaucrats' reorganized the initiation of policy, influenced by their local circumstances, and only by doing so did the system survive.

As the self-organizing process is not necessarily guided or determined by specific goals, it may be difficult to talk about the function of a system. Patterns emerge that satisfy the constraints put upon it. This concept runs against traditional organizational thinking that emphasizes control of organizational relationships as the system is engineered towards its strategic goals.

In human systems, precursors for self-organization are:

- shared principles – systems align themselves around core values even if system goals are not articulated.
- connectivity and feedback – self-organization emerges from non-linear processes arising from feedback at a local level
- dialogue – this involves a sensitivity to other perspectives and a willingness to change our mental models and paradigms
- memory – without memory the system can do no better than mirror the environment. As any system has a finite memory capacity, there must also be some form of selective forgetting.
- interdependency – self-organisation is driven by both competition and co-operation amongst system elements but against a background of interdependency.

A self-organizing system will attempt to balance itself at a point known as *self-organized criticality* (alternatively known as the *edge of chaos*), where it is able to adapt with the least amount of effort in response to a wide variety of external challenges. This phenomenon is considered in more detail below.

There is considerable debate over the concept of self-organization. In natural ecologies, the recursive interplay of competition and co-operation of system elements leads to the emergence of co-evolving patterns of behaviour that fit with environmental demands. However, we need to be cautious when applying this thinking to human systems. It may be wishful thinking to suggest that left to their own devises, individuals will self-organize to the benefit of the system of which they are a part. Human motivations can be destructive, leading to anarchy and system collapse. Experience suggests that we need formal structures to facilitate a constructive mode of human self-organization. For example, market economies can be successful methods of self-organization that allocate societies' limited resources but have strict rules of transaction to enable them to operate effectively. Perhaps the best we can say is that human systems will flourish with less external control than we currently think, and focus on more useful concepts such as the 'edge of chaos', which appears throughout this book and is considered in the next section.

Using complexity metaphors and analogies for understanding organizations

Complexity insights are being developed across a number of disciplines, and insights and metaphors from one area are invariably invoked in another. Caution is needed when transferring metaphors derived from non-human systems into organizational thinking. There is also a danger of importing complexity insights from commerce, where the focus is on competition, to public health systems where competition is usually limited. Some imported metaphors and their sources are shown in Table 3.1.

Different writers are attracted to different metaphors. I find the metaphors from chaos theory and self-organized criticality useful and these are expanded below. The other metaphors are briefly reviewed in Appendix 1.

Table 3.1   Some metaphors imported from other disciplines (*see* Appendix 1 for more details)

Metaphor	Discipline
• Chaos – phase space/attractors/fractals	• Mathematics
• Dissipative structures	• Chemistry and physics
• Auto-catalytic sets	• Biology
• Auto-poesies	• Biology, psychology
• Fitness landscapes	• Ecology
• Self-organized criticality ('the edge of chaos')	• Biology, ecology, physics

Insights and metaphors imported from chaos theory

I previously suggested that a useful starting point from an organizational perspective was to consider chaos theory as the quantitative study of non-linear systems and complexity as the qualitative approach, drawing upon chaos metaphors. This section explores how insights from chaos theory might be applied to the study of organizations viewed as complex systems. Four concepts are considered.

Simple rules

In Chapter 2 we saw how complex patterns could emerge from the recursive application of simple non-linear equations or 'rules'. An important but contested insight is that the capacity of systems to evolve to new patterns of order can emerge from the recursive application of a small number of simple rules. For example, the complex phenomenon of bird-flocking or fish-shoaling emerges from the recursive application of three simple rules: move to the centre of the crowd, maintain a minimum distance from your neighbour and move at the speed of the element in front of you.

The suggestion is that underpinning complex behaviour in organizations are a small number of simple rules or guiding principles. For example, Plampling[10] identifies three simple rules that have traditionally underpinned the NHS and offers an alternative set which maybe more applicable:

- I am responsible – I am responsible in partnership
- Can do, should do – maximize the health gain for the population within the available resources
- Doing means treatment – doing takes place within a broader social action.

Plsek[11] identifies three general types of simple rules for human systems: general direction pointing; system prohibition, i.e. setting boundaries; and resource or permission providing simple rules have found favour as a practical framework in which complexity insights can be utilized. Exposing and changing the rules is seen as a method of instigating change. Major concerns are that this approach reflects the ideology of control that the complexity framework seeks to avoid and the focus of attention is removed from the importance of interaction between system elements. The concept of simple rules is considered in more detail in Section 3.

Multidimensional phase space

An important use of metaphor drawn from chaos theory is to view complex systems as a multidimensional phase space. Each system variable is defined and

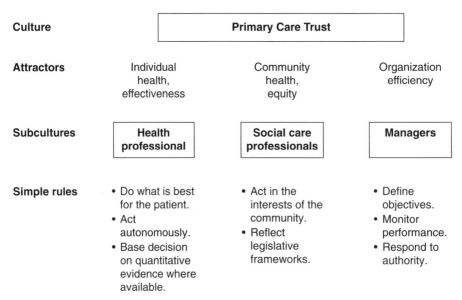

Figure 3.3   Subcultures within a primary care organization, their simple rules and attractors.

quantified in one dimension. The system is described in terms of a multidimensional phase space, with the number of dimensions depending on the number of variables required to describe it. Agents will follow trajectories through this space with time. Although trajectories cannot be predicted with certainty, they are bounded by areas of phase space known as attractors. These are areas of phase space where trajectories tend to be found and place limits on the room for manoeuvre.

For example, two current NHS attractors are equity and efficiency. In the US healthcare system, profit is a powerful attractor. One suggestion is that an attractor is a system property that emerges from the recursive application of simple rules at a local level. The attractor then feeds back and reinforces or modulates the simple rules. Figure 3.3 shows some possible simple rules and attractors for subcultures within the NHS primary care sector. At a more local level, Miller *et al.*[12] have offered insights into the organization of individual primary care practices by identifying practice attractors such as maximization of income or rapid access to healthcare provision.

Self-similarity at different scales

Fractals are patterns that repeat themselves at different levels of scale and we may expect to see this phenomenon in organizations. For example, a dissonance between rhetoric and reality occurs at every administrative level of the NHS!

The importance of initial conditions

What has gone before is important. For example, it would be inadvisable to consider the current developments in primary care in the NHS without an understanding of their historical context. Davies and Marshall[13] have warned of the dangers of comparing health systems where the historical context is often different. Systems develop within the framework that they have inherited, building on what has gone before. Often, organizations are memorials to old problems, institutional residues that reflect the historical processes through which problems have been tackled.[14]

The edge of chaos or self-organized criticality

This important metaphor is a recurring theme throughout the book. This insight was derived and explored using computer modelling, and despite its attractions we must be aware of the dangers of importing such models into human organizations.

In a complex network, three system states can be described depending on the strength and number of connections between elements: stable state, chaotic state and the edge of chaos.*

Stable state

In this state there are a limited number of strong interactions between system elements with little feedback. As a result, there is a simple linear relationship between cause and effect. The system is stable and predictable, and organizational decisions can be taken within a rational framework. This assumes that the costs and consequences of alternative courses of action can be predicted and a choice made that reflects explicit values and goals.

---

* We can look at the edge of chaos phenomenon in a different way using the metaphor of a multidimensional phase space. A stable non-linear system eventually reaches either a fixed point (a point attractor) or a closed set of points such as an oscillatory cycle (a periodic attractor). Such a system is stable and any disruption will be compensated by the system's tendency to resume limit cycle behaviour. Under other system parameters, the system response is represented by a more complex trajectory within a strange attractor, and under these circumstances the system's dynamics are chaotic. Between these stable and chaotic attractors is a phase transition where highly ordered structure emerges spontaneously. The attainment of this phase is only observed for an extremely narrow critical range of the system's parameters and it is here that the most productive information processing is thought to occur and the system responds adaptively to changes in its environment with the least amount of effort.

Chaotic state

Here there are large numbers of weak and rapidly changing connections. Although system behaviour appears random, there may be underlying features that can be described by the mathematical approaches of chaos theory. Chaotic systems have little memory and mental models change rapidly from novelty to novelty without consolidating gains.

The 'garbage can model' of organizational change is the antithesis of the rational approach and can be seen as one interpretation of this zone. It sees organizations as a continual mixture of people, choices and problems circulating aimlessly and occasionally coinciding to create a juncture at which a decision is made. A collection of choices looking for problems and solutions looking for the issues to which they might be the answer.[15]

There are advantages and disadvantages to both tightly and loosely coupled systems. For example:

- Loosely coupled systems allow parts of an organization to evolve independently rather than forcing the entire system to move at once. However, systems are not pressurized to discontinue non-productive practices.
- Loosely coupled systems are more sensitive to environmental changes, but this may subject the system to the whims of fads.
- Loosely coupled systems can permit isolated systems to experiment without committing the entire system, but may inhibit the diffusion of experiments that are productive.
- Loosely coupled systems are less vulnerable to problems or breakdowns.
- Loosely coupled systems may be cheaper to run than co-ordinated systems, but the trade-off is loss of control.

The edge of chaos

Many complex systems organize themselves to a state known as self-organized criticality (sometimes termed 'zone of complexity' or the 'edge of chaos'). Here, each element is optimally fit at a level that does not disrupt the fitness of others in the network.[16] This area has been defined as the transition band between chaos and predictable stability where systems are maximally fit and adaptive.[17] The important features of this zone are:

- Dynamics are still chaotic but they also possess characteristics of order.
- The organization is sufficiently rigid to carry information about itself and to perform its task adequately, but at the same time sufficiently chaotic to allow it to use its information creatively.
- The system is robust to the influences of external forces and operates at a point of maximum efficiency so that an increase in either order or chaos will reduce the system's efficiency.

- There is scale invariance, i.e. patterns repeat themselves at different levels of scale (or fractals).
- The system often demonstrates power-law scaling, i.e. where x and y are system variables and c and a are constants:

$$y = c \cdot x^a$$

y is usually plotted as the frequency of a system event and x is the size of the event. This power-law distribution is a footprint of the edge of chaos and not diagnostic of it. Nevertheless, a large number of physical systems ranging from earthquakes to traffic jams demonstrate this behaviour and evidence is beginning to accumulate that it exists in healthcare systems.[18]

Box 3.2   A surfer's guide to the edge of chaos

The edge of chaos isn't an edge – it is a class of behaviours where an orderly system starts to break down but before the system is chaotic. Some people find the analogy of a wave useful. Stability is represented by the ordered wave pattern out to sea. The edge of chaos is the area under the wave about to break which is known as the tube. Surfers are in tune with this complex region until the wave hits the beach and chaos ensues.

The edge of chaos metaphor has been interpreted diagrammatically by Stacey, who applies it to organizational understanding and decision making.[19] He identifies three areas of organizational life, depending on the certainty about the relationship between cause and effect, between system variables and the agreement between agents on this relationship.* This is shown in Figure 3.4.

When there is a high degree of certainty as to outcomes from actions and a high degree of agreement amongst the people involved in the actions about the relationship between actions and outcomes, machine systems thinking with detailed planning and control may be appropriate. The instinct of reductionist science is to resolve ambiguity and paradox and move into this linear, rational zone on the underlying assumption that there is a correct answer to any problem.

The upper right-hand segment represents a system of anarchy where chaos reigns and is to be avoided. However, most issues in healthcare are in the 'zone of complexity' where there are only modest levels of certainty and agreement

---

*Despite its attractions and use throughout this book, Stacey has rather distanced himself from this model. It is seen as too reductionist and diverting attention from the central role of human relating at a local level, from which outcomes emerge.

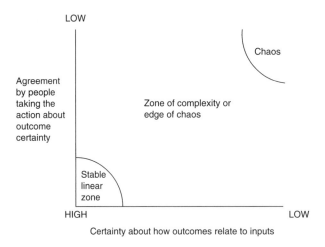

Figure 3.4 Three zones in networks – the Stacey diagram.[19]

and where it would be most appropriate to use the paradigm of complex adaptive systems. This perspective would be to accommodate paradox and value the inherent tension that arises from it. The attention focuses on things that seem to work best and learning incrementally.

A third dimension could be added to the model – the degree to which agents agree about the purpose or goals of a system.[20] For example, cause and effect may be uncertain with high agreement on system goals. In this area, detailed planning is of limited use and the emphasis is on the articulation of a vision and underpinning values of the system. Alternatively, there may be agreement amongst agents over system certainty but there may be disagreement over system goals. Here, decision making is based on compromise and negotiation. If there is disagreement in all dimensions, then all we can hope for is inspiration!

The Stacey model has been developed by a number of writers. For example, Kurtz and Snowden[21] emphasize the importance of boundaries between preferences for action (*see* Appendix 2).

Conclusion

Engaging with complexity challenges a number of current assumptions and offers an alternative perspective from which to analyse social systems. It cautions that complex systems cannot be described and predicted using simple linear models; that activity and performance cannot be precisely controlled by rational technical fixes that have predictable outcomes. Organizations cannot be re-engineered within hierarchical command and control frameworks and attempts to understand them by a reduction into their constituent elements will invariably destroy what they seek to understand. However, given certain dynamic relationships, patterns of behaviour can develop as organizations adapt in response to changes in their environment. By taking a broader view, perhaps we can retain some predictive power – concentrating on being vaguely right rather than being precisely wrong.

References

1   Cilliers P (1998) *Complexity and Post-modernism*. Routledge, London.
2   Waldrop M (1992) *Complexity: the emerging science at the edge of order and chaos*. Penguin, London.
3   Lewin R (1993) *Complexity: life on the edge of chaos*. Phoenix, London.
4   Collander D (2000) *Complexity in the History of Economic Thought*. Routledge, London.
5   Holland A (1995) *Hidden Order: how adaption builds complexity*. Addison-Wesley, Reading, MA.
6   Heath R (2000) *Non-linear Dynamics, Techniques and Applications in Psychology*. Lawrence Erlbaum Associates, London.
7   Greenberg D (1997) NIH resists research funding linked to patient load. *Lancet*. **349**: 1229.
8   Department of Health (1998) *The Health of the Nation: a policy assessed*. HMSO, London.
9   Lipsky M (1980) *Street-level Bureaucracy: dilemmas of the individual in public services*. Sage, New York.
10   Plampling D (1998) Changing resistance to change in the NHS. *BMJ*. **317**: 69–71.
11   Plsek P (2000) Redesigning healthcare with insights from the science of complex adaptive systems. In: *Crossing the Quality Chasm: a new health system for the 21st century*, pp. 309–22. Institute of Medicine, National Academy Press, Washington, DC.
12   Miller W, Crabtree B, McDaniel R *et al.* (1998) Understanding change in primary care practice using complexity theory. *Journal of Family Practice*. **46**: 369–76.
13   Davies H and Marshall M (2000) UK and USA healthcare systems: divided by more than a common language. *Lancet*. **355**: 336.
14   Pratt J, Gordon P and Plampling D (2000) *Working Whole Systems: putting theory into practice in organisations*. King's Fund, London.
15   Cohen M, March J and Olsen J (1974) A garbage can model of organisational choice. *Administrative Science Quarterly*. **17**: 1–25.
16   Bak P (1996) *How Nature Works: the science of self-organized criticality*. Springer-Verlag, New York.
17   Marion R (1999) *The Edge of Organization*. Sage, Thousand Oaks, CA.
18   Papadopolous M, Hadjitheodossiou M, Chrysostomu C *et al.* (2001) Is the National Health Service at the edge of chaos? *Journal of the Royal Society of Medicine*. **94 (12)**: 613–16.
19   Stacey R (1996) *Strategic Management and Organisational Dynamics*. Pitman Publishing, London.
20   Hopwood A (1980) The organisational aspects of budgeting and control. In: Arnold J, Carsburg C and Scapens R (eds) *Topics in Management Accounting*, pp. 221–41. Philip Allen, Deddington.
21   Kurtz C and Snowden D (2003) The new dynamics of strategy: sense making in a complex world. *IBM Systems Journal*. **Fall**.

Section 2

The spectrum of how we think about organizations

Introduction

What can we make of the overwhelming volume of organizational literature and where does complexity theory fit into the melting pot? In this section we review the range of perspectives on how we think about organizations.

The study of organizations has been conducted from within two main paradigms. Firstly, organizations have been approached as if they were machines – technical instruments for harnessing human energies and directing them towards set aims. Here, classical management theory seeks to deliver results in terms of economy, efficiency and quality. The second paradigm emphasizes the social dimension where people are attempting to make sense of their lives in organizational contexts. Organizations are seen as having a 'life of their own' where there is interdependence of the component parts and planned changes have unexpected consequences. This polarity between rational instrumental and natural system models of organization has provided a theoretical context within which most of organizational thinking has been developed.

I find it useful to think about organizations across this spectrum in terms of how we view movement of the organization towards the future and the perceived ability to stand outside of it and engineer it to a defined objective. Figure A shows the interpretation of this spectrum that this section considers.

On the 'right wing' sits *hard systems thinking*, the dominant voice in organizational theory. Here the discourse is of design, regularity and control within the context of a predictable future. Managers stand outside the system and engineer it towards a desired objective, searching for causal links that promise tools for manipulating behaviour. Feedback is used to keep the system from drifting off course, underpinned by mathematical models of the system wherever possible.

The first systems approach to healthcare was proposed by Florence Nightingale in 1836 when she advocated outcome measurement in terms of whether patients were 'dead, relieved or unrelieved' in an attempt to 'avoid an unnecessary waste

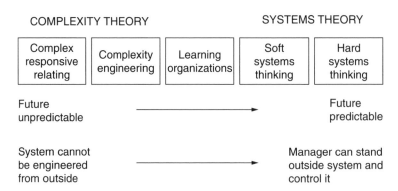

Figure A   The spectrum of organizational thinking.

of life'. Today, health economists are in the vanguard of this thinking. The focus is on management within a hierarchical structure and with an emphasis on quantitative analysis and information to model behaviour and change based on incentive manipulation. Implicit decisions undertaken by practitioners and managers are seen as incoherent, leading to inefficiency and inequity.

Soft systems thinking stands in contrast to the hard system engineering approaches. Appreciating the differences between the real and modelled world, it is essentially a learning process that seeks to converge and reconcile conflicting views of participants in order to derive actions which seem sensible to those concerned.

In Chapter 4, John Powell offers an overview of systems thinking. While recognizing its limitations, he argues that it can offer useful insights into the way that the organization behaves and give managers a useful framework for action.

On the 'left wing' of the spectrum sit the complexity sciences, united by a focus on local interaction and the unpredictability of the future. The extreme left views organizations as *complex responsive processes*. Here the focus is on the essentially responsive and participative nature of the human process of relating and the radical unpredictability of its evolution as we interact with each other in the co-evolution of a jointly constructed reality. The focus is on the 'going on together' and the creation of knowledge within our communicative activity. Jo Poole is a healthcare practitioner and, in Chapter 6, draws upon her own experience to make sense of change using this framework. She emphasizes the participatory and narrative approach to understanding change in organization. What an organization is emerges as a result of communication between individuals and groups at a local level. We are always participants in an organization and can never step outside it to shape it.

To the right of this approach is *complexity engineering*. Drawing upon systems theory and complexity insights, the emphasis is on using complexity theory to manipulate the system. The focus is on identifying and changing the simple rules, modulating system attractors or identifying organizational tipping points where a small managerial input can change the trajectory of the system. Success lies in the ability to recognize complex and subtle structures amid the wealth of details. To see patterns where others only see events and forces to react to. These themes will be visited throughout the book.

The mid-spectrum view is that as we participate we can observe and assess ourselves retrospectively, making adjustments as we continue. The focus is on *learning organizations.* The future can be anticipated over short time-scales, and through this process of reflection we can learn to design the patterns that will prove useful until next time we pause to reflect. Here the possibility of purposeful design of systems is offered by intervention in the human processes of learning. The future is potentially knowable if we have the resources to invest, but invariably we do not.

In Chapter 5, Huw Davies explores 'organizational learning', and the characteristics of the organizational cultures needed to underpin it. He argues that healthcare organizations may need to adopt some of the characteristics and cultural values of learning organizations if they are to deliver substantial quality improvements. Although organizational learning is currently enjoying a high profile within the NHS, it has been criticized for its utopian view of organizational life. Its usefulness is limited by the way in which it focuses on what ought to be rather than what is and how it ignores many of the processes such as ambition, self-interest, aggression and envy that are very much a part of organizational life.

CHAPTER 4

An introduction to systems theory: from hard to soft systems thinking in the management of complex organizations

John Powell

Systems theory has had a major impact in the military and industrial sectors and more recently is finding increasing application in human organizations. This chapter reviews the development of systems thinking and in particular the techniques available to managers for framing and solving problems in organizations.

Key points
- A system is a collection of components that communicate with one another to produce an output which transcends the output of the components standing alone.
- Systems applications were developed during the last war for military and industrial techniques, but during the last 30 years have been applied increasingly to human organizations.
- Systems can be hard – the systems state can be expressed in an unambiguous and usually numerical manner, or soft – they can not be defined by numerical methods.
- Alternatively, systems can be described as positivist – there is one single definition of the system, or pluralistic – there are multiple views of the system.
- Soft, pluralistic systems approaches are more applicable to healthcare organizations and are becoming a useful management tool.

Introduction

In this chapter we survey the range of system modelling and intervention techniques available to managers when dealing with messy systems. We concentrate primarily on what are known as human activity systems (HAS),[1] but we will also discuss briefly approaches deriving from the study of systems more familiar to other disciplines such as engineering, physics and ecology. Primarily we are concerned with approaches which provide practical proposals for action rather than unifying theories which help us make sense of system behaviour in the abstract.

Although we can trace the concept of a system back to the study of mechanical and astronomical systems in the seventeenth and eighteenth centuries, it was not until the middle part of the last century that the idea of a disciplined, procedural approach to system study emerged. Driven by the military and industrial need to design more complicated engineering devices, increasingly capable mathematical methods were developed to describe the overall effects produced by connected sets of essentially simple components. For example, a gun, a radar and its mounting needed to be treated as a connected group of components if the anti-aircraft gun were to perform correctly. The separate parts of these components can physically cohabit but it is the functional interconnectedness and communication between them that make the anti-aircraft gun a system. These attributes characterize what we mean here by a system. It has to have components that communicate one with another to produce an output (called the system response) which transcends the output of the components standing alone.

The discipline necessary to produce the military and industrial devices demanded by war was known as system engineering. Two early developments were cybernetics and operational research (OR). Cybernetics sought to provide rules for the design of systems which were 'governed', i.e. had to be controlled and guided to produce responses which they would otherwise not exhibit. Although many examples were drawn from nature, the essential objects of study were the engineering-type systems we will refer to below as 'hard' systems. Operational research, originating in the study of the effectiveness of military systems, soon came to be applied to industrial systems, for example in the modelling and study of production plants.

By the 1970s, however, the techniques of modelling (the mathematical representation of a system) were being applied to a wider set of systems which for the first time included human beings at their heart. These systems present fundamentally different problems to their would-be controllers, and a rising tide of dissatisfaction with the ability of the OR community to address this wider set of problems led to the establishment of a set of powerful techniques known as 'soft' methods. This chapter explores the differences between hard and soft methods and examines their respective applicability to healthcare organizations.

The nature of managerial systems

Before turning to a description of systems approaches, it would be wise to remind ourselves of the nature of managerial systems (of which health management systems are archetypal) and the difficulties they present. In engineering and allied disciplines, much effort is spent in maintaining the illusion that systems (and by extension organizations) are orderly and rational, i.e. the consequences of alternative courses of action, given adequate data, can be predicted, allowing objective decisions to be made based on explicit values. Managed systems, however, are *hybrid* – they contain both system elements which are bureaucratic or algorithmic in nature and components where effect is less closely connected to cause.[2-5] Due to limits in our information gathering and processing power, our ability to observe and predict is limited. In addition, the human components of the managed system cannot be guaranteed to behave in a way we would understand as rational. An example of this 'bounded rationality' is 'satisficing' behaviour[6] where, rather than attempting to produce the rational best solution, we satisfy and suffice to meet a reasonable expectation. We may seek to discipline our own and others' thinking onto the narrow path of logic, but we will fail.[2]

Checkland, whose work is summarized later, draws our attention to the idea of 'wicked' problems where, in contrast to other 'simple' problems, the investigator cannot access all parts of the problem. Here solutions affect the very problem being solved and differences in perception confuse and obfuscate, preventing incremental progress towards a solution.[1,7]

We also have to take account of the power and individual valuations of human participants, and solutions which fail to do so will not be implementable. This issue of power lies at the heart of a wide-ranging philosophical discussion of system matters and has informed much of the progress from an essentially mathematical view of systems (a positivist or modernist view) towards a more socially informed and essentially more realistic view of systems (the critical modernist view,[8-11] and ultimately towards post-modernism, where all truths are valid and as a result no truth is available for use.[12]

Characterization of systems

A useful method to characterize systems is to divide them into hard or soft, positivist or pluralist.

Hard and soft systems

A hard system is one where the system's state can be expressed in an unambiguous manner, usually numerically, for example a chemical plant, the economy, a queuing theory model of patients entering and leaving a hospital. Soft systems, in contrast, cannot be defined by numerical methods or even by a set of procedures.[1] Because they involve human beings they are not subject to the defining restrictions of hard systems, for example they do not always react in identical ways when presented with the same input. Consider, for example, the dynamics of relationships in a family, the buying behaviour of urban blacks or a model of patient admissions and discharges which took into account the patient as an individual. In none of these cases can we guarantee that even individuals acting alone will behave in a wholly predictable way; when we consider the interactions of those individuals we can see that any attempt to treat them as a hard engineering system is, at best, risky.

Positivist or pluralist systems

Participants in a system will have different views of the objectives and even define the system itself differently one from the other.[11] Much of 'hard' science, in contrast, assumes a *positivist* view. This asserts that with sufficient effort and care, different observers can gain access to a single truth and a single definition of the system. In the social context of human activity systems, this is inappropriate and unhelpful. For example, failing to recognize that patient and doctor may have different views of a consultation because of their different states of knowledge is important in understanding how failures of cognition may emerge. Systems where different participants can and do have different views and definitions of the system are known as *pluralist*.[13]

A taxonomy of systems methods

We can now proceed to characterize the different systems approaches by examining the nature of the assumptions which underpin them. These are shown in Figure 4.1.

In the top left-hand quadrant lies a large group of methods that are essentially mathematical in nature. These are designed for the study of positivist systems, for example something which is essentially numerically defined, such as a queuing system for a hospital. We discuss these methods in more detail later.

The methods in the right-hand half of the diagram are all soft methods and represent a reaction by the practical community to the serious shortcomings of the hard methods. In the top right-hand quadrant we see methods that assume that there is no serious disagreement between participants. Qualitative system

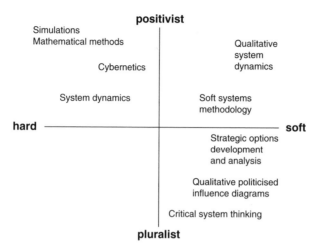

Figure 4.1   Characterization of systems approaches.

dynamics (QSD)[14-17] is a soft variation of a well-known hard numerical simulation technique of systems dynamics,[18-20] but it still assumes a positivist view of the problem in hand.

Strategic options development and analysis (SODA)[21] and soft system methodology (SSM)[7] lie near the boundary between positivist and plural approaches in that they allow the expression of different system views in the early phases of analysis, but assume that there is a single system owner.

Lastly, since almost by definition there are no hard pluralist methods, we see qualitative politicized influence diagrams (QPID)[17,22] and critical system thinking,[10,23-25] which seek to retain a multi-perspective view of the system under consideration, using a wide variety of non-numerical data for the system representation.

With that understanding of the inherent assumptions of the various approaches, we can discuss their relevance in the management of the type of system in which we are interested, and health systems in particular. For the remainder of the chapter we will divide these models into hard or soft approaches.

Hard approaches to organizational management

Conventional mathematical approaches to system modelling are of limited use to us in the context of health system management. The essential problem is that the very precision which a mathematical solution provides precludes it from being flexible enough to encompass the bounded rationality and arbitrariness of a HAS. In some areas it works extremely well, particularly when coupled with the ideas of simulation. For example, modelling the details of a hospital triage system using queuing theory. We could construct numerical models of patients arriving for triage and being allocated to various services in a hospital. Over time, the simulation records the waiting times in the various areas of the hospital and allows investigation of the consequences of allocating extra resources to minor injuries or basing specialists nearer the hospital when on call.

Cybernetics

Cybernetics, rather than being a method of practical solution of systems problems, is to be seen as a meta-theory – a set of statements about theories of systems. Emerging from the work of mathematicians such as Wiener in the Second World War,[26] it seeks descriptions of system behaviour based essentially on feedback loops (as opposed to feed-forward loops). There is an assumption that the system is sensing its environment and responding to it (often described as homeostatic behaviour). Success is a state of insulation from changes in the environment. While cybernetics clearly represents a coherent theory of system behaviour, its ability to produce detailed solutions which are implementable managerially is very limited.

System dynamics

System dynamics (SD) is a particular approach to simulation which to some extent overcomes the technical difficulties of using direct mathematical methods to model HAS. Jay Forrester, the father of SD,[18] was a servomechanism engineer and the application of feedback concepts to social and policy problems was a natural extension of his work. System (never systems) dynamics is now a minor industry with many consultancies specializing in this way of modelling feedback systems. Today it carries with it an assumption, particularly in the US, that the system under consideration will be modelled using a set of differential equations, normally using a software platform such as 'I-Think' or 'VenSim'. This takes all the mathematical labour out of the difficult step of moving from a diagram of the system flows to an accurate declaration of the equations.

The essence of SD, however, is not so much the modelling of the system through the differential equations,[20] as the idea of using explicit feedback models to explore policy options though the dynamics of the system behaviour.

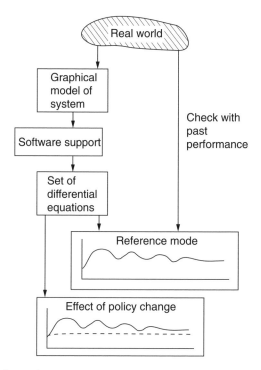

Figure 4.2   System dynamics process.

The idea is simple (*see* Figure 4.2) and the steps are:

- We declare a model of the system under consideration, usually using a form of causal map diagram (*see* Figure 4.2).
- Having turned that visual model into a set of equations, we trim the parameters of those equations so that the model behaves in a way we recognize, often using historical data to check the model is behaving properly. This is known as the reference mode.
- We then alter the parameters of the equations to reflect the effect of various policy options and observe the system behaviour. If this behaviour is an improvement on the reference mode, the option would be a good one to pursue.

System dynamics is immensely powerful when used in the contexts for which it is suited. However, it suffers from the inevitable criticism that the representation by numbers of variables which are inescapably qualitative can often seem arbitrary. SD has a huge literature and its own journal (*System Dynamics Review*), and is undoubtedly of use in those situations where the system description is dominated by numerical variables rather than qualitative ones.

Soft approaches to organizational management

As we have seen, the usefulness of hard techniques in the type of system with which we are concerned is, at best, limited. This became apparent to practitioners in the 1970s and their reaction was to attempt the codification of a set of system practices which came to be known as soft methods. These methods (particularly the three detailed here) are in wide use and have shown themselves most effective in the practical management of hybrid systems.

Soft system methodology

Soft system methodology[1] stands in contrast to the hard system engineering approaches which were its precursor. In the latter, great care is taken to achieve clarity in the objectives of the project. In practice, however, with HAS, this clear objective is frequently superseded during the implementation of the project. This is because of the interconnection between real world and modelled world. Because we have an imperfect knowledge of the real world, our model (be it mathematical or mental) is imperfect. As we progress our analysis, we learn more about both model and world and our objectives become refined as we proceed.

SSM is not objective-driven, it is essentially a learning process which seeks to converge and reconcile conflicting views of participants in order to derive 'actions which seem sensible to those concerned'. Figure 4.3 illustrates the process.[1]

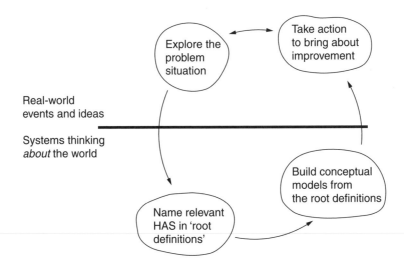

Figure 4.3   Basic structure of SSM approach.[1]

SSM declares six basic tenets:[27]

- It is concerned with managing as a process of organized action (as opposed to wholly emergent processes).
- The participants exhibit a variety of views (i.e. it is concerned with plural systems) and potentially desire different actions.
- Any objectives of the managed system must be seen as emerging from a process of ongoing examination of the world and models of the world.
- It is concerned with HAS rather than engineering or natural systems.
- Action proposals come from the comparison of conceptual models with the real world (*see* Figure 4.3).
- It is at heart a participative process.

Figure 4.4 summarizes the seven steps of the analysis process.[27]

One of the more technical steps of the method is step 3, the formulation of root definitions. Here multiple perspectives are advocated, encapsulated in the acronym CATWOE, standing for:

Customer – the beneficiaries of change
Actors – those who will carry out the activities

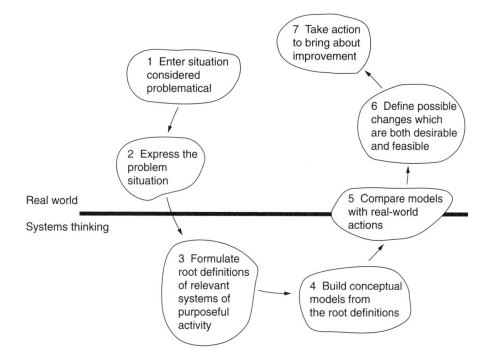

Figure 4.4   The seven steps of SSM method.

Transformation – what changes to its inputs does the purposeful activity of the system bring about?
Weltanschauung – what view of the world is appropriate?
Owner – who could stop the activity?
Environment – what constraints in the environment are taken as given?

For example, a drug purchasing system for a hospital would be described in the CATWOE framework:

Customers – administrators and doctors
Actors – not stated
Transformation – need to know: need met by recording information
Weltanschauung – monitoring spending on drugs is possible and is an adequate basis for joint action
Owner – hospital
Environment – hospital mechanisms; roles of administrators and doctors; budgets

The root definition would be: *a hospital-owned system which provides records of spending on drugs so that control action by administrators and doctors to meet defined budgets can be taken jointly.*

The subsequent process is to establish putative candidate models of such systems which would satisfy the root definition above and which can then be compared against existing systems.

SSM has enormous advantages when compared with the narrow ambitions of conventional systems engineering: it is responsive to the growing understanding which emerges during enquiry; it is responsive to different parties; and it expands the ambition of enquiry into the social context from the mere technical. On the other hand it does have a number of disadvantages: it needs experience to be performed successfully; because of its adaptive intent and emphasis on participative process, the carefully declared analytical process evades much that is tacit; and its strength in enabling high-level analysis tends to leave the detailed implementation to be defined somewhat sketchily within its defined process.

Cognitive mapping and strategic options development and analysis

Cognitive mapping[28,29] starts from the pluralist assumption that different participants in a system see it differently, but it goes further towards the idea of constructivism, whereby the participants are seen to construct the system through their perceptions and valuations. This is an important distinguishing

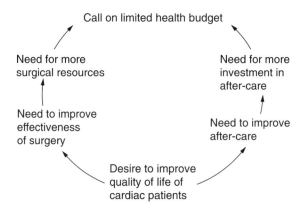

Figure 4.5   A small cognitive map – the perception of the hospital manager.

feature between SSM and cognitive mapping, of which SODA is a well-documented particular implementation.[21]

The heart of the approach is the cognitive map which records the viewpoints of participants. These partial viewpoints are then combined in order to produce an aggregated mapping of the issues and the connections between issues of participants. Figure 4.5 shows a very simple, highly summarized example. Here we see mapped out the essential conflict in the mind of a health system manager between competing demands on resources and two amelioration mechanisms – one surgical, one post-surgical.

Another participant who is a dietitian might have a cognitive map as shown in Figure 4.6, where the emphasis is on the education of the population of the benefits of exercise and good diet.

These two perspectives can be combined – they contain one common element, namely the desire to improve the quality of life of cardiac patients. Software is available for this purpose, but it can be done perfectly well by pen and paper methods. Figure 4.7 shows a combined cognitive map, demonstrating the link to overall government budgeting. In this way, an extended map of the perceptions of the participants is built up.

Having built up this extended map, the analyst now has the opportunity to identify areas of the map which appeal to, or come under the control of, particular parties. For example, the budgetary issues in Figure 4.7 would clearly be of considerable interest to the Treasury, whereas the professional remit of the hospital manager is limited to the subset shown in Figure 4.5. This may seem a rival benefit, but the advantage of cognitive mapping is that it gives us a mechanism to exhibit and jointly address the different perspectives on the system under consideration. This is no mean result when we bear in mind the ubiquitous difficulties of engaging different professional interests in cross-functional

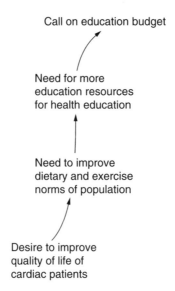

Figure 4.6   Dietitian's cognitive map.

discussion in the British NHS. This lack of internal communication is common to all large organizations and cognitive mapping is a most effective way of engendering and recording it.

The difficulty in practice with cognitive mapping is that the process of moving from mapping to action is ill-defined. The perceived mechanisms are recorded, but there is nothing in the representation method itself which cues us to look for action in particular areas. As with SSM, however, in the hands of an expert its effectiveness is undoubted.

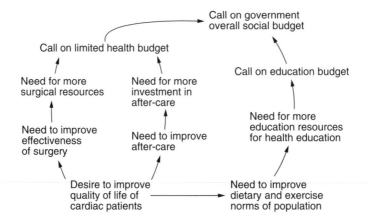

Figure 4.7   Combined cognitive map.

Qualitative system dynamics and qualitative politicized influence diagrams

It can be argued that what is needed for the management of the hybrid systems exemplified by health systems is a method which combines the crisp system descriptions of SD with the ability to include non-numerical data of SSM and the pluralist perspectives of cognitive mapping.

The first thrust was an attempt by Coyle and Wolstenholme[14] to include qualitative data in SD analysis in an approach now known as qualitative system dynamics.[16] The assumption is that we can tell to a sufficient extent the effect of elements of a system upon the overall behaviour to allow us to identify sensible managerial action. We may not know the precise results of that action any more than we do under assumptions of complex behaviour, but we know enough to be able to know what would be reasonable to do.

Figure 4.8 is an extract from a case study of patient access to general practitioners (GPs). It shows part of an influence diagram (ID), which is the equivalent of a cognitive map for SD. Both encapsulate the different perspectives of participants in the system, but they have slightly different grammars. In particular, IDs have as their variables only factors which can be expressed on a scale. This restriction is not necessary in cognitive maps.

The QSD method analyses loops extracted from IDs, such as that of Figure 4.8. The essential idea is that if we can identify actions which will cause such a loop to start moving in a beneficial direction, it will have a tendency to continue to move in that same direction. Similarly, if we can identify that a loop is moving in an undesirable direction, we can identify managerial actions to slow it down and reverse its motion.

Consider the reaction of the loop of Figure 4.8 to a small disturbance. Imagine that the demand for routine appointments were to rise (say, because of the

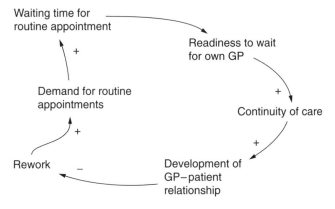

Figure 4.8   QSD loop.

opening of a large housing estate within the practice). The waiting time for appointments goes up and the readiness to wait for an appointment goes down. Because patients are then seeing doctors other than their own, continuity of care and the patient–doctor relationship decline (albeit slowly). More rework is needed and that puts further upward pressure on the demand for appointments. We can see that a small change in this type of loop propagates around the loop so that without external constraint the loop would run away out of control, something the practice would very much want to avoid.

In practice, QSD is highly effective. The grammatical rules are simple and natural and participants relish the construction of IDs in groups, thereby providing the collateral benefit of increased intra-system communication.

An important extension of QSD is qualitative politicized influence diagrams (QPID).[17,22] Each arrow has attached to it the person or persons who have control over the strength of that arrow. For example, in the connection between 'waiting time for routine appointment' and 'readiness to wait for own doctor', the receptionists will play a heavy part. If we can arm the reception staff with sound arguments as to why patients should wait for their own doctors, we can to some extent attenuate the effect of an increased desire on their part to see any doctor, with the resulting loss of continuity of care. This approach is considered in detail in Chapter 12.

Although apparently only a simple amendment to the QSD approach, the QPID attribution of actors to arrows provides a direction to the action considerations. Now the actions are no longer faceless, but are to be carried out by persons or groups of people. This in turn means that those people have a voice; they may not agree to carry out the actions we want and we must take that into account when we compile the actions into a coherent policy. QPID, of all these approaches, comes closest to reconciling the need for disciplined system representation with a plural approach.

Conclusion

Although as a general tool for system investigation and management QPID would seem to be the strongest practical candidate, the other methods have their role. There is an argument for proceeding from a very general exploratory method like cognitive mapping in order to determine the roles of different interest groups, via QPID to detailed simulation and quantitative SD representations of particular systems problems. In rare cases it might be possible to write a detailed mathematical model of a specific issue, but that is most unlikely to be a solution sufficient of itself.

The systems analysis approaches discussed here form an effective, even essential, part of the armoury of health systems managers. They must, however, be seen as part of a wide range of approaches, some of which are conventional general managerial tools while others are more the domain of specialists. The most insightful QPID analysis of actions aimed, say, at improving quality of life amongst cardiac patients is useless without the associated conventional cost–benefit analysis.

Hard methods, too, have their role in addressing those components of a health system which are amenable to a numerical approach. Determining the appropriate numbers of vehicles in an ambulance service or the matching of specialist facilities to uncertain demand are good examples of where a hard approach would be appropriate. In contrast, the examination of how the various 'constituencies' in cardiac care (surgeons, GPs, nurses, dietitians, educators, social workers) should work together for the benefit of patients is clearly a problem amenable only to the soft approaches we have described here.

To some extent, the availability of system tools limits our ambition as managers. If we only have the tools to address problems concerning numerical matters, it will be those problems that will command our attention. Soft systems allow us to address a wider set of problems that relate more directly to the human being form and take benefit from the systems we manage, and that can only be of benefit to recipients, practitioners and managers.

References

1 Checkland PB (1981) *Systems Thinking, Systems Practice*. John Wiley, Chichester.
2 Vickers G (1983) *Human Systems are Different*. Harper-Row, London.
3 Beer S (1985) *Diagnosing the System for Organisations*. John Wiley, Chichester.
4 Huff A and Reger R (1987) A review of strategic process research. *Journal of Management*. **13**: 211–36.
5 Rivett P (1994) *The Craft of Decision Modelling*. John Wiley, Chichester.
6 Simon H (1965) *The Shape of Automation*. Harper-Row, New York.
7 Checkland PB and Scholes J (1990) *Soft Systems Methodology in Action*. John Wiley, Chichester.
8 Flood R (1990) *Liberating Systems Theory*. Plenum, New York.
9 Wilson B (1990) *Systems: concepts, methodologies and applications*. John Wiley, Chichester.
10 Flood R and Jackson M (1991) *Critical Systems Thinking: directed readings*. John Wiley, Chichester.
11 Schwandt T (1994) Constructivist, interpretivist approaches to human inquiry. In: Denzin YS (ed) *A Handbook of Qualitative Research*. Sage, Thousand Oaks, CA.
12 Lyotard J (1984) *The Post-modern Condition: a report on knowledge* (trans. Berrington G and Masumi B). Manchester University Press, Manchester.
13 Denzin N and Lincoln Y (1994) *Handbook of Qualitative Research*. Sage, Thousand Oaks, CA.
14 Wolstenholme EF (1990) *System Enquiry*. John Wiley, Chichester.
15 Coyle RG (2000) Qualitative and quantitative modelling in system dynamics: some research questions. *System Dynamics Review*. **16** (3): 225–44.

16 Coyle R (2003) *Strategic Systems Modelling*. Pearson, London.
17 Powell J and Coyle R (In press) Identifying strategic action in highly politicised contexts using agent-based qualitative system dynamics. *Journal of the Operational Research Society*.
18 Forrester JW (1961) *Industrial Dynamics*. MIT Press, Harvard, MA.
19 Coyle RG (1977) *Management System Dynamics*. John Wiley, Chichester.
20 Coyle RG (1996) *System Dynamics Modelling: a practical approach*. Chapman and Hall/ CRC Press, London.
21 Eden C (1989). Using cognitive mapping for strategic options development and analysis (SODA). In: Rosenhead J (ed) *Rational Analysis for a Problematical World*. John Wiley, Chichester.
22 Powell J and Bradford J (1998) The security–strategy interface: using qualitative process models to relate the security function to business dynamics. *Security Journal*. **10:** 151–60.
23 Jackson M and Keys P (1984) Towards a system of systems methodologies. *Journal of the Operational Research Society*. **35**.
24 Jackson M (1991) The origins and nature of critical systems thinking. *Systems Practice*. **4:** 131–49.
25 Jackson M (1991) *Systems Methodology for the Management Sciences*. Plenum, New York.
26 Wiener N (1949) *Cybernetics*. RAND, Washington, DC.
27 Rosenhead J (ed) (1989) *Rational Analysis for a Problematical World*. John Wiley, Chichester.
28 Huff A (1985) *Mapping Strategic Thought*. Pergamon, London.
29 Mintzberg H (1995) Strategic thought as 'seeing'. In: Garrett R (ed) *Developing Strategic Thought*. McGraw-Hill, London.

CHAPTER 5

Organizations as learning systems

Huw Davies and Sandra Nutley

This chapter explores 'organizational learning', and the characteristics of the organizational cultures needed to underpin such learning. We have drawn on an existing literature base using an informal synthesis to summarize the key elements of learning organizations and relate these to recent developments of the NHS. Our aim is to encourage the transference of some of these ideas into the healthcare sector.

Key points
- The Government's national quality strategy for the NHS highlights life-long learning as a way of improving healthcare quality.
- Learning is something achieved by individuals but organizations can configure themselves to maximize, mobilize and retain this learning potential. Organizations that do this are called 'learning organizations'.
- Learning can occur at different levels. 'Single-loop learning' is about incremental improvements to existing patterns of practice (e.g. 'closing the loop' in clinical audit). 'Double-loop learning' occurs when organizations rethink basic goals, norms and paradigms (e.g. the development of day-case surgery, shifting services to primary care). Beyond this, 'meta-learning' reflects the attempts made by organizations to learn about (and improve) their ability to learn (e.g. by reflection on the experience of implementing clinical effectiveness initiatives).
- Learning organizations attempt to maximize learning capacity by developing skills in double-loop learning and meta-learning.
- Learning organizations exhibit several common characteristics and are underpinned by distinctive organizational cultures. Some of these characteristics may already exist in trusts and health authorities; others will need to be nurtured.
- Healthcare organizations may need to adopt some of the characteristics and cultural values of learning organizations if they are to deliver substantial quality improvements.

Introduction

Learning is something undertaken and developed by individuals but organizational arrangements can foster or inhibit this learning process – the organizational culture within which individuals work shapes their engagement with the learning process. More than this, there are real questions as to whether and how the organization is able to harness the learning achieved by its individual members. Thus, although continuing professional development (CPD) has long been a part of the NHS, evidence from other sectors suggests that learning needs to take a more central role. Organizations that position learning as a core characteristic have been termed 'learning organizations',[1–3] and this concept itself sits within the wider field of organizational development.[4]

Learning organizations

Individuals learn and enhance their personal capabilities within organizations, but what does it mean to talk of an *organization* learning? Can a hospital, a general practice or a primary care trust be said to learn? An organization is not simply a collection of individuals; the whole amounts to something greater than the sum of the parts. Similarly, the learning achieved by an organization is not simply the sum of the learning achieved by individuals within that organization. Individuals may come and go but the organization (even in the turbulent world of healthcare) usually endures. Robust organizations can still accumulate competence and capacity despite turnover of staff – individual learning can be retained and deployed in the organization. How well any organization can do this depends upon such factors as internal communication and the assimilation of individual knowledge into new work structures, routines and norms. *Learning organizations* see a central role for enhancing personal capabilities and then mobilizing these within the organization.

Organizations seek enhanced learning for two distinctive reasons.[2] First, to maintain flexibility and competence in the face of rapid change and profound uncertainty in their environment. Such change and uncertainty may arise, for example, from technological revolutions, economic turbulence, changing consumer expectations or increased competition. Because of this, rather than implement fixed responses, 'learning organizations' seek to develop structures and human resources that are flexible, adaptable and responsive. The second reason why organizations need to learn is in order to enhance their capacity to innovate, and hence to compete.

Change and uncertainty abound in the health arena, and flexibility and innovation are key requirements of modern healthcare delivery. Acute trusts are reshaping to face the transference of services to primary care; primary care trusts are gradually finding their feet; and both kinds of trust are facing mergers and other organizational upheavals. In Scotland, health boards are also seeing their role changing, and face challenging demands to foster innovative service arrangements and joint working. Thus healthcare providers of all types face many imperatives to develop effective learning – imperatives which operate across all developed countries' healthcare systems and are not confined to the UK NHS.

The key features of learning organizations are outlined in Box 5.1. They relate less to the ways in which organizations are structured and more to the ways in which people within the organization think about the nature of, and the relationships between, the outside world, their organization, their collea-gues and themselves.

Levels of learning

Crucially, learning organizations do not focus exclusively on correcting prob-lems or even on acquiring new knowledge, understanding or skills. Instead, they aim for more fundamental shifts in organizational paradigms and try to encou-rage development of learning capacity. In their seminal work on organizational learning, Argyris and Schön describe three different levels of learning.[1,5] At the most basic is the detection and correction of error (this they labelled 'single-loop learning' as it is analogous to maintaining a steady course through use of a feed-back loop). Such learning tends to leave organizational objectives and processes largely unchanged. Clinical audit, for example comparing existing practice with explicit standards, is typical of this type of learning.

Beyond basic error correction, a more sophisticated learning is possible – that which changes fundamental assumptions about the organization. Learning which, for example, leads to a redefining of the organization's goals, norms, poli-cies, procedures or even structures. This Argyris and Schön termed 'double-loop learning' as it calls into question the very nature of the course plotted and the feedback loops used to maintain that course. Development of new and innovative service delivery models, and service redesign from the ground up, represent attempts at this more radical form of learning. Unfortunately, many system pres-sures impede such a rethink and radical change often fails to materialize unless precipitated by crisis.[5,6]

One further (usually underdeveloped) aspect of 'learning capacity' is the ability of organizations to learn about the contexts of their learning. That is, when organizations are able to identify when and how they learn and when and how they do not, and then adapt accordingly. Thus successful learning organizations build on their experience of learning to develop and test new learning strategies. This can be thought of as 'learning about learning' (or

---

Box 5.1   Key features of a learning organization (adapted from Senge, 1994[3])

Open systems thinking. Individuals within organizations can tend to see activities in a somewhat isolated way, disconnected from the whole. The disease model prevalent in modern healthcare, which structures services by diseases or procedures, contributes to such isolationism. 'Open systems thinking' encapsulates the notion of teaching people to reintegrate activities, to see how what they do and what others do are interconnected. This reintegration needs to stretch beyond internal departmental boundaries, and even beyond the boundaries of the organization itself, to encompass other services and patients.

Improving individual capabilities. For an organization to be striving for excellence, the individuals within that organization must constantly be improving their own personal proficiencies. However, separate learning by the different professions in healthcare may be detrimental because individual virtuosity is insufficient – it is teams that deliver healthcare.

Team learning. Team learning is vital because it is largely through teams that organizations achieve their objectives. Therefore whole-team development is essential rather than piecemeal uni-professional learning.

Updating mental models. 'Mental models' are the deeply held assumptions and generalizations formed by individuals (internally and often implicitly). These models influence how people make sense of the world. They control, for example, how causes and effects are linked conceptually, and constrain what individuals see as possible within the organization. Changing and updating these mental models is essential to finding new ways of doing things.

A cohering vision. Empowering and enabling individuals within an organization has to be counterbalanced by providing clear strategic direction and articulating a coherent set of values that can guide individual actions. Encouraging a shared understanding of this vision, and commitment to it, is a crucial component of building a learning organization.

---

meta-learning). Experience in healthcare suggests that such learning will be difficult to achieve – standard approaches to continuing medical education (CME) appear to offer little real gains.[7]

Box 5.2 provides an illustration of these different forms of learning in healthcare.

Box 5.2 Levels of learning: an example in healthcare

Single-loop learning. A hospital examines its care of obstetric patients. Through a clinical audit, it finds various gaps between actual practice and established standards (derived from evidence-based guidelines). Meetings are held to discuss the guidelines, changes are made to working procedures, and reporting and feedback on practice are enhanced. These changes increase the proportion of patients receiving appropriate and timely care, i.e. care in compliance with the guidelines. This is an example of single-loop learning.

Double-loop learning. In examining its obstetric care, some patients are interviewed at length. From this it emerges that the issues which are bothering women have more to do with continuity of care, convenience of access, quality of information and the interpersonal aspects of the patient–professional interaction. In the light of this, obstetric care is dramatically reconfigured to a system of midwife-led teams in order to prioritize these issues. The standards as laid down in the evidence-based guidelines are not abandoned, but are woven into a new pattern of interactions and values. This is an example of double-loop learning.

Learning about learning. The experience of refocusing obstetric services to better meet patient needs and expectations is not lost on the hospital. Structurally and culturally, the organization encourages the transfer of such valuable lessons. Those factors that assisted such a reconfiguring (and those that impeded it) are analysed, described and communicated within the organization. This is done not through formal reports in writing but through informal communications, temporary work placements and the development of cross-service teams. Thus the obstetric service is able to share with other hospital services the lessons learned about 'learning to reconfigure'. This is an example of learning about learning or meta-learning.

The growth of 'problem-based learning' in medical schools and the rise of evidence-based medicine are both trends which seek to equip individuals with skills rather than a reservoir of facts.[8,9] As such they may contribute to a culture of both single- and double-loop learning in healthcare. They illustrate how teaching learning strategies and information skills can enhance learning capacity and flexibility.

However, learning is not always about acquisition. As so much of healthcare is time-served rather than evidence based,[10] there is also a need for learning strategies to focus on *unlearning* previously established practice.[11] This kind of unlearning is not just about individual practitioners making alterations to practice patterns. Even more important is that the organization should develop the ability to identify, critique and change whole routines embedded in organizational custom. For example, the moving of services from secondary to primary care challenges many deeply held assumptions about the role of specialists. Such unlearning may prove especially difficult because of the personal investments people have in current competencies. Experience after the healthcare reforms of the early 1990s showed that, despite the apparently radical nature of the changes, continuity rather than change was the dominant theme.[12]

Learning and the national quality framework

In the national context, the National Performance Framework[13] facilitates single-loop learning by providing clear measures of performance and benchmarks against which these measures can be judged. The Framework, however, provides less opportunity to call into question underlying assumptions and goals, and therefore contributes little to double-loop learning. In contrast, the 'lifelong learning' emphasized in *A First-class Service*[14] describes a notion of professional development that captures both single-loop learning and some elements of double-loop learning:

> *Continuing professional development (CPD) programmes need to meet both the learning needs of individual health professionals . . . but importantly they also need to meet the wider service development needs of the NHS.*
> (Para 3.30 in *A First-class Service: quality in the new NHS*[14])

However, how such 'wider service development needs' are to be met, and whether learning in the NHS is to embrace meta-learning, remains unclear. How are successes in transforming the NHS culture to be identified, analysed and communicated? What can NHS trusts and health authorities do to transform themselves, and what role should the central NHS infrastructure take in communicating models of good practice across the country?

Cultural values underpinning learning organizations

Building learning organizations is in effect an attempt to manage the culture of that organization.[15,16] It requires attention to some key cultural values if it is to be a successful undertaking. These values are outlined in Box 5.3.

Box 5.3   Cultural values underpinning learning organizations (adapted from Mintzberg *et al.* 1998[17])

Celebration of success. If excellence is to be pursued with vigour and commitment, its attainment must be valued within the organizational culture.

Absence of complacency. Learning organizations reject the adage 'if it ain't broke don't fix it' – they are searching constantly for new ways of delivering products and services. Thus innovation and change are valued within the organization.

Tolerance of mistakes. Learning from failure is a prerequisite for progressive organizations. This in turn requires a culture that accepts the positive spin-offs from errors, rather than seeks to blame and scapegoat. (This does not, however, imply a tolerance of routinely poor or mediocre performance from which no lessons are learned.)

Belief in human potential. It is people that drive success in organizations – using their creativity, energy and innovation. Therefore the culture within a learning organization values people and fosters their professional and personal development.

Recognition of tacit knowledge. Learning organizations recognize that those individuals closest to processes have the best and most intimate knowledge about their potential and flaws. Therefore the learning culture values tacit knowledge and demonstrates a belief in empowerment (the systematic enlargement of discretion, responsibility and competence).

Openness. Because learning organizations try to foster a 'systems' view, sharing knowledge throughout the organization is one key to developing learning capacity. 'Knowledge mobility' emphasizes informal channels and personal contacts over written reporting procedures. Cross-disciplinary and multi-function teams, staff rotations, on-site inspections and experiential learning are essential components of this informal exchange.

Trust. For individuals to give of their best, take risks and develop their competencies, they must trust that such activities will be appreciated and valued by colleagues and managers. In particular, they must be confident that should they err they will be supported, not castigated. In turn, managers must be able to trust that subordinates will use wisely the time, space and resources given to them through empowerment programmes and not indulge in opportunistic behaviour. Without trust, learning is a faltering process.

> *Outward looking.* Learning organizations are engaged with the world outside as a rich source of learning opportunities. They look to their competitors for insights into their own operations and are attuned to the experiences of other stakeholders such as their suppliers. In particular, they are focused on obtaining a deep understanding of clients' needs.

Some of these values are already central to the healthcare professions and the NHS (e.g. the celebration of success); others may need more work (e.g. openness and trust). Inculcating the cultural values outlined in Box 5.3 into a knowing and at times sceptical workforce will be no easy matter. Integrating these values with other organization-wide initiatives such as strategic planning, financial restructuring and clinical governance will be harder still. In addition, long-ingrained cultural values emanating from outside bodies such as the Royal Colleges will certainly impinge on, and may even impede, this process.

Interactions between attempts at internal cultural change and external accountability mechanisms may add further complications and conflicts. For example, the high levels of trust needed to underpin learning organizations may be damaged by some of the more judgemental aspects of the National Performance Framework.[18] Finally, the values underpinning learning organizations (those described in Box 5.3) have themselves in-built tensions requiring careful balance between their sometimes conflicting demands (for example, celebrating success while tolerating and learning from mistakes). Precious little empirical work specific to the NHS yet exists to inform strategic and managerial actions in these areas, and this lack needs urgent attention if the Government's ambitions for the NHS are to take shape as more than rhetoric.

Concluding remarks

It is clear from official policy documents that the Government would like to see the NHS undergo a cultural transformation, incorporating considerable attention to learning. If the NHS is to make progress towards such a goal then a number of considerations are germane:

- A substantial literature exists on learning organizations and the cultural values that underpin them.[16,19–22] This framework will undoubtedly be helpful in shaping policy and managerial strategies. However, much more empirical work is required to put flesh on these bones in the health arena, and most especially fresh work is needed in the context of the reformed NHS.
- Experience from other sectors shows that learning strategies tend to focus on single-loop learning, with relatively little double-loop learning and virtually

no meta-learning.[5] If the NHS is to learn how to adopt in any meaningful way the key features of a learning organization and the concomitant underlying values, the issue of meta-learning will need considerable attention.

- The emphasis on team delivery of healthcare reinforces the need for team learning. Uni-professional learning and traditional approaches to CME may be insufficient to bring about substantial changes in learning capacity.
- Different strands of the Government's quality strategy (for example, internal learning and external oversight) may interact in deleterious ways, for example by damaging trust and increasing defensiveness.[23,24] Ways of minimizing these collisions need to be found.
- Developing learning capacity may lead to more flexible healthcare delivery and enable service providers and health authorities to deliver on some of the quality agenda. However, there is no guarantee that learning will lead healthcare organizations in predictable directions. Indeed, the growth of capable and reflective organizations may highlight dissonance between what organizations perceive as appropriate goals (and the means of achieving them) and the directions stipulated by national policy or overseeing bodies. Managing these conflicts will require care, especially as hospitals gain greater freedoms under 'earned autonomy' or achieve 'foundation' status.
- Within any busy organization there is a tension between 'doing' and 'learning about doing'. Providing incentives as well as resources to develop the latter over the former may help ease this clash of priorities.

The Government often talks of its reforms as 'a ten-year modernization programme'.[14] This is probably a realistic estimation of the extent of the task. Cultural remaking of the sort envisaged is rarely quick and never simple.[25] Even the introduction of widespread single-loop learning into healthcare (clinical audit) proved troublesome and not especially effective.[26] However, there does exist some clear guidance on the sorts of cultural changes required to underpin the transformation of the NHS into a learning organization. Rapid evaluation and diffusion of the best ways of operationalizing these will be required if success is to be anything but sporadic and localized.

References

1 Argyris C and Schön DA (1978) *Organizational Learning*. Addison-Wesley, London.
2 Dodgson M (1993) Organizational learning: a review of some literature. *Organizational Studies*. 14: 375–94.
3 Senge PM (1994) *The Fifth Discipline: the art and practice of the learning organization*. Currency Doubleday, New York.
4 Garside P (1998) Organisational context for quality: lessons from the fields of organisational development and change management. *Quality in Health Care*. 7 (Suppl): S8–S15.

5   Argyris C and Schön DA (1996) *Organizational Learning II.* Addison-Wesley, Reading, MA.

6   Galvin RS (1998) What do employers mean by 'value'? *Integrated Healthcare Report.* **October**: 1–15.

7   Davis DA, Thomson MA, Oxman AD *et al.* (1992) Evidence for the effectiveness of CME: a review of 50 randomized controlled trials. *JAMA.* **268 (9)**: 1111–17.

8   Sackett DL, Rosenberg WMC, Gray JAM *et al.* (1996) Evidence-based medicine: what it is and what it isn't. *BMJ.* **312**: 71–2.

9   Sackett DL, Richardson WS, Rosenberg W *et al.* (1997) *Evidence-based Medicine: how to practice and teach EBM.* Churchill Livingstone, London.

10 Smith R (1991) Where is the wisdom . . . ? [editorial]. *BMJ.* **303**: 798–9.

11 Hedberg B (1981) How organizations learn and unlearn. In: Nystrom P and Starbuck W (eds) *Handbook of Organizational Design*, pp. 3–27. Oxford University Press, Oxford.

12 Broadbent J, Laughlin R and Shearn D (1992) Recent financial and administrative changes in general practice: an unhealthy intrusion into medical autonomy. *Financial Accountability and Management.* **8 (2)**: 129–48.

13 NHS Executive (1998) *The New NHS: modern, dependable – a national framework for assessing performance.* NHS Executive, Leeds.

14 Secretary of State for Health (1998) *A First-class Service: quality in the new NHS.* Department of Health, London.

15 Garvin DA (1993) Building a learning organization. *Harvard Business Review.* **71**: 78–91.

16 Marquardt MJ (1996) Building the learning organization. McGraw-Hill, New York.

17 Mintzberg H, Ahlstrand B and Lampel J (1998) *The Strategy Safari.* The Free Press, New York.

18 Davies HTO and Mannion R (1999) Clinical governance: striking a balance between checking and trusting. In: Smith PC (ed) *Reforming Markets in Health Care: an economic perspective.* Open University Press, Buckingham.

19 Cavaleri SA and Fearon DS (eds) (1996) *Managing in Organizations that Learn.* Blackwell Business, Cambridge, MA.

20 Moingeon B and Edmondson A (eds) (1996) *Organizational Learning and Competitive Advantage.* Sage, London.

21 Starkey K (ed) (1996) *How Organizations Learn.* International Thomson Business Press, London.

22 Pedlar M and Aspinwall K (1998) *A Concise Guide to the Learning Organization.* Lemos and Crane, London.

23 Davies HTO and Mannion R (1999) The rise of oversight and the decline of mutuality. *Public Money & Management.* **19 (2)**: 55–9.

24 Davies HTO and Lampel J (1998) Trust in performance indicators. *Quality in Health Care.* **7**: 159–62.

25 Deal TE and Kennedy AA (1992) *Corporate Cultures: the rites and rituals of corporate life.* Penguin, London.

26 Hopkins A (1996) Clinical audit: time for a reappraisal? *Journal of the Royal College of Physicians of London.* **30 (5)**: 415–25.

This chapter is a revised version of an earlier paper: Davies HTO and Nutley SM (2000) Developing learning organizations in the new NHS. *BMJ.* **320**: 998–1001.

CHAPTER 6

Making sense of organizational change in practice: change as complex responsive processes

Jo Poole

The need for change in the health service is widely recognized but poses an enormous challenge to managers and professionals. Change is seen as achievable by structural change, cultural change, or the imposition of targets and measures. However, in reality change is messy and contextual. Frustration and anxiety can be provoked when things don't go to plan. In this chapter I will be asking how a development of complexity thinking that sees organizations in terms of complex responsive processes can offer an alternative perspective. I will draw upon my own experiences as a healthcare practitioner to make sense of change using this framework.

Key points
- A systems perspective sees change as desirable and controllable but research and experience suggests that change is contextual and messy.
- Drawing upon psychology and sociology, a new theory of *complex responsive processes of relating* builds upon insights from the complexity sciences to understand human patterns of relating.
- The theory of complex responsive processes points to a participatory and narrative approach to understanding change in organization.
- What an organization is becoming emerges as a result of communication between individuals and groups at a local level. This includes co-operation and conflict; identity and difference; and power as enablement and constraint.
- We are always participants in an organization and can never step outside it to shape it. The organization's future cannot be determined solely by the choice of powerful individuals.

Introduction

My own interest in change emerged from experiences as a nurse in a primary healthcare setting. Having completed my first degree in 1997, I was fired with enthusiasm to use newly learned models of change and leadership. After initial perceived success I was appointed to a new post to lead an integrated nursing team. However, attempts to develop the team were to prove frustrating.

> *I am responsible for improving teamworking at the practice. I arrange a meeting where I ask people to talk about the work they do in their own discipline. I expect that we will find some common ground and develop a common vision of how we can achieve improved care by working together on a common health initiative. However, there is little enthusiasm for this idea as my new colleagues express their despair at previous interventions and away-days with facilitators, aiming to promote team-working. There is hostility between people at these meetings. Where am I going wrong? I feel frustrated and anxious that I have failed and reason that I need to get better at 'managing change'.*

This example shows a common organizational development approach to change, based on agreeing common goals and visions and setting objectives to achieve the change that is desired.[1-3] However, I sensed a dissonance between theories of change studied on my degree course,[4,5] and my real life experience. Similarly, my experiences of instigating change in a new NHS structure as a primary care group board nurse and primary care trust nurse executive also proved unfulfilling. What seemed to be lacking in my tools and models was a recognition of the context and history of what had gone on before. There was not a strategy that could be lifted and applied to any people in any context.

Subsequently, I came across the theories of complexity which resonated with my experience,[6] suggesting that change happened spontaneously but unpredictably from local interactions. The developing theory of complex responsive processes of human relating also suggested that change could be understood by focusing on these local interactions.

In this chapter I will be taking an alternative view of change in organizations which recognizes its messy contextual nature. I will first explore the dominant way of viewing change in organizations, then look at how the study of complex adaptive systems has been used metaphorically for this purpose. I will then examine the theory of complex responsive processes of relating and give examples of how change can be experienced in practice from this perspective. My aim is to offer an alternative way of viewing change by exploring change from the perspective of a practitioner/researcher participating in the process of change as it is happening. I hope this will help you to make sense of your own experiences as a 'change agent', whether you are leader, manager or practitioner in a healthcare organization.

The dominant paradigm of systems thinking

The dominant and implicit view of change arises from a systems view of the world. This perspective, derived from science and engineering, assumes the position of an objective observer of a 'system' which is open to manipulation. This is unproblematic when there is a clear boundary, as in mechanical systems, but less clear with human organizations and human interaction.

The NHS Plan reflects this view by focusing on organizational structure, culture and a proliferation of targets and measurement as ways of achieving change.[1] The prevailing view is that we must get better at understanding how change takes place, how to make it happen, and that this is indeed possible.[7,8]

Whilst a systems view can be helpful in understanding patterns emerging in organizations, or causal links distant in time, the tendency is to forget that we are viewing an organization as if it were a 'thing' or a spacial object.[9] The following narrative demonstrates a systems view of organizations as if they are wholes.

Measuring the 'organization'

A primary care trust (PCT) is measuring its performance relating to a number of target areas. For example, measures are related to whether the PCT has the structures and systems in place to deal with risk. Although the PCT has performed well in comparison with other PCTs, it has a number of 'red' or 'amber' lights for particular areas. However, where it has scored 'green', an Executive member points out that patient care relating to this area is not as good as it could be. The Executive members discuss this and conclude that the measures are not looking for quality indicators about service, but more about measuring the organization itself as a structure, i.e. did it have systems and procedures in place to deal with problems.

This example shows how an organization is viewed as a 'thing' or spacial whole rather than processes of people interacting with one another. Formal structures were being measured or reified (i.e. an abstract idea was being made concrete) as opposed to understanding what was really happening in interactions between people. Formal systems and plans only work due to the informal day-to-day interactions between people, rather than their controlling action. In this example it is questionable what indicators of quality were being measured, as formal structures themselves are not capable of ensuring interaction. This distancing and reifying may result in paying less attention to what is happening in the quality of our local interactions in the here and now.

Complex adaptive systems

There has been increasing interest in insights from the complexity sciences amongst organizational and management theorists over the past decade.[10,11] 'Complexity sciences' is the name given to a number of theories from diverse disciplines such as biology, physics, mathematics and chemistry, studying the nature of complex adaptive systems, i.e. systems made up of a number of agents with non-linear interaction.[12-14] Computer modelling of complex systems has demonstrated that self-organization and emergence arise spontaneously and unpredictably from local interactions between agents. In other words, order or patterns arise unpredictably from local interactions.

Business writers have metaphorically transferred ideas from the study of complex adaptive systems for use as tools in organizations. These approaches are considered in more detail in Section 3. For example, whilst choosing 'simple rules' to guide behaviour[15-17] or advocate more caring relationships[10,11] can be helpful, they may have unpredictable results and continue to focus on systems open to manipulation. Health writers have also interpreted insights for health organizations in a number of ways: by viewing the health system as an ecosystem,[18] looking for levers for change[19,20] or advocating increasing variables used in research to reflect complex relationships.[21,22] Plsek[15] advocates using 'simple rules' or 'minimum specifications' to guide behaviour of a system. This idea is taken from a simple computer simulation showing that 'flocking' behaviour of homogeneous agents, or 'boids', emerges from a few simple rules. However, this does not explain novelty, as that is all that these agents do. Furthermore, once the rules are decided it assumes that people will follow them.

These approaches remain firmly within the paradigm of systems thinking. What is dismissed is the problem of taking ideas from one domain, i.e. the scientist or computer programmer designing an experiment and observing the outcome, to the domain of human beings.[9] Stacey et al. argues that it is impossible for a human being to stand outside the processes of relating to observe them, as they are inevitably part of the same process.[9]

So what is the alternative to thinking about systems when dealing with human patterns of relating? Stacey uses the analogy of interaction between agents in computer modelling as interaction between human beings.[23] Interaction itself is capable of spontaneously self-organizing into emerging themes of conversation. This is a bit like the pattern or themes of conversations at a dinner party that can only be seen at the end. The focus then becomes the experience of a process of continual interaction between human beings from within that interaction.

Complex responsive processes of relating

One development of insights from the study of complex systems as a source domain by way of analogy for human processes of relating is known as complex responsive processes of relating. This theory is relatively recent and also draws upon sociology and psychology to explain the processes of human relating in organizations.[9]

The theory of complex responsive processes of relating:

- draws on insights from the complexity sciences as a source domain for understanding human relating
- draws from sociology and psychology for theories of human relating,[24,25] and suggests that we come to know the world primarily through gestures/ language
- acknowledges the messy, contextual and unpredictable nature of change and paradoxical nature of organizational life, which includes power, politics and conflict
- points to the importance of difference, diversity and spontaneity
- provides a different perspective on change, where structural, cultural and change by measurement and targets are considered to arise from interactions, rather than determining the future in themselves
- reality is understood as participation in processes of relating.

What becomes important is focusing on our own participation in our interactions, underpinned by a participatory, narrative methodology as opposed to an 'observer'/'observed' relationship.

Drawing on the work of social psychologist Mead[24] and sociologist Elias,[25] Stacey et al.[9] define 'complex responsive processes' as a development of complexity theories for human processes of relating, located within social and psychological theory, as opposed to thinking derived from engineers. They suggest that the individual and the group are continually forming and being formed by one another by gestures/responses. Elias suggests that the individual and the group are the singular and plural of the same phenomenon, namely human relating. My conversations within my own head (singular) and with others (plural) are perpetually creating the future as both continuity and with the potential for change or new themes of conversation to emerge.

Stacey et al. do not dismiss systems thinking as having no value in understanding human beings and organizational life. However, they argue that this way of thinking does not pay attention to what it is excluding, and does not deal

Table 6.1   Some differences between the dominant systems view and the perspective of complex responsive processes

Dominant view	Complex responsive processes view
• Experience is explained in terms of linear cause and effect	• Explains experience in terms of making sense in everyday conversations, which are stable but potentially transforming at the same time
• Refers to individuals as autonomous and organizations as wholes	• Refers to the emergence of the self in local interaction and *conversation as organizing*
• Views the past, present and future as separate wholes	• Views the present as including the past and intention about the future
• Results in anxiety about a radically unknown future with a focus on controlling the present	• Accepts and lives with anxiety inherent in conversations resulting in change, i.e. creativity or destruction, which involves shifts in power relations
• Tends to idealize and reify wholes	• Deals with the wholes which appear continuously as ideology, which exists only in the speaking of it, not something stored anywhere or shared

adequately with the paradoxes of organizational life. Rather they suggest we need to understand how we use systems thinking as a way to talk about an abstract idea. These tools are complex processes that are much more than tools alone.[9]

Table 6.1, adapted from Griffin,[26] highlights some differences between the dominant systems view and the perspective of complex responsive processes.

Complex responsive processes then suggest a very different perspective on change. Change is seen as spontaneously emerging as paradoxically both stability and change, at the same time, as we interact with one another in processes of human relating. It is a participatory process whereby the local interaction between humans is based on the past, with an intention towards the future, experienced as the movement in the 'living present' or here and now.[26] It provides an overarching view of how change occurs whether structural, behavioural or cultural. Looking closely at what happens when those in 'power' produce policies, they can provide a gesture (e.g. the 400 *NHS Plan* targets), but individuals locally choose how they respond. All these forms of change result themselves from local interactions between human beings, e.g. a politician with other colleagues, secretary and spouse.

From this perspective power is seen as a constraint, rather than something fixed or held by one person. When relating to each other we are all constrained to some degree based on what has gone on before, but there is always the potential for this to change in the dynamics of an interaction. Even leaders or those traditionally seen as powerful are constrained by what they are 'allowed' to do by those traditionally seen as 'followers'.

> *Instead of taking it for granted that powerful chief executives individually change organizations directly through their intended actions, the complex responsive processes perspective invites one to explore the communicative processes in which the mere presence of, the images of, and the fantasies about leaders all affect local processes of communicative interaction in the living present.*
>
> (Griffin, 2002[26])

Making sense of change in practice through the perspective of complex responsive processes

Anxieties arising from uncertainty about the future are paradoxes of organizational life. Fear of disasters such as the Bristol and Shipman cases make systems thinking comforting if we imagine we can control change, predict the future and manage risk. Models and tools allow us to categorize things and look at them from the outside, thereby removing the paradox. However, when tools and models fail, this defence can be worse than the original anxiety it tries to avoid.

What would it be like to experience change from the alternative perspective I am proposing? I have been asking this question as I participate as a practitioner/researcher in my daily work within primary healthcare, where I often find dissonance between the dominant way of viewing change and this new way of understanding. Seeing change from a complex responsive processes perspective has changed the way I make sense of my experiences as a practitioner/researcher and this final section offers some of my personal observations.

The first example illustrates some of the difficulties from a systems perspective when trying to reorganize healthcare. Deciding on who is in the 'system' to consult with can be problematic and the number of diverse views only adds to the complexity.

Planning the future

A health authority is planning a reconfiguration of health services county-wide, including local hospitals and primary care trusts. Many stakeholder workshops have been held to obtain views of local people, health professionals and managers. This has been taking place for some years with no decision being made. At a local workshop people are discussing what quality services would look like. A member of the public describes how he would like to have better communication with his GP and improved information about his appointment at the local hospital. The facilitator feeds back that although many of the qualities suggested don't need a ten-year plan to achieve them, there needs to be a decision about reconfiguration of health services to continue working with certainty about the future.

As we talk about and try to plan for the future, we are co-creating that future in our local interactions. Plans and procedures may feature in these interactions without determining their pattern.[8] When the aim is to agree a common vision of the future, frustration and anxiety can arise when difference is expressed. Systems, from a complex responsive processes perspective, can be understood as a temporal (i.e. over time) process of inclusion/exclusion, identity/difference at the same time. I may temporarily feel part of a 'system' or group of people, whilst at the same time experiencing feelings of exclusion from other groups or individuals. I may identify with but also feel different from others. I am continually living with these paradoxes, rather than trying to resolve them.

My next example thinks about how we interact with a patient. A traditional view would be to elicit an accurate history, agree a treatment plan and observe outcomes. This assumes there is a straightforward history and diagnosis to be found if only I had the required skill to discover it. However, a complex responsive processes perspective challenges me to think differently about what it is I am 'discovering'. I may have had conversations with a patient many times, but each occasion may differ slightly as we negotiate what to do on this occasion. This is the paradox of acting into the known, unknown. Meaning arises in the interaction in the living present.

Meaning in the here and now

A patient is telling me about a recent illness. I ask several questions and the patient thoughtfully responds. I am puzzled by the history and decide to ask a colleague to join us. I give a brief summary to my colleague concerning what we have discussed so far and the patient chips in. I find that my colleague is asking similar questions but the patient has changed their response, and gradually a pattern emerges about the patient's illness which seems meaningful.

Initially I may feel as if I have not understood the patient correctly and I will appear stupid to my colleague. However, from a complex responsive processes perspective, I would expect the story to change as we relate to one another. The patient's story emerges depending on my own responses, or questions I have asked. This in itself triggers new responses by the patient as conversations in our own heads, with each other and with my colleague who joins us, as we try to make sense together based on the past, with intention about the future, in the living present, or here and now.

In my own work setting I notice where things have changed and stayed the same, although not necessarily due to planned change initiatives. My final example describes the introduction of traditional management tools at a general practice aiming to produce desired change.

Improving teamworking

A GP at a practice is trying to improve teamworking and decides this may be achieved by introducing 360 degree appraisal (appraisal of all staff by each other), whereby staff are encouraged to give feedback to one another. This is received with some hostility by administrative staff, who believe they will not be able to give honest feedback to the GPs who employ them. After conversation with her colleagues, a member of the administration staff approaches one of the GPs to say that they are not happy to proceed with this new form of appraisal. The GP is taken aback but agrees to meet with the administrative staff to discuss further. The 360 degree appraisal is not implemented, although meetings between administration staff and the GPs continue.

The example suggests that there were changes in the way the administrative staff related to the GPs, although not in an expected way, due to introduction of an appraisal system. This is another example of the shifting nature of power relations in the moment, and of the potential for change to occur spontaneously although unpredictably.

Making sense of my experiences in this way has highlighted to me the importance of what I say and do in my interactions with others in the here and now. I notice how themes of conversation develop. Then, just by one comment they can take a different turn. Think about how quickly gossip and rumour spreads among people, but a different view or a disruption of the pattern may change the theme of conversations. I also notice how a mix of rational thought, emotion, fear, self-preservation, concern, hope and anxiety are all present in what we like to think of as rational decision-making processes.[28] I therefore try to act more on my feelings of dissonance during, say, a meeting or when with a patient by saying something in the moment and noticing what happens as a result. The disturbance of patterns of interaction, allowing new ones to emerge, is what organizational change is really all about.

Furthermore, notice how easy it is to become aware of patterns with hindsight. We then often assume that we should have known better, or think we can rationally choose to avoid mistakes in the future. How often time is spent planning how we can better manage meetings, time, discussion and outcomes.[27] I wonder how much more we could achieve if we did less, rather than more?[23]

What becomes evident then is the responsibility for our actions/interactions in the here and now. When I act with intention in the here and now, I am both responsible and yet cannot know the results of my actions, paradoxically at the same time. This theme can be explored further in Griffin's book on leadership and ethics.[26] Indeed, the future is both known and unknown, stable and changing, creative and destructive, at the same time. From this perspective one lives with the tensions of these paradoxes of organizational life, rather than trying to resolve them.

Conclusion

This chapter explores what it is like to experience change in primary healthcare from a complex responsive processes perspective. Traditional assumptions see change as controllable, yet research recognizes its messy contextual nature. This new theory offers a different way of viewing change which may lead to a new way of thinking. Attempts to change the system by changing structures, or by measurement and targets, appear to distract from the anxieties and paradoxes of providing healthcare, but may result in even greater anxiety when these attempts fail. The theory of complex responsive processes suggests that continuity and change emerge from local processes of relating, and focuses on paying attention to our own participation in our own local interactions as we make sense of our experiences, with others, in co-creating our futures.

> *It means questioning ourselves when we think that our role is to 'get them' to think differently, when we ask what 'you do' about complexity ... when one moves away from thinking that one has to manage the whole system, one pays attention to one's participation in one's own local situation in the living present.*
>
> (Stacey, 2001[23])

References

1 Department of Health (1997) *The New NHS: modern, dependable*. HMSO, London.
2 Department of Health (2000) *The NHS Plan: a plan for investment, a plan for reform*. HMSO, London.
3 Berwick D (1996) A primer on leading the improvement of systems. *BMJ*. 312: 619–22.
4 Lewin K (1951) *Field Theory in Social Science*. Harper-Row, New York.
5 Senge P (1990) *The Fifth Discipline: the art and practice of the learning organization*. Doubleday/Century Business, London.
6 Foulkes SH (1948) *Introduction to Group Analytic Psychotherapy*. William Heinemann Medical Books Ltd, London.
7 National Co-Ordinating Centre for NHS Service Delivery and Organisation Research and Development (NCCSDO) (2001) *Managing Change in the NHS*. London School of Hygiene and Tropical Medicine, London.
8 Ham C (1999) Improving NHS performance: human behaviour and health policy. *BMJ*. 319: 1490–2.

9   Stacey RD, Griffin D and Shaw P (2000) *Complexity and Management: fad or radical chal-lenge to systems thinking?* Routledge, London.

10 Lewin R and Regine B (1999) *The Soul at Work: embracing complexity science for business success.* Orion Business, London.

11 Wheatley MS (1992) *Leadership and the New Science.* Berrett-Koehler, San Francisco, CA.

12 Kauffman S (1995) *At Home in the Universe.* Oxford University Press, New York.

13 Holland J (1998) *Emergence: from chaos to order.* Oxford University Press, Oxford.

14 Prigogine I (1997) *The End of Certainty: time, chaos and the new laws of nature.* The Free Press, New York.

15 Plsek P (2001) *Redesigning Healthcare with Insights from the Science of Complex Adaptive Systems.* Institute of Medicine Report, Boston, MA.

16 Plsek P and Greenhalgh T (2001) The importance of complexity in health care. *BMJ.* **823:** 625–8.

17 Plsek P and Wilson T (2001) Complexity, leadership and management in health care organizations. *BMJ.* **323:** 746–9.

18 Royston G and Dick P (1998) Healthcare ecology. *British Journal of Health Care Management.* **4 (5):** 238–41.

19 Anderson A and McDaniel RR (2000) Managing health-care organizations: where pro-fessionalism meets complexity science. *Health Care Management Review.* **25 (1):** 83–92.

20 Arndt M and Bigelow B (2000) The potential of chaos theory and complexity theory for health services management. *Health Care Management Review.* **25 (1):** 35–8.

21 Griffiths F and Byrne D (1998) General practice and the new science emerging from the theories of 'chaos' and complexity. *British Journal of General Practice.* **48:** 1697–9.

22 Hayles NK (1999) From chaos to complexity: moving through metaphor to practice. *Complexity and Chaos in Nursing.* www.southernct.edu/scsu/chaos/nursing

23 Stacey RD (2001) *Complex Responsive Processes in Organisations: learning and knowledge creation.* Routledge, London.

24 Mead GH (1934) *Mind, Self and Society: from the standpoint of a social behaviorist.* Chicago University Press, Chicago.

25 Elias N (1989) *The Symbol Theory.* Sage, London.

26 Griffin D (2002) *The Emergence of Leadership: linking self-organisation and ethics.* Rout-ledge, London.

27 Shaw P (2002) *Changing Conversations in Organisations: a complexity approach to change.* Routledge, London.

Section 3

Complexity perspectives on healthcare organization

Introduction

Within the spectrum considered in Section 2 are a wide range of models for understanding organizations. This diversity reflects a lack of theoretical consensus surrounding definitions and interpretations of how organizations do and should operate. Each academic discipline approaches this study within their own conceptual paradigm, resulting in discourses that are invariably inaccessible to those who actually get on and do the work. Chapter 7 offers a brief overview of the development of organizational thinking.

Chapter 8 sets the search for the correct organizational solution for the NHS in a historical perspective. It alerts us to the fact that recent organizational models have been imported from the US. Reflecting a consumer-based focus, they see the patient as the central unit of organizational activity. I argue that a more relevant organizational unit would be the patient–healthcare professional, emphasizing the importance of relationships in complex adaptive systems. Although there are signs that the Department of Health may be getting the message about the implications of complexity theory, the political perspective remains within a linear model and a framework of central control.

Chapter 9 explores the concept of organizational culture. Although culture is a common theme that runs throughout the organizational literature, there is little consensus over what it means or whether it offers opportunities for manipulation. The chapter compares the concept from a reductionist and complexity perspective and argues that culture emerges from the interplay between formal and informal organizational channels.

A central feature in any organization is the role of leadership and Chapter 10 reviews this important concept. The traditional leader was seen as a decision maker who guided the organization through times of change. More recently, an alternative perspective sees a leader who is sensitive to the complex nature of organizational life. Leadership is seen as the management of meaning and symbolic action and the articulation of the organizational vision. Caught between the imperatives of central control and a political rhetoric of localism, leadership in the NHS is currently in a bit of a muddle.

Readers who would like to see some examples of how the theoretical constructs outlined in this section have been applied in practice may like to turn to Section 7.

CHAPTER 7

Complexity and the development of organizational theory

David Kernick

Despite an overwhelming literature, there is no convergence to an understanding of how organizations do or should operate. The common experience seems to be that organizational change does not yield the promised results and, invariably, managers end up managing the unwanted side-effects of their own efforts. This chapter briefly reviews how we think about organizations and where complexity sits in the theoretical menagerie. The dual nature of organizational life is highlighted – on the one hand, institutions designed to enact a specific purpose; on the other, communities of people who interact with each other to make their activities meaningful at a local level.

Key points
- There is no agreement on how organizations work and how they can be managed.
- No effective organizational model has emerged and the existing discourses remain largely inaccessible to those who actually get on and do the work.
- Studies suggest that a network may provide the most effective form of organization in environments of uncertainty and ambiguity.
- Complexity does not offer ready solutions to organizational change but shifts the gaze. It focuses on the patterns of relationships within organizations, how they are sustained, how they self-organize and how outcomes emerge.
- Organizations may manage just as well without the plethora of organizational theory.

Introduction

There are two frameworks within which organizations can be considered. Firstly, we come together in organizations in areas that require social regulation or integration that could not be achieved by individual action. Organizations bring together numbers of people and imbue them for a sufficient time with a sufficient similarity of approach, outlook and priorities to enable them to achieve collective, sustained responses, which would be impossible if a group of unorganized individuals were to face the same problem. In this model:

- Change takes place within a bureaucratic system of rules and norms that shape individual behaviour.
- Organizations contain structured activity that is goal-directed with an identifiable boundary.
- Activity consists of the allocation of limited resources (*physical*, e.g. buildings, equipment or *human*, i.e. skills, capabilities, information and knowledge) against criteria of effectiveness, efficiency and equity.
- Individuals behave in such a way as to maximize their utility or well-being.
- Power is enacted within a hierarchical framework, i.e a submission of some to the will of others against a background of conflict of interest.*

The second perspective sees people coming together in organizations to make sense of their world within a framework that is largely socially constructed. Weick[1] argues that sense making in organizations is retrospective. Remembering and looking back are the primary sources of meaning. Because of this, justifying and legitimizing play important roles and organizational action is as much goal-interpreted as goal-directed. In this model:

- The focus is on paying attention to the quality of one's own relationship with others.
- What an organization becomes emerges from the relationships of its members based on an intrinsic human need to individually and collectively express their identities and thereby their differences, rather than being determined by the choices of individuals who are in charge.
- The emphasis is on informal channels (who talks to whom, who is in and who is out) rather than formal channels (bureaucratic structures such as plans, organizational charts, contracts).

---

*Originally, power was a culturally defined position of authority on which the community relied for the resolution of conflicts and decisions about how to act wisely and effectively. Authority consisted of empowering others to act in ways that benefitted society as a whole. As society has become more complex, resolutions of conflicts become more organized within an administrative structure. Organizations are ultimately rules of behaviour that facilitate decision making and embody relationships that invariably imply the power of self-interest.

- Power is not an attribute or a possession of a single person but is character-istic of human relating – it arises between us in our relationships. To sustain a relationship with another person is to actively engage in a jointly created process of mutual constraint that affords each of us opportunities while at the same time limits us.

Across this spectrum are a number of interpretations of how organizations do and should work in an overwhelming literature drawing upon a range of disciplines that include sociology, psychology, philosophy, economics and

---

Box 7.1   Metaphors through which organizations can be viewed[5]

- Organizations as machines. The emphasis is on predetermined goals and objectives and the organization is expected to operate in a systema-tic, efficient and predictable manner. This can result in a lack of adapt-ability and a dehumanizing experience for those working within such frameworks.
- Organizations as organisms. The attention is focused on understanding organizational needs and the relationship with the environment. Orga-nizations go through cycles of birth, growth, development, decline and death – living systems that have to adapt to changes in their environ-ment. The needs of the individual and organisms must be integrated.
- Organizations as brains. The attention is focused on the importance of information processing, learning and intelligence. Innovative organiza-tions must be learning organizations open to enquiry and self-criticism.
- Organizations as cultures. The system is based on the ideas, values, norms, rituals and beliefs that sustain it as a socially constructed frame-work. The focus is on the human construction of organization within the cultural directives.
- Organizations as political systems. This sees systems as creating order and direction amongst people with potentially different views and interests. The organization is a system of government drawing upon political principles within different types of managerial frameworks.
- Organizations as psychic prisons. Here people have become trapped by their thoughts, ideas and beliefs that often originate in the unconscious mind. This can inhibit the organization's ability to change and mem-bers of the organization may share similar delusions.
- Organizations as instruments of domination. Here organizations use those who work for them and the environment in which they operate to achieve their own ends. It is a process of domination where certain people impose their will upon others.

anthropology and interpreted through metaphors as diverse as a machine to the narrative aspects of poetic logic![2,3]

One of the earliest categorizations of organizations was by Weber.[4] He classified organizations as charismatic, patrimonial, feudal or bureaucratic. Morgan[5] offers a range of metaphorical interpretations, some of which are shown in Box 7.1.

However, none of these constructs have provided effective models for public policy analysis and implementation. These élitist discourses remain largely inaccessible to those who actually get on and do the work, and from the organizational front line a number of observations are relevant:

- The literature has been generated by observers standing outside of organizations.
- The field is dominated by organizational gurus who are intent on promulgating their own perspective.
- There is a bewildering array of ideas and values without convergence to similar organizational themes – everything remains contested.
- Caution is required when importing insights from an organization that subserves one function to another where the function is very different. This is particularly relevant in healthcare. The aim of most of the organizational literature is to improve organizational profitability.
- Despite efforts to maintain the illusion that organizations are rational and orderly, much of our time is spent managing messes not of our own making and that have no simple solution.

In the next section we consider perspectives on organizations from a historical perspective, concluding with insights from complexity theory.

The evolution of ways in which we think about organizations

Taylorism

Towards the end of the nineteenth century, management had become a necessary function for a productive organization. However, the public sector was to lag behind. The predominant approach in the management of public affairs for some time was to remain one of 'leave well alone'.

The first formal theory of scientific management was introduced at the turn of the last century by Taylor.[6] The worker was seen as an individual with a predetermined function who undertook repetitive action backed by scientific analysis. This method focused on the efficient production of one item in an organization and reached its apogee in 'Fordism', typified by the Ford production line. The emphasis is on hierarchical control operating at the interface between organizational levels and putting constraints upon them.

Systems thinking

The 1950s saw the development of systems thinking, which we have met in Chapter 4. Organizations are seen as systems interacting with their environment and producing more than the sum of their parts. Although the importance of feedback is recognized, managers are still able to stand outside the system and control it towards defined objectives. A typical systems approach is shown in Box 7.2.

Box 7.2   A simple systems approach

- Identify system goals
- Develop alternative strategies for obtaining the goals
- Rank the ability of system components to meet the goals
- Initiate strategy
- Review and refine strategy as necessary

Within systems thinking a large number of techniques and approaches have developed. Hard systems thinking draws upon engineering principles and involves modelling techniques and explicit quantification of system elements. Soft systems approaches recognize that problems do not always lend themselves to quantification and may be ill-defined and ill-structured.[7] Many changes that have been introduced into the NHS, such as process re-engineering under the guise of a modernization agenda, have drawn upon systems thinking.

Organizations as learning systems

An important development of systems theory that overlaps with complexity thinking is the development of 'learning organizations' (*see* Chapter 5).[8] Here the emphasis is on teamwork, flat non-hierarchical structures, individual empowerment, information sharing and an ability to risk failure and learn from mistakes. Single-loop learning leads to incremental improvement in existing practice by comparing existing behaviour with a predefined model, e.g. clinical audit where existing practice is compared with explicit standards. Double-loop learning occurs where organizations rethink basic goals, norms and paradigms, i.e. they reflect upon their mental models and organizational objectives.

A number of applications from learning system theory have been introduced into the NHS,[9] including the plan-do-study-act (PDSA) learning cycle and improvement collaboratives.[10] However, despite the rhetoric, the success of these approaches in practice has been disappointing.[11]

Complexity and organizational thinking

All the above approaches attempt to manipulate social activity underpinned by an understanding of the psychology of the individual. The focus is on the individual's needs and motivations within an organizational context. For example, Maslow[12] postulates a spectrum of individual needs that need to be addressed, ranging from basic needs such as food and shelter to higher needs such as self-actualization. Le Grand[13] sees individuals are either knights (public-spirited altruists), pawns (passive recipients of state largesse) or knaves (self-interested), but suggests that unravelling the web of human motivation is difficult if not impossible.

By the late 1980s attempts at organizational change were having limited success. The limitations of systems thinking and the prevailing view that organizations demonstrated goal-seeking behaviour in a rational, planned and ordered way was being increasingly questioned. For example, in a study of large UK companies, only 15% of those who formulated long-term plans subsequently monitored and reviewed action against them.[14] There was an increasing gap between the dominant management discourse of being 'in charge' and the reality of not being in control. This paradoxical nature of life in organizations and an awareness of the limitations of predictability led to the accommodation of complexity insights as an alternative perspective on organizational life.

The focus moves from the control of individuals in an organization to the patterns that emerge from the relationships between them within a network that is inherently non-linear and self-organizing. The traditional description of organization in terms of structure, process and outcome changes to structure, process and pattern.[15] Outcomes are not an end in themselves but part of a learning process. Individual agents show patterns of communication, relationships and values that change with time and form critical elements of system behaviour.

We will visit the practical aspects of complexity thinking in future chapters, but Table 7.1 summarizes some of the main differences between the traditional and complexity approaches.

The application of complexity theory to organizational change is still in its infancy. There are concerns that important directives such as ambition,

Table 7.1   Traditional and complexity organizational perspectives (adapted from Stacey, 1992[16])

Traditional organizational thinking	Complexity organizational thinking
• Decision made by logical, analytical processes with emphasis on managers controlling and driving strategy. The generation of new ideas is undertaken by experts.	• Decisions made by exploratory and experimental processes. Intuition and reasoning by analogy encouraged. New ideas can emerge from anyone.
• Focus on experts and charismatic leaders.	• Focus on the group. Managers create favourable conditions for learning.
• Importance of future, goal setting and strategic plans. The focus is on the replication of processes that have worked well elsewhere.	• Emphasis is on the here and now. Local structures, processes and patterns are important.
• Organization understood by analysis on component parts.	• Holistic perspective. The organization is different from the sum of its parts.
• Emphasis is on measurement and system quantification.	• Qualitative aspects of measurement important. The importance of process factors are emphasized as part of a learning process.
• Attempt to rationalize decision making even when problems are 'messy', reducing uncertainty and ambiguity.	• Recognizing the creative potential of ambiguity and the importance of resolution through dialogue.
• Teams are permanent and part of a hierarchical reporting structure. Managers decide who participates and what the boundaries are.	• Teams are informal, spontaneous and temporary. Participants decide who takes part and what the bounds of their activities are. The focus is on self-organizing networks with an appreciation of the importance of both co-operation and competition.
• Organization based on strong shared culture.	• Organization is provoked and constrained by culture.

financial incentive, envy and the desire for a quiet life, all inevitable parts of organizational life, are not accommodated in the model. Many areas remain contested. We have seen in Section 2 how some see complexity insights as re-engineering opportunities. Others emphasize the importance of local interaction between agents on the basis of their historically evolved identities without knowing in advance how the system is going to evolve or understanding the current system as a whole. Managers are unable to step outside the system, make objective observations and choose the organization's dynamics. These dynamics emerge through their participation, not their act of design.

Conclusion

Five key elements have been suggested for successful organizational change:[17]

- the nature of relationships – how they are built and maintained
- the nature of decision making – how it is done and by whom
- the nature of power – how it is acquired and how it is used
- the nature of conflicts – how they arise and what are the ways of dealing with them
- the importance placed on learning – both individually and collectively.

Complexity theory can have a useful input into all these elements and offers an alternative perspective to traditional thinking on how organizations function. If we accept that organizations are not just rational structures but people who are trying to make sense of the situations in which they find themselves, then theories of organizations are theories of people's lives and their relationships with others. From this perspective, complexity does not offer ready solutions to organizational change but helps to shift the gaze.

It focuses on the patterns of relationships within organizations, how they are sustained, how they self-organize and how outcomes emerge. It explains why some interventions may have unanticipated consequences and how intricate interrelationships within a complex system give rise to multiple chains of dependencies. It emphasizes the limits to knowledge, the importance of history and the limits to predictability. It changes the focus from outcomes to process and counsels that analytical and predictive power can only be gained by standing back – not analysing a system in more detail. It emphasizes network over hierarchy, the importance of trusting rather than checking and guards against reductionism. This does not obviate the need for the scientific method – both approaches are complementary. But simple structures in healthcare organizations are rare and in many cases boundaries, relationships and attributions are uncertain.

The history of organizational development has been characterized by an overwhelming volume of literature that means nothing to those who actually get on and do the work. Is the application of complexity theory merely the latest fad? Organizations may manage just as well without the plethora of organizational theory. If nothing else, complexity theory challenges the dominant ways of thinking about organizations. If it only sensitizes us to the interplay of patterns that perpetually transforms the system against all attempts to the contrary, it may just help us to do things a little better.

References

A relatively user-friendly review of the organizational literature that has been commissioned by the NHS can be found at www.sdo.lshtm.ac.uk.

1   Weick K (2001) *Making Sense of the Organisation*. Blackwell, Oxford.
2   Morgan G (1986) *Images of Organisation*. Sage, London.
3   Skoldberg K (2002) *The Poetic Logic of Administration*. Routledge, London.
4   Weber M (1946) *The Theory of Social and Economic Organisation*. The Free Press, New York.
5   Morgan G (1997) *Images of Organization*. Sage, London.
6   Taylor F (1911) *Scientific Management*. Harper Brothers, New York.
7   Checkland P (1999) *Systems Thinking, Systems Practice*. John Wiley, Chichester.
8   Argyris C and Schön D (1996) *Organizational Learning*. Addison-Wesley, Reading, MA.
9   Davis H and Nutley S (2000) Developing learning organizations in the NHS. *BMJ*. **320:** 998–1001.
10 Berwick D (1998) Developing and testing changes in delivery of care. *Annals of Internal Medicine*. **8:** 651–6.
11 Bate S and Robert G (2002) Knowledge management and communities of practice in the private sector: lessons for modernising the NHS in England and Wales. *Public Administration*. **80 (4):** 643–63.
12 Maslow A (1954) *Motivation and Personality*. Harper-Row, New York.
13 Le Grand J (1997) Knights, knaves or pawns: human behaviour and social policy. *Journal of Social Policy*. **26:** 149–69.
14 Goold M and Quinn J (1990) *Strategic Control: milestones for long-term performance*. Hutchinson, London.
15 Capra F (1996) *The Web of Life: the new scientific understanding of living systems*. Anchor, New York.
16 Stacey R (1992) *Managing the Unknowable: strategic boundaries between order and chaos in organizations*. Jossey-Bass, San Francisco, CA.
17 Graham P (ed) (1995) *Mary Parker Follatt, Prophet of Management: a celebration of writings from the 1920s*. Harvard Business School Press, Boston, MA.

CHAPTER 8

The search for the correct organizational solution for the NHS

David Kernick

This chapter will set the search for healthcare policy instruments in a historical perspective before considering how insights from complex adaptive systems theory might be applied to NHS policy formulation and delivery. It suggests that recent changes may have inhibited a move towards a state of self-organized criticality and shifted the health service to a less adaptable and efficient one. Although there are signs that the Department of Health may be getting the message about the importance of complexity insights, political election cycles will always encourage quick fixes by government rather than programmes designed to bring about emergent change. The emphasis remains on deliverable targets that can be linked to government policies.

Key points
- The search for new ways of realigning healthcare organizations reflects a broader agenda to modernize and improve public services as a whole.
- A major problem is that healthcare organizational theory has drawn almost entirely upon literature from the commercial and industrial sectors where there are a number of important differences.
- Understanding the health service as a complex adaptive system offers new insights into healthcare delivery.
- Current NHS changes may be inhibiting the development of an effective service.
- The focus should be on developing a conversational competence amongst stakeholders rather than the current emphasis of an increasingly methodologically driven agenda.

Introduction

Demographic and socio-economic developments are driving demands for improvements in the efficiency and quality of the health service. The past 20 years has been a period of continual upheaval in the search for new policy instruments, but organizational change continues to have little effect on health service provision.[1] Despite considerable academic effort and a voluminous literature, research has had little direct influence on health service policy[2] and there is no convergence to any satisfactory priority-setting framework.[3] The correct organizational framework remains elusive.

A major problem is that healthcare organizational theory has drawn almost entirely upon literature from the commercial and industrial sectors where there are a number of important differences. These are shown in Box 8.1.

Box 8.1   Some differences between healthcare and other sectors

- Unlike most productive organizations, the nature of the final product (health) is contested.
- There is a tenuous relationship between healthcare and health.
- Consumers of healthcare have imperfect knowledge about the product that they receive. There may be a reliance on clinicians to make choices on behalf of their patients, but these same clinicians as suppliers may have conflicting incentives.
- Managers have an imperfect knowledge of the product they oversee.
- There are unique features of the relationship between the healthcare professional and the patient that include trust and empathy.
- The delivery of healthcare retains a public ethic and a concern for equity that may be absent in the commercial sector.
- Healthcare retains a high priority within the political agenda.

Recent organizational change in the NHS reflects a broader agenda to modernize and improve public services as a whole that translates into four elements:[4]

- the acceptance that all clinical decisions have resource dimensions against a background of limited healthcare budgets
- the recognition of the need to balance clinical autonomy with a more transparent accountability
- a systemization of clinical work underpinned by external evidence
- an acceptance of the power-sharing implications of team-based approaches to clinical work.

To these, a fifth element may be added. An increasing focus on the patient as the unit of organizational activity – 'a vision of the health service designed around the patient'.[5]

This chapter will set the search for policy instruments in a historical perspective before considering how insights from complex adaptive systems theory might be applied to NHS policy formulation and delivery.

The development of healthcare policy – the road to post-normal healthcare

To illustrate the evolution of NHS healthcare organization, a framework proposed by Ouchi[6] is developed, as shown in Figure 8.1. This approach sees the organization form as related to how well the transfer process that relate inputs (resources) to output (health) is understood and how well outputs can be defined. The historical stages are:

- the first way: managerial command – a focus on hierarchy and control
- the second way: the purchaser–provider split – developing market forces
- the third way: integrating co-operation and competition – attempting to get the best of both worlds.

Inputs (Resources)	Transfer process	Outputs (Health)	Mode of operation
	Well understood	Easily measured	Hierarchical, managerial system (the first way)
	Poorly understood	Easily measured	Market system (the second way)
	Partially understood	Partially measured	Mixed system (the third way)
	Poorly understood	Not easily measured	Complex adaptive system (the fourth way)

Figure 8.1 Four models of health systems depending on how well the transfer process that relates inputs (resources) to outputs (health) is understood and how well outputs can be defined.[6]

To these three historical approaches, a fourth is added:

- the fourth way: understanding the health service as a complex adaptive system – post-normal healthcare.

The first way – managerial command and control

For the first 25 years of the NHS, there was little in the way of formal management and the focus was on the centrality of clinical freedom. Management was perceived as diplomacy in which every effort was made to reach an accommodation between interested parties in matters of a sensitive or controversial nature.[7]

In the early 1980s a fundamental shift took place that reflected government interest in more systematic approaches to public service organization. In the healthcare sector, the Griffiths Inquiry was directed to examine ways in which NHS resources were controlled with the aim of securing the best value for money. The report highlighted the lack of managerial accountability and was critical of the system of consensus management. As Griffiths wrote, 'if Florence Nightingale were carrying her lamp through the corridors of the NHS today, she would almost certainly be searching for the people in charge'.[8]

Although powerful medical interests still prevailed, managerial approaches were introduced that focused on objectives, performance and accountability. The dominant metaphor of policy analysis and implementation was the machine – each part of the health service with a predefined function contributing to the overall purpose with government pulling the levers.

The second way – from hierarchies to markets

When it is perceived that the transfer process between inputs and outputs is poorly understood but outputs are readily measured, Ouchi's model suggests that a market approach may be the best framework within which to distribute resources.[6] Hierarchical control shifts to a network where exchange is mediated through contracts set within a competitive environment. However, during the late 1980s there were more practical concerns. A number of financial crises instigated a wide-ranging review of the NHS that was conducted largely in secret. The problem was seen to be inefficiencies produced by entrenched professionals and administrators operating in an environment of perverse incentives with no impetus for change. Influenced by a small number of health economists and finding spiritual support from the market tendencies of the Thatcher Government, the White Paper *Working for Patients*[9] outlined a radical agenda.

The main features of reform were the separation of purchaser from provider function and the development of general practitioner fund-holding within a quasi-market framework. This highly politicized atmosphere split professional allegiances, bewildered the public and caused considerable managerial conflict. In fact, the implementation of managed competition required more rules and regulations than the system that preceded it and overall, despite some changes in culture, measurable changes were small.[10]

The third way – integrating co-operation and competition

By the end of the 1990s a political consensus acknowledged that the essential features of the reforms were worth keeping but advocated a mixed economy based on co-operation and competition. The theoretical framework had been developed in the mid-1990s by Giddens,[11] who argued that rigid hierarchical state structures were increasingly incapable of fulfilling the diverse needs of citizenry and markets alone would not provide economic success or acceptable social outcomes. The third way, Ouchi's mixed system,[6] aimed to promote a synergy between public and private sectors, utilizing the dynamics of markets but with the public interest in mind.

This pragmatic approach was reflected in the government White Paper *The New NHS: modern, dependable*.[12] The aim was to retain the elements of the purchaser–provider split but emphasize a more collaborative approach with longer-term arrangements.

Elements of the third way are shown in Box 8.2 and have demanded some difficult balancing acts, for example between central direction or local autonomy or the use of sanctions or incentives to direct behaviour.

Box 8.2   Elements of the third way

- Striking a balance between central direction and local autonomy
- The recognition of competition as a lever to efficient use of resources
- An emphasis on longer term co-operation
- A shift to a private sector management style away from a public service ethic
- An emphasis on performance management and output measurement
- An emphasis on patient involvement and empowerment
- An emphasis on national frameworks of care with subsequent monitoring

---

This search for a mid path has resulted in a cocktail of organizations and directives issued under the guise of a 'modernization agenda'. One interpretation is that by making use of a variety of instruments, ministers will increase their chances of getting something right!

The Modernisation Agency was charged with delivering the new *NHS Plan* and, like the quasi-market approaches that preceeded it, drew heavily upon American influence. The new mantra placed the patient as consumer at the heart of the health service and consolidated a reductionist approach to policy – a confident assumption that the NHS could be understood by breaking it down into its constituent elements with the aim of engineering the system towards a predetermined future. This approach had three important practical consequences.

- Clinical discretion was to be reined in and doctors were to be brought under control within a scientific-bureaucratic framework.[13] Valid and reliable knowledge was now obtained from research conducted by experts and applied within a framework of clinical guidelines and service frameworks. Professional activity was to become instrumental in problem solving, applying general principles to specific problems.
- Performance management was introduced both to assess the extent to which healthcare organizations achieve defined social societal objectives and as a part of a continuous feedback process to improve performance.
- There was to be a commitment to service redesign based on a collaborative methodology that sought to cut across professional boundaries. Drawing upon commercial and industrial practice, the emphasis was on the quality of the patient experience and their pathway of care.

Unfortunately, the early indications are that the impact of modernization initiatives has been limited. Doctors are unhappier than ever;[14] the impact of large-scale collaborative interventions has been disappointing;[15] the ability of health organizations to influence system performance has been limited;[16] and managers and practitioners collude to avoid the dissonance between top-down performance management frameworks and the realities of the healthcare environment.[17] The system does not seem to want to do as it is told.

In summary, what has made the third way so difficult to achieve in practice and attract so much criticism is a failure to recognize the importance of a complexity frame of reference – the fourth way.

The fourth way – recognizing the NHS as a complex adaptive system

The fourth way, or post-normal healthcare,[18] views the NHS as a hierarchy of interrelated systems that interact in a non-linear fashion. The unit of activity shifts from the patient to the patient–professional unit in a perspective that sees all elements within the system co-evolving. The emphasis is on the relationships amongst a system's components and an understanding of what creates patterns of behaviour among them. The important features are diversity, connectivity, feedback and the existence of self-ordering rules that give systems the capacity to emerge to new patterns of order. Each agent cannot be understood in isolation.

From machine to ecosystem

Viewing the NHS through the metaphor of an ecosystem[19] can offer useful insights. All parts are adapting by learning to survive in a topography that is provided by co-existing and changing parts. Table 8.1 shows some comparisons and implications for organizations when viewed through the metaphors of machine (linear hierarchy), market (linear network) and ecosystem (non-linear network).

Practical consequences of the fourth way

How do the three practical consequences of the third way that were considered above – clinical discretion, performance management and service redesign – change with this new perspective?

Firstly, we must be aware of the importance of the nuances in the patient–healthcare professional interaction. In many areas, the production of health is an emergent phenomenon arising out of the healthcare professional–patient interaction which cannot be articulated within a scientific-bureaucratic framework. For example, Schon[20] argues that practitioners usually know more than they can say. They reveal a capacity for reflection on their intuitive knowing in the midst of action and use this tacit capacity to cope with the unique uncertain and conflicted situations of practice. The focus must change from a patient-centred service to one based on the unit of the patient–healthcare professional.

Secondly, we must be cautious over the use of quantitative measures to capture the performance of complex systems such as healthcare. Soft, qualitative information may play an important part with hard information acting as a safety net.[21] The extent to which healthcare organizations can influence indicators may be limited in a number of areas, and dysfunctional consequences may occur if organizations are held accountable for measures that are beyond their control.[22] An overemphasis on hard measures of effectiveness and efficiency may have a detrimental effect on social networks and the development of organizational emergence.

Thirdly, we need to recognize the limitations of redesign programmes. Complex systems can not be engineered – there are no causal links that promise sophisticated tools for analysing and predicting system behaviour. But, given

Table 8.1 Organizational metaphors and their implications

Principle	Machine: first way (linear hierarchy)	Market: second way (linear network)	Ecosystem: fourth way (non-linear network)	Implications for the health service as a non-linear network or complex adaptive system
Relationships within the system	Simple, static relationships pre-set	Contractual relationships. Directed by price, supply and demand	Diverse and dynamic relationships	Central tasks are: maintenance of effective relationships, monitoring of changing relationships, the encouragement of diverse types of relationships, the need to exploit new emerging relationships
Relationship to environment	Closed	Relatively open	Open	Consist of systems embedded within other systems. Working environments contain embedded overlapping networks of different functions and purposes
Diversity of elements	Static diversity designed in	Some diversity of elements, little diversity of structure or process	Diverse elements, structure and processes continually changing	Encourage diversity of people, skills, implementation and pathways
Knowledge management	Intelligence designed into the machine and remains fixed	A degree of learning	Learning perspective	As systems can't anticipate the range of problems they must evolve solutions on the basis of experience
Power	Power remains at the top of the hierarchy and is generally unresponsive	Power resides with the larger player and is responsive to resources	Power and influence are distributed locally and reside in relationships	Encourage open relationships and free exchange of dialogue
Strategic focus	Little strategic focus	Some strategic focus, particularly by major players	Emphasis is on local level	Focus on local interaction rather than strategic planning

the correct nurturing conditions, ecosystems can self-organize and adapt to changes in the external environment.

Bate and Robert[23] argue that the failure of collaboratives has been their focus on data and information within a framework of rules, regulations and reporting activities rather than the development of knowledge or wisdom that occurs in communities of practice. This approach recognizes the importance of social capital and that implicit knowledge is often the primary source of the organization's innovative potential.[24] Unfortunately, the social and professional networks of trust and the norms of reciprocity that characterize the NHS have been neglected during the years of organizational change.[25] This neglect will be further accelerated by a focus on a patient-centred NHS.

Conclusion

This chapter has reviewed the development of the NHS since its inception and argued that complexity insights may offer a useful perspective for further evolution. Policy making is seen not as a set of explicit goals that are engineered from above, but an ongoing maintenance of activities and relationships underpinned by guiding principles. The future state of the NHS is inherently uncertain but emerges from the result of interaction of its constituents at a local level. An essential first step is to move away from a consumerist perspective of a patient-centred NHS to one where the patient–healthcare professional is at the centre of an analytical framework.

It may be that the current emphasis on central performance frameworks, targets and monitoring may be inhibiting the NHS from operating at its most effective state. Evidence is beginning to emerge that the NHS may operate at the edge of chaos. For example, Papadopoulos[26] analysed the variations in hospital waiting times and demonstrated a power–law relationship independent of speciality and hospital location. He concluded that the length of waiting lists could be an emergent property of a system of patients, doctors, nurses and managers. Scale invariance was also shown, i.e. the same power–law relationship occurred on the waiting list of individual consultants as across the system as a whole. The conclusion was that the service may be operating at the edge of chaos and that external interventions may have little effect on system behaviour. It may also suggest that waiting times are a very poor indicator of system performance. If the NHS already operates as a system close to the edge of chaos, it could explain why the numerous measures introduced over the last 25 years have had so little impact on the way in which healthcare is delivered.

Unfortunately, checking performance and introducing measures to coerce behavioural changes to secure performance improvements may have counterproductive effects. These changes may have actually shifted the health service to a less efficient one by focusing on narrow short-term objectives at the expense of longer-term global or strategic ends. The fear of falling short on measured performance also leads to a disinclination to innovate. Of particular relevance within the NHS has been the emphasis on waiting-list targets which has led to a considerable amount of distortion and game playing within the system. There is also little support for the principle of publishing comparative information from the public, who are more inclined to trust their own experience or that of friends and family than comparative data.[27]

But are there signs that the Department of Health may be getting the message? David Fillingham, Director of the NHS Modernisation Agency, suggests that 'the NHS is the epitome of a complex adaptive system and that such systems do not always respond well to mechanistic formulae' (*Health Service Journal*, February 2002). Nevertheless, policy continues to be dictated from the Treasury where mandarins see a very linear world based on hard outcomes. Political election cycles will always encourage quick fixes by government rather than programmes designed to bring about emergent change, and the emphasis remains on deliverable targets that can be linked to government policies. Performance measures are expected to drive healthcare improvements within the context of *The NHS Plan*,[28] and the emphasis on target-driven incentives has been confirmed in the new general practitioner contract.

Inevitably, stakeholders will have to be prepared to sacrifice some of their core values in order to move forward. The edge of chaos is characterized by reasonableness and a sensitivity to the understanding and language that each of us uses. A useful first step for healthcare policy makers would be to recognize the dynamic, non-linear characteristics of the healthcare system, to appreciate the importance of developing a conversational competence amongst stakeholders rather than the current emphasis on an increasingly methodologically driven agenda. By encouraging open-ended creative and expressive language, we give rise to innovation from its capacity to invent and continually reinvent the ways in which we relate to our shared worlds.

References

1 Sheldon T (2001) It ain't what you do but the way that you do it. *Journal of Health Service Research and Policy.* **6 (1):** 3–5.
2 Black N (2000) Evidence-based policy: proceed with care. *BMJ.* **323:** 275–9.
3 Holm S, Sabin J, Chinitz D *et al.* (1998) Goodbye to the simple solutions: the second phase of priority setting in health care. *BMJ.* **317:** 1000–7.
4 Degeling P, Maxwell S and Kennedy J (2003) Medicine, management and modernisation: a 'dance, macabre'? *BMJ.* **322:** 649–52.
5 Department of Health (2001) *The NHS Plan: a plan for investment, a plan for reform.* HMSO, London.

6   Ouchi W (1980) Markets, bureaucracies and clans. *Administrative Sciences Quarterly.* **25:** 129–41.

7   Harrison S (1988) *Managing the NHS: shifting the frontier?* Chapman and Hall, London.

8   Department of Health and Social Security (1983) *NHS Management Inquiry Report.* DHSS, London.

9   Department of Health (1989) *Working for Patients.* HMSO, London.

10 Le Grand J, Mays N and Mullingan J (1998) *Learning from the NHS Internal Market.* King's Fund, London.

11 Giddens A (1994) *Beyond Left and Right: the future of radical politics.* Cambridge Politics Press, Cambridge.

12 Department of Health (1997) *The New NHS: modern, dependable.* The Stationery Office, London.

13 Harrison S, Moran M and Wood B (2002) Policy emergence and policy convergence: the case of 'scientific-bureaucratic medicine' in the USA and UK. *British Journal of Political and International Relations.* **4 (1):** 1–24.

14 Smith R (2001) Why are doctors so unhappy? *BMJ.* **322:** 1073–4.

15 Øvretveit J and Gustafson D (2003) Using research to inform quality programmes. *BMJ.* **326:** 759–61.

16 Hauck K, Rice N and Smith P (2003) The influence of healthcare organizations on health system performance. *Journal of Health Service Research and Policy.* **8 (2):** 68–74.

17 NHS Public Accounts Committee (2003) *Inappropriate Adjustments to NHS Waiting Lists.* 46th Annual Report. Public Accounts Committee, London.

18 Kernick D (2002) The demise of linearity in managing health services: a call for post-normal health care. *Journal of Health Service Research and Policy.* **7(2):** 121–4.

19 Royston G and Dick P (1998) Healthcare ecology. *British Journal of Healthcare Management.* **4 (5):** 238–41.

20 Schön D (1983) *The Reflective Practitioner.* Basic Books, New York.

21 Goddard M, Mannion R and Smith P (1999) Assessing the performance of NHS hospital trusts: the role of hard and soft information. *Health Policy.* **48:** 119–34.

22 Hauck K, Rice N and Smith P (2003) The influence of health-care organizations on health system performance. *Journal of Health Service Research and Policy.* **8:** 68–74.

23 Bate S and Robert G (2002) Knowledge management and communities of practice in the private sector: lessons for modernising the NHS in England and Wales. *Public Administration.* **80 (4):** 643–63.

24 Wenger E (1998) *Communities of Practice.* Cambridge University Press, Cambridge.

25 Welsh T and Pringle M (2001) Social capital. *BMJ.* **323:** 177–8.

26 Papadopoulos M, Hadjitheodossiou M, Chrysostomu C *et al.* (2001) Is the National Health Service at the edge of chaos? *Journal of the Royal Society of Medicine.* **94 (12):** 613–16.

27 Marshall M, Hiscock J and Sibbald B (2002) Attitudes of the public release of comparative information on the quality of general practice: qualitative study. *BMJ.* **325:** 1278–81.

28 Department of Health (1998) *The New NHS: modern, dependable – a national framework for assessing performance.* DoH, London.

CHAPTER 9

Organizational culture and complexity

David Kernick

Organizational culture is a common theme that runs throughout the organizational literature. However, there is little consensus over what it is and whether it offers opportunities for influencing organizational change. This chapter compares the concept from a reductionist and a complexity perspective. It is suggested that culture emerges from the interplay of formal and informal organizational channels and that there are factors that can facilitate or inhibit satisfactory emergence.

Key points
- Although the concept of culture is recognized by those who work in organizations, its description and the opportunities it offers for engineering change are contested.
- A reductionist approach sees culture as something an organization has that can be dissected and described in terms of rules and norms that shape individual behaviour.
- From a complexity perspective, culture emerges through the continuing negotiation about values and meaning between the members of an organization.
- This emergence is underpinned by the recursive interplay between formal and informal organizational elements and the rules that direct them.
- Cultural emergence can be inhibited by an excessive dissonance between formal and informal rules, hegemony between subcultures and an inappropriate leadership style.

Introduction

In the sixteenth century, the term 'culture' was used to describe the cultivation of crops or breeding of animals. In the nineteenth century, anthropologists adopted the term to designate distinctive ways of life. Culture was seen as the integrated system of socially acquired values, beliefs and rules of conduct that define the range of acceptable behaviours in a society. This analytical framework was adapted and came to prominence from the 1980s onward with the hope that the culture of an organization could be described and manipulated to achieve desired organizational objectives. For example, the current NHS reforms are based on the premise that a major cultural transformation of the organization must be secured to deliver desired improvements in quality and performance.[1]

The concept of culture resonates with all who work in organizations. Healthcare managers at all levels recognize the significance of culture, and are actively interested in shaping it or feel constrained by its influence.[2] We make sense of our organizations in terms of the cultural patterns within which we are situated – patterns that define our latitude for interpretation, improvisation and unique action. Culture preserves lessons learned from the past and can shape action without our awareness. But despite our acceptance of the concept, there is no convergence to an agreed definition.

In this chapter I compare reductionist and complexity approaches to the concept of culture. I conclude that healthcare culture emerges from the interplay of formal and informal organizational channels that can hold the organization at its most effective state. It is suggested that this emergence can be inhibited by an excessive dissonance between formal and informal rules, hegemony between subcultures and an inappropriate leadership style.

Culture from the reductionist perspective

There has been an increasing interest by policy makers in using cultural management as a lever for healthcare improvement. This approach assumes a number of steps:[2]

- the healthcare system possesses a discernible culture
- the nature of culture has a bearing on performance
- it is possible to identify positive and negative cultural attributes
- policy makers can design strategies that can influence beneficial cultures and these benefits will outweigh any dysfunctional consequences.

These assumptions reflect the prevailing view that culture is constructed from a hierarchical system of rules and norms that shape individual behaviour – a reductionist approach that sees culture as something an organization has that can be dissected and described.

Describing the culture

Cultures can be integrated – there is wide consensus amongst system elements, or differentiated – there are diverse and often incompatible views and norms amongst subcultures. The NHS is a differentiated culture, each subculture with its own value system affiliations and groupings. Box 9.1 shows some elements of these subcultures.

Box 9.1   Elements of subcultures in the NHS (taken from Scott *et al.*, 2003[3])

- Occupation – each occupation has a distinctive sense of identity and purpose arising from training, education and interaction with peers. For example, doctors and nurses.
- Specialization – the occupational groups are subdivided, e.g. obstetrics, cardiology, general practice, each of which has its own distinctive subculture.
- Gender – this is related to the distribution of the sexes within occupational subgroups. Historically, the medical profession was dominated by men and the nursing profession by women.
- Class – in the UK there is a strong relationship between professional entry and socio-economic class status. This may be an important factor in mediating between different professions and patients.

An alternative descriptive framework describes culture as a three-layered structure that co-ordinates organizational action:[4,5]

- Artefacts – these are the superficial manifestations of culture and include physical and behavioural elements. For example, dress code; medical language; the way of running services; performance assessment; the rituals, rewards and ceremonies.
- Values – the basic foundations for making judgements and distinguishing right from wrong. They are used to justify particular behaviour patterns and as the basis for choosing between alternative courses of action. For example, the traditional medical value has been to put the patient first before broader societal objectives.

- Assumptions – the 'taken for granted' views of the world. For example, medical research is predicated on the use of linear science and the feasibility of transferring generalizable knowledge.

Within the context of a reductionist model, the hope is that elements of culture can be isolated, described and re-engineered towards a desired organizational form. But how do we know where we want to be?

Defining a cultural strategy – what do we want to be?

The conventional approach to cultural analysis assumes that change is required and we know where the organization needs to go. Historically, the focus of cultural strategy in the NHS was on *first-order change*, i.e. 'do what you do better'. However, a number of highly critical reports have highlighted the need to reduce the gap between the prevailing culture of the NHS and the broader societal cultural changes that have occurred since its inception. *Second-order change* invokes a more fundamental view – 'do what you do differently'.

Powerful evidence is emerging that the culture of the NHS must change. For example, the Kennedy Report, published after the inquiry into children's heart surgery at the Bristol Royal Infirmary, described the prevailing culture at the Bristol Royal Infirmary as a 'club culture' which focused excessive power and influence around a core of senior managers and surgeons. These inadequacies were an underlying factor that adversely affected the quality and adequacy of care which children received.[6]

But where should the organization go? Some desirable cultural shifts for the NHS have been articulated by the Government[7] and echoed by commissioners and providers:[3]

- from hierarchical to devolved local networks
- from detailed guidelines with targets to clear long-term outcomes with latitude about method
- from a focus on institutions to working through networks
- from small pockets of excellence to mainstream quality improvement
- from risk avoidance because of fear of penalties to incentives as a key part of improvement with penalties seen by all as fair.

Changing the culture – how do we get to where we want to go?

Assuming we know where we want to go to, how can we get there? This question has confounded organizational theorists without convergence to any satisfactory answer. The NHS has encompassed frameworks ranging from command and control to competitive markets. The current focus is on a balance between co-operation, competition and top-down direction. However, experience shows that whereas the artifactual elements of culture may be manipulated, the deeper seated values and assumptions may prove more resistant to change.

Davies and Mannion[8] have suggested a number of practical considerations to be taken into account when initiating cultural change:

- Changes need to take into account the concerns and motivations of all staff.
- All stakeholders should participate in any decision-making process.
- The organizational structure needs to be such that stakeholders have a sense of long-term obligation and can offer support to change without having to calculate the cost or expect immediate return.
- Stakeholders should be allowed to communicate freely and openly and able to accommodate failure.
- There needs to be a balance between techniques that seek to compel performance and approaches that trust intrinsic professional motivation to deliver high-quality services.

Perhaps the most important element in enabling cultural change is trust. It has been linked to a wide range of desirable organizational outcomes, including improved communication, teamwork and organizational learning. An additional benefit is a reduction in transaction costs as the overheads associated with contracts and control mechanisms are reduced or eliminated. Trust reflects control based on shared goals and values rather than incentives and fault-finding. However, the diversity of cultures within the NHS, each with its own value system and incentive structure, proves a formidable barrier. Box 9.2 shows some characteristics of high- and low-trust organizations.

Box 9.2   Characteristics of high- and low-trust relations (taken from Fox, 1974[9])

High trust

- Share ends and values
- Have a sense of long-term obligation
- Offer support without calculating the cost or expecting an immediate return
- Communicate free and openly with each other
- Are prepared to risk their fortunes in the others party
- Give the benefit of doubt in relation to motives and goodwill if there are problems

Low trust

- Have divergent goals and interests
- Have explicit expectations which must be reciprocated through balanced exchanges
- Carefully calculate the costs and benefits of any concessions
- Restrict and screen communications in their own separate interests
- Attempt to minimize their dependence on others' discretion
- Are suspicious about mistakes or failures

The above analyses have been set within a reductionist framework. Culture can be reduced to a number of elements and the nature of organizational culture reflects the sum of these elements. The hope is that these elements can be identified and re-engineered towards a desired policy objective. What insights can complexity theory offer on the nature of cultural change?

Culture from the complexity perspective

An alternative approach to understanding culture is to see it in terms of not what it consists of, but an emergent property arising from the continuing negotiation about values and meanings between the members of an organization.[10] A property created by a social network involving multiple non-linear loops through which values, beliefs and rules are continually communicated, modified and sustained. Often, these elements are transmitted through the use of organizational stories that are told and retold within the webs of relationships of organizational alliances and friendships. Culture then feeds back on the organization, closing a network by creating a boundary of meaning and expectation that limits the access of others and producing constraints on interaction.

These networks of relationships form a 'shadow organization' of people who interact with each other and by doing so make sense out of their lives and establish their identities. A common practice develops underpinned by a shared way of doing things, a collective identity and informal rules of conduct. These networks have been termed 'communities of practice',[11] a concept that is considered in Chapter 21.

Formal and informal channels in organizations

Here we set the emergence of culture within the context of formal and informal organizational channels, or more specifically through the interplay of the interpretation of formal and informal rules that define these two channels.

Rules can range from informal and unstated agreements on how we act to more formal directives within a bureaucratic framework. North[12] describes

Table 9.1   The formal and informal strands of organization

	Formal channels	Informal channels
Power	Hierarchical	Relational
Predictability	Cause–effect certain Future predictable	Cause–effect uncertain Future unpredictable
Organizational function	Discharge specific functions and social obligations	Make sense of the situation in which people find themselves

rules as humanly devised constraints that shape human interaction and incentives in human exchange. They reduce arbitrary and opportunistic behaviour that can occur due to the potential for individual personal gain at the expense of others.

The suggestion is that culture emerges from the recursive interplay between formal and informal organizational elements in a way that holds the system at the edge of chaos where it is most robust and efficient. But before this concept is explored in more detail, we consider the formal/informal organizational channels and then the rules that underpin them. These two strands are shown in Table 9.1 and are characterized by:

- the view of how causes are related to effects and the consequent predictability of the future
- the nature of power and its enactment
- whether people come together to discharge specific functions and social obligations or to make sense of the situations in which they find themselves.

The formal organizational structures

We come together in organizations to discharge social functions. Physical and human resources are organized for a specific function that operates with a defined bureaucratic framework. The organizational metaphor is the machine. Systems are viewed as linear, reductionist and deterministic. In this model of technical rationality, an observer can stand outside the system and engineer it towards a predefined future. Predictive limitations are viewed as data or processing inadequacies. Discrepancies due to contextual factors are removed by statistical manipulation. Power is used in the behavioural sense and implies control of one person over another. External rules are imposed and enforced within a hierarchical system, having been designed within a political process. Violations are coupled with explicit sanctions that are imposed in formal ways.

The informal organizational structures

Here the focus is on people coming together to make sense of the situations in which they find themselves. The organizational metaphor moves from machine to an ecosystem of co-evolving elements. The system cannot be understood by a reduction into its component parts or engineered by an outsider. The future is unpredictable and emerges as a result of local interaction. There are no final outcomes or end-points but a continual system transformation. Internal rules evolve from human experience and incorporate solutions that have served people best in the past. These are the customs, norms and conventions, and violations are sanctioned informally. The focus of power in this analysis is not something that exists in agencies or structures but resides in the relationships that people have with each other as they try to understand who they are and construct their identities with each other.

Stacey[13] develops this theme and argues that organizations can never possess true identity because they are not things but processes, continually responding and changing. He focuses on the central role of ordinary everyday conversation in organizations – the shadow conversations. Here we struggle to understand each other in fluid, spontaneous conversation from which meaning or know-ledge emerges within the conflicting restraints of power relationships. Through these informal and local interactions, the future is continuously created in the present. Power is seen as constraint that excludes some communicative actions and allows others. (These themes have been considered in more detail in Chapter 6.)

The emergence of culture from the interplay between formal and informal rules

In this analysis, culture emerges from the recursive interplay of formal and informal channels. This dynamic holds the organization in its most efficient and adaptable state of self-organized criticality (*see* Chapter 3). Both are equally important for system functioning, both determine what an organization is.

This mechanism was identified over 20 years ago by Lipsky,[14] although he was unable to set it within a complexity perspective. He identified how 'street-level bureaucrats' – police, local government officials, healthcare staff – process work by modifying their roles and organizational expectations, thereby reducing the gap between available resources and system objectives. Paradoxically, he suggested that these coping strategies were essential to the long-term survival of the system. The importance of this interplay between formal and informal channels becomes apparent when employees 'work to rule' and the function of the organization becomes severely restricted.

What insights can this analysis of culture offer us? How can we hold the culture of an organization at a state of self-organized criticality? I want to focus on three areas: avoiding an excessive dissonance between formal and informal rules, reducing hegemony within subcultures and the role of leadership.

Dissonance between formal and informal rules

Diversity and difference is needed for emergent change. However, if the dissonance between formal top-down rules and the reality of practice and its informal rules is too great, there may be dysfunctional consequences. For example, in a study of decision making in NHS healthcare organizations, McDonald[15] demonstrated an environment characterized by multiple goals, ambiguous and competing objectives, and uncertain relationships between cause and effect. When confronted with the dissonance of policy directives and what was deliverable, managers developed coping strategies that were often dysfunctional. In many cases, doing something appeared better than doing nothing and became an end in itself. Anxiety was reduced and the illusion of an NHS that is both modern and dependable was maintained. This dissonance also produces 'gaming' in the system that utilizes resources inappropriately. For example, untenable waiting-list targets on hospital trusts can lead to a subversive subculture of cover-up and mutual protection.[16] During a recent monitoring week to ensure casualty units were meeting waiting-time rules, two-thirds of hospital departments used temporary agency staff to reduce patient waiting times.[17]

Subculture hegemony

If one subculture dominates, emergence will be limited. For example, the medical profession has dominated the NHS on the basis of their special expertise consolidated within a legal framework. Organizational conversation has traditionally been restricted and there have been limited opportunities for innovation and exploration of system possibilities. But the converse is also possible. If there are too many subcultures, the system will be too loosely coupled and operate inefficiently. For example, 14 subcultures of healthcare professional operate out of my health centre!

The role of leadership in complex systems

Historically, NHS leadership has focused on promoting ready-made solutions within a framework of top-down direction and control. This is known as transactional leadership and focuses on organizational compliance using a number of incentives and bureaucratic mechanisms. Current thinking sees leadership as playing a key role in facilitating the emergence of culture and inappropriate leadership has been identified as a key factor when attempts to change culture fail.[18] Transformational leadership focuses on removing obstacles to communication and change with an emphasis on encouragement rather than direction. The aim of the leader is to articulate the organizational vision and work with the informal networks of relationships to incorporate their knowledge into the organization. These themes are considered in the next chapter.

Conclusion

Despite acknowledging problems with defining culture, organizational members can engage with the concept as a framework in which they think about and do things. They are also able to identify traits that they think will facilitate cultural change and ones that will inhibit or delay it.[19] Policy makers also recognize the limitations of a reductionist framework – that cultural change cannot easily be wrought from top-down exhortation and the danger of eroding beneficial cultural traits that already exist, for example a commitment to equity in the NHS. But if culture in organizations is an emergent property, even if strategies account for the needs, fears and motivations of staff, policy makers are offered few levers for change. What are the options?

Firstly, there must be a realistic anticipation from the centre of what can be delivered. Untenable formal rules lead to organizational anxiety and dysfunctional consequences. At a fundamental level, the commitment to a health service based on need and not the ability to pay and that is effective, efficient, equitable and patient-centred may be over-realistic. Secondly, hegemony within the system must be reduced, a process that is already underway with the erosion of medical power. For example, many areas of first contact that were historically the preserve of GPs are being provided by other workers. Thirdly, the emphasis of leadership must change from transactional to transformational, a change that has already been acknowledged within the NHS.

What underpins these options is the development of an organizational conversation competence both between and across levels of the service – conversations which may not otherwise have occurred. By removing existing barriers and facilitating interactions, new cultures can emerge, ensuring that the organization can respond to the changing demands placed on it.

References

1   Department of Health (2000) *Shifting the Balance of Power within the NHS: securing delivery*. DoH, London.
2   Mannion R, Davies H and Marshall M (2003) *Cultures for Performance in Healthcare: evidence of the relationship between organisational culture and organisational performance in the NHS*. Department of Health, London.

3   Scott T, Mannion R, Davies H *et al.* (2003) Implementing culture change in health care: theory and practice. *International Journal for Quality in Health Care.* **15 (2):** 1–8.

4   Schein E (1985) Getting control of the corporate culture. In: Killman R, Saxto M and Serpa R (eds) *How Culture Forms, Develops and Changes.* Jossey-Bass, San Francisco, CA.

5   Davis H and Mannion R (2000) Organisational culture and quality of health care. *Quality in Healthcare.* **9:** 111–19.

6   Kennedy I (2001) *Learning from Bristol: public inquiry into children's heart surgery at the Bristol Royal Infirmary.* Department of Health, London.

7   Department of Health (2001) *The Balance of Power: the next steps.* DoH, London.

8   Davies H and Mannion R (2000) Clinical governance: striking a balance between checking and trusting. In: Smith P (ed) *Reforming Markets and Healthcare.* Open University Press, Buckingham.

9   Fox A (1974) *Beyond Contract: work, power and trust relations.* Faber and Faber, London.

10 Seal R (2000) New insights on organisational change. *Organisations and People.* **7:** 2–9.

11 Wenger E (1998) *Communities of Practice.* Cambridge University Press, Cambridge.

12 North D (1990) *Institutions, Institutional Change and Economic Performance.* Cambridge University Press, Cambridge.

13 Stacey R (2001) *Complex Responsive Processes in Organisations.* Routledge, London.

14 Lipsky M (1980) *Street-level Bureaucracy.* Sage, New York.

15 McDonald R (2002) *Using Health Economics in Health Services.* Open University Press, Buckingham.

16 NHS Public Accounts Committee (2003) *Inappropriate Adjustments to Waiting Lists.* 46th Annual Report. Public Accounts Committee, London.

17 Mayor S (2003) Hospitals take short-term measures to meet targets. *BMJ.* **326:** 1054.

18 Schien E (1995) *Organizational culture and leadership: a dynamic view.* Jossey-Bass, San Francisco, CA.

19 Marshall M, Sheaff R, Rogers A *et al.* (2002) A qualitative study of the cultural changes in primary care organisations needed to implement clinical governance. *British Journal of General Practice.* **52:** 641–5.

CHAPTER 10

Leadership and change

David Kernick

The traditional function of a leader is to have an overview of the big picture with the aim of directing and co-ordinating the activity of an organization. However, organizations rarely do what they are told and leaders find themselves less able to respond to the demands placed upon them – in charge but not in control. This chapter suggests why this might be and how a new type of leader can be identified from a complexity perspective.

Key points
- A unified science of leadership and management has proved elusive and its study has merely generated more contested models and theories.
- Transactional leadership has a strong sense of direction and comes to an agreement with subordinates about what should be done within a defined bureaucratic structure.
- Transformational leadership adopts a complexity perspective. The focus is on the articulation of an organization's values and an understanding of the importance of local relationships within a socially constructed organizational network.
- In the NHS, theoretical leadership frameworks have been imported from commercial settings that are very different from the context of the health service.
- Caught between the imperatives of central control and a political agenda of 'localism', leadership in the NHS is best described as a bit of a muddle.

Introduction

Management and leadership have been prominent themes in organizational theory, but consensus on their exact definition or role in organizational change remains elusive. A useful starting point is to see management deriving from the Latin word *manus*, meaning hand, and the subsequent Italian word *maneggiare*, to control. Leadership is from the old English derivation *lithan*, meaning to show the way or guide.

The simplest analysis is to view leaders as developing more strategic concerns, for example articulating the organization's mission and overseeing its development. Managers take lower-level resource decisions within a bureaucratic framework devised by leaders. Administrators rarely take resource decisions but ensure the smooth day-to-day running of the organization within a framework defined by managers. A number of leadership objectives have been defined for health systems:[1]

- safe – patients should not be harmed by the care they receive
- effective – patients should receive services based on the best available scientific knowledge
- patient-centred – wherever possible, individuals' preferences, needs and values should be taken into account
- timely – care should be delivered on time and without harmful delays
- efficient – waste of all forms should be avoided
- equitable – care should not vary in quality because of differences between patients.

Examples of more specific management aims for health systems are:

- redesign of care based on best practice
- use of information technology to improve access to clinical information and clinical decision making
- improvement of knowledge and skills across the workforce
- development of effective teams
- co-ordination of care across patient conditions, services and settings
- incorporation of performance and outcome measurements for improvement and accountability.

Traditional leadership theories have focused on the factors that make an effective leader and what shapes them. For example, Goodwin[2] suggests that leadership style is influenced by a number of interrelated factors:

- an understanding of the history of organizational decision making
- the quality of the executive team as perceived by the local stakeholders
- the extent to which organizational networks have been developed
- the extent of organizational power sharing.

Although the leadership literature recognizes the importance of networks and relationships, the focus remains on someone outside the system who is able to influence it. For example, the NHS Leadership Centre defines leadership as: 'the art of getting things done by enabling others to do more than they could or would do otherwise'. Control systems in the form of procedures and processes ensure necessary actions are taken to achieve the organization's objectives. Instruments available for manipulation can be 'hard' (e.g. policy, rules, standards, incentives) or 'soft' (e.g. culture, ethics, commitment, communication, training).

This approach sits within a linear model and has been termed transactional leadership. There is a strong sense of direction of some future state towards which the organization will move and an agreement with subordinates about what each will do to make a reality of that given vision. Specific goals are articulated and quantified within a bureaucratic framework. These are the formal structures, rules and regulations that define relationships of power. Boundaries are established by contractual agreements that delineate departments, budgets and plans. However, instructions will always be modified and reinterpreted, ignored in parts and added to. A system survives by not working to rule.

In certain conditions, change can be transacted successfully. For example, the introduction of the NHS in 1948 was politically managed despite opposition from powerful medical interests. But successive governments have attempted managed reorganization without the desired effects. The resulting 'glossy corporate images belie the problems of working in organizations as complex as the NHS' as managers realize that although they may be in charge, they can never be fully in control. They find themselves working in 'organizations under siege, barely coping'.[3] To survive, managers and leaders manipulate the controls placed upon them. For example, during a recent NHS monitoring week, two-thirds of accident and emergency (A&E) departments in England put in place temporary measures so that they appeared to meet waiting-time targets. Casualty units used agency staff to reduce patient waiting times and existing staff worked double or extended shifts during this time.[4]

In this chapter, we review insights from complexity theory that can be used by a new type of leader before looking more specifically at leadership within the NHS.

Change, leadership and complexity insights

Within the complexity field, there is a fundamental divergence of views on the extent to which we can stand outside systems and engineer change. These themes have been discussed in Section 2. Some would argue that a human system cannot be controlled and that the focus must be on change emerging from interaction at a local level. Others look for leverage or tipping points where the system is sensitive to external inputs. A pragmatic stance acknowledges the contribution of both these elements.

From a complexity perspective, the focus is on transformational leadership. A transformational leader sits within an organizational network and need not be at the top of a formal hierarchical structure. The main features of the transformational leadership model are:

- A recognition that the organizational future is boundable but essentially unpredictable in detail. In most cases there are no final outcomes or endpoints but a continual system transformation as organization members co-evolve.
- A transformational leader helps an organization to articulate its vision. Holding a vision is central to the success of any organization. We need to feel that our actions are meaningful as we negotiate our identities and relationships with one another in organizational contexts.*
- A transformational leader helps an organization to articulate its values around which the system will transform itself – what is right, what is wrong and the criteria we should place on our decisions. When the values of a transformational leader are declared and followed they are the basis of trust. When they are stated and not followed, trust is broken.[5]
- The interplay between the organization's formal design structures and its informal self-generating networks is understood together with the importance of socially constructed networks where meaning often remains implicit. Power does not exist in agencies or structures imposed by the transformational leader, but resides in the relationships that people have with each other as they try to understand who they are and construct their identities with each other.
- Change is rarely initiated by top-down instructions or force. There may be dysfunctional consequences in doing so. For example, the current obsession with NHS waiting-list targets focuses attention in one area to the detriment of others where resources may be utilized more beneficially.
- The inherent non-linearity of the system is recognized. The emphasis is on understanding what creates patterns of order and behaviour and how these patterns evolve. From a practical perspective, a transformational leader sets boundaries and removes obstacles to development; facilitates

---

* An alternative perspective (Weick K [2001] *Making Sense of the Organization*. Blackwell, Oxford) suggests that a vision is an interpretation of where an organization has got to. Meaning, purpose, vision and mission emerge from what people have done and are doing – they are not prior organization intentions. People can only understand what they are doing by interpreting what they have done. An organizational vision is therefore retrospective and not prospective.

Table 10.1   Some features of transactional and transformational leadership

Transactional leadership	Transformational leadership
• Assumes predictable context with short-term targets	• Accepts uncertain context with longer-term targets
• Change focused on planning and monitoring within a hierarchical command and control structure	• Change focused on setting intent, creating values and purpose, encouraging and coaching within a network structure
• Change introduced on a need-to-know basis	• Change needs extensive involvement
• Top-down direction	• Bottom-up, self-initiated change and learning
• External redesign of organization as lever to change	• Facilitate emergent change from within existing structure

communication through increasing organization connectivity and feed-back; amplifies the voices of employees who would not otherwise be heard; works with the informal networks of relationships; and tolerates experiments and marginal activities in the hope that they will lead to innovation.

Table 10.1 shows the main features of the transactional and transformational approaches.

Plsek has identified four main issues that must be addressed by transformational leaders:[6]

- How can conditions in the healthcare system be established to allow new ideas to emerge, see what happens then decide what to do next without undermining the system?
- How can diverse people be brought together to share information and stimulate creative connections that do not normally exist?
- How can desirable variation or innovation be separated from the variation that ought to be reduced?
- What is a 'good enough plan' to begin the change?

Although some commentators argue that there are no 'complexity tools' as it is not possible to stand outside of a system and manipulate it, there are a number of complexity insights that others have found useful. Zimmerman *et al.*[7] offer transformational leaders a wide range of principles for managing complex adaptive systems (interpreted here as 'complexity engineering'), many of which are already finding acceptance within the NHS. Some examples are shown in Box 10.1. In this chapter, I focus on the concept of organizational simple rules and attractors.

Box 10.1 Some principles for managing complex adaptive systems (after Zimmerman *et al.*, 1998[7])

- Good enough vision – build a good enough vision of the future rather than plan out every little detail.
- Tune the system to the edge of chaos. Foster the right degree of information flow, diversity and difference, connections inside and outside the organization, power differential and anxiety.
- Uncover and work with paradoxes rather than shying away from them as if they were unnatural.
- Listen to the shadow system – informal relationships, gossip and rumour contribute significantly to mental models and subsequent actions.
- Grow complex systems by 'chunking', i.e. allow them to emerge out of links amongst simple systems that work well and are capable of operating independently.
- Balance co-operation and competition.

Working with system attractors and simple rules

One approach is to view the trajectory of health systems in a multidimensional phase space, self-organizing around attractors (*see* Chapter 2). A transactional approach attempts to overcome resistance to change using imposed structures, incentives and sanctions. For example, the Thatcher government tried to bring about major organizational change by 'forcing' a new attractor into the system – a quasi-market (although its impact was negligible[8]). A transformational approach recognizes the importance of working with the natural system attractors.

The 'simple rules' concept is perhaps the most widely used application of 'complexity engineering'. The contention is that system characteristics emerge from the recursive application of simple rules at a local level. (More specifically, 'rules of thumb' rather than rules that must be adhered to.) This approach is contrary to current organizational assumptions that plans must provide detailed specifications that must be implemented across the whole system (for example, the current National Service Frameworks of the NHS and the proposed GP contract).

Three types of simple rules for human systems have been proposed:[6] general direction pointing; system prohibition, i.e. setting boundaries; and resource or permission providing. The key questions are:

- What are the existing and often implicit rules that underpin the existing system?
- How can they be identified and modified?
- How can new simple rules be disseminated and introduced?
- What are the simple rules that might guide the development of the health-care system?

One way to expose and change our simple rules is through the use of dialogue. By facilitating a conversation between disparate stakeholders and encouraging feedback, the system can change to new levels of organization. Dissemination of new rules succeeds when the basic concept is modulated in a way that reflects the local setting and is meaningful to the individuals concerned. Rogers[9] has identified five characteristics of change that spreads easily: clear advantage compared with current ways of doing things; compatible with current system and values; simplicity of the change and its implementation; ease of testing before making full commitment; and observability of the change and its impact.

An example of new simple rules and their precursors that might apply to a healthcare system are shown in Table 10.2.

Table 10.2   Some new organizational simple rules (adapted from Plsek, 2001[10])

New rules of thumb	Old rules
- Be innovative - Take risks and foster innovation - Develop new ways of working	- Don't fail - Prescribe the detail and minimize risk - Avoid diversity, seek a uniformly excellent health service
- Learn from failure - Change needs to be bottom-up - Reflect local needs	- You're fired - Change is driven from the top - Follow national priorities

---

Box 10.2   An example of some simple rules and their classification. The use of thrombolysis after heart attack (adapted from Plsek and Wilson, 2001[11])

- Ensure patient receives thrombolysis within 60 minutes of chest pain (*direction pointing*).
- Administration can occur in any environment by a properly trained individual (*direction pointing, boundary setting*).
- Remain within the overall project budget (*boundary setting*).
- Any group with an idea can draw resources from the pooled budget that has been established (*resource providing*).

An example of a more specific use of simple rules applied to the development of thrombolysis after a heart attack is shown in Box 10.2. Goals and resources are established with a view towards the whole system rather than artificially allocating them to parts of the system, encouraging generative relationships amongst stakeholders that may provoke more creative ideas.

Leadership in the NHS

There are three important features of the NHS leadership agenda. Firstly, theoretical frameworks have been imported from industrial and commercial settings that are different from the context of the health service. Secondly, there are constraints on the freedom of public sector managers arising from targets and policy-making deadlines imposed by national governments. But perhaps the most important factor is the strength of historical precedent reflected in an environment of differentiated subcultures with competing terms of reference.

From its inception, doctors have retained a central role as NHS leaders with an organizational focus on administrative support to the clinician. The development of the internal market in the early 1990s and the subsequent emphasis on clinical governance and resource constraint saw the development of managerial power with the aim of developing a 'networked community' of managers and doctors.[12] More recently, the emphasis has shifted to one of central control with leaders as agents of government and a further erosion of medical leadership.

Fortunately, within the NHS we do not have to worry about what leaders are suppose to do. The NHS has its own leadership centre developed under the auspices of the Modernisation Agency (www.modern.nhs.uk) that defines the role of NHS leaders as:

- to improve patients' care, treatment and experience
- promote a healthy population
- enhance the NHS's reputation as a well-managed and accountable organization
- motivate and develop staff.

A framework has been devised which describes the key characteristics that leaders in the NHS should aspire to (www.nhsleadershipqualities.nhs.uk). These characteristics have been derived from the qualities of existing leaders who seem to be doing a good job! (The 'John Wayne approach' – a leader's got to do what a leader's got to do.)

Fifteen qualities are defined which come under three broad headings:

- *setting direction* – broad scanning, intellectual flexibility, seizing the future, political astuteness, drive for results
- *delivering the service* – leading change through people, holding to account, empowering others, effective and strategic influencing, collaborative working
- *personal qualities* – self-belief, self-awareness, self-management, drive for improvement, personal integrity.

This rather confusing framework, the production of which has a considerable opportunity cost to the service, sits midway between transactional and transformational approaches and sets the new leader under the guise of 'change agent'. The impact on the delivery of care of the new leadership approach has yet to be fully evaluated but early indications are mixed.

Perhaps the most generous comment we can make is that leadership in the NHS is in a state of flux.

Leadership, government and the NHS

Foucault[13] has described the concept of governmentality. This recognizes a move away from government as a 'master institution'[14] – a dominant status that lies outside the citizenry, setting objectives and directing policy. The emphasis becomes one of managing and overseeing a population so that they flourish. The focus is on the 'conduct of conduct' – the shaping and guiding of people so they do what is best for themselves and society as a whole. This approach emphasizes the transformational leadership role of government, facilitating rich interaction within the system from which satisfactory solutions will emerge. The emphasis is on encouragement to explore the system's environment, sharing feedback and clearing pathways, but always within defined boundaries and clearly articulated values.

But there is also a fundamental need for government to stand outside the system. Funtowicz and Revetz[15] draws a distinction between *ordinary complexity* and *emergent complexity*. Ordinary complexity is characterized by a complementarity of competition and co-operation within a diversity of elements and sub-elements. Stability and simple system goals are the main features. By contrast, emergent complexity frequently oscillates between hegemony and fragmentation as diversity and innovation are impeded. The hegemonies of the NHS are well recognized – precedence, tradition and vested interests still remain.[16] To some extent, a degree of transactional government is necessary.

There is evidence that complexity insights are being accommodated by government leaders. For example, a recent report from the Cabinet Office acknowledged that although short-term results can be achieved through direction, in the long run it is more efficient and effective to motivate and empower than to issue detailed commands;[17] the encouragement of diversity through such initiatives as Health Action Zones and PMS pilots echoes complexity themes; the national quality strategy for the NHS[18] highlights lifelong learning as a way of improving healthcare and draws directly upon insights from complexity theory; and recent government policy emphasizes learning from mistakes in an organization with a memory rather than the perpetuation of a blame culture.[19]

However, despite these indications, political leaders are unable to acknowledge publicly the limitations on their ability to act rationally and continue to maintain their 'masquerade of potency'.[20] The result – a gap between the expectation of government and the aspirations and capabilities of the health service. Confusion arises when government articulates values which are not demonstrated in practice. For example, government policy still sees an NHS free at the point of entry and based on need alone and has repeatedly refused to accept the practical necessity of making hard rationing choices.[21] The political election cycle always favours quick fixes rather than programmes designed to bring about lasting change in service culture and the emphasis continues to be on deliverable targets that can be linked to government policies. Government remains a master institution. The simple rules remain unchanged – ministers decide/professionals deliver; politicians centralize credit/diffuse blame.

Conclusion

Historically, organizations have been viewed as changing in predictable ways, engineered by leaders to defined objectives. Failure to control correctly is seen as lack of system information. This chapter has outlined some complexity insights that may be useful for thinking about change from the perspective of leaders and managers. The new leadership acknowledges the fact that organizations are complex adaptive systems which limits the opportunities for prediction and control. Leaders articulate a clear vision of organizational history, a clear vision of where the organization is now and a clear set of values on which to base the future. Learning and sense making replace control and the focus changes to managing connections between people who have roles that are constantly changing.

Against this background, perhaps we can postulate two types of leaders? 'Covert leaders' can be found in any part of an organization where they exhibit natural transformational leadership characteristics, however menial their role in the organization. 'Overt leaders' are found in the upper hierarchy of an organization and are able to accommodate both transactional and transformational approaches, depending on the context in which they have to operate. They are cognizant to the importance of non-linear networks but are not afraid to impose hierarchical control when relevant, and by doing so are able to hold the organization at a state of self-organized criticality where it can function most effectively.

Although the application of complexity theory to organizational leadership and the management of change remains contested, its insights are increasingly attractive to policy makers. Whether they simply offer a framework to reduce anxiety against a background of the paradox of being in command but not in control, or whether they offer real opportunities for genuine change, remains to be seen.

References

1 Institute of Medicine (2001) *Crossing the Quality Chasm: a new health system for the 21st century*. National Academy of Sciences Press, Washington, DC.
2 Goodwin N (2003) Making leadership work in today's NHS. *British Journal of Healthcare Management*. **9**: 179–81.
3 Marshall M (1999) Improving quality in general practice: qualitative case study of barriers faced by health authorities. *BMJ*. **319**: 164–7.
4 Mayor S (2003) Hospitals take short-term measures to meet targets. *BMJ*. **326**: 1054.
5 Pendleton D and King J (2002) Values and leadership. *BMJ*. **325**: 1352–5.
6 Plsek P (2001) In: *Crossing the Quality Chasm: a new health system for the 21st century*, pp. 322–30. National Academy of Sciences Press, Washington, DC.
7 Zimmerman B, Lindberg C and Plsek P (1998) *Edgeware: insights from complexity science for healthcare leaders*. VHA Publishing, Irving, TX.
8 Le Grand, J Mays N and Mulligan J (1998) *Learning from the NHS Internal Market*. King's Fund, London.
9 Rogers E (1995) *Diffusion of Innovations*. The Free Press, New York.
10 Plsek P (2001) *Why Won't the NHS Do As It's Told and What Might We Do About It: rethinking performance management*. NHS Confederation, London.
11 Plsek P and Wilson T (2001) Complexity leadership and management in healthcare organizations. *BMJ*. **323**: 746–9.
12 Bate P (2000) Changing the culture of a hospital: from hierarchy to networked community. *Public Administration*. **78**: 485–512.
13 Foucault M (1991) Governmentality. In: Burchell G, Gordon C and Miller P (eds) *The Foucault Effect: studies in governmentality*. Harvester Wheatsheaf, London.
14 Light D (2001) Managed competition: governmental and institutional response in the UK. *Social Science and Medicine*. **52**: 1167–81.
15 Funtowicz S and Revetz J (1994) Emergent complex systems. *Futures*. **26 (6)**: 568–82.
16 Seedhouse D (1994) *Fortress NHS: the philosophical review of the National Health Service*. John Wiley, Chichester.
17 Performance and Innovation Unit (2001) *Better Policy, Delivery and Design: a discussion paper*. Cabinet Office, London.
18 Department of Health (1998) *A First-class Service: quality in the new NHS*. DoH, London.
19 Department of Health (1988) *An Organization with a Memory*. DoH, London.
20 Traynor M and Rafferty A (1998) Context, convergence and contingency. *Journal of Health Service Research and Policy*. **3 (4)**: 195–6.
21 Kernick D (2002) An introduction to rationing. In: Kernick D (ed) *Getting Health Economics into Practice*. Radcliffe Medical Press, Oxford.

Section 4

Facilitating emergence in healthcare organizations

Introduction

In market systems, individuals make decisions that affect their own well-being. Cost and the ability to pay determines who gets what and who goes without. In public systems, difficult choices must be made in two areas. Firstly, how are public resources allocated against a background of finite budgets? Secondly, how does the organization reconfigure itself as changing demands are placed upon it?

Historically, these decisions were taken implicitly within a hierarchical framework, often by one person. In healthcare this was usually the doctor. Recently there has been an acceptance of a wider input into the decision-making process within an explicit framework. But just how this should be accomplished is an area hedged with arguments and counter arguments without convergence to a workable framework. In reality, despite attempts to provide technical and evidence-based frameworks, we muddle through in an environment of conflicting policies.

An alternative approach is to work with paradox rather than attempt to contain it; to trust the human resources of the organization to develop solutions that may not be optimal but which satisfy the constraints placed on the system. This section explores approaches to how that may be achieved by facilitating emergence.

Emergence is a key concept within complexity theory. It recognizes that patterns are formed in systems that could not be predicted by an analysis of the system elements; that systems can self-organize to satisfy the constraints placed upon them given the right conditions. In this section we expand upon the emergent nature of decision making and change. How we can create environments that can facilitate the emergence of solutions that may not have been predicted. This does not of course exclude 'evidence-based' inputs such as the results of scientific trials, but offers a complementary approach.

It would not be practical or possible to involve all stakeholders in every organizational decision. In many areas, choices must be taken by a small number of decision makers. In Chapter 11, I set decision making within the emotive context of healthcare rationing. I argue that attempts to develop practical frameworks to support decision makers have failed as a result of applying linear analytical models to an inherently non-linear system. I conclude by suggesting some practical descriptive and prescriptive insights from complexity theory that can support an emergent perspective on resource decision making.

We then consider two systems-based approaches that are being used in healthcare organizations. Although the concept of emergence would be rejected by traditional hard systems thinking, the approaches described aim to facilitate to varying extents this process.

In Chapter 12, Will Liddell and John Powell demonstrate how a systems approach known as qualitative politicized influence diagrams helped a large NHS medical practice to improve patient access to general practitioners. Drawing upon quantitative and qualitative data, a practical diagram was developed to allow the views of stakeholders to be accommodated and form a picture of what was going on in the system. The model allowed options to be explored and capture the possibility of unexpected effects elsewhere in the system.

In Chapter 13, Sean Boyle and Julian Pratt take a different systems approach using as an example an urgent care situation in the NHS. In a technique they term 'agent-based working', they combine the insights from whole-system working with a computer modelling technique that reflects more closely the workings of a complex adaptive system. Although agent-based working shares the aims of the QPID approach in that it enables a more informed appraisal of the system-wide consequences of proposed actions, the emphasis is on giving attention to the parts and their interconnections.

Chapters 14 and 15 take a very different perspective, drawing upon the arts. Julian Burton shows how the visual arts can facilitate communication in organizations by supporting more non-rational and emotive forms of self-expression, and can create the conditions for the sorts of conversations in which new meaning or knowing can arise naturally. Pictures are also able to reflect dysfunction within organizations that may not otherwise be articulated and can avoid intellectual obstructions and jargon.

In Chapter 15, Marian and Shaun Naidoo follow a similar line using the performing arts. They describe how the creative skills they have developed over a number of years' experience can enable practitioners to understand the complexities of working together in organizations, with an emphasis on our perceptions of self, others, the context within which we interact as well as the process of interaction itself.

CHAPTER 11

Allocating limited
healthcare resources

David Kernick

This chapter views life in healthcare organizations as a continuum of resource allocation decisions. It argues that the failure to develop a workable framework to support decision makers is the result of applying existing linear analytical frameworks to an inherently non-linear system. An alternative model is suggested, emphasizing the emergent nature of decision making.

Key points
- Against a background of increasing demands on limited resources, difficult decisions are inevitable on how healthcare budgets are spent. Not everyone can receive the healthcare from which they will benefit.
- There has been no convergence to any workable framework to support resource decision making in public health systems.
- One solution is to match the approach with the complexity of the task.
- Most decisions are taken in an environment where there is an uncertain relationship between cause and effect, and the aims of stakeholders often differ. Complexity theory can offer useful prescriptive and descriptive insights for decision making in this area.

Introduction

Life in healthcare organizations is a continuum of decisions on how physical and human resources are allocated. Invariably, this process involves multiple stakeholders operating within a framework where goals often conflict and the relationship between cause and effect is uncertain. Against a background of limited healthcare budgets, resources invested into one area are at the expense of a lost opportunity in another and difficult decisions are inevitable. Every decision in healthcare is a rationing decision. Expanding one service means there is less for another, an extra five minutes spent with one patient will be at the expense of the next.

Attempts to use rational or technical solutions to this problem face substantial barriers that cannot always be overcome by methodological refinements. This chapter draws upon complexity insights to develop a framework that recognizes that systems cannot always be understood by breaking them down into their constituent elements and the application of rule-based decision frameworks. The focus changes from rational analysis and predictability to an emphasis on local interaction and the emergent nature of decision making. The 'edge of chaos' metaphor (*see* Chapter 3) is used to understand the interplay between formal and informal channels in decision making. This state has been defined as the transition zone between chaos and predictable stability where systems are maximally fit and adaptive. The metaphor can offer useful descriptive and prescriptive frameworks for understanding decision making in a healthcare system that is inherently dynamic and non-linear.

Making resource decisions in public systems

Not everyone can receive the healthcare from which they can benefit and the need to make resource allocation decisions is a pervasive feature of all healthcare systems. In market-based models, individuals make the choices based on three factors:

- cost determined by the interplay of supply and demand
- their ability to pay
- their perceived well-being or utility from the options that are available to them.

Public decision making involves a wider range of inputs (*see* Box 11.1) and the allocation of resources involves a number of participants.

Box 11.1   Questions to ask when resources are being distributed

- Appropriateness – is it appropriate that the intervention is delivered under the auspices of a public system?
- Efficacy – does it work in a research setting?

- Effectiveness – does it work in the intended setting?
- Efficiency – is the additional cost commensurate with the additional benefit?
- Equity – is it fairy distributed across the population?
- Affordability – do we have enough money to pay for it?
- Audit – are we doing what we claim?

The NHS decision-making process is characterized by:

- A framework where system goals often conflict; for example, efficiency and equity.
- The relationship between cause and effect is uncertain.
- There are a number of stakeholders that have different perspectives and specialized knowledge.
- The area attracts an emotive overlay that is often lacking in other public sectors. For example, rationing is often used as a pejorative term for decision making – patients are having care taken away from which they would benefit.

There is a voluminous policy analysis and decision-making literature that includes:

- social perspectives – the power relationships in decision making
- psychological perspectives – the cognitive elements of the decision process
- economic perspectives – the behaviour of individuals as they maximize their well-being against a background of choice and complete information.

Nevertheless, a workable framework to facilitate the difficult healthcare rationing decisions that are inevitable remains elusive.

This chapter reviews the three historical approaches to resource decision making in the NHS and sets them within a spectrum of decision making. Finally, some descriptive and prescriptive insights are suggested, invoking the 'edge of chaos' metaphor.

Approaches to healthcare decision making – the rhetoric and the reality

In general, approaches to resource decision making fall into three camps:

1 *The whole thing is so complex that the best approach is to leave it to the professionals and keep things out of the public eye as much as possible.* Historically, decision making in the NHS has been 'a combination of guidelines, exhortation and obfuscation, leaving it largely to the coal-faced workers to jiggle a quart of services from a pint-pot of resources'.[1] Stakeholders were happy to acquiesce to this system where doctors made implicit rationing decisions without challenge, an approach that was flexible and reflected the heterogeneity of patients, doctors and their treatments[2] and avoided the disutility of rationing.[3] However, despite concerns that what is right and what is feasible must keep in step with each other,[4] over the last decade there has been a call to make decision making more explicit. The suggestion is that implicit decision making may be influenced by professional interests rather than those of patients.

2 *Resource decision making should be explicit and based on rational technical frameworks.* Health economists have been in the vanguard of a more robust approach. While recognizing the conflict with equity, they argue that resource decisions should be directed by considerations of efficiency within a rational model. This framework assumes clarity of objectives and values and the ability to evaluate the costs and consequences of all options explicitly.

Unfortunately, international attempts at rational rationing have suggested that rationing is inherently complex and that there are no explicit frameworks that are acceptable both publicly and politically.[5] Simple solutions such as cost-effectiveness are often impossible to implement and priority setting by explicit trade-offs are too simplistic to reflect decision making in action. The Oregon experience demonstrated that, ultimately, the primary influence on health service priority rankings was subjective judgements.[6] In practice, new decisions are invariably compared with previous ones and their rationales in a 'case law' that helps to ensure consistency.[7]

3 *There is no simple answer but decision making must be open and transparent.* As the 'first phase' of decision making based on simple solutions such as economic evaluation has proved illusory, it has been suggested that the 'second phase' should focus on the priority-setting process itself.[8] As citizens are reluctant to make rationing decisions directly,[9] the suggestion is that policy makers should act as agents for citizens but that citizens should be involved in developing principles upon which these agents should act.[10] For example, such a framework should include public accessibility, relevance, the right to appeal and public regulation.[11] In the NHS, this approach has already been consolidated within a legal framework that directs treatment decisions taken by health authorities should be fair, consistent, set within a general framework of values, able to make an allowance for exceptional cases and open to appeal.[12]

Box 11.2 summarizes the main features of what has become a rationing debate. Here rationing means that resources are not available to provide the patient with an intervention from which they would benefit.

Box 11.2   Some features of the current rationing debate

- A desire to minimize implicit rationing
- A recognition of the difficulties of explicit rationing
- An acceptance of the difficulty of meeting efficiency and equity objectives
- A realization of the difficulty of engaging the public
- A lack of convergence to similar solutions across healthcare systems
- A general view that rationing is complex and messy

The spectrum of decision-making frameworks

There is a bewildering array of analytical models and frames that seek to illuminate public policy and decision-making processes (*see* Parsons[13] for a comprehensive and accessible overview). The spectrum of approaches includes:

- rationality – an explicit articulation of objectives and values and examination of the costs and consequences of alternatives
- bounded rationality[14] – recognizes the limits to rational behaviour due to limited information and processing power. The concept of 'satisficing' is emphasized – courses of action that are good enough
- incremental models – change by mutual adjustment and negotiation, and underpinned by pragmatism and learning[15]
- garbage can decision making – problems and solutions are messy and their resolution depends arbitrarily on the time they are picked up and the availability of cans in which to put them.[16]

Recognizing the inappropriateness of implicit rationing and the limitations of the rational framework, a number of healthcare commentators have emphasized the incremental and contextual features of healthcare decision making. For example, Klein[17] sees decision making as experimental and incremental, an 'approach that may represent a more sophisticated and realistic form of rationality rather than attempts to devise technical fixes'. Hunter[18] describes decision making as an 'iterative process of muddling through elegantly'. Light and Hughes[19] identify how economic transactions are embedded in social relationships and argue that rationing is a socially constructed reality that is shaped by cultural beliefs, social norms and power differentials between stakeholders.

Mannion and Small[20] set resource decision making within a post-modern perspective, emphasizing the importance of non-mechanistic, metaphorical language. They warn against the increasing esoteric set of concerns of health economists, a trend epitomized by the continual elevation of the mathematical, and suggest that knowledge is necessarily multiple, contingent, malleable and dynamic.

Although these commentators recognize the limitations of rational decision making and the need for a more contingent and incremental decision model, the development of their critiques has been limited by a failure to set their analyses within a non-linear frame of reference.

Complexity insights into healthcare decision making

Complexity theory offers a useful overarching model to understand the spectrum of decision making outlined above. Figure 11.1 shows how these approaches can be mapped onto the Stacey diagram that we met in Chapter 3. The important point is that the analytical approach must match the zone in which the problem sits. If the problem sits within the rational zone then an economic analysis underpinned by a randomized controlled trial will be appropriate. If the problem sits within the chaotic zone then the system may need a degree of stability imposed upon it before a decision can be made. However, most decisions in healthcare will be in the mid-zone where complexity theory can offer us a number of useful insights.

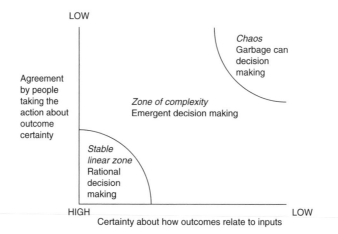

Figure 11.1   Decision making mapped onto the Stacey diagram (*see* Chapter 3).

Prescriptive insights of complexity

Perhaps most importantly, complexity theory tells us what we should not be doing. It cautions that we cannot analyse a system by reducing it into its component parts – there are no causal links that promise sophisticated tools for analysing and predicting system behaviour. Rather than spend time on detailed planning and striving to calculate a solution by the continuous addition of rules and measurement, decision makers should be content with setting minimum specifications, establishing boundaries and letting the system settle into a condition that satisfies the constraints placed on it.

Nussabaun[21] argues that the faculties of mind and the resources of language are best suited to the expression of complex problems; that appropriate emotions are useful in showing us what we might do and also morally valuable in their own right, providing the emotion is that of a reflective spectator and not derived from a personal interest in the case. Schön continues this theme in his analysis of professionals in action.[22] He suggests that competent practitioners usually know more than they can say and exhibit a 'knowing in practice'. They reveal a capacity for reflection on their intuitive knowledge in the midst of action, and in doing so do not solve problems but manage messes.

The essence of this approach would be to recognize that the resources of complexity are best suited to the expression of complex problems through the reiterated and integrated judgement of a collection of stakeholders and experts, whose interactions organize themselves into emergent processes from which decisions can emerge as 'a shared moral sensitivity'.

The emphasis should be on the interactions between stakeholders rather than their individual properties, interactions that are often inappropriately configured by power relationships. This approach runs counter to the model of technical rationality which sees professional activity as instrumental problem solving, made rigorous by the application of scientific theory and technique involving the application of general principles to specific problems.

Resource decision making as an emergent process – a practical framework

From a practical perspective, how could complexity insights facilitate the resource decision-making process? A useful first step for policy makers would be to recognize the dynamic, non-linear characteristics of the healthcare system; that complex systems operate most satisfactorily at the edge of chaos where they can learn and adapt and are most responsive to environmental change. Here technical and linear approaches are still relevant but coexist within a non-linear framework.

> **Box 11.3** Some 'simple rules' that could underpin emergent decision making (adapted from Williams, 2000[23])
>
> - To treat equals equally with due dignity, especially when near to death
> - To meet people's needs for healthcare as efficiently as possible (imposing the least sacrifice on others)
> - To minimize inequalities in the lifetime health of the population

The key is to develop a conversational competence amongst stakeholders rather than the current paradigm of an increasingly methodologically driven one. The edge of chaos is characterized by reasonableness and a sensitivity to the understanding and language that each of us uses and an ability to escape from one's own limited vocabulary of knowledge, skills and attitudes.

Underpinned by the recursive application of a small number of simple rules or guiding principles, solutions will emerge that may not have been predicted by an examination of the views of each individual stakeholder, are satisfactory rather than optimal, and provide a platform for the whole process to start again. Box 11.3 shows some possible simple rules.

Important factors in the success of this framework would be high levels of trust, a mutual understanding of each stakeholder's perspective and a reduction of power differentials. Here power is used not only in the behavioural sense within a hierarchical framework that implies control of one person over another, but power that resides in the relationships that people have with each other as they try to understand who they are and construct their identities with each other. Power as the constraint that excludes some communicative actions and includes others.

In summary, the emphasis is on creating the conditions for emergent solutions by facilitating the interaction of relevant stakeholders at the edge of

> **Box 11.4** Features of emergent decision making
>
> - Promoting a conversational framework between relevant stakeholders
> - Reducing professional hegemony and power differentials amongst stakeholders
> - Developing an environment of high trust
> - The definition of a small number of guiding principles or simple rules
> - Recognizing the importance of reiterative judgements – the source of standards is the previous history of the system
> - Allowing solutions to emerge that are not necessarily optimum but satisfy the constraints placed on the system

chaos, promoting a conversational framework in an environment of high trust, egalitarian relationships and underpinned by transparent simple rules.

Box 11.4 summarizes the main features of emergent decision making.

This process may already be taking place. Figure 11.2 shows the framework used by the National Institute for Clinical Excellence (NICE) that integrates both objective and subjective input. For example, NICE 'through the synthesis of all available evidence reaches a *judgement* as to whether *on balance* an intervention can be recommended as a cost-effective use of NHS resources'.[24] Setting this process within the framework articulated in this chapter might offer descriptive and prescriptive insights.

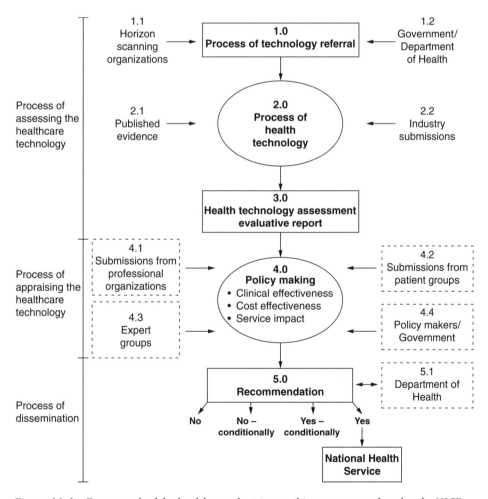

Figure 11.2   Framework of the healthcare decision-making process undertaken by NICE within its Technology Appraisal Programme.[25]

Conclusion

Healthcare resource decision making is an area hedged with constraints, intermediate positions, arguments and counter arguments characterized by a common perception that healthcare decision making takes place within a linear, reductionist and deterministic framework over which there is political and managerial control. The reality begs to differ.

In her study of resource decision making in health authorities and primary care organizations, McDonald[26] found that the use of technical solutions to resource allocation dilemmas at a local level face substantial barriers which cannot be overcome by methodological refinements or the collection of greater volumes of data. Faced with multiple goals, competing objectives and uncertain cause and effective relationships, relating ends to means is highly problematic. In many cases, doing something appeared to be better than doing nothing and became an end in itself. These unresolved ambiguities are also present at a national level as the case of beta-interferon for the treatment of multiple sclerosis demonstrates.[27]

Complexity theory challenges a number of traditional notions but offers us useful descriptive and prescriptive insights into decision making in the real world. It emphasizes the need to learn by reflection on the difference between rhetoric and experienced reality, forcing us to rethink our ideas on causation and intervention. In many cases, organizations do not move towards a defined future. Outcomes are not an optimal solution to a problem but a learning that leads to a decision to take certain actions in the knowledge that this will lead in general not to the problem being solved but to a new situation in which the whole process can begin again.

It is an approach that resonates with the experience of practitioners and healthcare decision makers who operate under constraints of limited time, knowledge and processing power in an environment that seeks to establish and modify relationships through time rather than follow goal-seeking behaviour. A model that reflects reality rather than attempting to force it into a disciplinary matrix, offering an explanatory framework for decision-making approaches that are already evolving.

Petros[28] reflects on the art of medicine – the ability to intuitively tune into all the patient's complex elements, absorbing numerous stimuli that are referenced against the accumulated knowledge of previous factors. The process is continuously modified until the diagnosis and its relevance to a person is reached. Emergent decision making takes a similar approach, but is applied by relevant stakeholders at a broader level as they are held at the edge of chaos. The first important step is to recognize the limitations of the dominant discourse in organizations and encourage decision makers to tune in to the dynamic, non-linear state that characterizes the healthcare system.

References

1   Butler J (1999) *The Ethics of Healthcare Rationing*. Cassell, London.
2   Mechanic D (1995) Dilemmas in rationing healthcare services: the case for implicit rationing. *BMJ*. **310**: 1655–9.
3   Coast J (1997) Rationing within the NHS should be explicit: the case against. *BMJ*. **314**: 118–22.
4   Butler J (1999) *op cit*.
5   World Health Organization (1996) *European Healthcare Reforms: analysis and current strategies*. WHO Regional Office for Europe, Copenhagen.
6   United States Office of Technology Assessment (1992) *Evaluation of the Oregon Medicaid Proposal*. Washington, DC.
7   Martin D, Pater J and Singer P (2001) Priority-setting decisions for new cancer drugs: a qualitative study. *Lancet*. **358**: 1676–81.
8   Holm S (1998) Goodbye to the simple solutions: the second phase of priority setting in healthcare. *BMJ*. **317**: 1000–7.
9   Kneeshaw J (1997) What does the public think about rationing? In: New B (ed) *A Review of the Evidence in Rationing Talk and Action in Healthcare*. BMJ Publishing, London.
10   Mooney G (1998) Communitarian claims as an ethical basis for allocating health-care resources. *Social Science and Medicine*. **49 (9)**: 1171–80.
11   Daniels N and Sabin J (1998) The ethics of accountability in managed care reform. *Health Affairs*. **17**: 50–64.
12   Newdick C (2002) Rationing and the law. In: Kernick D (ed) *Getting Heath Economics into Practice*. Radcliffe Medical Press, Oxford.
13   Parsons W (1995) *Public Policy: an introduction to the theory and practice of policy analysis*. Elgar, Cheltenham.
14   Simon HA (1957) *Administrative Behaviour*. The Free Press, New York.
15   Lindblom CE (1959) The science of muddling through. *Public Administration Review*. **19**: 78–88.
16   Cohen M, March J and Olsen J (1972) A garbage can model of organizational choice. *Administrative Science Quarterly*. **17**: 1–25.
17   Klein R (1998) Puzzling out priorities. *BMJ*. **318**: 959–60.
18   Hunter D (1997) *Desperately Seeking Solutions*. Longman, London.
19   Light D and Hughes D (2001) Rationing: constructed realities and professional practices. *Sociology of Health and Illness*. **23**: 551–69.
20   Mannion R and Small N (1999) Post-modern health economics. *Health Care Analysis*. **7**: 255–72.
21   Nussabaun N (1995) *Poetic Justice*. Beacon Press, Boston, MA.
22   Schön D (1982) *The Reflective Practitioner: how professionals think in action*. Basic Books, Cambridge, MA.
23   Williams A. Quoted in Hutton J and Maynard A (2000) A NICE challenge for health economists. *Health Economics*. **9**: 89–93.
24   National Institute for Clinical Excellence (1999) *An Appraisal of New and Existing Technology: interim guidance for manufacturers and sponsors*. NICE, London.
25   Taylor R and Mears R (2002) Making decisions at a national level: a NICE experience. In: Kernick D (ed) *Getting Health Economics into Practice*, p. 217. Radcliffe Medical Press, Oxford.

26   McDonald R (2002) *Using Health Economics in Health Services: rationing rationally.* Open University Press, Buckingham.

27   Kernick D (2002) Beta-interferon, NICE and rationing. *British Journal of General Practice.* **52:** 784–5.

28   Petros P (2001) Art and science of clinical knowledge [letter]. *Lancet.* **358:** 1818–19.

CHAPTER 12

Improving patient access in a large medical practice: a complex and complicated system problem

Will Liddell and John Powell

This chapter demonstrates how a systems method known as qualitative politicized influence diagrams helped a large NHS medical practice to improve patient access to general practitioners. Not only did the technique ensure that the views of all stakeholders were accommodated in the decision-making process, but that the possibility of unexpected effects elsewhere in the system were captured.

Key points
- Problems in healthcare contain both linear mechanistic components and non-linear human ones.
- QPID is a practical and effective method of representing and identifying the effects of action in complicated and complex systems, particularly those exhibiting multiple viewpoints and where there is a mixture of quantitative and qualitative data available.
- This approach helped a large practice to reconfigure their arrangement for access in a way that accommodated the perspectives of all stakeholders.

Introduction

In this chapter we look at how a large NHS general practice used an explicit system-modelling technique to facilitate a policy decision that was both complex and complicated and which contained both quantitative and qualitative components. Interactions between the components of such systems are frequently highly non-linear and there are a number of perspectives on the desirability of any particular action aimed at managing the system. Doctors, nurses, receptionists and patients form a complex, interconnected structure and unilateral changes may have unintended consequences in other parts of the system.

We use a technique called qualitative politicized influence diagrams to capture the complexities of such a highly interconnected system. Although this approach is used in general organizational management, it has only recently come to the attention of healthcare managers. The relationship of QPID with other system approaches has been discussed in Chapter 4.

Characterization of managerial problems in general medical practice

Although the problems facing general practice management are specific in some respects, they are typical of a wide class of management activities known as 'hybrid system problems'. Such systems contain both mechanistic components and human ones. The mechanistic components are reflected in the bureaucratic processes whose outputs are dependent solely on their inputs in a linear manner. A general practice has some components which are essentially bureaucratic, for example an information retrieval system, a detailed rule-based appointments policy and a practice formulary governing the prescription of drugs. This is in contrast with the human components which are at best boundedly rational,[1] but form the very heart of the organization's capacity for success.

Frequently these hybrid systems exhibit the inherent non-linearity, but they must be managed even when the precise definition of the system is inaccessible to the manager. Opting out on the basis of insufficient data and structural definition is not an option. There will also be a number of different perspectives on how the organization should be run and its criteria for success. This plurality of viewpoint and the associated need for accommodation among system stakeholders is characteristic of hybrid systems.[2]

The patient access problem

The NHS Plan[3] expresses a commitment to make the NHS more responsive and accessible to the needs of patients and sets out a range of targets for general practice. This has been driven in part by a desire to make the public services more accountable, but also by rising expectations of service provision within society. A key target was that by 2004 patients would be able to see a primary care professional within 24 hours and a GP within 48 hours. Against a background of limited healthcare resources, this represents a significant management challenge for general practice when GPs are already under considerable stress. A number of changes in health service provision are already underway to meet these demands, for example alternative points of direct access and advice, including NHS Direct and NHS walk-in centres, and development of practice nurses in the first-line management of both acute and chronic illness.

Another important initiative has been to encourage practices to try to match the availability of appointments more closely to demand. Traditional appointment systems are being replaced by first-generation open-access systems which attempt to predict same-day demand and reserve capacity in anticipation. These systems still tend to overflow and are open to manipulation by patients and practice staff. Second-generation open-access systems assume demand can be set aside if enough capacity is available and have been introduced widely across the NHS under the auspices of the primary care collaborative of the NHS Modernisation Agency.

The QPID approach to hybrid system problems

QPID is a development of system dynamics, a widely used approach to the hybrid managerial problems and described more fully in Chapter 4. The SD approach is to prepare a graphical model of the system under consideration by considering the flows and levels of certain variables which together define the state of a system. This graphical model is called an influence diagram.

In considering our present topic, there are a large number of relevant variables which include GP hours available for appointments, waiting time for a routine appointment and demand for a same-day appointment. Causality is expressed in the form of arrows connecting these variables, as shown in Figure 12.1. This is an extract from a larger diagram (*see* Appendix B, Figure 12B.1 at the end of this chapter) which will feature centrally in our subsequent analysis.

Here we see that as the waiting time for a routine appointment increases, the demand for same-day access will increase (as patients become impatient at the delay). This positive correlation is indicated by the '+' sign on the relevant arrow. Figure 12.1 also indicates that as the number of GP hours available for consultation goes up, the waiting time for a routine appointment will tend to go down. This negative relationship is indicated by a '−' sign on the appropriate arrow. In both cases there will be other factors which will affect the variables as the larger diagram shows.

The essential analysis tool in this qualitative embodiment of SD[4,5] is the concept of loop behaviour. Figure 12.2 shows another extract from the full patient-access ID of Figure 12B.1. It has two cyclic structures marked **A** and **B**.

Figure 12.1   Expression of causality in SD diagrams.

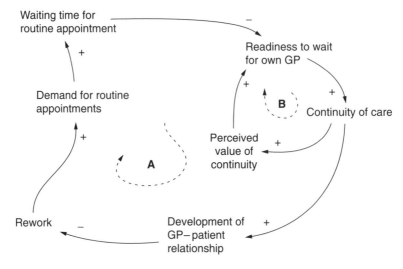

Figure 12.2   Two loops extracted from the full model.

Loop A shows how, as patients become more ready to wait for a consultation with their own GP, the continuity of care improves. The GP–patient relationship develops and rework is reduced, easing the pressure on routine appointment waiting times, which in turn encourages patients to wait that little bit longer for an appointment with their own doctor. If there were no other mechanisms in operation, a slight decrease in waiting times would propagate round the loop, reducing rework and eventually producing a further decrease in waiting times and an increased willingness to wait for the patient's own doctor. This type of loop is called a reinforcing loop. Clearly, if system managers can initiate a beneficial rise in the variables in this loop and, critically, can act so as to increase the strength of desired connections, the effect on healthcare provision will be positive. A loop with an odd number of negative signs on its arrows is known as a goal-seeking loop and has the potential to reach steady state without external intervention.

The qualitative form of SD uses such arguments to move directly from the structure of the system under consideration (the ID) to proposing sets of actions

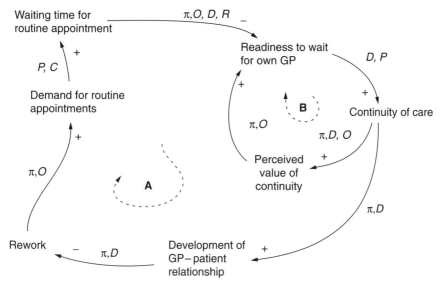

Figure 12.3   Two loops showing the actors which control the strength of correlation between variables.

aimed at manipulating the system variables and the strengths of the connections. The recent refinement[6,7] of this approach that we describe here attaches symbols to the causal arrows, indicating the actors or agents who are able to affect the strength of the connection. Figure 12.3 shows the actors for the loops of Figure 12.2.

The key to the symbols for all of these diagrams is shown in Box 12.1. Thus we see that the degree to which patients are willing to wait for their own GPs is influenced by the patient (π), the relatives and friends (O), the GP (D) and the reception staff (R). To the extent that we can identify actions aimed at motivating these actors to encourage patients to wait for their own doctors (even though the waiting time for such an appointment has increased) the more we will be able to use the inherent dynamics of loop **A** (Figure 12.2) to our patients' benefit and vice versa.

Box 12.1   Key of symbols designating actors

π = individual patient
D = GP
P = the partnership (practice executive)
C = primary care organization
R = reception staff
O = patients and relatives and friends

The final stage in the QPID method is to identify the set of actions that should be taken by the system's 'owners' to persuade the actors (which can include the system owners) to strengthen or weaken appropriately their effect on the system connections.

The case described below illustrates the practical use of the QPID method in deriving a set of actions from an ID from which Figures 12.1, 12.2 and 12.3 were taken.

Application to patient access in a general medical practice

Context of study

In 2000 the Frome Medical Practice, a large practice with 26 000 registered patients, changed from a traditional appointment system where same-day urgent access was achieved through provision of an unbooked 'emergency surgery' for urgent cases at the end of the day, to a first-generation system with twice-daily booked 'same-day surgeries'. Capacity was increased with the employment of more salaried GPs. The practice also started to gather data on waiting times and patient satisfaction. These changes were embraced by reception staff and demonstrated improvements in waiting times and patient satisfaction. However, two years later the appointment system was once again saturated and there was a growing sense of dissatisfaction amongst the GPs.

Access and workload were identified as a key area for management attention and as a direct result the investigation reported here was started. The objective was *to derive actionable policies for the practice which would improve patient access* (under existing and predicted NHS policy) *consistent with the needs and motivations of all stakeholders*, i.e. GPs, patients, nurses, receptionists and the local primary care organization.

Study method

The study was designed as an action research project. One of the authors (WL) was a partner in the practice and was formally engaged in the reconciliation of access needs with the strategic needs of the practice. The methodology was broadly based on an approach by Hazell and Powell.[8] In essence, their procedure is to establish a basic reference model which is used to structure interviews with the relevant stakeholders or participants. A final ID is then produced which incorporates the different hypotheses or assertions of the participants about the system. Proposed actions then emerge from an examination of the desired behaviour of each loop and these are reconciled into a coherent action plan. Resource implications are taken into account at this last stage. The model was constructed using pencil and paper. One of the authors (WL) acted as facilitator.

Developing the model

GPs, practice nurses, managers and reception staff participated in the development of the model. All participants quickly grasped the principles of constructing an ID and participated readily in the process of exploring relationships between different parameters. It was notable that none had difficulty perceiving the access and workload issue from a systemic perspective. A number of themes emerged repeatedly, for example the balance between the number of patients seen and the quality of the consultation, the responsiveness of the practice and the tendency of patients to seek advice about minor illness, speed of access and continuity of care. The final ID is shown in Figure 12B.1.

Undertaking the analysis

Analysis of the final ID comprises two stages. The first stage is to identify the important loops within it and determine the nature and strengths of the relationships depicted. The second stage is to determine the actors or agents able to affect those relationships and analyse their actual and potential roles. Space does not permit a discussion of all the loops, but three are highlighted for particular attention.

    1 *Continuity of care*. Continuity of care has traditionally meant that the patient visits the same GP over a long period of time,[9] resulting in the development of trust satisfaction and enablement.[10–12] Having a personal GP is highly valued by patients, particularly for dealing with more serious, psychological or family issues.[13,14]

    In the ID the first pair of reinforcing loops that involved continuity of care were discussed earlier in this chapter and are shown in Figure 12.3. In loop **A**, the short-term result of a patient consulting with a GP whom they did not know well was a greater likelihood of that patient returning for further reassurance or for a follow-up with their own GP, resulting in more rework. This perception was confirmed by analysis of data on repeat presentation after a same-day surgery appointment. The effect of rework is to increase the demand for routine appointments, leading to longer waiting times. Longer waits result in less patients being prepared to wait to see their own GP, thereby reducing continuity of care and completing the loop. Another loop (**B** in Figure 12.3) operates concurrently, in that reducing experience of continuity is likely to reduce its perceived value so that patients are even less willing to wait and see their own GP if they do not know them well.

2 *Minor illness.* GPs frequently express frustration at the level of consultations for minor ailments.[15] In the present study, several GPs felt they were more likely to issue a prescription for a minor ailment in the context of a busy same-day surgery. The issue of a script for a minor ailment like a sore throat increases the likelihood that the patient will re-attend in the future with the same ailment.[16] Figure 12.4 shows two minor-illness reinforcing loops (**C** and **D**) which describe the relationship between same-day demand, time pressure and doctors' consulting behaviour. Increased demand for same-day appointments under an open-access appointments system results in more patients seen on the day and greater time pressure on the GP responsible.

3 *The work of the receptionist.* The third pair of reinforcing loops (**E** and **F** in Figure 12.5) concerns the work of receptionists. Enhancing the skills of receptionists and allowing them greater discretion (loop **E**) may enable them to offer a signposting service, rather than acting as a barrier (under traditional appointment systems) or as a passive conduit for access to a GP (under open access). The skilled receptionist exercising discretion has the potential to direct the patient to an alternative source of help and advice, thus often avoiding the need to see a GP first. For example, medical secretaries, nurses or health visitors may be able to deal with the problem more quickly than a GP appointment. Diversion of work should reduce the time pressure on GPs, leading to better quality consultations and more effective preventative work. Since GPs' remuneration is in part

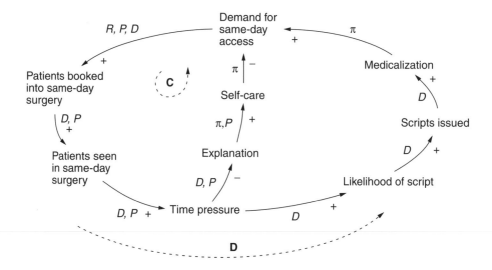

Figure 12.4   Minor illness loops.

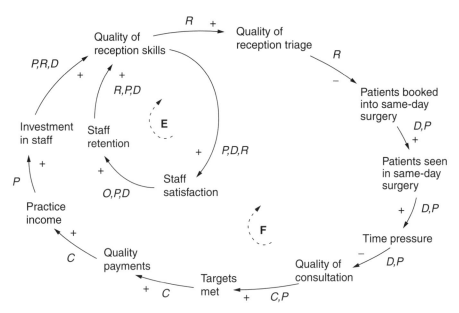

Figure 12.5   Reception skills loops.

target based, this trend should increase practice income. Higher levels of income could make more resources available for training and remunerating receptionists. Concurrently, enhancing receptionists' skills (loop **F**) is likely to increase job satisfaction and retention.[17]

Results of the exercise

Table 12A.1 in Appendix A sets out as an example the results of analysing one of the three loops in terms of the desired effect on the strength of each relationship, the actors influencing each relationship and the actions likely to achieve the desired outcome. The key actions implemented immediately following the study model-building exercise are shown below:

- *Telephone triage* – a nurse-led telephone triage service was set up to work jointly with a salaried GP who offered face-to-face consultations every morning for patients requesting same-day appointments. Approximately 70% of these requests are now dealt with over the telephone.
- *Clinical receptionists* – receptionists were trained to elicit more information from callers to allow them to identify the most appropriate source of advice. Receptionists developed a routine for use on calls to ensure consistency and respect for patient confidentiality.

- *List size adjustment* – patients were transferred from some GPs' lists to others so that the size of each list more closely reflected the availability of each GP for routine consultations. This measure has improved continuity.
- *Availability of health visitor and social worker* – these professionals agreed to make themselves available to answer patients' requests at defined times during the day.
- *Guidelines for the use of same-day surgery* – a definition of the purpose of same-day surgery was agreed so that patients are given consistent advice on how to use the service appropriately.
- *Guidelines for minor illness management* – evidence-based guidelines for the management of minor ailments were prepared to ensure consistency between GPs and nurses with respect to treatment and advice given to patients.
- *Increasing nurse capacity* – the working patterns of nurses have been closely examined to maximize effectiveness and certain services withdrawn as a result of reviewing the evidence on effectiveness.

Conclusion

The QPID process proved easy and practical to use in the context of general practice. The problem addressed was a complex one affecting the work of almost everyone working in the practice, clinical and non-clinical. Prior to the exercise it had proved difficult to achieve consensus on the best way to tackle the access problem. Several different viewpoints existed within the practice decision-making body and, while all agreed on the importance of addressing access, little progress was being made in developing a strategy.

It could be argued that some of these actions which followed the exercise could have been identified without the use of an explicit system description method, but there are a number of clear benefits from such an approach:

- The consequences of taking action and thereby altering the system dynamics can be explicitly identified. Moreover, these consequences are assessed within a system diagram which has been developed jointly by participants with different views and opinions. While the parties may not agree about which loop is the strongest, they will have agreed on the behaviourial mechanisms of the system under consideration.
- The consequences of not taking action are easily seen. Even if an option for action is rejected because of resource limitations, the codification of the system behaviour allows investigation and debate of the effects of such inaction.
- Within the system representation all actions and influences can be investigated, ensuring that no voice is excluded. The incorporation of ideas and views from people usually excluded from the decision-making body was a

notable strength. There is a sense of completeness about the study. Within the inescapable limitations of the system representation, we can be sure that all actions have been investigated. There is a political point here; because all action options emerge equally and formally from the loop analysis, it is rather difficult for some interested party to suppress arbitrarily debate about a particular style of response. While at times this may be managerially uncomfortable, the benefits in achieving wide consensus and assessment of action are well substantiated.

- The QPID method makes it impossible for participants to ignore the consequences of their own behaviour on the behaviour of the system as a whole. In this case, the effects of individual GPs' consulting behaviour with respect to prescribing in minor illness and eliciting patients' needs and expectations were made clear.

- This approach enables areas to be identified where the collection of additional numerical data can provide a useful input into decision making (such as the number of patients returning following a same-day surgery appointment).

In conclusion, QPID is a practical and effective method of representing and identifying directed action in complicated, complex systems, and particularly in those exhibiting multiple viewpoints and where there is a mixture of quantitative and qualitative data available. We anticipate its further use in such medical and health management problems as cardiac care, paediatric care policy and socio-medical systems such as the wider treatment and prevention of diabetes.

References

1 March J and Simon H (1993) *Organizations*. Blackwell, Cambridge, MA.
2 Quinn J (1978) Strategic change: logical incrementalism. *Sloane Management Review*. 20: 7–21.
3 Department of Health (2000) *The NHS Plan: a plan for investment, a plan for reform*. HMSO, London.
4 Coyle RG (2000) Qualitative and quantitative modelling in system dynamics: some research questions. *System Dynamics Review*. 16 (3): 225–44.
5 Wolstenholme EF (1990) *System Enquiry*. John Wiley, Chichester.
6 Powell J and Bradford J (1998) The security–strategy interface: using qualitative process models to relate the security function to business dynamics. *Security Journal*. 10: 151–60.
7 Powell J and Coyle R (In press) Identifying strategic action in highly politicised contexts using agent-based qualitative system dynamics. *Journal of the Operational Research Society*.
8 Hazell PJ and Powell J (1997) The future strategic dynamics of ceramic armour technology. *Defense Analysis*. 16: 53–72.
9 Freeman G (1985) Priority given by doctors to continuity of care. *British Journal of General Practice*. 35: 423–6.

10 Howie J, Heaney D *et al.* (1999) Quality at general practice consultations: a cross-sectional survey. *BMJ.* **319:** 738–43.
11 Mainous A, Baker R *et al.* (2001) Continuity of care and trust in one's physician: evidence from primary care in the United States and the United Kingdom. *Family Medicine.* **33:** 22–7.
12 Hjortdahl P and Laerum E (2002) Continuity of care in general practice: effect on patient satisfaction. *BMJ.* **304:** 1287–90.
13 Kearley K, Freeman G *et al.* (2001) An exploration of the value of the doctor–patient relationship in general practice. *British Journal of General Practice.* **49:** 273–6.
14 Schers H, Webster S *et al.* (2002) Continuity of care in general practice: a survey of patients' views. *British Journal of General Practice.* **52:** 459–62.
15 Morris C, Cantrill J *et al.* (2001) GPs' attitude to minor ailments. *Family Practice.* **18:** 581–5.
16 Little P, Williamson I *et al.* (1997) An open randomized trial of prescribing strategies for sore throat. *BMJ.* **315:** 350–2.
17 Pfeffer J (1998) *The Human Equation.* Harvard Business School Press, Boston, MA.

Further reading

Anon. (2002) *A Focus on General Practice in England.* The Audit Commission, London.
Coyle RG (1977) *Management System Dynamics.* John Wiley, Chichester.
Coyle RG (1996) *System Dynamics Modelling: a practical approach.* Chapman and Hall/CRC Press, London.
Coyle RG (1998) The practice of system dynamics: milestones, lessons and ideas from 30 years' experience. *System Dynamics Review.* **14 (4):** 343–65.
Department of Health (2002) *Achieving and Sustaining Improved Access to Primary Care.* HMSO, London.
De Maesener J, Hjortdahl P *et al.* (2000) Fix what's right, not what's wrong with general practice in Britain. *BMJ.* **320:** 1616–17.
Gillam S and Pencheon D (1998) Managing demand in general practice. *BMJ.* **316:** 1895–8.
Grant C, Nicholas R *et al.* (2002) An observational study comparing quality of care in walk-in centres with general practice and NHS Direct using standardized patients. *BMJ:* **317:** 1556–63.
Guthrie B and Wyke S (2000) Does continuity in general practice really matter? *BMJ.* **321:** 734–5.
Luthra M and Marshall M (2001) How do general practices manage requests from patients for same-day appointments? *British Journal of General Practice.* **51 (1):** 39–41.
Murray M (2000) Patient care: access. *BMJ.* **320:** 1594–6.
Murray M and Tantau C (1999) Redefining open access to primary care. *Managed Care Quarterly.* **7:** 45–55.
Pencheon D (1998) Matching demand and supply fairly and efficiently. *BMJ.* **316:** 1665–7.
Salisbury C, Mnaku-Scott T *et al.* (2002) Questionnaire survey of users of NHS walk-in centres: observational study. *British Journal of General Practice.* **52:** 554–60.
Simon H (1957) *Models of Man.* John Wiley, New York.
Sterman JD (2000) *Business Dynamics.* McGraw-Hill, Boston, MA.
Stoddart H, Evans M *et al.* (2002) *The Provision of 'Same-day' Care in General Practice.* Unpublished.

Appendix A

Table 12A.1 Action list resulting from loop analysis of loops **A** and **B**

Loop	Arrow	Intent	Actor	Action
Rework loop (loop A of Figure 12.3)	Waiting time > readiness to wait for own GP	Weak	π	• Ensure patients understand importance of seeing own GP.
				• Ensure that 'other' GPs make patients aware of limitations of treating 'other' patients.
			D	• Ensure that 'other' (i.e. not patient's) GPs refer whenever appropriate.
			O	
			R	• Instruct to advocate waiting as beneficial.
	Readiness to wait for own GP > continuity of care	Strong	D	• Ensure that if a patient chooses to wait they do get to see their own GP.
			P	• Ensure that IS system allows visible use of patient's history.
	Continuity of care > development of GP/patient relationship	Strong	π	• Ensure patients know the benefit to the doctor of personal, continuing consultation.
			D	• Ensure GPs use and are seen to use case history and informal knowledge in that case history.
				• Make sure patient understands the value to GP of consistent consultation.
			O	• Encourage other practices to agree on benefits of continuity.

Table 12A.1 *(continued)*

Loop	Arrow	Intent	Actor	Action
	Development of GP/patient relationship > rework	Strong	π	• Use close relationship to impart realistic time-scale information on curative processes to patient – expectation setting.
			D	• Use close relationship to investigate and deal with medical/social context.
	Rework > demand for routine appointments	Weak	π	• Set realistic expectations for rate of progress of condition.
			O	• Encourage other local practices to establish expected standards of service.
	Demand for routine appointments > waiting time for routine appointments	Weak	P	• Consider demand shaping (putting more GPs on at busy periods). • Consider alternative routes to treatment (practitioner nurses, for example).
Perceived value loop (loop B of Figure 12.2)	Continuity of care > perceived value of continuity	Strong	π	• Seek examples of positive and negative effects.
			D	• Explain to patient the role of knowledge in the diagnostic and curative process.
	Perceived value of continuity > readiness to wait for own GP	Strong	π	• Convince patient of worth of waiting relative to benefits.
	Readiness to wait for own GP > continuity of care	Strong		

Appendix B

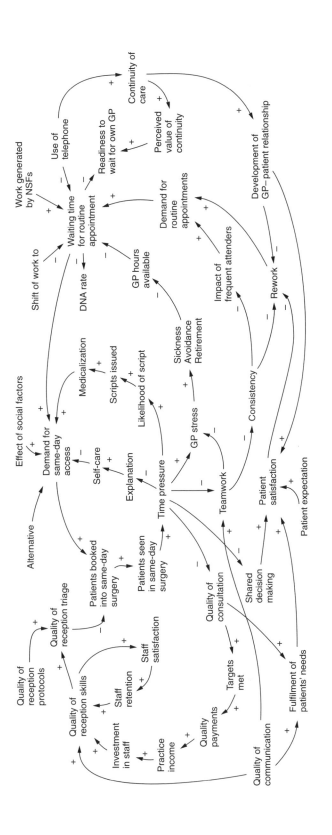

Figure 12B.1 Full ID of patient access study (without allocation of actors).

CHAPTER 13

Agent-based working: a device for systemic dialogue

Sean Boyle and Julian Pratt

This chapter describes a new approach to facilitate dialogue in organizations that we call 'agent-based working'. It brings together two ways of working based on the experience of the authors. Sean Boyle has worked with colleagues to explore the application of agent-based computer simulation to healthcare.[1,2] Julian Pratt draws upon his experience with a group that has developed an approach known as 'whole-system working', that enables local systems to get together to find solutions to their shared concerns.

Key points
- Agent-based working is a response to the challenge in complex adaptive systems – how to engage in dialogue with the parts and connections while at the same time maintaining an awareness of the whole.
- It combines agent-based computer simulation with whole-system working to foster dialogue across a whole system.
- Both these ways of working arise from a mental model of human systems as complex adaptive systems, or more broadly as living systems. Each has limitations, but in some situations their strengths can be complementary when deployed as an integrated approach.
- The process requires, and is able to sustain, the contributions of people working at policy, strategy and implementation levels in all the organizations involved, as well as people who use the system.

Introduction

When people seek help from the health and social care system, what happens is influenced by the many choices and decisions made by themselves and by all of the service providers they encounter. The journey of care that each patient follows is a consequence of the interactions of these choices with the resources available to the system. Each choice is contingent and has knock-on effects elsewhere in the system.

When all of these journeys of care are taken together, it is possible to provide descriptions and measures of the system as a whole. If you look at the aggregate of the whole experience of individuals you see envelopes of journeys of care. If you look at the performance of the service provider organizations you see aggregate flows (e.g. referral patterns) and stocks (e.g. numbers of people waiting at a particular point in their journey).

All of us have mental models that we use to make sense of what is going on in this system. These are likely to be partial and incomplete – each of us knows a lot about the bit of the system that we encounter on a daily or weekly basis, but little about parts of the system we never interact with.

When the system is not working as we would like, we may try to stand outside and form a picture of what is going on. In doing this, we are attempting to formulate our personal mental model; this can take several forms – images or text, maps or numbers, charts or computer models. Each of these can help to clarify our thinking and to share it with others.

NHS clinicians and managers have until recently approached computer modelling from quite different perspectives. Managers, encouraged (or driven) by performance targets and indicators such as waiting times, have focused their attention on aggregate measures of service provider organizations. They have used spreadsheet models or, less often, system dynamics or stochastic (discrete event) simulations to explore the implication of proposed organizational changes. Clinicians, whose focus is on the experience of individual patients, distrust aggregate models because these fail to engage with the highly contingent decisions they make every day. Moreover, both clinicians and managers recognize that these models are driven by historical data that they know to be unreliable.

Our experience is that clinicians and managers find common ground over computer modelling when the model engages not just with what is going on at an aggregate level but also with the behaviours that underlie this.[3] This can be achieved through a form of computer modelling called 'agent-based simulation', which is constructed by specifying within the model the people or groups of people in the system, and the rules they use to make choices and guide decisions.

Modelling in the NHS has generally been used in an analytical way of 'standing outside and forming a picture of what is going on'. A quite different approach is to find ways for the people who make up the system to share their own experience and understanding of how things are now, and to explore together ways they might change it. This approach, exemplified by whole-system working, brings people together for this purpose – often including people who are generally excluded from strategic thinking. It relies on providing devices that foster productive conversations.

Constructing an agent-based simulation requires conversations about 'what is going on around here' and 'what are the behaviours that give rise to it'. These conversations have traditionally been carried out in a series of individual interviews carried out by a modelling team acting as external expert. We suggest that constructing such a simulation can provide a device for conversations that include mixed groups of people, including managers, front-line providers like clinicians, and people who use the services. When these conversations include 'how we might change things', simulation can support them to explore 'what would happen if we ...' with far more nuanced understanding about unexpected consequences and knock-on effects than would be possible in unsupported conversations.[4] We call such an approach, in which agent-based simulation is used as a device for systemic dialogue, 'agent-based working'.

In this chapter we provide a framework for describing the range of approaches taken to computer modelling of complex systems. We outline why an agent-based approach is particularly apt when working with a whole system from the perspective of complex adaptive systems, and we describe how we have introduced this approach as a system intervention in several local areas, and their positive response.

Computer modelling of complex adaptive systems

Computer modelling includes a wide range of methods. These range from simple constructions of relationships between two or more variables (for example, simple demand–price relationships) to models in which individual agents, and their behaviours, are described, animated and followed over time (for example, the Boids animation where the behaviour of a flock of birds is modelled using local rules of interaction between neighbouring birds[5]). We describe the commonalities and differences in current approaches to modelling using the following six dimensions:

- *Individual/aggregate*. Is the model specified at the *individual* level, based on a bottom-up description of agents and their behaviours from which aggregate numbers can be obtained by summation, or is it specified at the *aggregate* level, based on top-down descriptions of the macro level behaviour of the system as a whole which are then disaggregated, when necessary, according to a set of assumptions about behaviours?

- *Functional/rule-based.* Does the model consist of a set of *functional* (mathematical) *relationships* between object variables that describe the relationship between the individual elements or aggregates, or is it based on sets of *rule-based relationships* (heuristics, guiding principles, simple rules, rules of thumb, strategies) that describe the local interactions of a group of autonomous decision-making agents?
- *Static/dynamic.* Is the model *static* in the sense that actions at one point in time do not affect actions at another point, or is it *dynamic* in the sense that there is an interdependence between actions over time?
- *Responsive/adaptive.* Is the model *responsive* in the sense that individual behaviour may change as a result of what happened in the past, without a change in underlying rules and relationships, or is it *adaptive* in the sense that the population of decision rules changes in response to what has happened in the past – either through the creation of new rules or through a change in the distribution of rules in the population?
- *Expert-led/involving.* Is the creation of the model *expert-led* in the sense that the modellers mainly use pre-existing knowledge and/or elicit information from some people within the system, or is it *involving* in the sense that people in the system are involved in the specification of the model and hence in conversations about their own behaviours and how these are revealed in the model?
- *Predictive/explorative.* Is the model used in a *predictive* way, i.e. to give estimates of (usually) aggregate variables, or is it used in an *explorative* way, i.e. to foster conversations about the possible impact of behaviours, and ultimately to lead to changes in behaviour?

Referring to the above dimensions, a model of a complex adaptive system needs to be specified as a set of rule-based relationships between individual agents that interact in a dynamic environment. We suggest that if the model is to make a difference, it should be part of a process that is adaptive, involving and explorative. The modelling approach that lends itself most readily to the task of modelling complex adaptive systems is agent-based simulation. This involves the construction of autonomous decision-making agents, with individual dynamic behaviours that are *rule-based* or heuristic. These behaviours may be responsive or adaptive. Whether it is used in ways that are expert-led or involving, predictive or exploratory depends very much on the approach taken by the modelling team.

Whole-system working

Thinking of organizations and networks of organizations as complex adaptive systems provides insights that may be useful to everybody, no matter what their role, whether chief executive, manager or front-line worker.

We have, over the last ten years, chosen to engage with systems from this perspective in a facilitative role. We have called this approach, which is both a way of seeing the world and a wide variety of ways of perturbing it, 'whole-system working'.[6] It seeks to influence the connections and communications of people and organizations in the system. We are interested in enabling the system to find its own solutions, not in acting as problem-solvers.

We find that this requires us to give attention to nine aspects, which are summarized below. Giving attention simultaneously to all of these enables agents (individuals, teams and organizations) to:

- explore and reach agreement about the *meaning* and purpose of this human system
- recognize whether they are part of the system or not, and join in if they feel *passion* to make a difference for this purpose
- take responsibility for *participating* and playing their part
- bring *many perspectives*, each with their own mental models
- begin conversations about what is actually going on around here, now. All the work takes place in the *here and now* too, and the approach involves crafting time and space to allow these conversations to happen
- develop a *web of connections and communication* in what is frequently otherwise an under-connected system
- recognize *patterns of order* arising from these communications
- recognize that they constitute a whole as well as parts. A *system that knows itself* will talk about 'we' as well as 'us' and 'them'
- *trust local resourcefulness* – trust that, if all the aspects have been given attention, the local system will organize around the shared meaning.

Combining agent-based simulation with whole-system working – agent-based working

Whole-system working enables people to engage in conversations in which they make explicit their often implicit mental models, guiding principles and what they know about capacities in the system. If these are encoded in a computer model, which is then shared with the people who contributed their knowledge, the formalism of the model makes them aware of gaps and inconsistencies and stimulates further dialogue.

The model enables each person to understand the consequences that their *own* rules of thumb and work patterns have for others in the system, enabling the healthcare system to adapt more intelligently. We envisage iterated interactions between the simulation and the real system (or at least mixed groups bringing

Healthcare system
(complex adaptive
system)

Agent-based
model
(complex system)

Figure 13.1   Lots of people exploring solutions through modelling.

perspectives from different parts of the real system) as the simulation is introduced, constructed, validated and used to explore what-ifs (*see* Figure 13.1).

What we believe is happening here is that the computer model, though not
adaptive in itself, provides a mechanism for the 'real' healthcare system to
adapt more intelligently. What makes it particularly apt is that its structure, of
agents and their mental models and rules of thumb, directs attention to exactly
those aspects of the 'real' system that an understanding of the theory of complex
adaptive systems would suggest require attention. The conversations and interactions with the real system are about 'what happens around here'.

The simulation itself provides additional benefits:

- it acts as a system memory, both literally and as an icon, so work that has
  been done in various groupings is not lost. Indeed it provides a means by
  which the work of otherwise disconnected work programmes (for example,
  those to improve elective care and to improve emergency care) can contribute to each other
- it provides the possibility of exploring what would happen *across the system as
  a whole* if agents changed their mental models and rules of thumb
- by providing a tangible representation of the intangible system, it can function as a transitional space that contains people's anxieties and enables them
  to engage in systemic conversations.

In the next section, a practical example is used to demonstrate the way this
combined approach has been introduced.

An example of agent-based working in the 'urgent care system'

We have been encouraged by the response to the first stage of a programme in
which we brought together whole-system working with agent-based simulation

as agent-based working, and applied it to the 'urgent care system'. In 2001, we were selected by the Winter and Emergency Services Team (WEST) at the Department of Health to develop local capacity, in four places, to support mapping of flows of patients in the emergency care system; and to explore whether they would find simulation modelling helpful in understanding and improving their local system as a whole.

Setting system boundaries and establishing meaning

We began by bringing together an 'Urgent Care System Group'. Simply bringing together a group from across the system was valuable in itself, and revelatory – in one place the initial belief was that general practice would not be interested in playing a part, while they ended up as a major contributor. Participants recognized that they had never had an opportunity to think together about the way the urgent care system functioned as a whole. The groups provided a firm nucleus when the Department of Health asked all areas of the country to form emergency care networks.

The next step was to clarify the boundaries of the urgent care system, and so who was in and who was out. Each group discussed the geographical boundaries of the system they felt made sense locally, and this led to changes in the membership of the group. Sometimes an issue as apparently simple as 'Do we have one urgent care system in this city, or are the north and south distinct?' led to new dialogue across boundaries. The geographical boundaries that seemed to make sense to outsiders like WEST and ourselves were rarely those identified by local people – and we believe that when using agent-based working, these are not issues for an outside 'designer' but for local participants in the system to identify for themselves.

Even more fundamentally, the group discussed the meaning and sense of purpose of the system. Since the key agents in the urgent care system are citizens and patients, clarifying the purpose of the urgent care system has meant challenging a professional definition of what is urgent and what is not (this often surfaces in discussions about whether to use the word 'urgent' or 'emergency'). The groups have recognized the difference between a citizen-defined sense that something needs to be done *now* (which is often referred to as 'urgent') and the professionally defined group of services that respond to these urgent events (which are usually described as 'emergency care services'). This avoids labelling the citizen's concern to receive 'urgent' attention as inappropriate use of 'emergency' services. Urgency is also salient for people working in the system – a GP wanting an outpatient opinion; a nurse in A&E who requests an X-ray.

Exploring the system

In order to support mapping of flows of patients in the urgent care system, we asked each place for any information that was readily available about the movement of patients around the system. They were able to bring together some details of the various service providers, though interestingly just doing this was an innovation. It rapidly became clear that, though each unit held information about its own performance (numbers of patients seen, waiting times and so on), which was of variable quality, there is almost no information collected that informs the way the system works as a whole.

For example, A&E departments know how many people attend at each hour of the day and how long they wait, but not the proportion who have arrived there after seeing their GP (let alone the number who arrived there after deciding that the anticipated delay in seeing their GP was too great to tolerate). It seems clear that the information that units are encouraged and required to collect is intended for performance monitoring of parts of the system. It is not the sort of information that would stimulate systemic learning. This became even more apparent when we asked people to provide 'guesstimates' of the numbers. Because they see numbers as serving the purpose of monitoring not learning, it was not considered to be legitimate to provide approximate numbers that might inform what was going on.

We worked with the Urgent Care System Group to identify the sorts of people who are at present getting a good, or a bad, service when they have urgent needs. These conversations began to reveal within the group some of the key local issues, for example in one place there seemed to be almost no alternatives to 'send them to A&E'. Out of these stories, in each place we identified one or two that illustrated the key issues and were immediately recognizable as real to local people – they were, in a sense, archetypal situations.

Understanding what is going on

The Urgent Care System Group then invited a group of about 40 people from a much wider range of perspectives to a half-day system mapping workshop.[6] We put a large sheet of paper on the wall and introduced the first instalment of the story – in one place this was 'A woman in her seventies goes to open the door to somebody bringing her lunch and falls behind the door. She injures her wrist and is unable to get up. What happens next?' As people describe the range of possible ways services might respond, these are mapped on the paper. An example is shown in Figure 13.2.

The purpose is to identify what is currently going on, not to develop agreement about the way things should be. Indeed the power of the approach is that, provided there is a genuinely wide mix of participants and a moderate willingness

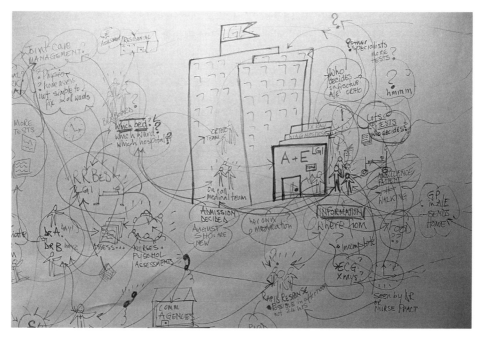

Figure 13.2   Urgent care wall map – capturing the system's complexities.

to speak the truth, it is possible to get beyond the 'authorized version' of the way things are supposed to happen to what really happens around here. Healthcare delivery systems are, and will always be, complex. Individual patients are not items on a production line, and the services delivered require interaction between a wide range of health professionals over space and time.

Once the complexity has been acknowledged people have a strong desire to tidy it up, and sometimes there are indeed gaps and duplications that need to be tackled. This is how a process mapping workshop would be used for process redesign. By contrast, we encourage participants to accept and continue to engage with the complex whole.

During this workshop everybody finds that they learn something about how things work locally. There is some service they did not realize existed, or operated in ways that they never knew. They learn about the 'rules of thumb' that people use in their day-to-day work. They can also see how the behaviour of their part of the system affects the other parts, and the experience of the patient.

For example, as we followed the range of possible things that might happen to the woman who had fallen, it became clear that everybody was trying, through their own actions, to reduce the risk to her. Because of the difficulties in keeping her safe at home, this resulted in her admission to hospital and to deterioration in her health. The systemic consequences of individuals trying to reduce risk in their part of the system led, perversely, to increased risk across the whole patient journey. It was not just to keep her safe – people did not want to seem uncaring once she was in hospital, and sending her home seemed less caring than looking after her in hospital.

The approach engages managers and planners because it gives them a way of understanding the behaviour of the system as a whole, and it is particularly effective in engaging clinicians as they are contributing their clinical expertise – the day-to-day choices that they have to make. The wall map remains an icon that people continue to refer to after the workshop, usually meaning 'this complex interconnected system in which we are all doing our best but which somehow doesn't add up to what we want'.

Making a difference

After mapping what goes on now, participants have both the energy to make a difference and insight into how things might be improved. They are also aware that, whatever changes they might make, there will be unexpected knock-on consequences for other parts of the system.

At this point in the workshop they are ready to engage with a presentation of a demonstration version of an agent-based simulation of an urgent care system.

The simulation is run on a laptop connected to a data projector, and participants can watch the simulation unfolding. They understand that it has been constructed by a process of surfacing implicit knowledge, just as they have been surfacing their own in the workshop. They understand that the simulation contains the representations of hundreds of thousands of individual patients seeking urgent care, each similar to, but different from, the archetype they have been discussing. When they see some of the outputs from the simulation, they understand that the aggregate numbers are not inputs to the simulation but are outputs resulting from the actions of all the individuals represented in the simulation.

A 'snapshot' of one of the output screens is shown in Figure 13.3. The lines represent flows of patients between parts of the system. The numbers (which build up as the simulation is run and here describe the activity in a simplified model of a borough at the end of a one-week period) describe aggregate numbers of patients. The dotted lines represent patients who have applied their own rule of thumb, 'I've waited long enough', when they have found themselves waiting in a queue for more than their threshold of patience and have taken themselves off (from the GP surgery to A&E or from several places back to self-care at home).

Other screens can be set up to explore a wide range of questions about the system – to follow the journeys of all patients with a particular diagnosis, for example, or to show the experience of a particular service provider.

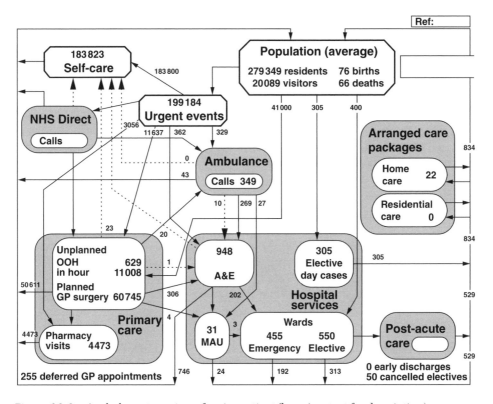

Figure 13.3   A whole-system view of major patient flows (see text for description).

Each of the sites had, by this stage, a realistic idea of what it would take them to construct a local model – in particular that it would involve clinicians as well as managers talking about their day-to-day decisions in caring for patients. It would involve information managers in providing aggregate numbers of activity and patient flows, but these would be used for validating the model, not for constructing it.

They could see, too, the potential benefits. It would be easy to be seduced into thinking of the model as predictive, something that would tell them what to do when they were thinking about staffing levels, opening and closing new units, or changing clinical protocols. But they were canny enough to recognize that what the modelling process really provides them with is not 'the answer', but better informed and connected conversations about possibilities, and practical help in their work too – for example, something that would allow them to inform their option appraisals from a system-wide perspective that is otherwise very difficult to include.

Conclusion

The benefits of agent-based working could be fundamental and long-lasting. It provides a device for conversations that engage a much wider range of people than usual in discussions about service provision. In particular, it engages clinicians in a way that other modelling processes do not (because it relates to what is most important to them – the care of individual patients) while also engaging managers by providing what they really need (not just the aggregate figures but an understanding of what lies behind them).

It also enables people to understand system-wide behaviours and knock-on effects that even a room full of well-informed people can only guess at. It enables much more informed appraisal of the system-wide consequences of proposed actions.

A key feature of agent-based working, as we describe it, is that it is embedded in the planning and service delivery mechanisms of local organizations, and so is far more likely to give rise to changes in service delivery than research projects or external expert opinions. Like some other developmental approaches, it derives its energy from the passion that people have to provide and have as good a service as they can.

Its particular strength is that it provides a device for informed and purposeful conversations and a way for these to build on each other. It provides a summary of the conversations over time that does not degrade as people move jobs. It also enables separate development programmes to contribute to each other. Finally, it provides an icon that represents 'the whole' that has to be held in the attention while simultaneously giving attention to the parts and to the interconnections.

References

1   Boyle S, Harrison A, Tansley J et al. (1998) Modelling Urgent Events. King's Fund, London.
2   Jessopp L (1999) Urgent/Emergency Care in Lambeth, Southwark and Lewisham: developing a systems approach. Lambeth, Southwark and Lewisham Immediate Access Project, London.
3   Currie C and Bryan-Jones J (2002) The latest models. Clinician in Management. 11: 55–6.
4   Jessopp L and Boyle S (2001) Developing whole-systems learning: a linked approach. In: Ashburner L (ed) Organizational Behaviour and Organizational Studies in Health Care: reflections on the future. Palgrave, New York.
5   Reynolds CW (1987) Flocks, herds and schools: a distributed behavioural model. Computer Graphics. 21: 25–34.
6   Pratt J, Gordon P and Plamping D (1999) Working Whole Systems. King's Fund, London.

CHAPTER 14

Using the visual arts to facilitate emergence in organizations

Julian Burton

Poor communication in organizations is currently a major barrier to successful change. It can cause misunderstandings and confusion that are rarely clarified. This creates the sort of organizational distress that inhibits service delivery and improvement. Because of the lack of adequate space to make sense of the chaos at work, the problems often go unvoiced and are compounded by jargon and abstractions. Informal, honest and grounded conversations, undertaken in an appropriate space to reflect, are the key to making sense of what is going on and lead to the clarity needed for change.

At the heart of all successful organizational change are honest conversations about what is really going on and what really needs to change. In this type of conversation, people speak in a way that encourages action in themselves and others. Speaking more openly and honestly about one's own experience naturally promotes shared understanding, which is is the key to developing the better working relationships that lead to improving performance.

My purpose here is to show how the use of pictures can stimulate these type of conversations through a facilitation process called 'visual dialogue'. The process can encourage people to speak more directly and personally. This naturally promotes sharing of experience, which is the key to developing the better working relationships that lead to improving performance. This chapter describes an NHS trust workshop where the use of visual art facilitated emergence, helping to create a reflective space in which people can speak in a more grounded way and engage in rich, meaningful and productive dialogue.

Key points
- The locus of change in an organization is never within an independent or autonomous individual but always emerges from within the relationships between people.
- The conditions for emergent change and self-organization can be encouraged by using more non-rational and emotional forms of self-expression.
- Visual art can create the conditions to encourage more spontaneous and grounded conversations, the sort in which new meaning or knowing can arise naturally for individuals in a group.
- Visual metaphors and stories are concrete and powerful ways of representation knowledge.
- Pictures can be used to provide a non-linear way of knowing.
- Pictures that reflect the causes of anxiety and frustration can often trigger conversations on difficult and normally avoided issues.
- This type of picture is a good way for a group to share their experience, and help them talk in a way that cuts through intellectual abstractions and jargon.

Introduction – why do we want emergent change?

There is a growing interest in complexity thinking as a different way of understanding how change happens. In social systems, change emerges in and from the space between us – in the dynamics of our relationships, in the constant flux of intention and expectations, and in the way we interact, relate and co-ordinate our activities. It is our conversations that can create the context for new and creative action. Alongside this development is a growing interest in using the arts to enhance people's understanding and sense making in organizational settings. The visual arts are a particularly powerful way of representing important themes symbolically, non-verbally and aesthetically. Pictures are also useful artifacts that can be used to stimulate conversations and can present knowledge in a more concrete form that words alone.

Many people I meet working in large organizations are struggling to work out how to 'facilitate emergence' or lead 'emergent change'. To facilitate is to make something easier and emergence means to arise naturally, so the aim is to 'make it easier for something to arise naturally'. Precisely what is it that we want to arise naturally? In the abstract language of complexity, this something is usually called novelty or 'new order'. But what is this 'new order'? I often wonder what, in my personal experience, reflects this term? When I am silently struggling to make sense of a complex situation in which I need to make a decision, it helps me to discuss it with someone. By expressing the contradictions and dilemmas at hand, socializing what I think and feel to a trusted friend, I can engage with the dilemma in a different, often more powerful, way. Things make more sense when I speak of them to another, and suddenly I have a better grip on the situation. This to me means having clarity on where I am and what I need to do next. By articulating my experience in symbols, I can feel energized and inspired. In my opinion, facilitating the emergence of new order is nothing more complex or theoretical than creating the conditions for good conversations.

As an artist working as a facilitator in organizations, I have developed a process of listening and reflecting back to clients their experience in visual metaphors and stories. Seeing pictures of important themes that often go unvoiced can give people an opportunity to express themselves and discuss issues not normally approached. In the process of making these pictures for clients, it is usually the most grounded and personal language that makes the best picture. If I am hearing lots of abstractions or jargon in a meeting or workshop, I immediately ask 'What does that mean to you? What would it look like?' This normally prompts people to redescribe what they are doing in a more personal and grounded way. Grounding the conversation like this has the effect of putting real human beings back into the communication process and brings more energy to any engagement. Clients find my pictures catalyse lively and animated conversations – the sort of conversations in which people could experience some clarity or movement in their situation. They can move from feeling stuck to a feeling of having a sense of hope, possibility or clarity that comes from having talked about what is happening to them. It seems to me that this is experienced as an outcome of having engaged in a creative and constructive conversation.

Pausing for a day of reflection – a practical example

A specialist NHS trust commissioned me to help facilitate a session at a one-day workshop for 50 senior managers, leaders and clinicians. The theme of the day was based around the idea of pausing for a day to reflect on what was going on in the trust (*see* Figure 14.1).

Not surprisingly there was high attendance as many people's daily experience involved: coping with the chaos at work; email mountains; the feeling of drowning in detail; horrific diaries; confusion; lack of clarity on priorities; going off sick because of stress; a constant struggle to keep their head above water; and trying to cope with the anxiety and uncertainty caused by always being in the midst of a new restructuring. A particular cause of stress was due to fear of

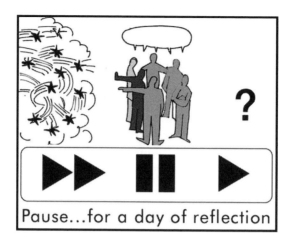

Figure 14.1   Part of the workshop invitation.

the uncertainties of future employment. Like many people in organizations, they spent much time and energy trying to make sense of the formal communications and directives intended to effect an improvement in performance and service delivery, yet that are couched in impenetrable jargon that goes unchallenged.

As a warm-up, the first session of the day was designed to engage participants in discussion around their current experience at work by using a picture to open up the conversations. Before the workshop, I talked with several people about their experiences at work and what metaphors would best describe them. I created a picture of the metaphors called 'Where are we now?' that reflected what they were currently dealing with. For example, I rang one manager to arrange an appointment, and he said he couldn't because he had a horrific diary (*see* Figure 14.2).

Their descriptions were distilled into a composite picture that reflected their experience in metaphorical themes. Copies of the picture were distributed at the beginning of my session. The participants were asked to pair up, look at the picture and ask each other questions like 'What do you see? What does it mean? How does it relate to your work?' The picture created a real buzz as people discussed it in pairs. Very quickly the hum of conversation grew and the energy in the room rose noticeably. The release of a lot of energy helped to create some initial conditions for a successful day. It is often difficult to find space to feel confident enough to overcome the fear of being vulnerable, to express one's feelings about current realities. At this workshop I saw people create a space within which they could reflect together, acknowledging and validating each other's experiences, and express feelings about what was going on. In this process new meanings arose naturally, creating clarity, a sense of new possibilities, energy and movement.

Figure 14.2   The horrific diary (detail from 'Where are you now?').

One interesting outcome was that a group of doctors found the picture quite negative. This was because it visualized the pressures and issues of managers. When this was pointed out to them, they suddenly understood what managers were really going through, with some sympathy. This is always a good first step in creating better relationships.

Using visual dialogue

My experience is that in many organizations conversations on change can be smothered in abstractions, generalizations and theories. The language used is distant and vague. The result is that meetings and workshops become disconnected from people's experience, leading to confusion, a lack of clarity and little or no action, yet the difficult but important subjects are avoided, or made safe and unthreatening – the truth gets hidden away and lost. This way of speaking is so ingrained that people are barely aware that they do it.

Simplifying abstraction and jargon

The language I hear used in many formal meetings is quite abstract and distance from our lived experience. It can cause confusion and ambiguity in

Figure 14.3   You have mail! (detail from 'Where are you now?').

organizations. Equivocation has become a tool to hide a lack of knowledge, something that is often stigmatized in our culture. This doesn't help when people are trying to understand each other and make sense of their daily experience at work. Pictures that are created from concrete descriptions of experience can cut through intellectual abstractions and jargon in a very powerful and liberating way (*see* Figures 14.3 and 14.4).

Generating symbolic artefacts

Another aspect of this process is to look at visual art as symbolic artefacts. Symbols help us organize our human systems. For example, the symbols of verbal language play a central role in organizations and are the primary means for co-ordinating our activities. When we speak we can make things happen and create new possibilities for action. Symbolic artefacts and material objects structure our experience. Whoever makes them has the potential to influence others.

What do we symbolize? What do we translate into tangible, visual form? Organizational structures, policy, statistics, strategies, etc. What are not usually represented are relationships and process, inner states and feelings, and

Figure 14.4   Overwhelmed by detail (detail from 'Where are you now?').

values, much of which cannot be formally talked about. Art can articulate these tacit elements and help generate new meaning in organizations.

Symbols themselves don't carry direct meaning but are interpreted locally by people in context. Meanings are symbolic, created in interactions, but if they are not constantly negotiated, refreshed or replaced they create contradictions and subsequently distress. Most formal symbols in organizations are closed and fixed, and often are vigorously defended from mutual negotiation, such as most strategies, policies and directives! For mutually meaningful and hence useful symbols to be currently relevant and useful for everyone in an organization, there needs to be space for everyone to be able to create new ones.

Visual art can be seen as the graphic representation of experience in a concrete artefact. It can convey meaning and, paradoxically, clarity and ambiguity at the same time. Pictures convey different meanings to different people so can stimulate dialectical movement in their understanding of each other. They allow for continuous and local interpretation of our experiences in a way that

Figure 14.5   A day at the office.

can keep meanings moving and flowing. In doing so, the consolidation of meaning into rigid and fixed frameworks that are used to maintain power relations is prevented.

Creating a reflective space

Creating pictures that represent what people experience at work can create a reflective space in which people step back and disengage from the chaos at work, getting some critical distance from the mass of details. By reflecting back their immediate concerns, frustrations and dilemmas, pictures serve as a mirror to provoke new conversations and offer an opportunity to explore and share organizational experiences. People can visually and orally explore and examine the picture together, providing a vehicle to encourage mutually focused discussion. By translating verbally articulated themes into symbolic artefacts that represent experience metaphorically, a trigger for the types of spontaneous and improvised discussions is created that can lead to emergence of new order, i.e. the clarity one feels when things make sense and one can then proceed with confidence. It offers an opportunity for people to speak about what is really going on for them within the organization and to share their hopes and aspirations of where they have come from and where would like to be. This creates understanding between people and is the key to developing better relationships and improving performance.

Conclusion

There is a desperate need to create space in organizations for people to engage in reflective practice, share their subjective experiences and talk about their working relationships. Informal, open and honest conversations are the key to sense making and hence change. I hope I have shown how visual art can facilitate this by stimulating productive dialogue. I believe that grounded conversations are at the heart of change and that visual art has potential to make a major contribution to creating better organizations.

CHAPTER 15

Using the performing arts to facilitate emergence in organizations

Marian Naidoo and Shaun Naidoo

For several years we have been engaged in the use and development of creative tools and techniques that can be used within organizations to improve practice. In this chapter we will describe how creative skills and processes can enable clinical practitioners to develop a practical understanding of the intrinsic value of identity, communication, relationships, leadership, problem solving, group interaction, teamwork, trust and the coping strategies necessary for working as part of a complex adaptive system.

Key points
- The creative arts can play a major part in making us become more effective by focusing on the way in which we as individuals interact both as people and professionals.
- This approach develops transferable skills that can be utilized in the workplace using a range of techniques.
- The emphasis is on the refocus of our perceptions of self, others and the context within which we interact as well as the process of interaction itself.

Introduction

Against a background of efficiency and productivity demands, life in healthcare organizations has become increasingly complex and demanding. The dominant management model is based on the machine. This style of management sees problem solving as reduction into smaller, more manageable problems. The emphasis is on the reduction of uncertainty and a workplace culture that places more value on status and control than teamworking and patient-centred caring.

In our work as clinical development facilitators within the NHS and other healthcare organizations outside of the UK, we found ourselves in a role where we were constantly trying to bridge the gap between theory and reality. At one level we were being asked to facilitate the development of new policies or strategies and at the next level trying to work with clinical teams who were desperately trying to make sense of these policies at the point of implementation.

The teams we worked with were complicated in their make-up and their boundaries were often fuzzy. In many cases they were multi-professional and crossed several boundaries, e.g. social care and/or education. Individuals were often members of more that one team and tension and conflict was a natural phenomenon in contrast to the traditional organizational management perspective that encourages harmony and compromise. Many healthcare professionals found it difficult to embrace modernization and the directives of the Modernisation Agency, whose role is to address the inconsistent qualities of care and develop more patient-centred healthcare provision.

These tensions, which are the source of organizational anxiety, are well recognized in the organizational literature. For example, Stacey *et al.*[1] discuss these challenges to a current management theory where the dominant discourse sees the role of the manager as one of 'removing ambiguity and conflict to secure consensus'. Capra[2] also refers to tension, particularly that experienced by those engaged in creative activity: 'The experience of tension and crisis before the emergence of novelty is well known to artists, who often find the process of creation overwhelming and yet persevere in it with discipline and passion.' He emphasizes that there are degrees of crisis and not all of them are as extreme, but what they have in common is uncertainty: 'Artists and other creative people know how to embrace this uncertainty and loss of control ... After prolonged immersion in uncertainty, confusion and doubt, the sudden emergence of novelty is easily experienced as a magical moment.'

We recognized that the teams we were working with had the potential for self-organization and needed to have ownership of any changes that were required to their clinical and organizational practice. In this chapter we describe how we use the creative arts to enhance the quality of interaction within healthcare organizations and encourage people to embrace the tension and conflict that is a part of everyday life.

Expressing complexity through the performing arts

The principles of complexity science are a key feature of the creative processes that artists undergo in pursuit of their art. In the performing arts, people, narrative (storytelling), relationships and learning are at the centre of everything we do. Whether actor, dancer, musician, playwright or singer, processes and techniques are developed that welcome contradiction, uncertainty, novelty and spontaneity as an everyday part of the professional experience.

Actors are trained to develop for themselves methodologies that embrace the use of insight and intuition that they can channel back into the creative process. Dancers, like actors, are trained to develop techniques that enable them to reproduce fractals (dancers call them motifs) that are based on observed behaviours and relationships. Indeed, all practitioners in the arts who retain a passion for their profession have well-developed abilities to put complexity into practice in order to explore for themselves and consequently others.

As spectators, we experience the multidisciplinary teamwork and a demonstration of complexity science through art as the characters played by the actors recreate behaviours, values, contradictions and emotions that have been drawn from their observations and life experience. We see the end product of a long and sophisticated process that involves the continuing development of skills (their very own plan-do-study-act cycles), techniques and understandings that launches the creative practitioner on an uncertain journey that offers new challenges and learning for the performance team every time.

Creative theatre practitioners, like any other professional, need to ensure that as creative entities they maintain their abilities to tap into their creative potential and apply these techniques to the interactive work that they engage in through each production and processes of preparation for production. They 'play' through a series of games designed to explore different areas or concepts that involve people. They explore form and content and the relationship between the two in order to identify what would be the most effective relationship to communicate their work. They use improvisational techniques to explore their own constraints and develop new and innovative ways to create and problem solve. They learn to adapt, self-direct and adopt change while pursuing the ideal that will always elude them – perfection; this nevertheless is the process of continuing improvement that is an integral part of the artistic experience.

Rediscovering the creative skills that are in all of us

Actors use a variety of exercises and games throughout their education and professional development. The purpose of this play is primarily involved with the development of creativity and spontaneity.

Human beings are naturally playful. As children we learn and make sense of the world we live in through our play. We also use play to explore and develop our physical selves in relation to others. Children are much happier than adults to physically express their play; they do not rely solely on words when they are creating imaginary scenarios.

Around the time we enter secondary education this process stops and we begin to develop our social masks to portray to the world the image of ourselves we wish others to see. We very soon forget how to play and even worse find the suggestion of play terrifying – play is silly and reserved for small children. Paradoxically, our system of education contributes to these diminishing abilities as we prepare for the world outside of our schools, colleges and universities.

In our roles as clinical development facilitators and educators, we explored the possibility that clinical practitioners could use the same creative skills and processes to develop a practical understanding of communication, identity, relationships, leadership, problem solving, group interaction, teamwork, trust and coping strategies for working as part of a complex adaptive system.

We felt very strongly that this development of our creative selves is essential when we are looking to improve services, albeit in a 'scientific' way. When the late physicist, David Bohm, was asked if he saw creativity as a cornerstone of science, he replied in the following way:[3]

> . . . many people have realized that creativity is an essential part of science. Creative insight is required for new steps. I feel that creativity is essential not only for science, but for the whole of life.
>
> If you get stuck in a mechanical repetitious order, then you will degenerate. That is one of the problems that has grounded every civilization: a certain repetition. Then the creative energy gradually fades away, and that is why the civilization dies.

Applying the creative arts to the development of healthcare organization

The NHS has invested a great deal of resources into the creation of models for improvement. All these improvement approaches worked on the principle that if everything was reduced to its smallest component, we could understand and control the system. The process that achieved the improvement wasn't important so long as a structure was developed that could be objectively measured. It wasn't surprising that most improvement projects were seen to be failing, and despite the huge amounts of financial support there was concern that nothing very much had actually improved.

As so much of the activity within healthcare organizations is non-linear and unpredictable, it is important to focus more on relationships and how people interact with each other. Lewin and Regine call this 'relational practice':[4]

Relational practice starts with you and how you interact . . . It's a practice of developing personal awareness through reflection and action – an awareness of our impact on others and their effect on us, and being aware of the quality of the relationship itself and taking responsibility for 'it'. If 'it' doesn't feel right, it needs to be addressed.

By engaging clinical teams in creative activities, it is possible to see an improvement not only in the way that they work together as a team but also in the way that they transform their services.

The use of image theatre

One of the ways that we would deal with addressing 'it' is with the use of image theatre. The group, using a series of images in a montage style, recreates a situation in an abstract way. They have to understand and agree on how each of the parts of the image interacts and relates in order to recreate or 'codify' the situation. Having to critically reflect in this way in order to reach agreement forces them to 'decodify' in order to identify the problem. A better understanding of their reality is usually the outcome of this process (the quality of which has a correlation to the quality of the group dynamic) of de-codification with a clearer identification of the fractals that affect and contribute to the complexity of experience. They are then asked to change the image to the way they would like it to look, requiring a recodification of the situation.

Recodification is important as it confirms a number of key factors within the process of interaction. It confirms *identity* either of self or the issues affecting self, particularly in the broadest sense. It confirms the power of *relationships* through the process of interaction. It reifies the significance of *communication* as a necessary but nevertheless complex activity, within which lies a whole range of useful people-centred skills that can be harnessed and developed organically to help self, groups and organizations to move forward with clarity:

Individuals who were submerged in reality, merely feeling their needs, emerge from reality and perceive the causes of their needs. In this way, they can go beyond the level of real consciousness to that of potential consciousness much more rapidly.

(Friere, 1970[5])

We approach our creative work in the health service in a similar way as we would when working with a new theatre company at the start of an ensemble rehearsal process. We take the group through a creative process that begins with the individual and the identity of that individual and moves into the relationship of the individual with others in the group. Our relationship with the group is improvisatory, in constant dialogue with the group as we act and react to their needs. It is important to focus both on the body and on the emotions, in this way incorporating both the physical and the psychic. Boal also makes this point in a discussion on the importance of games and exercises:[6]

> *This concept is easily grasped in its most obvious manifestations – the idea of eating can produce salivation, the idea of making love can produce erection, love can bring a smile to the face, hate can produce a hardening of the features, etc. The phenomenon is less obvious when it relates to a particular way of walking, sitting, eating, drinking, speaking. And yet all ideas, all mental images, all emotions reveal themselves physically.*

The playing of these games and exercises also demands the use of all of their senses; they are encouraged to feel, touch, hear and speak in a way that would alert them to those senses in a more heightened way than is usual in our day-to-day lives. Here is an example: a person tells another person a story from their life that has strong emotional significance to them, especially a situation involving a perceived and felt oppression. The teller tells with their eyes closed so that they don't tell the story with any visual feedback from the listener. At the end of the storytelling, the teller and the listener (now the copilot) make independent image representations of the story using people from the rest of the workshop. Here image theatre is used to compare critically two related contents – that told by one and heard by the other. This exercise thus takes the group into the phase of using the language of physical imagery (image theatre) as a way of externalizing internal states (decodifying and recodifying) for the purposes of discussing perceived differences and similarities.

Improvisation occupies a special place in the range of techniques that actors use. It is often used to help solve problems where conventional thinking, particularly within a creative context, is not working. It is also used to develop new ways of working that can be spontaneous and innovative. Through improvisation we create relationships with other improvisers that utilize our imaginations and explore the differences that exist in relating that lead to creative emergence. Improvisation happens without the use of complex structures and codes, other than those which we bring as individuals.

Conclusion

Complexity science encourages individuals to live within uncertainty. Through the use of the creative arts, we have developed creative processes to improve provision and bring a quality of interaction across teams and professions that enable new emergent cultures to occur in localized contexts. We encourage people to embrace the tension and conflict that is a part of everyday life.

We have used improvisation extensively within our work in the health service to demonstrate how complex the human response is and how complex the behaviour codes that we use to determine our identity, status and emotional state are. Used together with the work of Boal and that of Friere, we can experience how difficult we find communication, relating and identity. We can discover things about ourselves as professionals as well as our personal skills. Placed in the context of development of team identities and creation of multi-professional interactive dynamics, discovering the complexity within this process is always a revelation where paradox is a constant practical feature.

Shaw, in *Changing Conversation in Organisations*, writes:[7]

> ... *practitioners in the arts have an acute sense of the paradox of 'being in charge but not in control' as we strive to play out creatively the evolution of our interdependence and conflicting responsibilities and aspirations, forming and being formed in the process.*

It is therefore by focusing on professionals as people that we enable a clearer access to understanding relational practice within the workplace. The use of creative processes to enable the individual to reflect and renew the core values of their own stories and individuality is the best way to reaffirm one's identity from which authentic relational practice can emerge. McNiff understood the emergent qualities that are rooted in the relationship between story and identity:[8]

> *People create their own theories through their lives, and they explain (theorise) their lives through story.*

In the context of healthcare improvement this also presents an interesting paradox. How can healthcare professionals be expected to improve their practice by placing the patient at the centre while the organizations they work for do not do the same for their workforce?

> *The most important thing to remember about organisations is that they are not structures; they are people. Take away the structures and you still have organisations. Take away the people and you have none. Theories of organisation are theories of people's lives. Traditional theories of organisation are theories about places. New theories of organisation are story-theories by people for people.*
>
> (McNiff, 2000[8])

The same set of improvement principles that applies within healthcare systems also applies to organizations and embraces the very essence of complexity science. At its heart are creativity and creative processes and our capacity as individuals to transform ourselves through relational practice.

References

1   Stacey RD, Griffin D and Shaw P (2000) *Complexity and Management: fad or radical challenge to systems thinking?*, p. 124. Routledge, London.
2   Capra F (2002) *The Hidden Connections: integrating the biological, cognitive, and social dimensions of life into a science of sustainability*, p. 118. Doubleday, New York.
3   Bohm D (1998) *On Creativity*, p. 108. Routledge, London.
4   Lewin R and Regine B (2000) *The Soul at Work. Listen ... Respond ... Let go: embracing complexity science for business success*, p. 306. Simon and Schuster, New York.
5   Friere P (1970) *Pedagogy of the Oppressed*, p. 98. Penguin, London.
6   Boal A (1992) *Games for Actors and Non-actors*, p. 61. Routledge, London.
7   Shaw P (2002) *Changing Conversation in Organisations: a complexity approach to change*, p. 117. Routledge, London.
8   McNiff J (2000) *Action Research in Organisations*, p. 243. Routledge, London.

Section 5

Going on together in organizations: perspectives on healthcare provision

Introduction

Section 5 offers four complexity perspectives on healthcare provision.

Although the word governance has a wide range of connotations, it is traditionally viewed as the systems and processes by which organizations lead, direct and control their functions in order to achieve organizational objectives and by which they relate to their partners and the wider community. Kieran Sweeney is Head of Primary Care Policy at the Commission for Health Improvement (CHI) and offers a complexity perspective on clinical governance. Using a number of illustrations taken from practice, he shows how the embedding of clinical governance within primary care can be understood in terms of the evolution of a complex adaptive system.

In Chapter 17, I review the area of skill mix from the perspective of doctors and nurses. The NHS is the largest single employer in the UK and the Government has recently called for a radical change in the way in which the medical workforce is planned and trained. I explore the concepts of adaptability and efficiency by comparing the linear model of economics with the non-linear emergent perspective of complexity theory.

The Modernisation Agency was established under the auspices of *The NHS Plan* and is charged with 'modernizing' healthcare delivery around the needs of the patient. One objective is to improve services through collaborative programmes of work. A recent review by an expert group highlighted a number of problems in the area and made recommendations for action. The report did not specify precisely how care should be organized, but laid minimum specifications to be interpreted and implemented locally.

In Chapter 18, Ceri Brown describes how developments and improvements in the service following from this report have been made using a complex adaptive system approach.

A key element to a modern health service is a well-trained and flexible workforce. In Chapter 19, Jim Price examines recent changes in education theory and how insights from complexity theory may help with the changing educational needs of the modern healthcare professional. Complexity is used as both a guide for improving teaching and learning, and as a metaphor for the teaching environment in today's health services.

CHAPTER 16

Progressing clinical governance through complexity: from managing to co-creating

Kieran Sweeney

The chapter reviews the components of clinical governance and the challenge facing primary care organization leads who are responsible for monitoring and developing it. A résumé of a three-year study into the development of clinical governance in general practice (and in one region of England), and a series of three short vignettes from clinical governance issues encountered by the author in his work as primary care lead for the Commission for Health Improvement, are described. These illustrate how the embedding of clinical governance within primary care can be understood in terms of the evolution of a complex adaptive system.

Key points
- Understanding the principles of complex adaptive systems allows us to observe systems such as the implementation of clinical governance in a more informed way.
- These principles help us understand how such systems evolve with an inherent uncertainty but recognizable direction.
- We can develop a range of management strategies to adapt to such evolving systems in a way that sustains their receptive context and facilitates their evolution.
- Complex systems are not managed in the sense of standing outside them and manipulating some of their elements towards a precise outcome. Command and control is out.
- Observation, negotiation and facilitation are the clinical governance lead's main tools. Co-creation is the aim.

Introduction

Invariably, commentaries on clinical governance begin with the hallowed definition of Scally and Donaldson (1998):[1] 'Clinical governance is a system through which NHS organizations are accountable for continuously improving the quality of their services and safeguarding standards of care by creating an environment in which excellence flourishes.'

But what did it feel like on the ground, to the courageous band of first-time clinical governance leads charged with translating this rather woolly definition into practice? 'I had this image of a kind of vast amoeba which has all these things going through it, pulling it in different directions, and it does virtually include the world, the universe and everything,' wrote one clinical governance lead.[2] In an observation truly prescient of the developing understanding of complexity, this same clinical governance lead continued, 'And I think it takes the shape of the people who – often by accident – have got involved in it and are driving it.' Let us begin with this striking image of co-evolution to explore how complexity theory might help us understand how clinical governance can become embedded within communities of healthcare professionals in order to improve quality in the NHS and benefit patients.

Complexity is an off-putting term: it deters people from an exciting enquiry by using a theoretical term that evokes an enigmatic opacity. It is much easier to understand complexity by reflecting on its application in the routine activities of clinical governance leads. This is the direction which this chapter will take. Our starting point is that the theory is subservient to the examples – and that it is from the examples one can learn. We will first review the components of clinical governance before describing a number of studies that illustrate how the embedding of clinical governance within primary care can be understood in terms of the evolution of a complex adaptive system.

The components of clinical governance

The components of clinical governance are shown in Box 16.1. These components are subject to cyclical assessment through the Commission of Health Improvement's clinical governance reviews and show two trends.

Firstly, in general practice, the best developed elements are clinical audit and clinical effectiveness. The remaining components are repeatedly included in the primary care organizations' action plans – a set of milestones agreed between CHI and the host organization which is monitored by the strategic health authorities.[3] Developments in the other contractor professions (dentistry, pharmacy and optometry) lag some way behind.

Box 16.1   The components of clinical governance

- Clinical effectiveness
- Clinical audit
- Use of clinical information
- Risk management
- Continuing personal and professional development
- Human resources
- Patient experience

Secondly, organizations have developed a 'silo' structure for developing their clinical governance policies. While each of these silos might contain very detailed activities within each of the designated areas, what they failed to capture is the crucial integration of these components of clinical governance into a coherent strategy. This notion of the importance of balancing the structure of a system (and here we are using the term 'system' to mean the implementing of clinical governance) with the interactions between the structural elements is absolutely central to complex adaptive systems and we shall return to it later in the chapter.

Clinical governance and primary care – the first three years

The implementation of clinical governance in primary care was the subject of a recently published three-year qualitative study in the South West of England. This described the progress of the first cohort of clinical governance leads as they struggled to come to grips with new and statutory responsibilities. It also followed up the demise of a small group of resigned leads, producing a rich narrative of success and failure.[2] We present its main findings here, and will show later in the chapter how the progress (or lack of it) reported in this study exhibits some of the key features of complex adaptive systems.

The first year – difficult beginnings

Clinical governance suffered a faltering and often painful introduction into primary care in this region. To many of the participating leads, clinical governance seemed initially vague and nebulous – the 'vast amoeba' referred to above. Its perceived lack of substance and direction meant that leads felt obliged to interpret it locally and develop it idiosyncratically. Volunteers were not queuing up for the role of clinical governance leads, which they perceived lacked clarity. Some felt threatened and described the negative impact of the role on their professional and personal relationships, complaining as one lead did 'that the kids were often asleep when I got home'. But the majority, certainly at the beginning, relied on goodwill and pre-existing professional relationships with their GP colleagues to move the process forward, while remaining unsure about the carrots and sticks at their disposal to monitor and improve quality.[4]

The second year – consolidation and the development of multidisciplinary teams

By the beginning of the second year, core governance teams had become more multidisciplinary against a historic background of doctor-dominated primary care organizations. Accountability and responsibility issues were becoming clearer, and most practices were receiving the framework of clinical governance relatively well.[5] But while one lead described clinical governance as having 'the potential to be the change agent which the Government is seeking in modernizing the NHS . . . it is still seen and treated as a kind of poor relation and as a bolt on' (PCOCG lead, September 2001). Facilitative and development approaches were clearly favoured in most cases *faute de mieux*. The workloads and shortage of protected time for many clinical governance leads meant that they were unable to engage more continuously (or forcibly) with constituent practices.

The third year – embeddedness in primary care

By the summer of 2002 (the last period of data collection for this three-year longitudinal study), participating clinical governance leads reported developments in three broad domains – cultural shift, systems approach and team focus. It was now legitimate to monitor an accountability that was becoming increasingly embedded in the culture of general practice, and there was a greater acceptance of the notion of appraisal. An increase in reflective practice was evidenced in a wider team focus within general practices (clinical governance team meetings or significant event auditing, for example); there was evidence of greater networking too. For example, two practices becoming 'buddied', to share their views on prescribing or access. In some cases there was systematic sharing of ideas and information across entire primary care trusts, with the focus on developing systems to ensure that risky events were minimized or at least reviewed. In summary, while one clinical governance lead commented 'the philosophical battle has been won', lack of capacity remained the major issue with other clinical governance leads expressing concern about 'working on a wing and a prayer'.[2]

Key issues from this study

We identify five key themes from this report:

1   the use of pre-existing relationships to begin to develop a clinical govern-
    ance community
2   the development of clinical governance teams both at organization-wide
    and practice level
3   the broadening of the base of these clinical governance teams from initially
    doctor-dominated to multidisciplinary
4   the notion of buddying
5   moving the descriptive metaphor from a 'vast amoeba' to 'winning a philo-
    sophical battle', with a concomitant greater acceptance of cultural shift,
    systems approach and team focus.

We shall show later in the chapter how each of these illustrate the key features
of an evolving complex system.

Routine challenges for clinical governance leads

While each primary care trust is unique in many ways, the leads for these organizations often encounter similar types of problem. In this section we present
a small number of these vignettes drawn from one of the author's experiences
commenting on how the clinical governance lead approached the problem.
These commentaries, which relate to the real-life strategies adopted by these
leads, are included here because they illustrate some of the potential applications of complexity in understanding how the embedding of clinical governance
evolves.

Vignette 1 – Must do's: introduction of National Service Frameworks

The introduction of the National Service Framework (NSF) for Coronary Heart
Disease (CHD) conferred a new responsibility for clinical governance leads to
ensure that the milestones set out in this (and subsequent NSFs) were being
achieved by constituent practices. For many practices the milestones of the
CHD NSF were relatively straightforward: establishing a register of patients
with ischaemic heart disease and high blood pressure, being able to produce

data on aspirin prescribing and evidence of systematic call and recall of patients on the register.

Clinical governance leads tended to adopt a reasonably uniform approach to the challenge of the NSF. This was a must do, in an important area of general practice, where most general practice teams accepted the need to develop a systematic approach to care. In order to share data, and produce PCT-wide datasets, there had to be agreement on coding – a much greater challenge than one might think. Which of the 14 codes for heart attack could the practices agree on? While consensus had to be developed for this important taxonomy, the imperatives were fairly clear: there was a shared sense of obligation, a ready agreement that practices would produce this information and relay it to their PCT, and in many well-developed PCTs an agreement to share that data either anonymously or on a named basis.

Generally, the leads provided a very clear steer for their constituent general practices here. This is what you have to do; this is when you have to do it by; this is what we agreed to code; get your data in by the agreed date. The emphasis was on achieving targets rather than negotiating approaches.

Vignette 2 – Not over my threshold

A number of clinical governance leads faced the problem of practices who declined access to their premises for clinical governance assessments on behalf of the primary care trust. While this isn't a widespread problem, three sites were observed where clinical governance leads were challenged in this way. They recognized their dual responsibility: ensuring the quality of services to patients, and their statutory responsibility to ensure that clinical governance was being developed. But how to go about it?

While there wasn't a uniform solution to this problem, the three leads involved in these dilemmas recognized the importance of informal negotiations with these practices. They were able to draw on routinely available data to assure themselves of basic quality standards in these practices – none, for example, had a plethora of complaints or showed signs of droves of patients abandoning their registered practitioner. Negotiation seemed the best way forward, often taken opportunistically when leads met with colleagues at routine meetings, socially, or even during long on-call sessions for the local out-of-hours co-operative. Establishing common ground, for example the willingness to improve the NHS in primary care, seemed a good starting point, combined with a willingness to share the lead's own data and any primary care data that might help the constituent practices.

Finding common ground, trying to minimize any idea of threat or invasion, and recognizing the statutory legitimacy of the reluctant practitioner's position characterized the leads' approach to this dilemma.

Vignette 3 – Developing a PCT learning network

A recent educational initiative in one PCT has been taken up by a colleague in a programme entitled 'Developing a PCT Learning Network' (Kernick D, personal communication). Rather than establishing a curriculum for continuing education based on the lead's personal views, national targets or educational imperatives, this organization has decided to develop the educational activity through the notion of communities of practice. Communication, mostly electronic, invites professionals in any part of primary care to identify their educational needs. As individuals identify these, they find often that they are shared by other colleagues with whom they can form small groups, often multidisciplinary; the groups themselves set the agenda and are supported to some extent by the host organization itself. The perceived outcome of this process, which has just started, is to make sure that individuals address the learning needs which they themselves have identified, in collaboration with colleagues who identify similar needs. They address these needs creatively under the aegis of the primary care organization through the medium of a network which both builds professional as well as social relationships.

The key feature of this highly innovative approach to continuing education is that the curriculum is emergent – no one knows what it will consist of at the outset. It is through the interaction of the people in the system, their willingness to collaborate to set up appropriate structures and processes, and the sustaining of this receptive context by the host organization for professional development which are the key elements of this approach. We will see shortly how these are features of complex systems.

An overview of these developments

These reports from clinical governance are not intended to constitute a systematic or exhaustive account of the development of this initiative in the NHS over the last three years. They are presented here, with their commentary, because they illustrate some key principles of complexity theory. The idea here is this: the implementation of clinical governance in the NHS is an example of an evolving complex adaptive system. By understanding what a complex adaptive system is, how it operates and what its principle features are – the basics of complexity theory – we can both understand how and why these systems have developed as they have, and become better equipped to select from a range of management options when working within one such system. Understanding the theory isn't going to help us predict precisely how these systems will operate at some point in the future, nor will it help us manipulate or control such systems from outside. It will, however, help us to be vaguely right rather than precisely wrong.

In order to understand how these complexity principles operate in, and explain, these real-life situations, we now review a brief introduction to the features of complex adaptive systems upon which we draw.

Insights from complexity theory

We describe four insights that have been discussed in Chapter 3.

- *Self-organization.* Due to non-linear action at a local level, system properties emerge that allow the system to adapt to its environment and co-evolve with it. This co-evolution produces fresh forms of behaviour (emergent properties) whose nature and purpose could not have been predicted in advance. The process is called self-organization.[6]
- *Receptive context.* All complex systems need a receptive context within which to develop. This receptive context consists of an infrastructure of communicability which facilitates the interaction, emergent behaviour and self-organization within a human system. The contexts are co-created by the interaction between the agents in the system: quite simply this means through constructive dialogues which change each participant, alter the way they relate to each other, change the influence each agent has on the system and, by a ripple effect, change the nature of the system itself.
- *The edge of chaos.* All systems are complex. They express their dynamic evolution in both linear and non-linear ways (which isn't surprising as linearity is a subset of non-linearity). The degree of stability a system reflects is a reflection of its linearity – that is, its ability to proceed in a rational predictive way, with a good degree of certainty between cause and effect in its inputs and outcomes. Instability in a system reflects its non-linearity. The relationship between linear and non-linear elements holds the system at the edge of chaos, where it is both stable and creative (*see* Chapter 3).
- *Stacey diagram.* The Stacey diagram, explained in Chapter 3, shows how managers can identify an approach to a system by reflecting on the degree of certainty within which actions are related to outcomes, and the agreement amongst agents in the system about this relationship.[7] The 'Stacey diagram' identifies three zones – the linear or rational zone, the chaotic zone and the zone of complexity.
- *New dualities.* The complementarity between linearity and non-linearity set out in the second point above constitutes a new duality for the twenty-first century, replacing the discredited mind–body duality which dominated medicine for the last 200 years. When a system is predominately linear, the system is located in the bottom left-hand corner of the Stacey diagram, and the management approach can be classic, rational, theory driven. Not so when

the system is at the edge of chaos, balanced between linear and non-linear change. The management strategy there has to be emergent, responding to patterns and trends within the system. So, rational and emergent management approaches complement the linear and non-linear expressions of a developing system. Finally, a third duality consists in the knowledge brought to inform these management approaches. In broad terms, classical theory-driven operational knowledge informs rational strategies. Figurative knowledge – the stuff of daily lived experience, street knowledge – informs emergent strategies.

Management theorist, Phil Hadridge, has brought these features together in Figure 16.1. This describes the degrees of rational and emergent approaches to management strategy, and the features occurring within this notional space. Where issues are highly rational, pre-existing research, capitalizing on prior experience, can be used. Where issues are characterized by high degrees of both rationality and emergence (the top right-hand corner), systematic involvement of stakeholders are commended, allowing the characteristics of the system to evolve and its direction to become clearer. This is where the development of clinical governance would locate itself – a strong linear or rational component (must do's, statutory authority, mandatory reporting) balancing against emergence (but how exactly is this going to work, what if general practices won't play, how do you embed risk management). Hadridge locates real life as balanced between the two – at the edge of chaos.

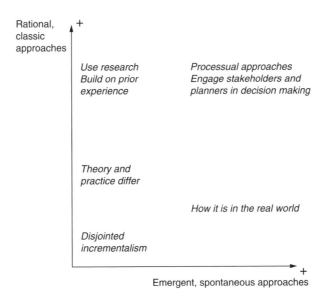

Figure 16.1 Approaches to governance.

Complexity insights for clinical governance

How do these insights from complexity help us understand the way clinical governance developed over the last three years? For each of the examples above we will suggest key insights from complexity which help us understand how clinical governance developed.

The evolution of clinical governance in the NHS over its first three years: receptive context, co-evolutions and self-organization in a complex adaptive system

The embedding of clinical governance in the NHS illustrates the evolution of a complex adaptive system which we set within the analytical framework of the Stacey diagram. Clinical governance started well out in the zone of chaos, with little agreement about its nature – the amoeba referred to at the beginning of this chapter – and very little certainty about how it might develop. It was clear that the Department of Health wasn't too sure either about how clinical governance might proceed: the key documents of the time[8] set out the principle domains for clinical governance with little guidance about how they might develop, or even more worryingly, no clear idea how they might be interwoven. The key textbooks of the time[9,10] explored these elements chapter by chapter but made little attempt to integrate them. The report from primary care[2] describes the clinical governance leads' committed attempts to shape clinical governance from something that they describe as 'vague and nebulous'. As they progressed, they reported feeling threatened and that their professional colleagues regarded them as 'Big Brother'.

As the clinical governance system evolved, the participating agents co-created a receptive context. Through encouragement by leads, coercion by the centre (shifting the system away from its initial state to a new disequilibrium) and acceptance of the idea, at least in principle, the system self-organized. Winning the philosophical battle, to which one of the participants refers, multidisciplinary teams were formed and committees, structures and processes established – not to any blueprint, but spontaneously through the agents' interaction. The system moved to the edge of chaos. The leads favoured facilitative and developmental management approaches to the implementation of clinical governance. Gradually they became aware that the environment in which they worked felt less threatening monitoring became more legitimate and accountability more accepted. Through the co-creation of this receptive context, rich interaction of the participants (of which 'buddying' is a good example) could be facilitated.

Remember, there was no blueprint for how clinical governance should be rolled out. Each PCT had to make its own choice about how high a profile clinical governance should occupy: some visionary PCT managers ring-fenced substantial sums of money to protect several days per week for the clinical governance leads (Gill Morgan, NHS Confederation, personal communication). In adjacent areas a single GP, allocated one half-day per week, drowned in the deluge of committee papers, Department of Health documents and requests for clarification. The complex adaptive system of clinical governance co-evolved with all the other influences impacting upon primary care over the last three years. If Bristol changed most things, Shipman changed everything, and clinical governance found itself co-evolving rapidly under societal pressure to clean up its act.

But another layer in the system, the clinical governance leads themselves, co-evolved with their clinical governance subcommittees but also with their practice partnerships and their home lives – at times despairingly commentating on the negative impact of the clinical governance workload on their private lives. Among the most conspicuous results identified through the three-year clinical governance study, a cultural shift, greater networking and sharing, and a degree of acceptance of reflective practice all illustrate the notions of co-evolution, receptive context and self-organization.

Vignette 1 – Must do's: introduction of National Service Frameworks – agreement, certainty and the Stacey diagram

This vignette is best depicted in the bottom left-hand corner of the Stacey diagram. The 'system', that is, the delivery of the NSF, is well understood – the milestones are all agreed; its delivery relatively straightforward – key information had to be recorded and made available to PCTs; and participation by the agents was assured – it was an agreed key area of healthcare. A receptive context existed, and the relation between inputs and outputs was uncomplicated. Management techniques were relatively straightforward. So, adopt a classic rational management approach. Get on with it, tick the boxes, achieve the milestones.

Vignette 2 – Not over my threshold: creating a receptive context, moving to the edge of chaos

The management strategy applied to the NSFs would be doomed to failure if applied to the second vignette, dealing with practitioners' reluctance to accept clinical governance visits, or to the clinical governance educationalist charged with developing his individually tailored programmes. These issues locate themselves in the zone of complexity in Stacey's diagram. Tightly crafted plans seeking elegant 'solutions' to these problems will lead only to frustration in the clinical governance leads, and resentments among fellow practitioners. Coalition building, negotiation and reverting to shared vision (something as broad as improved quality of care for patients, which all parties can embrace) might well lead to a satisfactory outcome, if not an elegant solution. What these represent is an attempt to co-create a receptive context. This can't be foisted on the system, it needs the rich interaction of agents to proceed. They move the *status quo* to the edge of chaos, with a little more stability in the system imbued by the agreements between the agents.[11]

Vignette 3 – Supporting the organization by supporting the individual: developing an educational strategy for continuing professional development in primary care – classic co-evolution and self-organization

The clinical governance educationalists' approach to devising a PCT-wide programme of education based on the unique needs of individual professionals is an approach which clearly implies an acceptance that the system (the educational activity within that PCT) is receptive to its own potential to self-organize around the rich interaction of its participants. This rich interaction is encouraged firstly by facilitating the development of a receptive context – the clinical governance leads' emails to fellow practitioners outlining the support for this programme and this approach, inviting topics for educational discussion and proposing, in only the broadest terms, that professionals may like to group themselves around similar educational issues. For the system to proceed, the receptive context will have to be co-created and then populated by the prospective participants – that is, they will have to express a willingness to engage in such a system which may seem to them unconventional or radical but which holds out the promise of addressing their very own educational needs.

In this way, complexity theory would say the facilitator and the participants co-create their receptive context, and through developing that, their system. Once that receptive context is established, the system proceeds with 'life' of its own; the rich interaction of participants suggesting a range of educational issues, those professionals then grouping themselves around different topics and acknowledging that its support for various activities under the identified area will be forthcoming from the host organization. As that part of the system proceeds, the participants self-organize into whatever groups, in whatever locations, with whatever educational approach they themselves deem to be appropriate. Only the broad agenda has been set by the host organization, with the broad specified outcome that after a period of time professionals will be able to demonstrate that they have engaged in an educational activity which specifically addressed their needs. This banishes the notion of the GP refresher course, with its set list of lectures served up by usually junior consultants under the aegis of 'updates', to the dark ages.

Conclusion

Healthcare policy is undergoing a paradigm shift,[12,13] both in the UK and the USA.[14] This chapter contributes to this shift by describing the implementation of clinical governance as a complex adaptive system. Recognizing this principle requires us to become familiar with the basic principles of complex systems, to understand the paradigm shift that this involves, and to rejoice in the complementarity of combining the linear and non-linear elements of all complex systems. Clinical governance leads need to draw upon the knowledge bases and the management strategies which underpin this balance with all complex systems; to balance rational and emergent strategies; draw upon classic operational as well as figurative knowledge; and recognize the crucial balance of linearity and non-linearity which holds a system at the edge of chaos. These will replace Descartes as the new dualities for healthcare policy in the twenty-first century.

References

1   Scally G and Donaldson L (1998) Clinical governance and the drive for quality improvement in the new NHS in England. *BMJ.* **317:** 61–3.

2   Sweeney G (2002) *Exploring the Implementation and Development of Clinical Governance within Primary Care Organisations in the South West Region.* Report to the South West Region Research and Development Forum, Bristol.

3   Sweeney K (2002) *The Early Experience of Clinical Governance Reviews Carried Out by the Commission for Health Improvement in Primary Care: a review of eight pilot reviews.* Briefing paper. Commission for Health Improvement, London.

4   Sweeney G, Sweeney K, Greco M *et al.* (2002) Softly softly – the way forward: a qualitative study of the first year of implementing clinical governance in primary care. *Primary Health Care Research and Development.* **3:** 53–64.

5   Sweeney G, Sweeney K, Greco M *et al.* (2002) Primary care clinical governance: what's happening on the ground? *Clinical Governance Bulletin.* **3** (1): 10–12.

6   Battram A (1998) *Navigating Complexity.* The Industrial Society, London.

7   Stacey R (1996) *Strategic Management and Organisational Dynamics* (2e). Pitman Publishing, London.

8   Department of Health (1998) *A First-class Service: quality in the new NHS.* DoH, London.

9 Lugon M and Secker-Walker J (1999) *Clinical Governance: making it happen*. Royal Society of Medicine Press, London.
10 Lugon M and Secker-Walker J (2001) *Advancing Clinical Governance*. Royal Society of Medicine Press, London.
11 Sweeney K and Griffiths F (2002) *Complexity and Healthcare: an introduction*. Radcliffe Medical Press, Oxford.
12 Cilliers P (1998) *Complexity and Post-modernism*. Routledge, London.
13 Sweeney K and Kernick D (2002) Complexity: a new model for post-normal medicine. *Journal of Clinical Evaluation*. **18**: 356–8.
14 Plsek P (2000) *Crossing the Quality Chasm: a new health system for the 21st century*. Institute of Medicine, National Academy Press, Washington, DC.

CHAPTER 17

Skill mix in the NHS: adaptability or efficiency?

David Kernick

The NHS is the largest single employer in the UK accounting for 5% of the working population. This workforce is characterized by its wide range of occupations, an emphasis on historical precedent and representation by strong professional institutions. This chapter focuses on doctor–nurse teamworking and the insights that the complexity model offers its development.

Key points
- All health systems need a cadre of healthcare professionals that are both efficient and adaptable.
- Doctor–nurse skill mix development can be explored by comparing the linear model of economics with the non-linear emergent perspective of complexity theory.
- When there is a high degree of certainty as to outcomes from actions, skill mix can be developed with an emphasis on co-ordinated teamwork within a linear or rational decision-making framework underpinned by the concept of efficiency.
- When there is a low degree of certainty as to outcomes from actions, the focus is on co-evolution within a framework of adaptability. Here complexity insights may be useful.

Introduction

Nearly one million people work for the NHS. A recent government review has called for a radical change in the way in which the medical workforce is planned and trained. The emphasis is on the integration of workforce development and flexible deployment of staff to maximize the use of their skills and abilities.[1] These developments have been driven by a number of factors:

- the need to ensure efficient utilization of what is the major expenditure of the NHS budget
- a more educated nursing sector has resulted in pressure on existing professional boundaries and access to many areas that were previously the prerogative of doctors
- an evidence base is developing which suggests that in many clinical areas, roles undertaken by doctors can be successfully transferred to nurses.

Over the past decade there has been a rapid expansion of the role of nurses within the NHS, but a number of historical influences remain. For example, power, status and gender are still important factors; many healthcare professionals are reluctant to relinquish their traditional roles; there is limited room for significant change over the short term due to extended lead times that reflect long training requirements; the organizational structure of healthcare has been determined by entrenched policy frameworks such as general practitioner reward systems that often inhibit new ways of working.

This chapter explores doctor–nurse skill mix development by comparing the linear model of economics with the non-linear emergent perspective of complexity theory. The suggestion is that we need a cadre of healthcare professionals that are both efficient and adaptable against a background of rapid technological change, financial constraint and increasingly complex healthcare needs.

What do we mean by efficiency and adaptability?

Within the context of complexity theory, there is confusion with these terms. This is because they have been developed within an evolutionary and biological perspective that may not be applicable to human organizations. Here we define these terms within an organizational framework.

Efficiency

Efficiency refers to getting the most out of limited resources, either by achieving a given output from the minimum possible input or producing the maximum possible from a fixed resource. Efficiency advocates the adoption of two basic principles: ensure that sacrifices entailed are kept to a minimum and make sure that no activity is pursued unless the benefits gained outweigh the benefits foregone. For example, it is efficient for nurses to manage minor illness in primary care as they can do so at lower cost but with similar outcomes to GPs.[2] Alternatively, a mix of nurses and doctors working in combination can enhance the dermatology care of patients in general practice for the same cost compared with doctors working alone.[3]

Adaptability

This is the ability of systems to continually change and evolve in response to environmental changes. It encompasses the elements of agility and capability – the facility of individuals and their organizations to generate new knowledge and continuously improve performance by using system feedback.[4]

Building a model to analyse doctor–nurse skill mix

A model for analysing the development of teamwork has been described by Pratt *et al.*[5] and is shown in Figure 17.1. Four types of partnership are identified: competition, co-operation, co-ordination and co-evolution. The mode of operation of the workforce depends on the extent to which goals are collective or individual and whether the purpose of the system and the behaviour needed to achieve that purpose can be known in advance.

This model will be used to plot the evolution of the NHS from a system of individual goals to one where the focus is on collective objectives. It will then

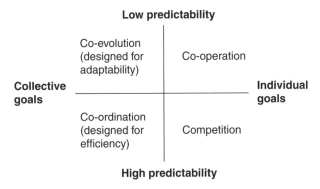

Figure 17.1   A model of partnership development.[5]

compare the rational economic approach that applies to co-ordinated team-work where there is high predictability, with the complexity approach that can offer insights for team co-evolution when predictability is low.

From individual to collective goals in the NHS

In the US, elements of a competitive environment exist (high predictability and individual goals). For example, nurses can find themselves competing with doctors over prescribing and hospital admitting rights.[6] In the UK, the histori-cal focus has been on individual professional goals in an environment of low predictability. Everyone knew their place and co-operated within a defined hier-archical structure based on delegation of task, consolidated by professional colleges and associations. The evolving subcultures had well-defined individual goals that inhibited the development of alternative forms of care.

However, by the 1990s the need to tackle professional boundaries had been recognized. Encouraged by fund-holding, changes in the primary care sector such as the introduction of nurse practitioners led to a large number of local experiments with different ways of providing services. The emphasis was on teamworking and a broader view of the delivery of healthcare with the patient at the centre.

The NHS Plan[7] consolidated a further shift away from a health service based on individual professional goals with a recognition that the NHS may have evolved in part to subserve the requirements of the professionals within it, rather than the more logical converse. The radical talk was one of 'shattering existing demarcations' and the 'breakdown of the barriers between staff and individual services'. The new health service was to be underpinned by a number of collective goals that included high-quality care and a decentraliza-tion of the NHS around the convenience and concerns of the patient. There was also a growing recognition that the training of the workforce was detached from the day-to-day process of service delivery, despite having a profound influ-ence upon it.[8]

If we are moving to an environment of collective goals, how can we analyse skill mix changes from a descriptive and prescriptive perspective? Drawing on Pratt *et al.*'s model,[5] when there is a high degree of certainty as to outcomes from actions, skill mix can be developed with an emphasis on co-ordinated teamwork within a linear or rational decision-making framework underpinned by the concept of efficiency. When there is a low degree of certainty as to out-comes from actions, the focus is on co-evolution within a framework of adapt-ability. Here non-linear complexity insights may be useful.

We first look at designing for efficiency.

Designing for efficiency – co-ordinated teamwork

From an economic or co-ordinated perspective, the concept of skill mix seeks to match clinical presentation to an intervention based on an appropriate level of skill and training.[9] The anticipation is that working in co-ordinated mixed teams will provide more effective and efficient care.

This approach is underpinned by the linear economic model. This assumes that it is possible to identify and measure system outputs and that the transformation process that relates inputs to outputs is understood. The focus is on maximizing outputs for any given resource allocation or minimizing resources utilization for a given output. For example, a primary care organization has £100 000 to improve asthma care. What is the best mix of doctors and nurses to maximize population health in this area? Alternatively, asthma care targets have to be reached. What is the mix of staff to do this at lowest cost?

A linear analysis would focus on a number of areas. For example, how can we match rewards to job attributes in a way that can recruit, motivate and retain labour? How can centralized pay bargaining reflect local requirements? However, economic evaluation forms the central model for the analysis of efficient skill mix.

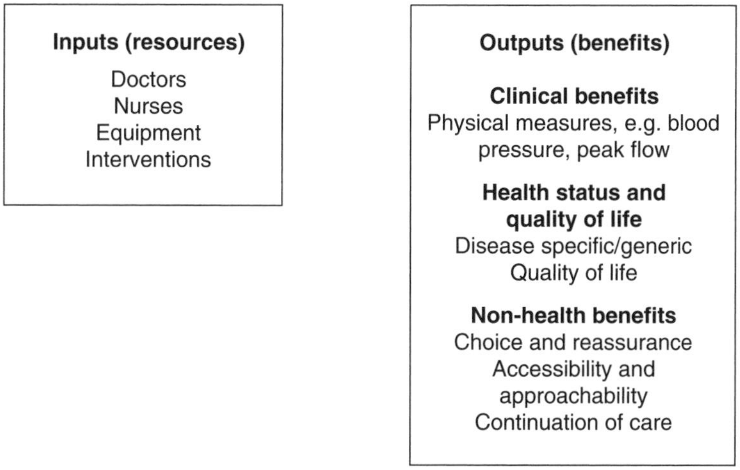

Inputs (resources)	**Outputs (benefits)**
Doctors Nurses Equipment Interventions	**Clinical benefits** Physical measures, e.g. blood pressure, peak flow **Health status and quality of life** Disease specific/generic Quality of life **Non-health benefits** Choice and reassurance Accessibility and approachability Continuation of care

Figure 17.2   An economic analysis relates inputs (resources) to outputs (benefits and the values attached to them) of alternative interventions to facilitate decision making when resources are scarce.

The concept of economic evaluation

Economic evaluation compares the costs and consequences of alternative health-care interventions to facilitate decisions from the perspective of efficiency.[10] Figure 17.2 shows the costs and benefits that may be relevant in an economic study. Skill mix issues focus on the extent to which different labour inputs are substituted, and the effect this has on output. This framework requires values to be made explicit, objectives to be set and assumes that the system can be engineered towards those defined targets.

There are three assumptions in this model:[11]

- There is a spectrum of tasks in healthcare based on task complexity and uncertainty.
- The correct level of skill and training can be matched across this spectrum.
- This will result in limited healthcare resources being used more efficiently.

Figure 17.3 shows an example of this spectrum taken from primary care.

Problems with economic evaluation

A recent review of skill mix in primary care found that it was difficult to form a coherent overview of service provision in terms of cost-effectiveness.[12] This is due to a number of problems applying economic evaluation to skill mix that include:

- Difficulty in clarifying strategic objectives. Skill mix options and their re-source implications are complex and include combinations of doctor/nurse investment/disinvestment and substitution/complementation. Increased nurse availability may also lead to unanticipated additional consultations by exposing unmet need. Patients who would not have previously consulted

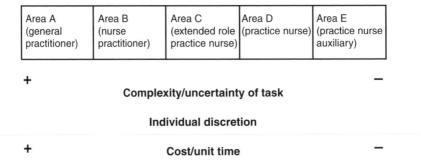

Figure 17.3   The spectrum of tasks in primary care.

may now do so. For example, a study on the impact of nurse practitioners in primary care showed no reduction in the rate of GP consultation.[13]

- Difficulties identifying the best mix to test. A *marginal analysis*[14] recognizes the importance of how the relationship between outcomes and costs changes as programmes expand or contract. For example, an asthma nurse rarely provides exclusive respiratory care but shares this role with the GP, and the extent of this sharing may differ. In principle, this relationship should be determined by undertaking trials across a number of skill mix options to identify the optimum doctor–nurse mix, but this will rarely be possible.

- Difficulties with developing an evidence base. A particular problem is measuring the outcomes of skill mix options. Although the broader aspects of health are recognized, other sources of benefit that may be of particular relevance for nurse interventions can be overlooked.[15] For example, benefit may be obtained from the process of care arising from information reassurance or choice. Outcomes are often multidimensional and assessment may be affected by timing and characterized by difficulties with attribution.[16,17] Due to the wide variation in case mix, training and organization, there will be problems with generalizability and estimates of the potential for doctor/nurse delegation may be sensitive to the methods of data collection and type of practice.

In summary, while recognizing its limitations, a linear approach underpinned by economic evaluation can facilitate skill mix decisions when there are clear objectives and well-defined roles operating within a framework where inputs and outputs can be measured and their relationship is well understood.

Designing for adaptability – co-evolving teamwork

Most areas of healthcare operate in the 'zone of complexity'. Here, everything is connected to everything else and changes in one element changes the context for all other elements. Developments takes place within a complex network of healthcare providers where there may not be a simple relationship between inputs and outputs or agreement over what outputs are important. Simple system goals are replaced by broader societal goals. For example, the new NHS walk-in centres aim to enhance the accessibility of public healthcare and reduce workload on other providers across the service.

In these areas of healthcare, the relevance of rational planning supported by economic analysis will be limited. The emphasis is on co-evolution and the design of systems that can adapt as the healthcare environment changes, creating the conditions for self-organization of agile and adaptable professional teams. Some characteristics of such teams are shown in Box 17.1.

Box 17.1   Characteristics of agile teams (taken from Fraser *et al.*, 2003[18])

- They constantly attune themselves to what the patients want.
- They don't slip into a paternalistic framework which offers a patient what the experts think.
- They engage in a continual dialogue around a genuine desire to improve the patient experience.
- They demonstrate an outstanding knowledge of what they actually achieve and how to measure and monitor it.
- They invariably know about teams who outperform them and are curious to know how this is achieved.
- They work in small cycles of planning and change their shape to fit what needs to be done.

Four complexity insights are important when designing for adaptability:

- A recognition of the importance of initial conditions. Organizations do not start from a clean slate but develop within the framework that has been inherited, building on what has gone before. An important factor that inhibits co-evolution is power. For example, Bull and Hart[19] explored the main themes in the development of the clinical nurse specialist. Problems arising from the conflicts of power in relationship to patients, doctors and other specialized nurses were the main areas identified. Although the environment of the health service has changed dramatically, professional groups still cling to their historical precedent and remain reluctant to relinquish their traditional power bases.[20]
- The importance of holding a shared vision. A vision articulates the simple rules or values of the system around which it will transform itself and is central to the success of any team. It not only gives direction but helps us to feel that our actions are meaningful as we negotiate our identities and relationships with one another in organizational contexts. There is no predetermined organizational end-point and any measured outcomes are not an end in themselves but part of a learning. Any trappings of rationality such as objectives and strategic plans are important largely as binding mechanisms.
- Doctor–nurse teams will be most adaptable operating at the 'edge of chaos'. The emphasis is on exploring purpose, fostering relationships and building on the strengths of each partner. This requires connectivity, openness and feedback. By encouraging conversation and creating dialogue, power shifts from the traditional hierarchical framework to a relational context with the emancipation of voices that were not previously heard. The key is the development of a mutual respect for each profession and an escape from each one's limited vocabulary of knowledge, skill and attitudes.

- We must be cautious in our evaluation of new skill mix initiatives that are highly connected within the healthcare economy. The information we obtain from a reductionist analysis may offer limited insights into changes in complex systems. For example, Chalder *et al.*[21] have identified the difficulty of obtaining robust quantitative evidence about the impact of NHS walk-in centres on other health providers and the extent to which they act as an additional, substitute or duplicate service. In fact, the initiative may have had the opposite effect to that desired and increased demand on general practice.

The need for difference – but not too much

From the perspective of both efficiency and adaptability, it is not what people have in common but their differences that make collaborative work more powerful than working alone. We must be wary of homogenizing tendencies in the workforce. For example, medicine has created doctors who are self-reliant, independent, expert and autonomous. They know more than they can say and exhibit a tacit knowing in practice. They demonstrate a capacity for reflection on their intuitive knowing in the midst of action and can use this capacity to cope with the unique uncertainty and conflictive situations of practice.[22] Nursing traditions have emphasized hierarchy and bureaucratic rule-based frameworks. Their professional activity focuses on instrumental problem solving and techniques that involve the application of general principles to specific problems.

Box 17.2   Clinical subcultures working out of one health centre

- Medical – general practice
- Medical – specialist community clinics
- Nursing – community
- Nursing – practice (auxiliary, nurse practitioners, practice nurses)
- Nursing – community psychiatric
- Midwifery
- Health visitors
- Chiropody
- Clinical psychology
- Counselling
- Physiotherapy
- Occupational therapy
- Speech therapy
- Dietitian

Although skill mix demands a difference between entities, too much diversity may lead to inefficiency. Box 17.2 shows the subcultures that are working out of my health centre.

One way of picturing these problems is by invoking the metaphor of a multi-dimensional phase space. In Chapter 3 it was suggested that each organizational subculture could be characterized by their simple rules and attractors. Too many weak attractors in the multidimensional phase space of healthcare will cause the system to lurch haphazardly between them. Too few strong attractors will inhibit the system from exploring its possibility space.

Conclusion

The NHS Plan[7] has set out a long-term programme for reform in the NHS. This emphasizes the importance of breaking down the demarcations between different professional groups and freeing front-line staff to use their skills to redesign services and improve performance around the needs of the patient.[23] A recurring theme in skill mix debate is the need to work 'smarter not harder'. However, the meaning of this term is never qualified. This chapter has suggested that a 'smart' system recognizes the context of the healthcare intervention. When there is high predictability, the system can be designed for efficiency with the emphasis on co-ordination within regulatory frameworks and guidelines. When there is low predictability, the system needs to be designed for adaptability, drawing upon complexity insights.

References

1 Department of Health (2000) *A Health Service of All the Talents: developing the NHS workforce*. Consultation document on the review of workforce planning. DoH, London.
2 Jenkins-Clarke S, Carr-Hill R, Dixon P *et al.* (1997) *Skill Mix in Primary Care*. Centre for Health Economics, University of York.
3 Kernick D, Reinhold D, Sawkins J *et al.* (2000) A cost–consequence study of a dermatology nurse in primary care. *British Journal of General Practice*. **50**: 555–9.
4 Fraser S and Greenhalgh T (2001) Coping with complexity: educating for capability. *BMJ*. **323**: 799–803.
5 Pratt J, Gordon P and Plamping D (2000) *Working Whole Systems: putting theory into practice in organisations*. King's Fund, London.
6 Kassiner JP (1994) What role for the nurse practitioner in primary care. *NEJM*. **20**: 304–5.
7 Department of Health (2002) *The NHS Plan: a plan for investment, a plan for reform*. HMSO, London.
8 Health Select Committee (1999) *Workforce Planning in the NHS*. Health Select Committee, House of Commons, London.

9   Rashid A, Watts A and Leneham C (1996) Skill mix in primary care: sharing clinical workload and understanding professional roles. *British Journal of General Practice*. **6:** 639–40.

10   Drummond M (1994) *Economic Analysis Alongside Control Trials*. Department of Health, London.

11   Kernick D and Scott A (2001) Economic approaches to doctor/nurse skill mix: problems, pitfalls and partial solutions. *British Journal of General Practice*. **52:** 42–7.

12   Sergison M, Sibbald B and Rose S (1998) *Skill Mix in Primary Care: a bibliography*. National Primary Care Research Centre, University of Manchester.

13   Touche Ross (1994) *Evaluation of Nurse Practitioner Pilot Projects*. Touche Ross, London.

14   Torgerson DJ and Spencer A (1996) Marginal costs and benefits. *BMJ*. **312:** 35–6.

15   Ryan M and Shackley P (1995) Assessing the benefits of health care: how far should we go? *Quality in Health Care*. **4:** 207–13.

16   Orchard C (1994) Comparing health outcomes. *BMJ*. **308:** 1493–6.

17   Wilson-Barnet J and Beech S (1994) Evaluating the clinical nurse specialist: a review. *International Journal of Nurse Studies*. **31 (6):** 561–71.

18   Fraser S, Conner M and Yarrow D (2003) *Thriving in Unpredictable Times: a reader on agility in health care*. Kingsham Press, Chichester.

19   Bull R and Hart G (1995) Clinical nurse specialist: walking the wire. *Contemporary Nurse*. **995:** 425–32.

20   Berwick D (1997) Medical Associations: guilds or leaders? *BMJ*. **314:** 1564–5.

21   Chalder M, Sharp D, Moore L *et al.* (2003) Impact of NHS walk-in centres on the workload of other local healthcare providers: time series analysis. *BMJ*. **326:** 532.

22   Schön D (1983) *The Reflective Practitioner: how professionals think in action*. Basic Books, New York.

23   Department of Health (2001) *Shifting the Balance of Power within the NHS: securing delivery*. DoH, Leeds.

CHAPTER 18

Adaptation in action: the NHS Modernisation Agency's Critical Care Programme

Ceri Brown

This chapter describes how the Modernisation Agency set up a collaborative improvement programme to address issues that had been identified in NHS critical care services. It describes how critical care can be viewed as a complex system and how complexity insights were used in the programme.

Key points
- A review of the NHS critical care services by an expert group gave general recommendations for improvement of critical care services in England.
- A complex adaptive system metaphor was used to put change and improvement into action at a local level.
- Multiple, iterative, non-linear interactions between elements of the system were used to generate new knowledge and ways of acting within the system, drawing upon a number of techniques.
- The precise nature of the adaptations was delegated to local clinical teams to make specific changes of local relevance.
- Due to its local focus, results of the global effect of the programme have been difficult to ascertain.

Background to the Critical Care Programme

The Modernisation Agency was created in April 2000 in response to the UK government document *The NHS Plan*[1] with the declaration 'rapid, effective service improvement requires targeted expert support to spread best practice and stimulate change locally' (para 6.14). Initially, the Agency set up collaborative improvement programmes to address issues of service improvements in the seven areas of coronary heart disease; cancer; mental health; older people; children; waiting times; access to services.

In 1998, prior to the setting up of the Agency, critical care services in England had received attention due to the excessive numbers of patients being transferred between intensive care units of hospitals. The associated untoward events that occurred were publicized in the press and led to a review of the critical care services by an expert group in 1999. The group's report, *Comprehensive Critical Care*,[2] contained several recommendations for action. In a major change in the thinking, the sobriquet of the report, 'Critical Care Without Walls', concluded that critically ill patients should receive care throughout hospitals, not solely in intensive care and high-dependency units. While it did not specify in detail precisely how this care should be organized, it laid minimum specifications for improved services. To implement the report, the Modernisation Agency set up the Critical Care Programme with the explicit aim 'to improve access, experience and outcomes for patients with potential or actual need for critical care based on the severity of their illness and not where their care is delivered'.

This chapter describes the programme, which has been running since September 2000 and using a complex adaptive system understanding to achieve developments and improvements in critical care.

Critical care as a complex adaptive system

A complex adaptive system has been described as 'a collection of individual agents with freedom to act in ways that are not always totally predictable, and whose actions are interconnected so that one agent's action changes the context for other agents'.[3] From its origins in cybernetic systems, Holland[4] noted four features of a complex adaptive system which extend the above definition:

1 All complex adaptive systems involve large numbers of parts undergoing a kaleidoscopic array of simultaneous non-linear interactions.
2 The impact of these systems in human affairs centres on the aggregate behaviour, the behaviour of the whole.
3 Their interactions evolve over time, as the parts adapt in an attempt to survive in the environment provided by the other parts.
4 Complex adaptive systems anticipate.

This more complete description highlights the idea that aggregate behaviour cannot be predicted from an analysis of individual behaviours alone because of the continual adaptation of those behaviours. The unpredictable, but observable, outcome of interactions is known as 'emergence'. Put simply, it is the conclusion that 'the whole is greater than the sum of its parts'. The evolution of interactions and anticipation of events by the system imply mechanisms for learning from past events and generating new ways of coping in response to external stimuli. It is to be noted that it is sometimes difficult to distinguish between a complex adaptive system and its external environment because the system and the environment relate intimately to each other,[5] a phenomenon known as co-evolution.

Setting boundaries

What is the system? A major problem in describing complex adaptive systems arises from the difficulty in determining the size of the system that is adapting to an external stimulus.[6] It has been pointed out that human beings themselves are composed of, and act within, a multiplicity of interacting systems.[7] For example, a professional within an organization responds to the behaviours of others within the same clinical department. Clinical departments within a hospital interact, hospitals interact with each other within geographical areas, and the NHS is one system of many within national boundaries.

Comparing the structure of the NHS in England with the features of an adaptive system, it can be argued that NHS services are provided by 'large numbers of parts undergoing a kaleidoscopic array of multiple non-linear interactions'. At a national level, feedback by the press of untoward events in critical care associated with transfers evoked two learned adaptive responses from the NHS – the provision of extra resource to increase the capacity of the NHS to deal with critically ill patients and the production of the report *Comprehensive Critical Care*,[2] which recommended changes in behaviour.

One of the recommendations of the report was that networks of critical care units should be set up 'to meet the needs of all critically ill people in their geographical area' (para 46). The Critical Care Programme assisted in setting up 29 networks which co-ordinate and deliver service developments and improvements. These networks of critical care units can be considered as an adaptive response by creating another layer of complex adaptive systems whose elements comprise of the hospital critical care services within their boundaries.

At individual unit level, the feedback for change was the report itself. The Critical Care Programme provided new ways by which behavioural change could come about. In broad terms, these different feedbacks led to adaptive responses eventually resulting in the way staff in critical care interacted with their environment.

Using complexity insights for improvements in critical care

A problem for applying complexity theory to a human situation is determining methods by which individual elements of a system gain feedback from, and generate new knowledge of, the environment and the system they are operating within. This facility of individuals (and by inference, their organizations) to generate new knowledge of the system and to continually improve performance by using feedback has been termed 'capability'.[8] Complexity theory suggests that the facility for 'generative learning'[9] is typical of a complex adaptive system 'at the edge of chaos'.[10] The phrase 'edge of chaos' has a specific meaning when used in complex adaptive systems (*see* Chapter 3). It is a point between two states of a system, one where the relationships and actions of elements of a system are fixed, and the other a mass of unco-ordinated action by the elements.[5] In the orderly state there is no ability or incentive for the system to adapt to the environment or create new knowledge. The system is in a steady state. In the 'chaotic' state, each individual element attempts to adapt optimally for itself with no consistent connections with other elements of the system and no generalized learning. An area of optimum adaptability and learning occurs at a critical density of connectivity between the elements, the 'zone of complexity'.[11] In order to adapt to the feedback, the elements change their behaviours. The next section demonstrates how complexity insights were used to facilitate emergent change in the Critical Care Programme.

Methods for feedback

In the programme, three techniques widely taught by the Modernisation Agency were used to elicit feedbacks and facilitate changes in behaviour – process mapping, a small-step change methodology known as 'plan-do-study-act', and a narrative feedback technique. The evolution of behaviours created by these feedback methods were means of improving the adaptive fitness of intensive care units to meet the needs of the external environment described in the document *Comprehensive Critical Care*.[2]

Process mapping

Process mapping in healthcare[12] involves a group of clinicians creating a representation of a clinical process on paper. Areas within the process which require improvement are identified. At a coarse level of analysis, the clinical process under investigation may be considered a 'series of connected steps or actions to achieve an outcome'. As such, the process resembles a linear system with few of the features of a complex adaptive system. However, at a finer level of analysis, precise relationships and timing between each step in the process are not accurately predictable because of the changing context of the system. The behaviour of the clinical process can be said to be 'emergent'. The process, or complex adaptive system, may be operating neither efficiently nor effectively in absolute terms, but its output is sufficient to avoid provoking adaptive changes. For example, patients may be an 'input' to a diagnostic process, such as in a radiology department, and become an 'output' of the process in a linear fashion. However, invariably the orderliness of the process breaks down into 'messy, fuzzy, unique and other context-embedded problems'.[7] The precise actions performed in the department are influenced by other events and situations. An analysis of a process map by clinicians, knowlegeable of the context, suggests areas for improvement in efficiency and effectiveness, which then give rise to new emergent behaviours. The process mapping exercise is a way of describing a desirable future state and simultaneously inventing ways of getting to that state – a 'generative learning' environment.

Small-step change methodology

This methodology allows for small changes to be made to individual parts of a system, observing the results and then making a judgement whether the results of the change were beneficial.[13] The four steps taken in sequence using this method are: *plan* (a change); *do* (perform a change); *study* (observe the response); *act* (judge the response and decide on other changes). Typically, one measure of the output of the process is decided upon and the value of the measure is displayed sequentially on a 'run-chart'. The graphical representation of a changing process measure has been shown to be useful in an intensive care setting. In achieving a reduction in time patients were sedated on a ventilator, Brattebo *et al.*[14] noted that 'graphically displayed results served as an important information resource'. They served as a synoptic feedback mechanism for the performance of the staff on the intensive care unit.

Both of these techniques focus on parts of a process of delivery of care to patients to determine how this could be optimized, and they have one important element in common. They allow individuals to reflect on their part of a system. This process of reflection has been documented in Schön's 'reflective practitioner' description of learning and behavioural change,[15] and Kolb's experiential learning.[16] Reflection by individuals has been described as an essential component of a 'learning organization'.[9] However, reflection should be only one phase of a cycle of learning that also involves doing something.[17]

A narrative feedback technique

The usefulness of stories to develop clinical care and alter the behaviour of clinical professionals has been described.[18] This technique of narrative 'analysis', with the object of organizational improvement by a clinical team, is a novel feedback mechanism in the complex adaptive system of critical care. Termed a 'discovery interview',[19] it makes use of a description of the chronological sequence of a patient's experience through the healthcare system. This is achieved by a semi-structured interview with patient and carer, with the resulting transcript being read out to clinical teams who had been involved with the patient. Reflecting on the transcript, clinical teams identify areas for improvement and use an appropriate methodology to achieve change. In this particular method of feedback, the narratives have two distinct attributes. They are simultaneously a focus for reflection by clinicians and a powerful motivator for change. Rather than simply relying on an objective measurement of a process, the subjective elements evoked when listening to the story of a patient's journey make process improvements more meaningful to clinical staff.[20] Thus, using a narrative feedback can be a more powerful driver for change than a graphical display.

For example, a patient had been admitted to intensive care as a result of septic shock following an urgent appendicectomy. A section of one of the transcripts read:

> *When I did wake up, I initially didn't know where I was but guessed I was in hospital. As I had a tube in my throat and was unable to speak, the nurse gave me a 'rattle'. She came over and asked if I was all right and said that I was in hospital, but she didn't say which one. I looked at this rattle and it said 'supplied by Eastbourne Hospitals'. I then suddenly thought why the hell am I in Eastbourne, so that made me panic as well. I was thinking, does anyone know I am here? I managed to get the nurse's attention and ask what hospital was I in. She then told me and I felt relieved, panic over.*

The patient knew that when he had been admitted to hospital he was quite far away from Eastbourne, giving rise to the anxiety over his location. When the transcript was read out to the unit staff, they realized that the labelling of 'rattle' had a greater significance than they had previously considered. The 'rattle' was a small pathology specimen pot with small plastic pieces inside which was used to get the attention of the nursing staff, and labelled with its origin, Eastbourne. The immediate action taken by the staff was to use only appropriately labelled containers for all purposes. The transcript highlighted a general need for precise geographical reorientation while waking up on an intensive care unit. As a result, all items on the unit which had a location printed on them, such as bed linen, were examined and removed from use if necessary.

Results of change using complexity insights

The precise nature of the changes made by local critical care teams was decided by them. Many of the different process redesign results have been directed towards improving efficiency by reducing unnecessary delays in the critical care system. Waiting times for investigation or equipment, and times to discharge patients from critical care areas, have been examined and beneficial changes made.

One example of the success of this technique was an effort to decrease the time delay in making blood results available on a high-dependency unit in the West Midlands. A process mapping exercise had identified this as a problem area and three sequential small-step changes were made. Firstly, phlebotomists gave priority to critical care patients and medical admissions when taking samples. While this gave some change in the availability of results, further improvement was only achieved by making a specific phone call for a porter to send blood samples to the pathology department. Finally, pathology porters adopted a continual cycle of collecting blood samples from all wards.

A similar issue involving the availability of blood gas results was identified at a different hospital. The initial arrangement was for doctors to take arterial blood samples, but a delay of two to three hours before the doctor could attend was common. The adaptive, behavioural change was that senior physiotherapists and nurses were trained to take arterial blood samples according to a protocol. After the change, there was a notable reduction in the delay from time of the request for the procedure to it being done. The enhancement of the roles of clinical staff benefited the patient, and also clinicians' own confidence.

More examples can be seen on the Critical Care Programme website, www.modern.nhs.uk/critical.care.

Conclusion

The complex adaptive system metaphor has proved a useful way of understanding how to put change and improvement into action in a section of the NHS in England. Multiple, iterative, non-linear interactions between elements of the system have been used to generate new knowledge and ways of acting within the system.

The aim of the techniques described was to provide individual practitioners, in the complex adaptive system called critical care, with the ability to gain feedback, reflect and change their behaviours. In each methodology – process mapping, plan-do-study-act or the discovery interview technique – participants in the process of care temporarily viewed the system as if from the outside, using their

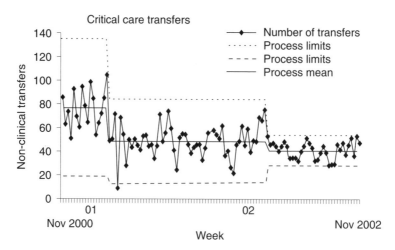

Figure 18.1   Mean, upper and lower control limits of the number of critically ill patients transferred per week for non-clinical reasons in England over a two-year period, November 2000 to November 2002 (based on unvalidated management information).

own or another person's perspective. Their rich contextual knowledge was then used to look at the system from 'outside' to provide a feedback to the system of which they are also a part. In each case, because feedback was made in a group setting, there are parallels with 'social-system management', which is concerned with organizational development rather than tight managerial control.[21]

While there was central sponsorship of the techniques for feedback, the precise nature of the adaptations was delegated to local clinical teams to make specific changes of local relevance, measured in a local context (as in the examples above). For this reason, results of the global effect of the programme are difficult to ascertain and a single indicator of national improvement has been difficult to develop. To date, the clearest indicator of the results associated with the Critical Care Programme is a reduction in the numbers of transfers of critically ill patients. Because this was the nature of the original feedback, it was important to note this particular change in activity of the whole critical care system in England. The graph shown in Figure 18.1, in the form of a statistical process control chart, covers a two-year time period from just before the inception of the Critical Care Programme until November 2002. It demonstrates a reduction in the mean, and the spread of the upper and lower control limits, of the number of critically ill patients transferred per week for what are now termed non-clinical reasons. This means the inability to admit an appropriate patient to an intensive care unit.

With such a large system being examined, it is difficult to attribute a single cause to the observed variation in activity. However, it does indicate the effect of an adaptive response of critical care services to a stimulus from the external environment. This large system effect, only observable over an extended time period, is made up of many different, small-scale improvements whose effect is more easily observed in individual hospitals and intensive care units.

References

1   Department of Health (2000) *The NHS Plan: a plan for investment, a plan for reform.* HMSO, London.
2   Department of Health (2000) *Comprehensive Critical Care.* HMSO, London.
3   Plsek PE and Greenhalgh T (2001) The challenge of complexity in healthcare. *BMJ.* **323:** 625–8.
4   Holland J (1994) *Adaptation in Natural and Artificial Systems.* MIT Press, Cambridge, MA.
5   Kaufmann S (1995) *At Home in the Universe.* Viking, London.
6   Hurst D and Zimmerman BJ (1994) From lifecycle to ecocycle: a new perspective on the growth, maturity, destruction and renewal of complex systems. *Journal of Management Inquiry.* **3:** 339–54.
7   Wilson T and Holt T (2001) Complexity and clinical care. *BMJ.* **323:** 685–8.
8   Fraser SW and Greenhalgh T (2001) Coping with complexity: educating for capability. *BMJ.* **323:** 799–803.
9   Senge P (1992) *The Fifth Discipline.* Random House, London.
10 Langton C. Quoted in Waldrop M (1992) *Complexity: the emerging science at the edge of order and chaos,* p. 120. Penguin, London.
11 Stacey R (1996) *Strategic Management and Organizational Dynamics.* Pitman Publishing, London.
12 Modernisation Agency (2002) *Improvement Leaders' Guide.* Modernisation Agency, Leicester.
13 Langley GJ, Nolan KM, Nolan TW *et al.* (1996) *The Improvement Guide.* Jossey-Bass, San Francisco, CA.
14 Brattebo G, Hofoss D, Flatten H *et al.* (2002) Effect of a scoring system and protocol for sedation on duration of patients' need for ventilator support in a surgical intensive care unit. *BMJ.* **324:** 1586–9.
15 Schön D (1983) *The Reflective Practitioner: how professionals think in action.* Basic Books, New York.
16 Kolb DA (1984) *Experiential Learning: experience as the source of learning and development.* Prentice Hall, Englewood Cliffs, NJ.
17 Zimmerman B, Lindberg C and Plsek P (1998) *Edgeware: insights from complexity science for healthcare leaders.* VHA Inc., Irving, TX.
18 Greenhalgh T and Hurwitz B (eds) (1998) *Narrative-based Medicine.* BMJ Books, London.
19 Wilcock PM, Brown GCS, Bateson J *et al.* (2003) Using patient stories to inspire quality improvement within the NHS Modernisation Agency collaborative programmes. *Journal of Clinical Nursing.* **12:** 422–30.
20 Wensing M and Grol R (1998) What can patients do to improve care? *Health Expectations.* **1:** 37–49.
21 Gharajedaghi J and Ackoff R (1984) Mechanisms, organisms and social systems. *Strategic Management Journal.* **5:** 289–300.

CHAPTER 19

Educating the healthcare professional for capability

Jim Price

When the world is predictable you need smart people, but when the world is unpredictable you need adaptable people.

(Henry Mintzberg)

The rapid pace of change in today's health services has important implications for future training and education of healthcare professionals. This chapter will examine how the changing educational needs of the modern health professional in the NHS may be linked with changing educational theory, and how insights from the notion of complexity might help both educators and health professionals learn to cope with this dynamic environment.

Key points
- An appreciation of the theory of how we learn is necessary to understand how capability might be developed.
- Teaching and motivating health professionals to learn how to learn will give them the best chance to become adaptive throughout their career.
- Educational providers at all levels need to be aware of the principles that underpin adult learning to maximize the engagement of health professionals.
- The importance for human learning and education is that any individual, group or system will learn best in the zone of complexity.
- 'Complexity' can be seen as both a guide for improving teaching and learning, and as a metaphor for the teaching environment in today's health services.

Introduction

The NHS Plan[1] was designed as a blueprint for reform of the NHS, and other government policy documents have also called for reform in the human resources domain.[2–4] Many suggested role changes for the workforce have been welcomed and are seen as appropriate professional development, but tensions can arise when traditional professional boundaries are challenged. Educational providers both in institutions and in clinical settings, such as within primary care trusts and those organizing clinical placement on the wards in secondary care, should be aware of these tensions and also of the principles that underpin adult learning to maximize the engagement of these health professionals. The new 'University for the NHS' (NHSU) strategy espouses these principles, although the practical application will be more challenging.[5]

With uncertainties about future roles and responsibilities, how can the teachers and learners of today prepare for an unknown tomorrow? Perhaps the concept of capability can help us.

Educating for capability

The notion of capability is important in that it combines two meanings:[6]

- the quality of being capable or 'competent' (i.e. either the academic 'know that' or 'understanding', or the operational 'know how' or 'effectiveness'.[7] Complexity thinking suggests that we should hold the paradox and consider both meanings at the same time)
- an undeveloped faculty or property, a condition capable of being turned to use.

The importance is that it encapsulates a present meaning of competence (as a prerequisite for current performance) at the same time as a future-orientated 'potential' for the development of competence.

Bandura[8] views humans as possessing five basic capabilities which underlie our ability to learn and function in all situations. These are shown in Box 19.1.

The last two of these are of prime importance in the development of skills to cope with uncertainty and maintain adaptability for health professionals, and they have become keystones for continuing professional development in the health services.[9] 'Capability' then is an amalgam of concepts, linked closely to the way in which adults learn. An appreciation of the theory of how we learn is necessary to understand how capability might be developed.

Box 19.1   Five human capabilities[8]

- *Symbolizing capability* (the ability to internalize experience in symbolic form to serve as a guide for future actions)
- *Forethought capability* (anticipatory planning of actions, and goals, which in turn motivates behaviour)
- *Vicarious capability* (learning by observing what happens to others, and modelling one's behaviour – a shortcut to experiential learning)
- *Self-regulatory capability* (self-evaluation against internal standards as the personal guidance system for action)
- *Self-reflective capability* (analysis of our experiences and our thought processes – also known as meta-cognitive capability)

Learning theory

In this section we consider approaches to learning theory before discussing how insights from complexity theory can add to our understanding.

The learning cycle

Adaptation is a key concept in complexity thinking. The 'system' as an individual or organization adapts its behaviour in the light of acting and interacting with other agents in the system. Feedback influences future behaviour and so learning occurs. The so-called 'learning cycle' (*see* Figure 19.1) was developed by David Kolb in the 1970s,[10] building on the thinking of Dewey[11] and Lewin.[12] The cycle describes such experiential learning for individuals. It is analogous to the plan-do-study-act cycle for quality improvement in organizations, again a form of adaptation.

An agent may have a preferred 'learning style' (e.g. 'activist' or 'theorist' – *see* Figure 19.1), but the suggestion is that for true learning to occur an individual (or indeed organization) should undergo the full cycle, and exhibit all of the 'learning styles' through this process of action and reflection on action. The cycle is continually repeated and becomes a developmental 'spiral' rather than a circle.

The concept of the 'learning spiral' underlies the 'constructivist' view of learning, i.e. that meaning is created by the learner on the basis of an internal collection of representations or models; action and reflection on the action change the models and represent learning. If the reflection is internalized and given a degree of permanence, 'deep learning' is said to have occurred.[13]

Figure 19.1   Kolb's learning cycle.[10]

'Deep' learning may be contrasted with 'surface' learning, which occurs when things are learned or memorized without true understanding of the bigger picture, or by making appropriate linkages between facts and details. In adults, deep learning is more likely to occur if they possess specific characteristics and certain conditions are met. These are considered in the next section.

Adult learning

'Andragogy' (or adult learning) was first proposed by Knowles *et al.* in 1973.[14] The difference between childhood learning and that of the adult concerns the differences in:[15]

- context (adults having assumed responsibility for their lives, and being a learner is only one of several roles)
- characteristics of learners (such as intellect, experience, internal motivation and the need for self-direction)
- learning process (e.g. the pacing of learning, meaningfulness and motivation).

The characteristics of adult learners are listed in Box 19.2.

It is therefore important that educational initiatives follow these principles in order to maximize engagement of health professional as learners. One of the most important aspects of adult learning is its relation to self-direction and autonomy in learning. In a complex adaptive system, self-direction and autonomy are also key characteristics of the agents in the system that may then interact to bring about emergent behaviour. So it is appropriate to consider this area now in more detail.

Box 19.2   Adult learning[16]

Adults are motivated by learning that:

- is perceived as relevant
- is based on and builds on previous experiences
- is participatory and actively involves them
- is focused on problems
- can be immediately applied in practice
- involves cycles of action and reflection
- is based on mutual trust and respect.

Self-directed learning

Self-directed, lifelong learning is becoming increasingly explicit as the hallmark of best practice in the development and maintenance of professional competence.[17] Candy[18] has described four dimensions of self-directedness, including personal autonomy, self-management in learning, learner control of instruction, and the independent pursuit of learning. He also described a large number of traits associated with self-direction, allowing the development of metric scales for the assessment of 'readiness' for self-direction.[19,20] The implications for educators are that learners need to develop and practise skills which directly enhance self-directed learning. These include competency at asking questions, and critical appraisal of new information.

The capability for deep learning is unsurprisingly a prerequisite for ongoing self-direction, as is that of critical reflection on one's own learning and experience.[17,21] Personal goals may then be set, for instance within a personal learning or development plan. Aligning learning and assessment with these goals then becomes the aim of the educational advisor or provider. Reflection, initially personally, and then with a peer in the form of 'challenged self-assessment' becomes the means to derive deep learning about oneself.[22] The concept of 'appraisal' when viewed from this perspective appears not only sensible and formative, but probably essential for personal and professional development.[23]

Teaching and motivating health professionals to learn how to learn (and to go on doing it) will give them the best chance to become truly adaptive throughout their career, and to avoid premature extinction or burn-out.

It cannot be assumed that all adults will engage in this form of learning, or be naturally self-directed and adaptable. In order to enable them to engage and develop their 'potential' capabilities, as well as their competencies, it may help to look at how teachers and learners bridge the gap between theory and practice, and interact in a complex learning situation. This is set within the context of curriculum development.

Curriculum development

Curriculum refers to the 'expression of educational ideas in practice', and has been classified into that which is planned, that which is actually delivered, and that which is experienced by the students.[24] The implication is that sometimes the differences between these 'levels' may be greater than they should be, but in rapidly changing times perhaps this is a necessary and 'emergent' property of curriculum design and delivery. There should also be a two-way interaction between the health curriculum and the clinical health services, in that they are mutually dependent for improvement.

In 1949, Tyler proposed the 'product' mode of a curriculum – emphasizing the acquisition of predetermined knowledge and skills.[25] This correlates with an 'instrumentalist' view of education (i.e. that education is about producing a health professional for a predetermined role with agreed competencies and skills). This is the 'traditional' view of education, e.g. teaching nurses a set curriculum to produce good nurses for society's benefit. The classical model of teaching would then be a teacher lecturing to passive students, i.e. 'the sage on the stage'.

More recently, a so-called 'progressivist' ideology, combined with a 'process' model of curriculum development, has been favoured.[26] Based on seventeenth-century empiricism and a reaction to rationalism (and thus similar to complexity thinking), this model places more value on the processes of learning and the learning experience itself, rather than a specified level of achievement. It therefore resonates well with the ideas of complexity and emergence from self-organizing, adaptive behaviour. Learning occurs through the process of interactions and experiences of the learners. The teacher becomes the 'guide on the side'.

Beattie[27] attempts to reconcile the two models in Figure 19.2, which juxtaposes two ideological concepts of knowledge (i.e. external and authoritative versus contextual and local) with the locus of justification for learning (i.e. intrinsic or extrinsic).

Many would say a balanced approach to the curriculum should involve all four elements – but complexity thinking might favour the 'process' approach – with 'minimum specifications' for the educational objectives and learning outcomes. Being too specific in setting learning outcomes may stifle the emergent nature of the teaching process, and although now popular because they are measurable and allow educators to be monitored, it can been argued that if not handled with care, learning outcomes can become a real hindrance.[28]

Nevertheless, a goal for learning is useful for the learner, and certainly the public does expect a certain level of competence in any qualified health professional. How does this progress occur and how do we know that is has occurred?

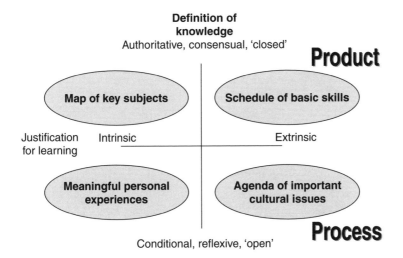

Figure 19.2   Product and process in the curriculum.[27]

Competency, performance and action

Pre-registration education and training has been based on a framework of competencies over recent years, in line with international trends.[29] At qualification, a certain 'minimum competence' is expected and assessed. Thereafter, continued learning is classed as 'continuing professional development', which has gradually become more formalized and effective.[9]

Miller[30] proposed a pyramidal model for competence which has major implications for assessment, in as much as only work-based assessment is likely to test the highest level, i.e. what the health professional actually *does* when seeing a patient when the door is closed. Most other assessment methods, such as multiple-choice questions, simulated cases and objective structured clinical examinations (OSCEs), target lower levels, i.e. what the professional shows they can do in an artificial situation.[31] Miller's hierarchy is shown in Figure 19.3 with two further dimensions, showing how different curricular aspects can be included, and validity in assessment gained by reiteration of the assessment with different patient groups or using different clinical procedures. Assessment of performance is a challenge for all professional groups, but 'capability' is necessary for 'performance' to be translated into 'action'.

The competency approach is reductive since there needs first to be a functional analysis of occupational roles, and the blinkered use of this approach has been criticized in mainstream higher education[33] and in medicine.[34] However, with the health service environment changing so rapidly, and doubt cast upon future professional roles, this functional analysis is now getting more

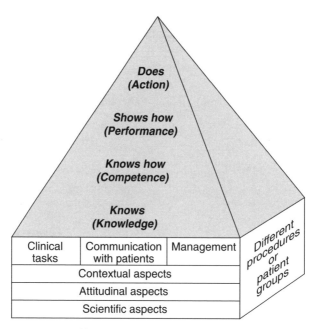

Figure 19.3   Miller's pyramid.[32]

difficult. Redesigning clinical education to reflect changing competency requirements is hard to do quickly due to the inertia in the educational systems, and
educational needs may not be met. So again this supports the notion of educating health professionals to remain adaptable and flexible, and educationally
autonomous.

Insights from complexity theory

Appreciating the complexity of both the educational system and the health service itself, together with an understanding of the implications of complexity
thinking, may help health professionals to cope with the anxiety of new situations and with their performance, and indeed action, in novel situations. The
non-linear nature of progress along the professional's journey, and the implications for learning, are now addressed and closer links made with the notion of
complexity and anxiety.

Non-linearity, anxiety and performance

A complex system may be seen as containing a number of agents which interact
in an unpredictable way. If educational systems are viewed in this way, it is

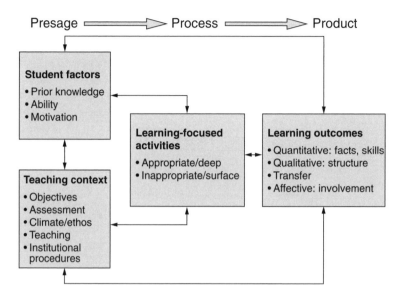

Figure 19.4   The '3P' model of learning and teaching.[35]

evident that trying to change an output, for example a learning outcome of a course, by only changing one aspect of the system may not result in what was intended. A complex four-agent model of teaching and learning has been pro-posed by Biggs[35] (*see* Figure 19.4).

Here each component of the system interacts with the others, and so changes in one area can influence all other parts of the system. Biggs argues for 'construc-tive alignment' of teaching and learning so desired outcomes can be achieved, linking it to a proposition about learning outcomes by Shuell:[36]

> *If students are to learn the desired outcomes in a reasonably effective manner, then the teacher's fundamental task is to get the students to engage in learning activities that are likely to result in their achieving those outcomes.*

Again, a mixture of 'process' and 'product' is suggested and this fits well with the concept in complex systems of having a general aim, but minimum specifi-cations and simple rules. The aim is to engage the learner, and using 'process' factors, enable maximal learning for both student and teacher alike.

Aligning teaching and learning with complexity

Process factors are important in complex systems and mapping the process may help. The Stacey diagram[37] (*see* Chapter 3) may help the reader to visualize

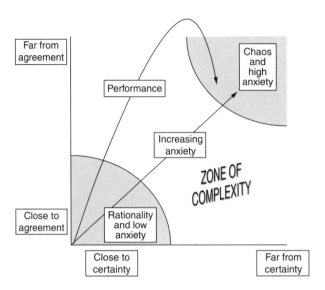

Figure 19.5   Stacey diagram – anxiety and performance.[37]

the transition from order to apparent disorder in a complex system, despite the author's recent rejection of the model. Represented in Figure 19.5, it also shows that *anxiety* (which equates with 'arousal' and also 'stress') increases as progress is made towards the 'edge of chaos'. It is well known that 'performance' of a human (or indeed an organization) increases as arousal and anxiety increase. After a peak, performance falls off rapidly as levels of anxiety and stress increase. This can be mapped onto the Stacey diagram so that the performance curve peaks as the transition into 'chaos' occurs.

The importance for human learning and education is that any individual, group or system will perform – or learn – best in the zone of complexity (peak of performance). Pushed too far, performance and learning will drop rapidly. So what does this mean for teaching and learning?

Teachers and learners need to be encouraged to move away from the safety of the left-hand corner and into the zone of complexity when deep learning may occur. This involves using tools and techniques which increase the opportunity for creativity and innovation, and usually involves a degree of risk taking. Pushed too far, the learning environment may become chaotic and inefficient, but in the 'zone of complexity', non-linear learning is likely to occur.

Non-linear learning

Sometimes a relatively linear course for the achievement of wisdom and capability may be followed, such as a training course to learn a new surgical technique.

Box 19.3 Non-linear learning methods (adapted from Fraser and Green-halgh, 2001[38])

- Case-based discussions, case presentations, significant event analysis
- Simulations, role-play and the use of actors
- Small group work and problem-based learning
- Team-building exercises
- 'Learning in the lay-by' (e.g. the district nurse in the car with the student, reflecting on the last case visited)
- Clinical conversations over coffee or in the lunch queue

However, many situations and methods lend themselves more readily to non-linear learning, i.e. that which occurs at unpredictable rates and times. It generally involves rich interaction, with the opportunity for creativity and innovation, but may occur in the one-to-one situation if the learning experience is powerful enough. Some possibilities are listed in Box 19.3.[38]

Tools and techniques

Various teaching formats may include complexity insights, and many seemingly linear formats may be adapted to allow for self-organization, emergence and creativity. Learning performance should then be maximized, allowing students to get used to novel situations and thus 'more used to the anxiety' in a changing learning environment. Aligning the aim of the education session

Table 19.1 Educational aims and methods[38]

Educational aim	Method
New factual learning	Lecture, symposium, seminar, project
Exploration of issues in depth	Debate seminar, symposium, project, module
Presentation skills	Mini-lecture, micro-teaching, teaching learning group
Communication skills	Micro-teaching using video material or role-play
Problem solving	Problem case analysis, brainstorming, buzz groups, significant event auditing,[39] action learning
Methodology of learning (learning and study skills)	Action learning, teaching–learning group, project learning (library project or dissertation)
Generation of themes and ideas	Open space technology, brainstorming, buzz groups

with the desired outcome may help, and Fraser and Greenhalgh[38] suggest some methods which might be associated with different educational aims (*see* Table 19.1).

Methods such as the formal lecture may seem difficult to 'push' into the zone of complexity, but, for instance, using buzz groups or 'snowballing' during a formal lecture can create an innovative environment and improve learning. Other small group formats, such as those used for problem-based learning,[40,41] are more naturally 'close to the edge of chaos', and usually favour deep and sometimes 'transformative' learning.

Transformative learning

In certain situations, at often unpredictable times, a deeper form of learning known as 'transformative learning' may occur:[42]

> *Transformative learning involves experiencing a deep, structural shift in basic premises of thought, feelings, and actions. It is a shift of consciousness that dramatically and permanently alters our way of being in the world.*

For example, in a significant event analysis meeting of a ward team after a failed resuscitation attempt on a 75-year-old lady, the team realize that in fact the patient had written a 'living will' and had requested not to be resuscitated. The relatives have been very distressed by the event and have requested that this 'never be allowed to happen to anyone else'. The learning for all involved is likely to be deep and, for some, possibly transformative. This holistic, quantum transformation may not happen in a linear way or at a planned time. However, it is again when the learning environment is pushed into the 'zone of complexity' that this is most likely to occur.

Conclusion

This chapter has linked learning theory and models and insights from complexity thinking with the practice of teaching and education. The rapidly changing nature of technology and roles for all health professionals in modern health systems means that teaching and learning must not only be continual and lifelong, but must prepare learners for constantly changing clinical scenarios and working environments. The current and future capabilities of all health professionals need to be identified and used to their most beneficial effect.

Clinical teachers are necessarily part of the complex system that is the classroom or the clinical attachment in practice, and their own insights and attitudes are as important as those of the student. Teaching teachers to be self-aware, self-directed and reflective learners in their own right will enable them to adapt teaching methods and styles as necessary. Both teachers and learners need to be adaptable, and need to develop the capacity for change by exploiting their innate capabilities. 'Complexity' in this context can be seen as both a guide for improving teaching and learning, and as a metaphor for the teaching environment in today's health services.

References

1   Department of Health (2000) *The NHS Plan: a plan for investment, a plan for reform.* HMSO, London.
2   Department of Health (1996) *'In the Patient's Interests': multiprofessional working across organisational boundaries.* NHS Management Executive, Leeds.
3   Department of Health (2001) *A Service of All the Talents: developing the NHS workforce.* HMSO, London.
4   Department of Health (2002) *Liberating the Talents.* HMSO, London.
5   Department of Health (2002) *NHSU – putting learning for everyone at the heart of healthcare.* HMSO, London.
6   Eraut M (1994) *Developing Professional Knowledge and Competence.* Falmer Press, Brighton.
7   Barnett R (1994) *The Limits of Competence: knowledge, higher education and society.* Open University Press, Buckingham.
8   Bandura A (1986) *Social Foundations of Thought and Action: a social cognitive theory.* Prentice Hall, Englewood Cliffs, NJ.
9   Grant J and Stanton F (2000) *The Effectiveness of Continuing Professional Development.* Association for the Study of Medical Education, Edinburgh.
10 Kolb D (1984) *Experiential Learning.* Prentice Hall, Englewood Cliffs, NJ.
11 Dewey J (1938) *Experience and Education.* Collier, New York.
12 Lewin K (1951) *Field Theory in Social Sciences.* Harper-Row, New York.
13 Marton F and Saljo R (1976) On qualitative differences in learning. 1: Outcome and process. *British Journal of Educational Psychology.* **46:** 4–11.
14 Knowles MS (1973) *The Adult Learner: a neglected species.* Gulf, Houston, TX.
15 Merriam SB and Caffarella RS (1999) *Learning in Adulthood* (2e). Jossey-Bass, San Francisco, CA.
16 Spencer JA and Jordan RK (1999) Learner-centred approaches in medical education. *BMJ.* **318:** 1280–3.
17 Kaufman DM, Mann KV and Jennett PA (2000) *Teaching and Learning in Medical Education: how theory can inform practice.* Association for the Study of Medical Education, Edinburgh.
18 Candy PC (1991) *Self-direction for Lifelong Learning: a comprehensive guide to theory and practice.* Jossey-Bass, San Francisco, CA.
19 Gugliemino LM (1977) *Development of the Self-directed Learning Readiness Scale.* Unpublished thesis. University of Georgia, Athens, GA.
20 Oddi LF (1986) Development and validation of an instrument to identify self-directed continuing learners. *Adult Education Quarterly.* **36 (2):** 97–107.

21   Schön D (1983) *The Reflective Practitioner: how professionals think in action*. Temple Smith, London.
22   British Association of Medical Managers (1999) *Appraisal in Action*. BAMM, Stockport.
23   Department of Health (2002) *Annual Appraisal of General Practitioners in the NHS* (letter from Chief Medical Officer, 1 March) and www.doh.gov.uk/gpappraisal/ (accessed 20 March 2003).
24   Prideaux D (2003) Curriculum design. *BMJ*. **326**: 268–70.
25   Tyler RW (1949) *Basic Principles of Curriculum and Instruction*. Chicago University Press, Chicago, IL.
26   Stenhouse L (1975) *An Introduction to Curriculum Research and Development*. Heinemann, London.
27   Beattie A (1987) Making a curriculum work. In: Allan P and Jolly M (eds) *The Curriculum in Nursing Education*. Croom Helm, London.
28   Hussey T and Smith P (2002) The trouble with learning outcomes. *Active Learning in Higher Education*. **3 (3)**: 220–34.
29   Department of Education (1986) *Working Together: education and training*. HMSO, London.
30   Miller GE (1990) The assessment of clinical skills/competence/performance. *Academic Medicine*. **65**: 563–7.
31   Norcini JJ (2003) Work-based assessment. *BMJ*. **326**: 753–5.
32   Ram P (1998) *Comprehensive Assessment of General Practitioners: a study on validity, reliability and feasibility*. Thesis. Maastricht University, Maastricht, The Netherlands.
33   Hyland T (1994) *Competence, Education and NVQs: dissenting perspectives*. Cassell, London.
34   Leung W-C (2002) Competency-based medical training: review. *BMJ*. **325**: 693–5.
35   Biggs J (1993) What do inventories of students' learning processes really measure? A theoretical review and clarification. *British Journal of Educational Psychology*. **63**: 1–17.
36   Shuell TJ (1986) Cognitive conceptions of learning. *Review of Educational Research*. **56**: 411–36.
37   Stacey R (1996) *Strategic Management and Organisational Dynamics*. Pitman Publishing, London.
38   Fraser SW and Greenhalgh T (2001) Coping with complexity: educating for capability. *BMJ*. **323**: 799–803.
39   Pringle M, Bradley CP, Carmichael CM *et al*. (1995) *Significant Event Auditing: a study of the feasibility and potential of case-based auditing in primary medical care*. RCGP Occasional Paper No. 70. Royal College of General Practitioners, London.
40   Bligh J (1995) Problem-based, small group learning. *BMJ*. **311**: 342–3.
41   Wood D (2003) Problem-based learning. *BMJ*. **326**: 328–30.
42   Transformative Learning Centre (2003) www.oise.utoronto.ca/~tlcentre/index.htm (accessed 25 Feb 2003).

Going on together in organizations: perspectives on whole systems

Introduction

Organizations have been studied using the model of an interacting network before complexity theory was developed. From a sociological perspective, social networks have been seen as providing efficient systems for processing, interpreting and storing information, shaping identity, and mobilizing resources for joint action. The concept of community implies that people's behaviour is embedded in ongoing systems of social relations and their well-being is influenced by their interactions with others.[1] The economic perspective sees the co-ordination of productive activities through a network of informal mechanisms within a market rather than the bureaucratic directives of an organizational hierarchy or a set of negotiated contractual regulations.[2] In this way, the costs of undertaking transactions (costs related to the exchange of goods and services rather than their production) are reduced.

However, these discourses see organizations as complicated systems where what each of the parts will do in response to a given stimulus can be predicted. As we have seen, the contribution of complexity theory is the appreciation of network features due to the non-linear interaction between component parts and, in particular, how unpredictable patterns emerge that satisfy the constraints placed upon a system through the process of self-organization. In this section we look at perspectives that help with our understanding of whole systems and our sense making within them.

Chapter 20 develops the concept of social capital. This emphasizes the social perspective of complexity and how benefits emerge from the interactions that we have with each other. Tim Wilson draws the links between social capital, community networks and complexity and suggests how this concept can be used within the context of improving health. Unfortunately, the social and professional networks of trust and the norms of reciprocity that characterize the NHS have been neglected during the years of organizational change. Although recent health service planning has attempted to address physical and human elements through good employment practices, the importance of social capital remains overlooked.

In Chapter 21, Alasdair Honeyman explores the concept of communities of practice. This refers to a description of relating that occurs through particular activities or practices undertaken by a group of people that facilitates their sharing of knowledge and negotiating of meaning amongst them. The emphasis is on the importance of implicit knowledge as the primary source of an organization's innovative potential.[3] Communities of practice are seen as appropriate social structures suitable for developing and sharing knowledge in the organization and consist of three structural elements:[4] *domain* – for example, knowhow or highly specialized professional expertise; *community* – the environment in which people interact, learn and build relationships; and *practice* – the set of ideas, tools and documents that they share. An important feature is the development of design elements that can be of assistance in supporting participation against a background of understanding. What emerges is a product of both the design and the participatory process that is owned and enacted by the group itself.

It has been suggested that the failure of NHS collaboratives to deliver their anticipated benefits has been their focus on data and information within a framework of rules, regulations and reporting activities rather than the development of knowledge or wisdom that occurs in communities of practice.[5] Alasdair argues that the concept of communities of practice has always sat within a political domain, but can offer a valuable support to the activity in the healthcare domain where the negotiation of meaning is rich, omnipresent and crosses many boundaries.

Finally, in Chapter 22, Will Medd rather spoils the party, arguing that a holistic perspective is at best a romantic dream. Taking as his example partnership working, he suggests that although it may be helpful to explore 'whole-systems thinking', the importance lies in the detail and examining how and where the emergent partnership is located. The conclusion is that the focus should be on the local constitution of partnerships, which requires reflexive considerations of one's own responsibilities and possibilities.

References

1   Thompson G (1991) *Markets, Hierarchies and Networks: the co-ordination of social life*. Sage, London.

2   Robinson R (2002) Transaction cost economics. In: Kernick D (ed) *Getting Health Economics into Practice*, pp. 79–87. Radcliffe Medical Press, Oxford.
3   Wenger E (1998) *Communities of Practice*. Cambridge University Press, Cambridge.
4   Wenger E, McDermot R and Synder W (2002) *Cultivating Communities of Practice*. Harvard Business School Press, Boston, MA.
5   Bate S and Robert G (2002) Knowledge management and communities of practice in the private sector: lessons for modernising the NHS in England and Wales. *Public Administration*. **80 (4):** 643–63.

CHAPTER 20

Social networks in organizations: social capital and health

Tim Wilson

Tim Wilson is a GP and policy analyst for the Department of Health. The views expressed in this chapter are his own.

Social networks in organizations: social capital and health

Social capital is a concept that is highly topical, especially with policy leads in the government. This chapter explores what social capital means and highlights how it may reflect a means of making sense of complex responsive processes at a community level. Whilst it has limitations because of its deconstruction of relationships into measurable values, it also offers a glimpse of how complex systems, like communities could be influenced.

Key points
- Capital is the name given to an asset that can generate changes in structure, process or outcome that yields a stream of benefits over time.
- Social capital is the institutions, relationships and norms that shape the quality and quantity of a society's social interactions.
- Social capital is measured for descriptive and prescriptive purposes. One of the most common measures is the degree of trust in society.
- Social capital could be a mechanism for making sense of the sum total effect of relationships in particular communities.
- There are distinct limitations to the concept of social capital; it applies linear, Cartesian thinking to something complex and tries to make predictions of something that may be unpredictable.
- There is a statistical association between social networks, measured in terms of capital and aspects of community life, including crime, employment, education and health.

> - There are mechanisms by which social networks can be influenced. These might reflect the means by which complex responsive processes in communities can be influenced.

Introduction

There is no such thing as society.
(Margaret Thatcher, *Women's Own*, November 1987)

Why is it that some areas are good to live in and some not so? Apart from environmental factors, the network of relationships you have with others is important. How well you get on with your neighbours; who was there to help when an elderly woman had to go into hospital, leaving her disabled husband at home; can you leave your car unlocked for a few minutes whilst you pop into the shop? This chapter explores how and why these social networks influence health, and the means by which they might be influenced.

Capital is the name given to the elements of a system that can generate changes in structure, process or outcome that will yield a stream of benefits with time. Within any organization, community or society, it is possible to consider six capital groups:

- *physical capital* – the buildings, equipment and concrete things within society and organizations
- *financial capital* – the ability to fund, acquire or invest
- *natural capital* – air, water and other natural resources
- *human capital* – the individual people that work within the community, their skills and knowledge
- *cultural capital*, including ethnic culture – the cultural aspects of a community
- *social capital* – the value or worth of the relationships between people in organizations, communities and localities.

Many would argue that social is the most important capital dimension; what happens between people is more important than with any individual, or building. Margaret Thatcher was certainly wrong; there is such a thing as society. Indeed, the totality of the relationships or interconnections making up social capital creates what might be termed, for the purposes of this chapter at least, society.

It is the relationships between people that create complex adaptive systems, and at a local level complex responsive processes.[1] We exist within family groups, work teams, groups of friends, organizations, travellers sharing a train journey, communities, neighbourhoods, towns, countries, and more. It is impossible to disentangle these different existences as they are all part of the same network (your colleague might be your friend, might live in your area, might be the mother of your daughter's best friend, might be your ex-lover . . .). Indeed, because the intertwining relationships that build these networks create complex systems, some would argue there is no such thing as an organization as an entity – we are all interconnected. If on average we have 300 or so acquaintances, then we are only three handshakes away from 27 000 000 others.*

Networks of family, friends and acquaintances will have many characteristics. The characteristics one person attributes to any network will very likely differ from another person's attribution, even in the process of attribution the nature of the network changes. The characteristics, and those that matter to you of a network around you, determine how you perceive your own part of that society. It is of course connected to the rest of the social network, but will have local *flavour*. If some *worth* is put to that flavour, it might be termed 'social capital'. The World Bank defines social capital as '. . . relationships . . . that shape the quality and quantity of a society's social interactions' (see www.worldbank.org/pverty/scapital/).

Many readers will blanch at the idea that a complex system such as a societal grouping has a tangible capital that arises from a network of interactions, and might doubt that this network could be influenced. I argue that such systems can be influenced, and that the results are unpredictable but boundable. Chapter 23 illustrates how developing capital by working with community social networks can transform health and well-being in addition to building physical, environmental and human capital.

Developing the concept of social capital

The most popular description of social capital comes from Robert Putnam in his book *Bowling Alone*.[2] In it he identified the decline of social fabric in the US, one marker of which was the increasing number of people ten-pin bowling in the US alone. He described the TV screen provided in alleyways for the lone bowler, as opposed to interacting with their neighbouring bowlers. Putman defines social capital in terms of four characteristics:

---

* *The five degrees of separation.* In order to decide how connected people were within society, psychologist Stanley Miligram gave participants in a number of US states each a package with a name and vague details (such as occupation, age and vague whereabouts). It did not have the full address on however. The participants were asked to pass the package onto a person that they thought might know the recipient. In almost every case the parcel was delivered through five or six intermediaries. That is, the first person was connected to the recipient through five or six other people.

- the existence of community networks
- civic engagement (participation in these networks)
- local identity and a sense of solidarity and equality with other community members
- norms of trust, reciprocal help and support.

A complementary perspective on social capital is:

- social networks – who knows who
- social norms – the formal and, more importantly, informal rules that guide how people behave
- sanctions – the formal and again, important, informal processes that ensure network members keep to the rules.

The assertion is that there is worth in communities and that the worth of social capital translates into many benefits. Putnam[2] used his measurements of social capital to show links between the measured amount of social capital (as opposed to the financial or physical state of communities) and a number of variables. By using multivariant analysis, he found that those who had higher social capital had lower rates of violent crime, were happier, had better school attainment, were wealthier and were more likely to pay their taxes.

Some of the measures of social capital used are shown in Box 20.1. An alternative approach is to use trust as a single, simple measure of capital.[3]

These measures have been criticized for their Cartesian, mechanistic and linear approach in a system that is highly complex. However, Putnam[2] realized that without using the right language, those with the power (political and financial) to help support communities would probably dismiss the concept, and the use of the term 'capital', with its financial connotations, was probably deliberate. (It is notable that the new Labour Government has held a number of seminars with Robert Putnam and that social capital provides a focus for health development in the Health Development Agency's paper *Social Capital for*

Box 20.1   Measuring social capital – examples used by Putnam[2]

- Community organizational life (e.g. serving on committees, club meeting attendance, number of local organizations)
- Engagement in public affairs (e.g. election turnout)
- Community volunteerism
- Informal sociability (survey responses to 'I spent a lot of time with my friends')
- Social trust (survey response to 'Most people can be trusted')

Health.[4]) It also highlights the potential to make a trade-off between financial, physical, human and social capital (especially when making choices).

Complex systems, social networks and social capital

Social capital is a means of measuring something within social networks or communities. However, the reification of a complex system such as a community to measure something like capital must lose meaning and sense in its process. Unarguably the measures used are oversimplistic and have a number of limitations:

- It is impossible to measure everything at once.
- The act of measurement distorts what is measured.
- Numbers can never convey real meaning.
- The interconnectedness of systems means it is impossible to compare the social capital of one part of the system with another. However, there will be local *nuances* and local *flavour*. One neighbourhood might be described as 'rough', one street as 'desirable', one town as being 'a great place to live'. In coming to these subjective decisions many factors are taken into consideration. But in the end it is a feeling.

However, if we accept these limitations and that we sometimes need to make sense of complexity to aid understanding, then these measures have utility. If social networks are a means of describing complex systems and social capital is a mechanism to measure social networks, we can begin to guess at how complex systems working at a community level affect health and how they might be influenced.

Does the level of social capital influence health?

It is accepted that health is determined only in small part by healthcare.[5] Trust and reciprocity within society have many advantages that include a more vibrant economy, effective labour markets, educational attainment, lower levels of crime, better government and better health.[6]

The connection between health and social capital was first demonstrated in the late nineteenth century by Durkheim, who showed that involvement and support led to lower suicide rates.[7] This evidence base has grown over the last ten years. For example, cardiovascular disease is less likely,[8] as are other aspects of disease.[9,10] Bonding, as a function of higher social capital, certainly seems to reduce depression and suicide.[11] Survival rates from major surgery or illness are predicted by marital status and presence of close relationships, and even the simple act of confiding has a positive effect on the immune system.[12,13] Figure 20.1 shows how survival of a heart attack is improved by the level of emotional support.

There is some speculation that social capital may protect more deprived populations, acting as a buffer,[14] whilst others have suggested that it is the impact of social capital on stress reduction.[9]

An important element of social capital for the generation of health is goodwill or altruism. Indeed, much of the health and social care system depends on altruism, most notably the vast input of carers. If they were to withdraw their multi-billion pound contribution to care, the health and social system would collapse. In Japanese society it is accepted practice to care for elderly relatives. However, in Sweden the opposite is true, but there is general agreement that taxation will fund proper care for the elderly. These are gross generalizations, and no doubt there are changes occurring in these countries (because of trends in neighbouring and connected societies). Even with these caveats, it is clear that there is some social decision to care for the elderly. There is capital in the caring system through accepted funding by taxation or direct care by relatives.

Lastly, every physician will recognize the phrase 'I didn't want to bother the doctor'. The truth is that the NHS, and all healthcare systems around the world, would collapse if everyone came with every ailment for which they had a need. Some element of social capital, reflecting the 'our NHS' sentiment, means that many patients, rightly or wrongly, avoid burdening the health system.

However, social capital may not always be beneficial. The 'accepted cultures' within social groups can continue to promote unhealthy activities like smoking, drug abuse, alcoholism, betel-nut chewing and sedentary lifestyles. Further, some groupings in society can work together to exclude others (see, for instance, the experience of the Oregon experiment where certain conditions like human immunodeficiency virus [HIV] were excluded).[15] This could also work at local levels with patient forums and other public involvement programmes.

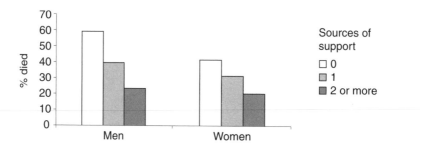

Figure 20.1   Six-month survival after heart attack, by level of emotional support.

Increasing levels of social capital to improve health

Managing complex systems is impossible. It is only possible to create the environment in which the desired outcomes may flourish, and even then untoward effects may occur. However, there are ways in which the healthcare organizations can interact with communities in an attempt to influence levels of social capital and with it the improvement of health. Examples from four areas are considered in this final section.

Building individual links towards greater social capital

Here the emphasis is on facilitating communication and feedback in complex systems. For example:

- Expert patients and mentoring – the notion that patients will support each other, either as an expert or through a mentoring process, is already underway in the NHS. It is proving to be an effective mechanism for education and helping people take greater control of their own health and illness.
- Educational input – working with the public, especially at school age, can be a mechanism to encourage them to help and support each other in times of illness. It can also be used for highly specific issues like first aid and basic resuscitation skills. The efficacy of this is uncertain.
- Group visits – many practices are now encouraging patients to attend in groups. The group dynamics create powerful and generally positive effects on health outcomes and utilization.
- Sure Start – this scheme, designed to help in the early years of motherhood, equips mothers with the means for better social skills. Its effect on social capital is uncertain.
- Volunteering – many local volunteer groups already exist, some with a formal structure (like the Women's Royal Voluntary Service [WRVS]) and others more informally based. The services can vary between running a canteen, offering a car service and sometimes a sitting service, giving carers a break. These undoubtedly improve social capital and can create large amounts of goodwill.
- Information technology networks – much has been made of the possibility of the internet and email in building social capital. Where this replaces face-to-face meetings it probably reduces capital. However, as an additional mechanism, especially for the housebound or distantly connected, it can build social capital and have large health benefits.

Building local communities or environments towards greater social capital

Health action zones, healthy communities and active communities are all ways in which entire communities can be engaged in developing networks with beneficial health outcomes. Their benefits are very variable. There are a number of examples of these, one of which is discussed in detail in Chapter 23.

Working with official policy channels towards greater social capital

Community health councils, variously successful in representing their constituents, are set to disappear and new bodies (including oversight committees, patients forums and PALS*) are being put in their place. The effect these official mechanisms will have on the ways in which healthcare organizations interact with communities and building social capital is unpredictable. It is quite possible their impact will be negligible, although that does not reduce either their symbolic function, utility or impact on health service design. One twist on this tale is the introduction of foundation trusts, owned and run by a board of local governors. This experiment has many potentials, or may have a limited impact on social capital.

Accountability and trust and social capital

Trust is a key measure of social capital, but the current emphasis in modern health care systems is on accountability. This takes place both through the public disclosure of performance data (for example, see www.drfoster.org) and performance league tables and star rating systems. Most importantly, the soon to be reformed Commission for Healthcare Audit and Inspection (CHAI) will inspect every part of the NHS and private healthcare, review the quality of patient care and how well the NHS is using its funds, and produce an annual report to Parliament on the state of the NHS.

In the recent Reith lectures, Anora O'Neill explored our new age of accountability. She examined the evidence that supports the hypothesis that greater accountability improves care and increases trust, but concluded the opposite. Increasing reliance on measurement reduces trust in health (and other public) services and it was suggested that professionals and public servants should be free to serve the public.[16] Trust, strongly correlated with the strength of social capital, would fail with current accountability mechanisms, with consequent disadvantages to the healthcare system.

---

* PALS = patient advisory liaison service.

Conclusions

For many, the mechanistic approach of measuring and determining social capital will be antithetical to their thinking about complex systems. I have argued that there are links between the concept of social capital, community networks and so complexity. Health is in large part determined by the state of the networks and how they behave. Although healthcare is not the only influence on the health of a community, healthcare organizations can engage with the community networks (they are, after all, part of that community) and attempt to influence them by building the asset base of social capital.

Finally, in attempting to build social capital through engaging with their communities, healthcare organizations could follow these principles:

1. Meet face to face with your community (not just their representatives).
2. Ensure those meetings have meaning, so:
   - a healthcare person with power must be there (e.g. chief executive or empowered deputy)
   - listen to what the community says
   - listen to what they want (it may not be the same as you)
   - pay attention to hygiene (seating, what people want to be called, language, time of meeting).
3. Do what the community wants, even if it conflicts with your own plans.
4. Engage with local opinion leaders and help them facilitate improvement.
5. Use volunteering.
6. Develop local people.
7. Delegate power to them.
8. Allow mistakes.
9. Help build places (real and virtual) where people can engage with each other.
10. Promote and support people's ability to care for themselves and, more importantly, each other.

References

1. Stacey R (2001) *Complex Responsive Processes in Organizations*. Routledge, London.
2. Putnam R (2000) *Bowling Alone*. Simon and Schuster, New York.
3. Norris P (2000) *Making Democracy Work: social capita and civic engagement in 47 societies*. Paper for the European Science Foundation Conference on Social Capital, Exeter, September 2000.
4. Swann C and Morgan A (2002) *Social Capital for Health: insights from qualitative research*. Health Development Agency, London.

5 Marmot M (1999) *Social Determinants of Health*. Oxford University Press, Oxford.
6 Aldridge S, Halper D and Fitspatrick S (2002) *Social Capital*. Discussion paper, April 2002. Performance and Innovation Unit of Cabinet Office, London.
7 Durkheim E (1893) *The Division of Labor in Society*. Republished 1984. Free Press, New York.
8 Kawachi I (1996) A prospective study of social networks in relation to total mortality and cardiovascular disease. *Journal of Epidemiology and Community Health*. **50**: 245–91.
9 Wilkinson RG (1997) *Unhealthy Societies: the afflictions of inequalities*. Routledge, London.
10 Kawachi I, Kennedy BP, Lochner K and Prothrow-Stith D (1997) Social capital, income equality, and mortality. *American Journal of Public Health*. **89 (9):** 1491–8.
11 Brown G and Harris T (1998) *Social Origins of Depression*. Tavistock, London.
12 Berkman LF and Glass T (2000) Social integration, social networks, social support and health. In: Berkman L and Kawachi I (eds) *Social Epidemiology*. Oxford University Press, Oxford.
13 Kennedy S, Kiecolt-Glaser JK and Glaser R (1990) Social support, stress and the immune system. In: Sarason I, Sarason B and Pierce G (eds) *Social Support: an interactional view*. John Wiley, Chichester.
14 Campbell C, Wood R and Kelly M (1999) *Social Capital and Health*. Health Education Authority, London.
15 United States Office of Technology Assessment (1992) *Evaluation of the Oregon Medicaid Proposal*. Washington, DC.
16 O'Neill A (2002) *Called to Account. A Question of Trust*. Reith lectures. Lecture three. Available at www.bbc.co.uk/radio4/reith2002 (accessed August 2003).

CHAPTER 21

Organization and communities of practice

Alasdair Honeyman

In this chapter I offer an introduction to the ideas of communities of practice. This is followed by a brief historical example which explores the politics of information sharing and sense making. I follow with background in theories of learning and finally I discuss how ideas of communities of practice may be valuable in supporting the richness of activity in the healthcare domain, where the negotiation of meaning is rich, omnipresent and crosses many boundaries.

Key points

- Communities of practice offer a valuable language for thinking about ways that sense making occurs amongst people.
- The politics of information control is as significant and as hot an issue as it was with the invention of the printing press.
- Theories of learning have their historical precedents in the history of understanding about the mind and the brain. Increasingly, sense making is understood to be informed by our interaction with the world around us – this impacts on our contemporary thinking about learning being social and situated.
- With the increasing complexity of healthcare provision, there are ever-increasing numbers of active communities seeking to optimize their own domain of expertise. This includes communities that are disease-specific and belong as much to patients as to professionals.
- The skills required in crossing the boundaries between and amongst communities are considerable.
- These communities do not follow the formal structures of healthcare organizations and some are more tribal than others.
- Patient communities are here to stay and will be a valuable resource for us and them in the future.

What are communities of practice?

The ideas encompassed within the model of communities of practice[1] offer a way of thinking about significant design issues that impact on the way information is shared amongst people engaged in a particular activity or activities. The boundaries of a community are determined by the nature of the practices of its members, and may extend and impact across many constellations of people both within and across organizations. Communities of practice encompass a developmental approach to the formation of identity, which is grounded in the sharing and negotiation of meaning amongst people. It is influenced by ideas of apprenticeship[2] and builds on Bandura's description of the dynamic interaction between our cognition, behaviour and environment in a social cognitive theory of learning.[3]

In communities of practice there is an interest in thinking about design elements that can be of assistance in supporting participation. This is with the understanding that what emerges as an outcome is a product of both the design and the participatory process and is owned and enacted by the practice group itself. In addition, any successful learning and change is predicated on a healthy ecology of information sharing and sense making amongst the people in the community.

Wenger's background in artificial intelligence[4] is significant in understanding the genesis of his ideas. With the advent of digital information storage and the ubiquity of its access via the World Wide Web, much information may now be technically seen as a public good. Questions still remain, however, about what the information means and for whom.

Wenger offers a useful way of looking at the creation of meaning. He describes it as including the paradoxical components of participation and reification. Participation describes the social experience of being together through which meaning is negotiated. Reification describes both the creation and use of artefacts that are endowed with that meaning and around which meaning is also negotiated. This could include a schedule of work as well as the work practices that have developed amongst people using the schedule. Reified health information may be read by a patient from an internet site or shared as folklore handed down between family members. 'Bush tea' UK comes up quite often in my consultations and 300 times on a Google search. As 'Bush tea' Jamaica it comes up 150 times. It doesn't appear at all in a search on the electronic Library for Health. Additional sense making may then occur through the renegotiation of its meaning via some participatory process with a health professional. Making sense of this chapter and the others in this book could grow and change if you spent time talking to its authors or discussing it with others online or face to face. Being part of a community of practice requires attention to both the nature of participation amongst people and the ways in which meaning is reified.

Knowledge as power – an early tale

In 1476, Willian Caxton set up the first printing press in England. This was in the precincts of Westminster Abbey. Fifty years later William Tyndale translated the Bible into English. The translation and the printing of the Bible were both done in secret and out of England. It was a dangerous activity Tyndale was undertaking. This was because the early 1500s were the time of the reformation with immense power struggles between the Catholic church and the reformers across northern Europe. Tyndale's argument and that of other reformers such as Luther, Calvin and Knox was that the authority of the Bible was independent of the authority of the Catholic church. The existence of a Bible that common people could read and interpret themselves had significant repercussions for the power of the church and the state. In England the only Bible available was one in Latin. The church was so concerned that they had Tyndale's translation prohibited by King Henry VIII. Tyndale was eventually betrayed, found guilty of heresy and finally burnt at the stake in 1536.

Henry VIII's first wife was Catherine of Aragon. She failed to produce an heir for him and from 1530 Henry tried to secure the Pope's permission to divorce her so he could marry Anne Boleyn. Anne was his dead brother's wife. Pregnancy intervened and he married Anne without waiting for papal approval. The Pope finally ruled against Henry and refused to annul his marriage to Catherine. Consequently, in 1534 by the Act of Royal Supremacy, Henry took over the church himself. The question remained about how to then mark or brand the church as his own. Notwithstanding the recent death of its translator two years previously, the presence of an English version of the Bible could not have been more serendipitous and by 1538 all churches were obliged to have an English version. Until this time the dialects of English were virtually incomprehensible to each other. The advent of an English Bible written in south-eastern English led to a diffusion of that way of speaking throughout the country.

A potted history such as this does not give credit to the richness of the history of this time. However, it does give an important flavour to understanding the significant ways in which meaning is negotiated and the power that appears to reign in its reification. Retrospection offers tantalizing explanations for cause and effect, although how true they can be is hard to delineate. It is unlikely that the consequences of the English Bible were particularly thought through, let alone predicted by the King, his ministers or the church. The contemporary ownership, control and manipulation of meaning was as central to the politics of change then as it is today. Politicking in healthcare in the UK is perhaps not as violent as 500 years ago. Some do, however, argue that we are yet to be freed from an NHS whose organizational form remains feudal in nature.[5]

Five hundred years ago, people had a very different sense of identity and agency from now.[6] The mysteries of the soul held sway over our understanding of ourselves, Descartes (1596–1650) hadn't made his exploration of the relationship between body and mind, and Locke (1632–1704) had yet to argue in *An Essay Concerning Human Understanding* for empiricism, the philosophical doctrine that regards experience as the only source of knowledge. These artefacts of making sense from the past still have an impact on our sense making today. This has been particularly significant in our sense making about learning.

Theories about learning

Theories of learning have traditionally been the province of psychology and have tended to focus on the individual. They can be divided into three categories: behaviourist, cognitive and constructivist. I shall examine each of these briefly followed by a description of social theories of learning as they relate to communities of practice.

The behaviourists built on Locke's empiricism and the ideas of the blank slate. Their preoccupation was with the manipulation of the environment as a way to alter animals' or people's actions. To them the inner workings of the brain were a black box and the contents of the mind such as beliefs and feelings were of no interest. The learner was a passive recipient of the learning that was 'fed' to them. Famously, John Watson (1878–1958) wrote 'give me a dozen healthy infants and I will guarantee to take any one at random and train him to become any type of specialist I might select – doctor, lawyer, artist, merchant-chief and, yes, even beggar-man and thief, regardless of his talents, tendencies and race of his ancestors'.[7]

The cognitive approach to the mind has similarities with ideas of digital information processing in that it is concerned with symbolic representations, rule manipulation and modification of information. It encompasses a computational systems-based and empiricist view of the mind with an increasingly sophisticated understanding of language and of memory. A leading theorist on working memory is Alan Baddely.[8] He describes the mind as having a central executive which co-ordinates information from different sources, directs the ability to focus and switch attention, and organizes incoming material and the retrieval of old memories through a phonological loop or slave system. This way of speaking invokes the 'dogma of the ghost in the machine', Gilbert Ryle's recapitulation of the dualism of body and mind.[9] Instructional design theories have relied considerably on the cognitivist attention to issues of memorization, understanding and application and have many valuable applications. In decision support systems, the number of choices offered is generally not more than seven because this is the number that people can hold in their short-term memory (the phonological loop).

Constructivists argue that knowledge resides in the individual and is an emerging characteristic of activities taking place amongst people in specific contexts. Meaning is determined by the learner. It is constructed by them; there is no knowledge independent of the meaning attributed to experience 'constructed' by the learner. Jonassen *et al.*[10] neatly summarize the tenets of the constructivist instructional design: multiple representations of reality are provided thereby helping represent the natural complexity of the real world. Attention is given to the construction of knowledge rather than its reproduction. Authentic contextualizing tasks are offered rather than abstracting instruction with real-world, case-based learning architectures rather than predetermined instructional sequences. These foster reflective practice which encourages context-dependent and content-dependent knowledge construction for the learner.

Social and situated theories of learning

Interest in the environment in which learning occurs is condensed in theories of social and situated learning. These offer a view of how human knowledge develops in the course of activity (what Wenger would call practice[1]), and how people together make collective sense of what they are doing. Human knowledge is viewed as a capacity to co-ordinate and sequence behaviour with which to adapt dynamically to a changing environment. In contrast to cognitivist models of internal representation, schemas and memory processing, in situated learning knowledge is treated as an analytic abstraction like energy. Learning is understood as 'a process of conceiving and enacting an activity', that activities are inherently social and that this puts the emphasis on addressing issues of membership, participation and identity. This then frames identity of an individual in a paradoxical way. To use Elias' words,[11] 'the concept individual refers to interdependent people in the singular and the concept of society to interdependent people in the plural'. Communities of practice offer one way of attending to the generic patterning of information sharing and sense making that occurs amongst interdependent people.

What of healthcare and communities of practice?

Primary care in the UK brings with it an interesting discipline of thinking about the negotiation of meaning between the doctor and the patient. This is embodied in a tradition of working and apprenticeship that spans the last 40 years. The domain of the patient's story meets that of the primary care clinician's expertise in a biopsychosocial model of health and well-being. Between them, a new story can be woven together, incorporating the strengths and weakness of both domains in a way that is hopefully satisfactory for both parties.

The reification of the patient's medical story in primary care is now manifest as a digital electronic record. The presence and sharing of this record in the consultation brings a third historical party into the consulting room. Ryle's[9] ghost in the machine has been subsumed by the 'historical' patient in the machine.

A community of practice could refer to people engaged in providing care but what about people who are receiving it? Imagine that the patient in front of you has a rare rheumatological disorder and also happens to be a member of a community that includes people from all over the world with the same condition. They have a website that someone maintains and a discussion list for all those who choose to be more active participants. They notice when people aren't around (James has not posted for a couple of weeks, is he ill again?) and they have a detailed knowledge of each other's healthcare systems, including the personalities of the people who look after them. A fellow sufferer in Australia has recently discovered a novel can-opener design that was invented by a resourceful physiotherapist in the hospital he attends and your patient asks you if he might have the contact details for the occupational therapists so he can send them one. In addition, he knows of a new treatment that is being offered in the US but felt patronized by the specialist he had seen recently, who did not want to discuss it even though he had kindly sent the specialist the web address and details of recent scientific papers. He has another colleague who speaks glowingly of another consultant at Saint Elsewhere's and was wondering if you could possibly refer him there. He also wants to know why NICE has not published their opinion on the value of the new drug X in the UK. This anecdote is made up of a collection of different conversations. Amongst an increasingly sophisticated population, these sorts of narrative are becoming more common. The knowledge exists not just in the expert patient, but in the collective voice of shared understanding amongst people with that condition as well as amongst the people whose task it is to look after them.

The health informatics community

The advent of the internet has revolutionized the possibilities for the sharing of information and the negotiation of its meaning amongst people who are distributed geographically, be it locally across GP practices in a primary care trust, in a particular city, across a country or around the world. Each specialism and sub-specialism has its multiple collaborative environments both as formal academic journals, conferences, meetings, newsletters, websites, discussion lists and web portals.

Health informatics is becoming a sub-speciality all of its own. It provides a valuable example of the significance of having people who can cross the boundaries between domains of expertise. Over the last 20 years, primary care healthcare information systems arose out of the enthusiasm of amateur programmers, who also happened to be general practitioners. Their number in primary care and enthusiasm was sufficient to swell the number of systems available up to 300 at one point. Multiple communities now exist for information system users and providers, academics and people involved in local data quality initiatives and system maintenance and development. These people are often embedded in these activities at many different levels. A GP may be a user of one of the systems, write academic papers about their use, and facilitate the local uptake of data quality initiatives or be involved at a national level politically. These people are valuable because of their local understanding and the sense they can make of it at many other levels. They have the personal and social resources to be able to improvise with others about how they might do things differently. They can both imagine and invent what the future might look like within their domains of expertise. Innovations in activity are bounded by the collective knowledge that exists amongst the people in the community who are creating it. Recreating that knowledge with another group of people may very possibly create a different result. The distribution of information about how to do things is not the same as the distribution of knowledge. The map is not the same as the territory.

It is important to think about the creation and support of communities. This is not done in a vacuum. There is no *tabula rasa* of community virgins waiting to join. There is considerable organizing of relationships already within and between the tribes of carers, administrators, managers, nurses, technicians, doctors and ancillary staff. Unless careful attention is given to the nature of relationships that already exist, community technologies and designs are unlikely to take root. Developing communities is resource intensive and complex, requiring a sophisticated understanding of, and relationship with, the people whom you are hoping to support. A youthful and enthusiastic person may be employed by the Modernisation Agency as an agent of change. They might find that despite their training and new found skills, they are party to political infighting, most of which they are not privy to, but which invisibly leads them into the labyrinths of people's personal vendettas and power struggles, rather than the apparent task of trying to improve a service. The ideas encapsulated in communities of practice, while strong on the structural design issues of the ecologies of communities, tend not to address the subtleties and pathologies of group relations, to which none of us are immune.

The healthcare environment attempts to contain considerable amounts of human distress. It is well accepted that healthy mechanisms need to be found for dealing with this if it is not going to impinge on the rest of our professional and personal lives. When there is much at stake, as in healthcare, it is no surprise that the negotiation of what needs to be done and how to do it in an organization such as the NHS can be fraught. The modernist agenda, and the ideologies of change which are predicated on a diet of positivism and the power of science and technology, may not account for the complexities of human relating whose co-evolution is not as fast as the science and technology the human race has been inventing.[12]

Live versus hypothetical communities

The discipline of the formal learning environment is far away from the hurly-burly and the pain and suffering of which day-to-day healthcare is a part. Invoking a rosy, cosy community where people are going to freely trust in sharing their knowledge and their ignorance is unlikely to succeed without considerable skill being offered in attending to the people who are doing the work. The body of people with the requisite skills required to attend successfully to the patterning of relations amongst clinicians and managers, for instance, will take a long time to develop. By the nature of its practice, and the nurturing of skills in primary care groups and primary care trusts, people working in primary care may have a head start.

One of the consequences of William Tyndale translating the Bible into English was his own demise. The risks of making information more accessible and understandable are less dangerous in the twenty-first century. Nonetheless, the renegotiation of power and responsibility across boundaries of expertise can instil considerable feelings of threat to people's professional and personal identities. The attendant sequelae will be familiar to many on a day-to-day basis.

The skill in supporting the negotiation of meaning amongst people, which is sensitive to the constraints and subtleties of human relating, is significant. Discovering how to successfully broker information and negotiate the meaning that is made of it may well reside amongst those for whom the information has the most potential value, namely a community of patients. As indicated, such stirrings already exist in the virtual sharing of stories, gossip and information through the World Wide Web amongst people suffering from chronic diseases. Their knowledge, fear and excitement are already giving them power in small ways to start organizing us. It would be good to find out how we might harness this to their and our benefit. Such explorations are not so much about the organization and communities of practice but about the nature of community in our society as a whole.

References

1   Wenger E (1998) *Communities of Practice*. Cambridge University Press, Cambridge.
2   Lave J and Wenger E (1992) *Situated Learning: legitimate peripheral participation*. Cambridge University Press, Cambridge.

3 Bandura A (1985) *Social Foundations of Thought and Action: a social cognitive theory*. Prentice Hall, London.

4 Wenger E (1987) *Artificial Intelligence and Tutoring Systems*. Morgan Kaufmann, San Francisco, CA.

5 Tyler L and Evans A (2003) Annual appraisal and liege homage: why the British NHS is fundamentally a feudal organisation. *Journal of Health Services Research Policy*. **8 (1):** 57–9

6 Armstrong D (2002) *A New History of Identity*. Palgrave Macmillan, London.

7 Watson J. Quoted in Pinker S (2002) *The Blank Slate*. Penguin, London.

8 Baddely AD (1999) *Essentials of Human Memory*. Psychology Press, Hove.

9 Ryle G (1964) *The Concept of Mind*. Penguin, London.

10 Jonassen DH, Wilson BG, Wang S *et al.* (1993) Constructivist uses of expert systems to support learning. *Journal of Computer-based Instruction*. **20 (3):** 86–94.

11 Elias N (1994) *The Civilising Process*. Blackwell, Oxford.

12 Gray J (2003) *Al Qaeda and What it Means to be Modern*. Faber and Faber, London.

CHAPTER 22

Imagining complex partnerships

Will Medd

There is no possibility whatsoever of an emergent overview, and this is not simply because it is neither possible nor necessary to make what is known fully explicit – there is no final coherence. There is no system, global order or network. These are, at best, partially enacted romantic dreams. Instead there are local complexities. Local globalities. And their relations are uncertain.

(Law and Mol, 2002[1])

This chapter will examine how we can use complexity theory to think about the characteristics of partnerships. While aiming to illuminate some of the complexities of partnership working, the chapter also demonstrates a particular social science approach to complexity. This requires identifying the emergence of partnerships as entities operationally distinct from the organizations that belong to them. Once partnerships are seen as emergent in this way, it leads to exploring their relationships within the wider networks that come to play a part in the partnership dynamic. Finally, this also means that the multiplicity of a partnership becomes important. The chapter aims to suggest that, rather than seeking to achieve consensus-based decision making in partnerships, decision makers need to develop ways of working that recognize the limits to such idealistic notions.

Key points
- Complexity theory can be applied to partnerships but this requires complex thinking, not just the straightforward application of models.
- Much of the problem of understanding partnerships is that they are often not seen as involving their own emergent, complex dynamic.
- Understanding partnerships as emergent systems leads to recognizing the complex relationships that come to play a part in partnership working.
- Complexity suggests we need to find ways in which to work with imperfect possibilities and yet we need to take responsibility in the local constitution of partnerships.

Introduction

Partnerships have proliferated in recent years across all aspects of government policy and especially in relation to issues of health and social care. 'Partnership working' is the mainstay of joined-up government. Partnerships might entail the provision of a seamless care plan for an individual patient, organized through a partnership arrangement between a GP and social services department; or they might involve a whole myriad of agencies engaged to develop public health strategies to prevent teenage pregnancy. The rhetoric of such partnerships is that they enable a joined-up, holistic and consensus-forming arrangement through which we can improve the nation's health. And yet the realities of partnership working suggest that successful collaborations in which such holistic and consensus-making approaches are developed might well be the exception rather than the rule. Anyone who has had anything to do with partnership working knows the struggle this can usually involve. And the benefits of such struggle are not always clear to see. Indeed, it might be fair to say we are reaching a point of 'partnership fatigue'.

What if, instead of using complexity to develop yet another analysis of the ten key stages of good partnership working, we consider that partnerships might actually be 'partially enacted romantic dreams'? That they cannot hold up to the expectation? What if they cannot be the all-encompassing, joined holistic, joined-up mechanisms that they are portrayed to be? The complexities of these partnerships are rarely revealed. When a partnership decision is being made – perhaps between a general practice and social services department – rarely is it explicit what is at stake. There are the immediate issues of the particular strategy or care programme, but entangled within this are a host of policy, strategy, organizational, professional, interpersonal, network and even material relationships. The approach I want to develop in this chapter is one that acknowledges partnerships can be an important means of co-ordination between disparate sets of organizations, professionals and policies, but that they are not a simple solution.

My approach to revealing some of the complexities of partnerships is also intended to highlight a particular approach to complexity. One that uses complexity science to elaborate the importance of the detail of the dynamics of health and social care. This is a different approach from that which is found in much of the complexity literature. Often complexity is presented as embracing a holistic perspective. In so far as a holistic account recognizes that everything has a part to play, that is fine. But if that account then moves to claim it can account for everything, it is problematic. When making a partnership decision we can't possibly hope to account for a full understanding of the partner –the person, organization, policy and so on. This is why 'trust' becomes so

important. We have no choice but to trust in building partnership arrangements. But again, building trust is not just about the development of interpersonal relationships, important though they are. Trust itself needs to be
understood as something achieved through a wide array of relationships. So to
understand the complexity of partnership working, we have to look beyond
what may appear as the immediate partnership dynamic. We have to look to
the wider relationships that come to play a part in the partnership.

The chapter is organized around three interrelated concepts important to
understanding complexity – emergence, relationality and multiplicity. I take
each in turn before drawing together some conclusions about the implications
for partnership working.

Emergence

At first sight, the concept of emergence offers a lot of resonance for partnership working. It is precisely because of the properties that can emerge through the
interactions of a range of problems that partnerships to tackle some health issues
are developed. The interacting issues that contribute to an individual's health
symptoms often require interventions that are beyond the remit of healthcare
organizations. Partnerships offer the opportunity to address the different issues
in a combined way, not only benefiting the individual but also avoiding organizational externalities. The same applies at the level of public health where issues
such as housing quality, income levels and water infrastructure require more
than public health intervention from within the NHS can offer. What partnerships do, it is argued, is bring together a range of perspectives, practices and
strategies in order to intervene to address health problems in a more holistic
way. As a solution to deal with such complex problems, however, what complexities do partnerships themselves entail?

The characteristics of partnerships are rarely predetermined. Indeed, much of
the celebration of partnerships comes with regards to the bottom-up approach
through which successful partnerships tend to form. Just as complexity emphasizes the characteristics that emerge through the self-organized processes of
interacting parts, so too successful partnerships are seen to emerge through the
complex negotiations between the various partners. As an emergent dynamic we
might understand partnerships in terms of properties that have a different characteristic than the parts of the system. The partnership offers more than, say, the
characteristics of a health agency and local authority working together. It has
an emergent quality that is not reducible to its parts.

In recent years the growing interest in partnership working has meant that
such 'bottom-up' partnerships are increasingly difficult to achieve, particularly
as partnerships have become a part of government policy – 'thou shall work

well together in partnership'. The authentic partnership is not always clear to see and the motivations of members can indeed come into question – are they really here to contribute to the issue or just to tick performance targets? Even though this might be the case, complexity science fits within those approaches to organizational analysis that suggest whatever the intention of a particular policy or strategy, the emergent outcome will be different. There will be emergent characteristics and dynamics that are not predictable even if the formation of the partnership is directed from government policy. Locality matters.

So whether formed authentically from the bottom up or imposed from the top down through some government initiative, the argument of complexity science is that the organizational dynamic of the partnerships will nonetheless have properties of emergence. It will have characteristics that emerge from the interaction between a range of interests that get entangled, from personnel, professional, organizational and policy issues. And the importance of emergence, particularly where non-linear dynamics are concerned, is that it is not predictable. A small change – such as a change in the representative from an organization – can have a dramatic impact on the dynamics of the partnership.

We could explore the characteristics of such emergence and the implications of different concepts within complexity science. For example, a partnership strategy cannot be seen as imposing plans based on predictions, but needs to be about ensuring the partnership is flexible, adaptable and able to learn. In this sense, strategy itself becomes an emergent process. Similarly, knowledge from an objective 'bird's-eye' view becomes impossible and undesirable. Instead, the partnership needs to find ways of enhancing 'agility and intelligence ... to respond to the incessant barrage of frequent unplanned change'.[2] Hence knowledge management becomes about allowing information to flow where intelligence must be seen as distributed in networks of relations. It means recognizing the constant and distributed production of knowledge throughout all of the 'ordinary' life of the partnership, and with that, humility about what one can know and do.[3] And so the structures of the partnership need to be seen as emergent, able to adapt and transform.

The problem of doing this is, however, that it is not always clear where the partnership is. Is it the meeting between two individuals? Is it the formal, written-down agreement? Is it the informal discussions between members of the partnership? All of these things?

Relationality

The idea of a partnership is often one in which the ideal – the romantic vision – is of two or more organizations coming together to form a new whole (*see* Figure 22.1).

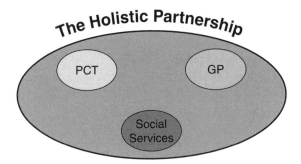

Figure 22.1   The holistic partnership.

When we consider how complex it is to identify and understand the dynamics of one organization – say a primary care trust, a GP or a social services department – it becomes clear that this coming together is likely to be difficult to achieve. However, if we think of the partnership as emergent, we need to think about what the partnership is in a different way. Seeing partnerships as emergent suggests we understand the partnership itself as a particular dynamic, as a particular organizational form. What this means is that partnerships are as much about differentiating (defining what is and is not the partnership) as they are about coming together. This suggests the partnership is not an all-embracing organization that encapsulates the involved organizations (as in Figure 22.1), but is about the formation of another organizational form (*see* Figure 22.2).

This point is rather simple but has important implications. There is something distinct about the partnership that makes it different to the organizations, and even the community, that are involved. The partnership forms another

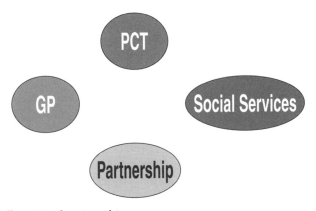

Figure 22.2   Differentiated partnership.

organizational form. The decisions made as a partnership are not necessarily the same that the organizations in the partnership have to make. When individuals make a decision in the partnership, this then has to be communicated as a decision in their own organizations. This point is particularly clear when we think of examples where the partnership thinks a decision has been made and later discovers that the member from a particular organization does not have the capacity to commit resources from their organization and that the partnership decision in effect could only be a recommendation.

If we see the partnership as distinct, as a new emergent form, then understanding some of the dynamics of the partnership becomes clearer. There are two processes of particular note at work here. First, we need to note the closure of the partnership. The partnership has particular meaning, makes particular decisions, includes particular members, takes place at a particular time. In other words, the partnership is inherently closed. As with all complex organizations, partnerships are closed in so far as they form organizational boundaries that determine their identity. This view of partnerships causes problems for conventional assumptions of partnerships, particularly the notions that they are inclusive, holistic and involve shared information and consensus decision making. The argument I am suggesting is that by necessity partnerships form boundaries anew, and this involves exclusion. It includes defining what is excluded from the partnership. Second, however, there is also openness in partnership working. As emergent phenomena, partnerships can only be understood in the context of the environment in which they co-evolve. Partnerships take in resources from their environment – time, money, technology and so on – and translate these into particular agendas of the partnership. It is the relationship between openness and closure that defines the dynamic of the partnership.

Multiplicity

So far my argument has been that we need to understand partnerships as emergent phenomena and that, as emergent phenomena, they form distinct organizations separate from the organizations that have representation in the partnership. There remains an interesting problem, however, which is, what actually is the partnership? What is this thing that I am suggesting becomes distinct? Indeed, how does one observe a partnership? Where does one look to see the partnership? This is the greatest challenge for how we understand complexity science in the social world, and in the world of healthcare organization in particular.

This is where the problem of the holistic partnership really gets into trouble. The key problem is what constitutes the 'whole' that is the partnership? What are the elements that interact to form an emergent whole? Can we identify the rule-based parts/elements that we find in models of complexity? Where indeed do we begin? If the partnership is between the primary care trust and the housing services department, for example, how do we represent these? What do they look like? The problems of internal complexity in each of these organizations mean that what each of these are, what they look like, is itself not clear.

One way to think about this problem is to think back to the quote that I cited at the start of this chapter. Our approach to partnerships might risk assuming that an underlying dynamic can be made explicit. The interesting thing is that both complexity science and approaches to partnerships tend to be associated with notions of assuming the possibility of understanding the complex dynamics of the organization. In the case of partnerships there is often an emphasis on being holistic by engaging all stakeholders, through developing a 'whole-systems approach' for example. And in complexity science, although it often uses an imagery of what Law and Mol[1] refer to as a 'romantic imagination', it tends to develop models that encompass more and more and assume all complexity can be understood. Both complexity science and partnership working move towards the idea of gaining an overview.

My suggestion is that to understand the complexity of partnerships, while it can indeed be a helpful process to explore 'whole-systems thinking', one can also find the complexity of partnerships by looking down to the details. This approach does not mean neglecting the arguments about emergence. What it means is examining how and where the emergent partnership is located. It is in the detail of partnership working that we find the partnership. In the detail of people's interactions, policy documents, formal meetings, resource flows, and so on. Partnership working becomes an accomplishment of bringing together a range of people, things, organizations and agendas. Looking at the detail of such accomplishment means recognizing that we cannot make all the partnership explicit. Both for the academic observer as well as the decision maker in the partnership, much about the partnership remains unknown.

This is important. Models of complexity science can sometimes give the impression of a clear system of interacting parts co-evolving and forming a dynamic emergent order. If it was possible to be clear what the parts of partnerships could possibly be, then perhaps it would be possible to identify clear demarcations between a partnership decision and other decisions. However, complex systems are distributed systems. As complex systems, partnerships are not located in one place. They are in many places, at the same time, being achieved through many negotiations and decisions across a range of networks. Indeed, since there are multiple locations, so to speak, then the partnership would seem to become multiple. When we recognize this, then we can begin to see the many things that interact and come into play in the formation of partnerships, for example computer technologies, telephones, policy documents, evidence-based reports, transports, the settings for meetings, people, emotions, and so on. These things all become significant for a distributed partnership.

Conclusions

My argument has been that we need to understand partnerships as complex emergent phenomena. As with all complex phenomena, they are defined through relationships which constitute what is and what is not the partnership. The partnership is not, however, a neat system onto which a model of complexity can be imposed. Partnerships are embedded within a whole host of complex relations between different people, professions, organizations, policies, buildings, technologies, and so on. They are manifest in these relationships in many ways; partnerships are complex multiplicities. This all sounds rather academic but the argument is of practical significance.

Much analysis of partnerships points to the ways in which a good partnership can be formed. Yet the picture of the complexity of partnerships that I am suggesting is one that means the types of characteristics of a 'good' partnership are always going to be the exception. Instead, complexity suggests we need to find ways in which to work with imperfect possibilities. Complexity offers no simple solutions to partnerships. However, it does point towards the local constitution of partnerships, to responsibility in every moment of the partnership. Working in partnerships requires reflexive considerations of one's own responsibilities and possibilities.

In summary, if a complexity perspective is to be useful to understanding partnerships in healthcare organization, we need to note:

- *Emergence.* Partnerships are not necessarily knowable. Partnerships create new forms of complexity, generate new forms of problems and involve dynamics that cannot always be rendered explicit; knowing them requires ignorance.
- *Relationality.* To understand partnerships requires understanding them relationally, for example in the abstract, to what are not the partnerships. However, the abstract is not enough because there are always local relations, and so we must always understand partnerships locally. This also means understanding the way in which partnerships transform other relations. The implication is that we examine the types of relations that partnerships form (for example as hierarchical, market, network and indeed combinations of these).
- *Multiplicity.* If partnerships are complex and relational then they are also multiple. A partnership has many different realities – not simply perspectives – that it performs. A partnership decision, for example, can produce many communications (economic, political, legal, health, social care). This means there become limits to shared understanding, for example, and the question becomes how to work with this.

References

1 Law J and Mol A (2002) *And if the Global Were Small and Non-Coherent? Method, Complexity and the Baroque.* Centre for Science Studies and Department of Sociology, Lancaster University, www.comp.lancs.ac.uk/sociology/soc096jl.html.
2 Wheatley MJ (1999) *Leadership and the New Science: discovering order in a chaotic world,* p. 38. Berrett-Koehler, San Francisco, CA.
3 Stacey RD (2001) *Complex Responsive Processes in Organizations: learning and knowledge creation.* Routledge, London.

Section 7

From theory to action: personal perspectives

Introduction

Sarah Fraser

One of the criticisms levelled against complexity thinking is that it is all very well in theory, but where are the demonstrations of practical benefit? This final section draws together a number of personal perspectives from practitioners who have found complexity insights useful in their work.

One of the key challenges for a book about complex adaptive systems is the dilemma of the printed media. Words on pages are insufficient to capture the nuances and essence of what interconnected human systems are about. Specifically, in healthcare and the public sector, the tradition of the academic or quasi-academic paper as a means of sharing information through the written word has its limitations. This section is intended to provide the reader with insights into the practice of complex adaptive systems through a less formal mode.

In the first chapter in this section, Robin Durie and his colleagues explain how the transformation of a deprived community took place with no hierarchical or traditional public sector interventions. It's a compelling story of the art of letting go across a whole community and enabling appropriate networks to merge, and stands as one of the most extraordinary examples of neighbourhood regeneration in the UK. The project has been widely recognized at a national and international level and resulted in Hazel Stuteley, one of the authors, being awarded the OBE.

Chapter 24 provides a different context, yet similar theme, of letting go as Peter Fryer provides the view within one organization. Through programmes such as 'Feeling Comfortable with Feeling Uncomfortable', removing budgets, developing innovative feedback systems and other truly empowering activities, this organization took on many of the recognizable features of a complex adaptive system. Peter, chief executive at the time, also includes his thoughts on the leadership requirements for running such an organization.

In Chapter 25, Barbara Douglas and her colleagues reflect on their experiences on a development programme for the elderly and how a house was adapted for independent living. They tell their story through a conversation, interspersed with reflective comments on how it related to complexity theory, of how they worked with elders in their community, and the myriad of departments, to design a house – for life. The conversational way in which this chapter is written usefully captures the emergent process they experienced.

In a shift from community-based experiential work, in Chapter 26 Leigh Hamby shifts the reader to a US-based hospital looking to improve their bed availability. Written in the first person, this narrative sweeps the reader through his reflective experience as he applies complexity theory instead of more traditional change and quality management techniques.

Paul Thomas next looks at applying complexity theory in primary healthcare organization and, specifically, he shares his view as a general practitioner who focuses on the importance of the narrative. He offers a personal interpretation of how he translated complexity into practice at the level of the individual practitioner, at the organizational level and at a systems level within the context of whole-systems participatory action research.

Vivian Rambihar was a very early advocate of chaos and complexity theory and describes his work as a community cardiologist working with a sizeable South Asian community in Toronto and elsewhere. He describes a number of projects which were the first of their kind to translate complexity theory into practice. The final chapter in this section summarizes these many years of work, explaining the key events and showing how they have arisen from a complexity approach.

The six chapters in this section each present a different view on how the theory of complexity has been applied or experienced. The context varies from community-based projects (Durie et al., Rambihar, Douglas et al.) to organizational approaches (Hamby et al., Thomas, Fryer), through to personal reflection and experience (Hamby et al., Fryer, Thomas, Douglas et al.). The timing is no less varied, covering Rambihar's 20-year project with South Asian heart health promotion in Ontario through to Hamby's quick-fix bed management improvement project in Atlanta that took place in a matter of months.

The authors have approached their stories in unique ways. For some, they have used a more formal reporting structure with which the reader may be more familiar, whilst other a more informal approach. Douglas et al. tell their story of the housing project as a conversation, reflecting at the start that when they wrote the more formal report it seemed too 'tidied-up'. Similarly, Hamby tells his story from the heart and as it happened.

Another difference in approach is the choice between retrospectively viewing the emergent practice and applying complexity theory (Durie et al., Douglas et al.) or whether the authors have takes the theories and then purposefully applied them in practice (Rambihar, Hamby et al.). In his chapter on how complexity can be applied in primary care, Thomas covers both angles, and in a similar way, Fryer explains how he started from a position of understanding complexity through what had been done intuitively, and then moved to a more 'theory into application' mode.

Despite their differences in content, approach and process, all these stories hold some common themes from which the reader can understand complexity in action. It is not intended for this section summary to identify all the features of complex adaptive systems in each chapter and to summarize them; that is left to the reader. However, there were two consistent and powerful themes than we can identify.

The first is that of meaning and purpose. Durie *et al.* explain that it was important for all those living in the housing estate to have a vision of what it might be like. Hamby *et al.* talk of goals and others mention sense making, meaning and the importance of providing a purpose – even if at some times, in the case of Douglas *et al.*, the purpose needed challenging and even changing.

The ability to make connections, to develop interactions and to have conversations, with all people, at all levels, is another critical theme. Again, all the chapters mention this, regardless of the setting or context. In addition, two chapters focus on the importance of feedback (Hamby *et al.* and Fryer), though it is implicit in many of the others. For both Hamby *et al.* and Fryer, feedback plays a crucial role in enabling individuals to develop their awareness and decision-making abilities; it is the means by which they continue to learn, and therefore adapt to changing conditions.

CHAPTER 23

Community regeneration and complexity

Robin Durie, Katrina Wyatt and Hazel Stuteley

Introduction

Over a period of five years, a remarkable process of change took place on the Beacon and Old Hill estate in Falmouth, Cornwall. Overlooking the gleaming boats in the multimillion pound marina below, by 1995 the estate had come to be known to the other communities in Falmouth as 'Beirut'. One of the most deprived areas in Britain, the estate was blighted by violent crime, drug dealing and intimidation.

The process initiated within the community that we describe stands as one of the most extraordinary examples of neighbourhood regeneration in the whole of the UK. Perhaps most strikingly, it has led to a series of notable health outcomes. In this chapter we describe the regeneration of the Beacon and Old Hill estate and advance our initial hypotheses, explaining how and why this process of regeneration occurred.

Background

In 1996, a Bristol University report[1] found that Penwerris, the electoral ward comprising the Beacon and Old Hill estate (having an overall population of 6000, living in 1500 homes), was the most deprived in Cornwall. The county is itself the most deprived in England. The report also found that it had the largest percentage of children in households with no wage earners and the second highest number of children living with lone parents. According to the Breadline Britain Index,[1] it had the highest proportion of poor households of the county's 133 wards. More than 30% of households were living in poverty, well above the national average.* The unemployment rate on the estate was 30% above the national average. Of 23 child-protection registrations in the council district of Carrick, 19 were on the estate. More than 50% of the 1500 homes were without central heating. Its illness rate was 18% above the national average.

By 2000, the overall crime rate had dropped by 50%. Affordable central heating and external cladding had been installed in over 60% of the properties. Child-protection registrations had dropped by 42%. Postnatal depression was down by 70%. The educational attainment of 10–11-year-old boys – i.e. standard attainment tests (SATS), level 4, key stage 2 – was up by 100%. The number of unwanted teenage pregnancies had been significantly reduced to the extent that in 1999 there were no unwanted teenage pregnancies. The unemployment rate was down 71% amongst both males and females. These achievements were recognized by central government when the community was awarded the Nye Bevan Award for Excellence. The sustainability of the regeneration process was further recognized in the form of the presentation of a Queen's Jubilee Award in June 2003.

Figure 23.1   'Beirut'.

---

*Falmouth docks, formerly the main employer in the region, had, during its heyday, a workforce of over 3000. By 1995, that had fallen to 100 part-time workers. There is a clear correlation between the demise of the docks and the degeneration of the estate.

The regeneration process

It is generally agreed by tenants and residents that, by 1995, the Beacon and Old Hill estate was in a state of terminal decline. It had the reputation of being a 'no go area' for the police. Crime and vandalism were spiralling out of control, and the community had become dissociated from the statutory agencies. At that time, there was no residents' association and therefore no place where people's voices could be heard.

This escalating decline was recognized by two local health visitors, Hazel Stuteley and Philip Trenoweth, to whose practice some two-thirds of the population of the estate were registered. Although this population group amounted to only a third of their overall caseload, they were devoting all of their time to problems arising on the estate. The turning point for the health visitors came in the form of a particularly horrific incident, which the author subsequently recalled:

> The flashpoint came simultaneously for us both, literally in Rebecca's case, when she witnessed the family car ignite following the planting of an incendiary device. She was 11 years old then and although physically unhurt, she was deeply traumatised by this. She was already in mourning for her friend's pet rabbit and tortoise, which had recently been butchered by thugs from the estate. This was the final straw.
>
> As family health visitor for the past five years, I was a regular visitor to her home. Her mum was a frequent victim of domestic violence and severely postnatally depressed. My caseload had many similar families with multiple health and social problems. Seeing Rebecca and her family's deep distress, I vowed then and there that change must happen if this community was to survive. I had been watching it spiral out of control for long enough.

During May to September 1995, the health visitors therefore initiated a series of meetings with representatives of health, education, social services, local government and police. From the outset it was recognized that community involvement would be essential to the success of the project. Twenty key tenants were identified by the health visitors as having the necessary skills to engage their peers and were invited to work in partnership with the statutory agencies. Of these 20, five agreed to participate. Resourced by the local government housing department, they received training to become proficient in submitting grant applications, and forming and maintaining a constituted committee. This group subsequently established a formal tenants' and residents' association. They went on to produce a hand-delivered newsletter, along with a 'one-to-one' chat to all households, informing residents of the plans for the estate. This proved to be fundamental in galvanizing the community to articulate and prioritize their concerns.

A series of increasingly well-attended meetings for residents were held, which were often stormy. This was interpreted as a good sign by the health visitors, who were convinced that, while an apathetic community can achieve little or nothing, an angry community has a potential energy that can be harnessed for positive effects. These meetings led the community to conclude that the main problems affecting their health were crime, poor housing and unemployment, together with the historical failure of the statutory agencies to address these issues. These were followed by joint meetings between residents and the relevant agencies, resulting in the foundation of the multi-agency, tenant and resident-led Beacon Community Regeneration Partnership in January 1997. The Partnership began meeting monthly, as it still does to this day.

Among the outcomes initially achieved by the Partnership was a successful bid for £1.2 million of Capital Challenge funding, with a further £1 million funding from Carrick District Council. This money was used to fund the central heating and energy efficiency measures, and led to the installation of central heating in 300 properties, with a further 900 properties being re-clad. An old butcher's shop was converted into a resource centre, offering training courses and advice on welfare and benefits, as well as being an informal drop-in centre and hub for communication of news about the estate. Another disused building was converted into a healthcare centre, providing a range of healthcare

Table 23.1   Impact of the regeneration project on health, environment and education

Health outcomes	Environmental outcomes	Educational outcomes
• Increased breast-feeding rate by 50%	• £2.2 million generated by tenants and residents	• On-site training for tenants and residents
• Postnatal depression rate down 77%	• Gas central heating to 318 properties	• After-school clubs
• Childhood accident rate down 50%	• Loft insulation in 349: cavity wall in 199; external cladding to 700	• Life-skills courses
• Reduced incidence of asthma	• Fuel saving estimated at £180 306	• Parent and toddler groups
• Sexual health service for young people	• £160 000 traffic-calming measures	• 100% improvement in boys' SATS results
• Beacon care centre providing on-site health advice	• Provision of safe play areas	• Information technology skills
	• Recycling and dog-waste bins	• Crèche supervisor training
	• Skateboard park	

such as physiotherapy sessions and health checks for over-65s, alongside confidential contraceptive advice and counselling, directly aimed at teenagers on the estate.

Over the last seven years, the Beacon Partnership has achieved a series of dramatic health, educational, law and order, and environmental outcomes, as detailed in Table 23.1. Today, a series of initiatives contribute to the ongoing maintenance of the regeneration process. A purpose-built nursery in being constructed alongside a new youth centre. There are plans for a sensory garden – money has been secured for landscaping the original Beacon site, from which the estate takes its name. A mosaic project for street names and signs aims to bring the young and elderly to work together with the long-term unemployed of the estate.

Setting the project in a complexity perspective

Our first motivation for seeking to understand this process of regeneration that came from the perspective of complexity theory emerged during a complexity workshop held in 2002. During the workshop, a presentation by Eve Mittleton-Kelly provoked the following response from the author:

> *Although the presentation was nothing to do with community development, I was mesmerized by it. What I heard being described was a process which, uncannily and exactly, mirrored my intuitive responses to 'kick-starting the Beacon Project'. It placed great value on widespread networking and the creation of relationships and dialogue based on trust. Conversations, humility and respect, I now realized, contributed hugely to the creation of that all-important enabling environment, which released the resourcefulness of this community to become self-organizing and achieve such significant and dramatic outcomes. Sitting through that presentation was one of those rare, life-changing moments of self-enlightenment.*

The importance of receptive context

Prior to the regeneration process occurring, it is important to understand how the receptive context for change was created. Not only was the community isolated from the statutory agencies, it was also isolated from and within itself. The common response, when others suffered the effects of crime and vandalism in the community, was one of relief that it had happened to someone else. There was little or no communication, either between the community and the authorities or amongst the members of the community themselves. Rather, as Bob Mears, the Police Community Liaison and Crime Reduction Officer, was later to reflect: 'There was an attitude among us and other people that everybody who lived on the estate was a criminal. That's obviously not true, but there was no exchange of information.'

The success of the residents' association, and then the partnership, consisted first and foremost in enabling relations to be formed amongst the members of the community – for people to begin to talk to each other again. As a consequence, vandalism and crime were no longer seen as other people's problems – rather, they were problems confronting the community as a whole. In turn, the formation of these relationships enabled relationships to begin to form with the authorities, such that chains of communication between the community and the statutory agencies started to emerge. As trust spread throughout the community, so the community began to be trusted by the authorities, and the community in turn began to trust the agencies. On the basis of the formation of such relations, therefore, we can talk of a co-evolution of trust between the community and its environment consisting in the authorities and statutory agencies. An initial series of 'listening forums' ultimately led to the situation where the agencies began actively to glean the views of the people in the community. The change in attitude was captured by Grenville Chappell, Co-ordinator of the Beacon Community Regeneration Partnership: 'You've got to get out there and find out what people want, not sit around and think you know best what people want.'

The importance of non-linearity

While these interrelations doubtless constitute a necessary condition for the regeneration process, the momentum for that process came from a different quarter – a quarter which bears all the hallmarks of non-linearity. In a linear relation, the cause is 'commensurate' with its effect. In non-linear relations, however, small causes can lead to disproportionately large effects. It is precisely this disproportion of effect that propels the regeneration process. In the case of the Beacon and Old Hill estate, perhaps the most striking example of this is the instance of dog-waste bins.

The provision of dog-waste bins on an estate is calculated according to a ration based on the number of residents in the estate, not the number of dogs. On the Beacon and Old Hill estate, where the number of dogs per capita is higher than average, there was a consequent lack of dog-waste bin provision. The estate was blighted by dog waste. The Partnership worked to deliver a dog-waste bin provision which reflected more accurately the number of dogs on the estate. Within a very short time, dog waste became a problem of the past. In a subsequent survey of tenants and residents, which sought to determine the single factor that had the most impact on the estate, a large majority identified the provision of adequate numbers of dog-waste bins and the resultant improvement to the living environment for the community. Here was clear evidence of a dramatic outcome following from a small intervention, and the momentum this gave to the change process was to lead, ultimately, to a community-wide commitment to the betterment of the environment.

Emergence through co-evolution

The most significant aspect of the regeneration process on the Beacon and Old Hill estate was that from the outset, there was no initial funding, no hierarchy, no targets, no business plan. Only a shared vision of what the community wanted to be, rather than an obsession with what it had to do. Thus, the regeneration process was not a result of a predetermined plan. Rather, the process emerged as a consequence of the interactions between the members of the community, and between the community and its environment, for example the statutory agencies, the police and the council. As the community evolved, so also the agencies and professional bodies co-evolved with the community.

Localized self-organization

A key element of complexity theory is the insight that, within a community or organization, knowledge is distributed and behaviour is necessarily localized. Macroscopic changes in the behaviour of the community or organization as a whole are then classified as emergent phenomena resulting from the interactions between the localized changes in behaviour. This necessitates a conceptual shift from the assumption that change must be 'managed' from the 'centre'. A fascinating example of this notion of localization occurred as a direct consequence of the award of the Capital Challenge funding. While this award provided further evidence to the community of its ability to achieve successful outcomes by working together, it also necessitated, as a stipulation upon which the funding was conditional, the formation of a formal Regeneration Partnership. The effect of the formation of this Partnership, not least in terms of the trust which it built up in the authorities, was a noteworthy break in the traditional working practices of local government. Rather than maintaining sole control of the budget and decision-making processes, Carrick District Council agreed to delegate some of its powers. This process empowered the Partnership, which remained a predominately tenant-led body, rather than a council committee to make recommendations to the full council concerning the estate's progress. As Mike Owen, Senior Housing Officer for Carrick District Council at the time, said: 'It was quite brave for the authority to extend responsibility to a body controlled by residents.' While the decision may indeed have been brave, it had the effect of ensuring that it was the specific local needs of the community which were being responded to, with local, directed changes being the result. Perhaps the most poignant expression of this localization of the decision-making process is to be found in the way that the Partnership worked together with the tenants to determine the order of priority for the improvement work on the buildings, enabled by the award of the Capital Challenge funding. Such localized self-organization in turn ensured that, for the community as a whole, there was clear evidence of the fairness of the prioritization of the re-cladding and heating improvement work to be undertaken.

Conclusion

The Falmouth Beacon and Old Hill estate is a living example of relevant order emerging out of what was in 1995 a chaotic system. The intricate web of interactions which have formed between the community and the agencies hold the Beacon Partnership at the edge of chaos and allow the exploration of adjacent possibles, where new projects can be tried out and new relationships formed. The self-organization of these emergent social structures patterns the behaviour of the Partnership and is able to adapt and respond to changes. There is a sense of agencies 'acting differently' in non-traditional ways, forging links

Figure 23.2   Post-regeneration – best garden award.

outside of their organizational remit, which contributes to this emergent order. The visibility of the change is captured in the wonderful gardens on the estate; where once old prams and mattresses flourished, there is now a riot of flowers and shrubs, rockeries and raised borders. Work is ongoing to determine whether exchange visits, where communities beginning the regeneration process are brought to Falmouth to 'see' and share stories, are able to act as a vehicle for the possible transference of successful change.

Reference

1   Gordon D, Payne S, Henson B *et al.* (1996) *Poverty and Deprivation in West Cornwall in the 1990s*. Bristol University.

CHAPTER 24

Running an organization along complexity lines

Peter Fryer

This chapter tells the story of the Humberside Training and Enterprise Council that was set up by the Government in the early 1990s to replace the Manpower Services Commission. It describes how the organization found complexity and how it influenced its development in terms of thinking and acting.

Key points
- Complexity insights can offer radical solutions to organizational frameworks that can work in practice.
- Organizations can function satisfactorily without a detailed grand plan.
- The key elements are trust, increasing connectivity and feedback between staff.
- Old style controls such as budgets can be successfully abolished.
- Introducing innovative change involves being comfortable with being uncomfortable.
- The role of chief executive changes to one of leader who creates and protects a space in which innovation can flourish.
- These ideas are fragile to start with and take time to grow, but the rewards are great for those who are brave enough to let go of the past.

Introduction

A word of caution. No matter how many times I tell this story and no matter how many caveats I put on it, it always sounds as though we knew where we were going and that we had some grand plan. But we didn't, and for those of you who have experienced complexity, you will know that we couldn't have because complexity just doesn't work that way. So please read this as a journey with success and failures, great surges ahead, blind alleys and steps back, and no clear idea of where we were going.

Humberside Training and Enterprise Council (TEC) was one of a national network of 72 TECs set up by the Government in 1991 to replace the then Manpower Services Commission. In their locality each was responsible for Government training programmes such as Modern Apprenticeships and Investors in People, development work with colleges of further education, economic development, business support, and developing local initiatives to meet local needs. Although their funding was largely from the public sector, they were independent private companies which 'traded' with the Government rather than receiving grant aid. They were limited by guarantee rather than shares so that all profits were ploughed back into the local community.

Humberside TEC was one of the larger TECs with an annual turnover of £35 million and with 200 staff. In many ways we had much more freedom than the Civil Service that we replaced, but we were restrained by our contract with the Government and we had the dubious pleasure of satisfying Government accounting and auditing as well as private company accounting and auditing.

Reversing into complexity

So how did we get into complexity? Well, it sort of found us. We had intuitively realized that our planning processes did not work and that the more freedom we gave our people, the harder they worked. So we had started implementing processes to take account of our intuition.

We had removed all reference to hours with our staff; they were free to come and go as they pleased and do what they wanted when they wanted as long as the job got done. This gave staff the responsibility and control over their own work which helped to relieve stress and increase commitment. It also began the process of demonstrating trust. It also massively decreased overtime working.

We had abolished hierarchy charts as we felt that they were a false construct, and told everyone that they could talk to anyone, and should. I suspect that most people actually constructed their own charts for reference, but that they would probably have all been different because they represented that individual's perspective of the business.

We realized that most of our rules and procedures were too bureaucratic and, what's more, were based on 'the worst person'. That is, when drawing up the rules we were thinking of who was most likely to get this job wrong and how could we ensure that they did not screw up, or who was most likely to try to take advantage. So we started drawing up rules and procedures based on our best people, and then to develop our worst people, or in extreme cases to get rid of them. This then led to us developing 'fuzzy policies' where rather than detailing the procedures to be followed, we just stated the outcome we wanted. The expenses policy became 'We will reimburse all staff all reasonable expenses incurred in the course of their duties', and our grievance procedure 'All grievances are to be resolved to the satisfaction of all concerned'. This put the emphasis on getting the right outcome rather than following laid-down procedures and processes.

It then occurred to us that our biggest waste was management and checking processes, and that if individuals could take full responsibility for their own objectives and actions, that would free up the managers and checkers to get on with other work. This was when we ran into trouble! It was getting increasingly difficult to persuade both our Board of Non-executive Directors and our Government Contract Managers that we were not just operating some kind of lackadaisical free-for-all. This was when complexity theory found us, first through a couple of management articles, and eventually through a Santa Fé Institute Conference where we met up with the London School of Economics that had a project looking at organizations as complex adaptive systems. This gave us a respectability which, although not necessarily understood by those who were sceptical, was sufficiently prestigious to allow us to experiment further.

This set the pattern for the rest of our journey through complexity. Rather than studying the theory and then trying to apply it in practice, we seemed to do it the other way around. We just kept trying things (many of which didn't work or we got wrong) and then we found the theory that explained what we were doing or what was happening. This enabled us to ask new questions and then to refine what we were doing, which led to us trying something new. Our view of complexity theory was very 'secular' in that its real value was that it gave us a different perspective on our organization, and we set about looking for other concepts that would also do that. We explored neuro-linguistic programming, the Herman whole brain model, soft systems and much more, but the concept that made the most sense for the whole organization, and helped us develop our new operating framework, was complexity theory because this was the one concept which also had room for all the others.

We had to accept that we were a complex adaptive system whether we wanted to be or not, and that if we were, then most of the traditional management and organizational approaches we had in place were at best ineffective and at worst harmful. We had to find ways to help the organization with its natural evolution and emergence, to improve the quality and quantity of its connections and to develop more effective feedback mechanisms.

Building on the complexity model

Freeing up staff and feeling comfortable with feeling uncomfortable

We considered first how could we help the organization become a more natural one, emerging and co-evolving with its environment. After much discussion and many mistakes, we developed an organizational form based on three key principles:

- all our staff were adults and were treated as such
- everyone was trusted to operate in the best interests of the organization
- we all gave each other loads of support.

In effect, we recognized that our organization was a community and that it would work best if we treated it like one.

Treating our staff as adults meant them not having to ask for permission, and not being told what to do and how to do it. We believed that people knew better than anyone what was needed in their job, what their objectives should be and whether they were meeting those objectives. We trusted them to act in the best interests of the organization and, most importantly, we told them that we trusted them to do so.

This approach had huge implications for us all. Critically, if staff were to operate in the best interests of the organization they needed to know what the organization was for, what was its purpose, and what did it want to be. They needed the skills of developing options, making choices, being accountable for their choices, coping with failure and learning from their mistakes. Although we were giving them immense amounts of freedom and effectively saying 'you decide', this was no soft option because they had nowhere to hide. They couldn't say when things went wrong 'I was only doing as I was told' because no one was telling them; they had to take full responsibility for their actions. But not responsibility to the 'management' because they didn't have a manager in that sense, but to everyone who was affected by what they did, because that was who they were accountable to.

It was impossible to move to this way of operating straight away because people needed to develop the skills and confidence to handle freedom; but on the other hand, you can't develop those skills and confidence without having the freedom. So, as we began gradually removing the controls on people, we introduced a wide-ranging development programme under the banner of 'Feeling Comfortable with Feeling Uncomfortable'. This was so called because we were asking people to move out of their comfort zone, and the normal tendency when that happens is to try to get back to the area in which one is comfortable. But we wanted people to stay in the area of discomfort and to learn how to become comfortable, and furthermore we wanted them to actively expand their comfort zone. People often said to me 'This is scary', and I would say 'Being scared is a really good management response'.

As part of the 'Feeling Comfortable with Feeling Uncomfortable' programme:

- We invested a lot of time on culture and values, eliciting from people what they thought they should be, and when we had broad agreement, asking them how they were going to get us there. This ensured that they owned the culture and values but also emphasized that it was 'they' who were running the organization and not 'the management'.
- We considered in depth over a considerable time-scale what were we for, what did we want to be and what was our purpose. After some initial attempts at writing down our answers to these questions, we realized that writing them down would do more harm than good. These were emerging and evolving issues and writing them down would fix them in a point in time, and also every time we attempted to write them we lost so much of their essence. We realized that as everyone was involved in the process of clarifying the concepts, they knew what the answers were, and also that the process was as important as the result. The nearest we got to codifying these concepts was to say 'When in doubt, do the right thing, even if it costs us'.
- We introduced a thinking and learning skills programme. If people were to take responsibility for their part of the organization, they needed to generate options and to be able to choose between them. This meant that they had to be able to develop a wide range of thinking and learning strategies. This part of the programme included the neuro-linguistic programming and the whole brain model mentioned earlier, as well as 'how to be a brilliant learner', 'thinking about thinking', De Bono's six thinking hats and much more.
- We also wished to develop people's confidence, self-responsibility and accountability. Much of this was done within the work context. For example, when people came to me for a decision, I initially helped them identify the options and choose the 'right' one. After a while I then sent them away to do this for themselves, and eventually, when they were ready, I wouldn't even let them tell me what they had decided until after the decision had been implemented. Also, most of our staff went on Dale Carnegie's 'High-impact Presentation Skills' course, not because we wanted them all to give presentations, but having to stand up in front of people to give a wide range of presentations can do wonders for building confidence.
- We introduced the concept of 'loving mistakes to death', meaning that mistakes are an essential part of learning and taking responsibility, and that 'if you are not making mistakes, you can't be trying'. The most important part of a mistake is that by definition you end up in an unexpected position and opportunities become apparent from that position that were not clear before.

- We introduced the 'power to commit'. Anyone attending a meeting on behalf of their team or the organization had the power, and the responsibility, to commit their team or the organization. This developed confidence and accountability, made us more responsive within our environment, and ensured that people were sufficiently trained and prepared for what they were being asked to do.

Building up connections

We implemented a number of measures to improve both the internal and external connectivity of our people:

- We ran a number of whole-organization away events to look at issues such as becoming more resourceful. Built into these events were devices which required people to work with others who they did not normally come into contact with in the organization.
- I used to give a quarterly update to all the staff to ensure that they all heard the same message from the same person at the same time. The format was a short input from me followed by a coffee break where the staff had to team up with others they did not know too well to discuss what were the issues they would like to hear about. The meeting then resumed with a question-and-answer session on those issues.
- Everyone was encouraged to belong to external groups and we facilitated many of our staff becoming school governors or mentors for young people. Support and, where necessary, training was given for this.
- We were attracted to the complexity concept that to function well a system needs some built-in redundancy, that is, available spare resource which can be called on in times of need. Therefore, when we came across interesting and challenging people who could add a different dimension to our organization, we recruited them whether we had a vacancy or not. There was always plenty for them to do, even if that amounted to them challenging us to think about things differently, and they were invaluable in times of pressure.
- We built a café right in the middle of the most used thoroughfare in our building so that people could meet and mix for recreational and business purposes. It became the most popular meeting area in the place and was even in demand by people outside the organization for their meetings.

Enhancing feedback

The third major area of complexity we worked on was feedback. We explored with everyone, as part of the development programme, the concept of consequences, and ensured that wherever possible the feedback loop was closed.

We encouraged everyone to appreciate that 'feedback is', that is, that it is all around us and that everything that happens is feedback. We also ran development sessions on 'giving and receiving feedback'.

Our biggest breakthrough on feedback, however, came when we examined our appraisal process. Up until then we had had a tick-box rating system based on the one we had inherited from the Civil Service and which was completed by managers. We wanted to 'get rid' of our managers, so we devised our own paperless 360° appraisal process. First, we gave responsibility for appraisal to the individual – they decided when, where, how and who should be there. The basic model was that a group of up to about ten people should be invited representing people you accounted to, people who accounted to you, customers and suppliers, and all of these could be internal or external people as appropriate. In the meeting room there would be a sheet of flip-chart paper on each wall, one headed 'stop', and the others 'start', 'continue' and 'change'. All the appraisers were given a different colour marker-pen and proceeded to put their thoughts on each of the sheets of newsprint. Then, under the guidance of a facilitator, they would discuss what was on the sheets of flip-chart paper to gain greater clarity. Following this, the appraisee returned to the room, read what was on the sheets and questioned the appraisers about what they had put and why. We found that people were more open and honest in this form of feedback and because the feedback was coming from a number of directions, it was more balanced and acceptable to the appraisee. But, most importantly, we found that the appraisers were getting just as much from the process because what was actually being appraised was the relationships between all the people present in the room – which takes us full circle to the emerging organization and connections.

Breaking down the traditional frameworks

Whilst running this programme, which was ongoing during the life of the TEC, we began to remove the old-style controls. Some we had already removed intuitively, as mentioned at the beginning of this chapter. Others were job descriptions, job titles, reporting lines and eventually targets and objectives. If people know best what is needed then targets and objectives are unnecessary, and the amount of time you free up in not setting, agreeing and reviewing targets is incredible. We were still being set targets by the Government but these were not being passed on to the staff. Because everyone was working so much more effectively and was so committed, we easily surpassed the Government targets – unless it was actually a poorly thought out target and we then had the evidence to demonstrate why it was a poor target.

The most contentious control we removed was budgets. The problem with budgets is that when people have them, that is what they focus on – their budget rather than what it is for. 'There's no money left in my budget', 'I need to get back on budget' or 'What shall I do with this money that is left in my budget?' were all commonly heard. A budget has no objective presence in reality, it is just a series of marks on a piece of paper. It is only the sense we make of it that makes it a budget – it is a construct. But we treat it as though it is real and we can actually see the cash associated with it – and it is ours! So we decided to take a different approach. We asked everyone to plan what they were going to do and to give us their best guess of how much it would cost and how much it would earn, if appropriate. We then took a view at the 'centre' on how realistic the plans were and drew up a central profit-and-loss account, and if necessary negotiated with people to adjust how much they would do. We then 'approved' the activities and told everyone that if the projected costs and income changed to let us know, but that it would not affect their plans because they had no budget. The outcome of this was that people focused on their activities, only predicted the amount they really needed and didn't spend like crazy at the year end to use up their budget (and therefore when attributing spend to cost codes, they now entered it where it really belonged rather than against their budget). Furthermore, we freed up a lot of resource that we could use on extra initiatives to benefit our local community.

Changing the leadership role

So, if everyone was responsible for themselves and managers were not needed, why did the TEC need a chief executive? Well, it didn't need a traditional chief executive and I had to reinvent the role. First, I adopted a 'holding leadership' style which is about the creation and protection of possibility space, and I saw my job as:

- *scanning the environment*, both external and internal, looking for regularities and patterns and analysing their likely impact on the organization
- *giving feedback* on the findings from the environment scanning, and helping to make connections between the various parts of the organization, again both internally and externally
- *clearing pathways* by identifying and removing the remaining vestiges of any inappropriate command-and-control mechanisms which were preventing people's natural potential to shine through
- *giving oceans of support* in terms of time, space, encouragement, etc. and by consistently living the philosophy
- *messing things up a bit*, in that if things were getting too comfortable and the organization was starting to drift back towards equilibrium, giving it a nudge back towards the 'edge of chaos'.

I was accountable for the organization's running but it wasn't my job to run it, rather to ensure the maintenance of all the parts of the system so that the whole exceeded the sum of the parts.

So did it work?

I believe it did because of the following feedback:

- visitors regularly commented on the buzz they could feel as soon as they entered our building and how pleasant and helpful everyone was
- we were awash with new ideas and innovations and external partners sought out our staff for the contribution they could make
- comments from our independently conducted stakeholder survey
- the findings of the London School of Economics' case study research on our TEC (www.psych.lse.ac.uk/complexity)
- the national awards we received
- the delivery of our Government contract and the renewal of our operating licence
- external benchmarking studies showed that we were getting better results with 20% less staff, although cost cutting was never on our agenda
- results from our staff attitude surveys.

All of which showed that we were getting our successes from going with the grain of the organization and by treating it as a community and a natural system – by working with it as a complex adaptive system.

So what happened next?

When TECs were abolished in 2001, Humberside TEC gave way to five successor organizations which took up the concepts and practices we had developed to varying degrees. It is important to stress that what Humberside TEC did was its response to how it evolved in its environment and that each organization has to find its own approach. The two smaller organizations have picked up the concepts and are running with them in their own ways. Sadly, however, the three larger successor bodies have not followed through with the complexity approach. This is primarily due to two reasons.

Firstly, the leadership of these successor bodies has not adopted the 'holding leadership' style but a more target-setting and checking style. The staff consequently feel frustrated and that they have less opportunity space within which to experiment and make mistakes, and no longer feel that they own the organization.

Secondly, several staff of the TEC took the opportunity to leave completely and to take their chances in the wider world. Included in this group were most of those who understood complexity best and who had been responsible for 'protecting the opportunity space'. Many of these people, myself included, are now helping in various capacities in organizations throughout the UK and several other countries to 'see things differently' and to gain the benefits of operating in this way.

Conclusion

Our story of Humberside TEC demonstrates what can be achieved by using the principles of complexity. Staff can take ownership of the organization, resulting in the development of a thriving community where innovation flourishes and traditional results improve and costs fall. However, if this is to happen, the change must start at the top with the leader living and breathing the culture, values and approach, and the concepts must be persevered with even when the going gets tough.

I firmly believe that using the concept of complexity heralds the way that organizations will have to be in the twenty-first century if they are to thrive. However, as with all new ideas, they are fragile to start with and take time to grow. But the rewards are great and the major benefits will go to those who are brave enough to let go of the past and prepared to see their organizations as the complex adaptive systems that they naturally are.

CHAPTER 25

Whole-systems working in practice: this house is for real

Barbara Douglas, Pat Gordon and Julian Pratt

This is a story about putting ideas into practice. It tells of a group of people in Newcastle who felt strongly about the quality of life of older people, especially around housing. They started to work with ideas of complexity and working whole systems as part of a development programme.[1] This story is about one of their practical achievements – adapting a house for independent living – along with a commentary about the theories that underpinned their actions.

The first draft of the chapter told the whole story, and then tried to illustrate how seeing human systems as complex adaptive systems leads us to intervene in particular ways. But it felt too tidied-up, as if it were all worked out in advance. So it seemed more honest and more interesting, as well as more in the spirit of the ideas that actually underpinned the work, to write it as a conversation. And that a good starting point would be for us to sit round the table, set the tape running, and talk about what we remember and what sense we make of what happened.

Our story is written as a conversation between the authors as a device to try to avoid the almost overwhelming temptation to tidy up the story retrospectively. The authors were part of the initial development programme. Barbara Douglas is Co-ordinator, Better Government for Older People Initiative, Newcastle. Pat Gordon and Julian Pratt are members of the Urban Partnerships Group based at the London School of Economics.

The narrative is interspersed with a commentary on complexity ideas in parentheses and italics.

The problem with telling stories

Looking back on it, it's difficult to be sure why things turned out as they did. Remember that wonderful Douglas Adams quotation? 'Anything that happens, happens. Anything that, in happening, causes itself to happen again, happens again. Anything that, in happening, causes something else to happen, causes something else to happen. It doesn't necessarily do it in chronological order, though.'[2]

It's so tempting to pretend at the beginning that you know exactly what you want to achieve and how you are going to achieve it – which means believing that you can trace the link from cause to effect. Actually, it felt as though we were having to make it up as we were going along a lot of the time. So often what makes the difference is being responsive to situations and seizing opportunities as they come along. As long as it's consistent with the meaning and overall purpose of what you are trying to achieve, and fits with the principles of how you want to work.

(Sounds like surfing a wave at the edge of equilibrium/edge of chaos. You have to be in the right place at the right time and then do something that is appropriate to the local conditions. Sometimes you catch the perfect wave, sometimes it just fizzles out. You can't expect just to roll out a standard method or toolkit.

But we are also doing things to keep the waves sweet, to keep things at the edge of equilibrium, using a pretty clear body of theory and a whole load of practices that we have tried out repeatedly and found to be consistent with the theory.)

How it began

I think we need to hear about what you actually did, but where do we start this story? In the report[3] you went back to 1995, which was six years before you actually got the house. That makes complete sense to me, but do you think other people would see the link?

I think there are a lot of people in Newcastle who would. People who were at Eldon Square keep popping up in the story.

So what do we have to say about Eldon Square? That 200 people from a wide range of agencies, and lots of older people, spent three days exploring how they could, together, work towards 'a better life in later life'. And that at the end they formed groups to work on issues they felt strongly about. That it was a *Whole System* event,[4] using a more or less straight *Future Search* design,[5] and it took place in a leisure centre called Eldon Square in the centre of Newcastle. But I'm beginning to sound like the press release.

When people say 'since Eldon Square', I think one thing they mean is people from lots of agencies took part – but there have always been interagency meetings, and partnerships have exploded since 1997, sometimes it seems as though there's no end to them. Another thing is the number of older people – 20% meant that it wasn't just tokenism, there were enough of them to stop professionals from fudging the purpose and hiding in their professional boxes. Eldon Square's become a label for a way of working that people recognize.[6] Not about fixing problems but about getting to understand each other and explore possibilities together. Older people not just being consulted but recognized as part of the solution. 'No elders, no meeting' became a kind of mantra.

Human systems

*(Everything about Eldon Square was heavily influenced by what we understood about complex adaptive systems, or perhaps more widely, living systems and ecosystems. Human systems are multiple and overlapping and what defines each one is its **meaning** and purpose, so getting clear the purpose was critical. With a purpose like improving the quality of life for older people, there were a huge number of people who **recognized themselves as a system**, and were astonished to find each other. The work of getting people in from all the **many perspectives** was vitally important, and the event provided lots of time for people to tell each other how they saw things. This provided a container for the conversations and **communication** they needed to have so that they could understand each other better and sometimes alter the way they saw things and behaved. It happened in the **here and now** and was fun. It took the whole two days – you can't do it in a two-hour meeting with a tight agenda. And we all **trusted local resourcefulness**, believing that something useful would come of it and the local system between them would know what needed to be done. That people could organize themselves during the event (within the structure of the process) and afterwards, that **patterns of order** can arise from lots of people interacting with shared purpose without anybody directing them.)*

It's pretty astonishing that two of the 'action groups' that got together then are still meeting, more than seven years later, and one of them has some of the original members. *(The two things that the whole approach really relies on are the combination of the **passion** and **responsibility** of individual people. It means that they are prepared to do a bit more, give and take a bit more, if that's what is going to make a difference.)*

Perhaps that's all you need, people who really care just getting on and doing things.

No, no, no, that's a recipe for disaster on its own. Surely you're not advocating lone heroes?

You did say that people who were at Eldon Square keep popping up in the story. Perhaps what you have here, what's made the difference, is that there is a group of you who encourage each other but also stop each other from rushing off on your own.

We understood the purpose we shared and the overall principles of how we were going to work. So we could trust each other's judgement and also take risks, knowing that we would be backed up by each other. I remember when we first talked about getting an actual house for the *House for Life*,[3] I thought 'what a crazy idea'. But I mentioned it to Vera and she said 'yes, why not' and then I took it to the housing group and it went on from there.

So where had the housing group come from?

The importance of purpose

It was one of the groups that came together after Eldon Square with people from the health authority, the housing department, Anchor Housing Trust and older people. One of them was really keen on producing a directory of housing options for older people, and that's what they did.

As usual, once people get together and start the groundwork, other people find them and give support – the printing costs for the directory came out of some end-of-year joint finance, for example. It very nearly became something much more interesting as the information people from the council, who had also been at Eldon Square, could see how this could become a web-based resource updated by residential homes themselves. It never went ahead in that form, but the ideas were developed later and something very like it is now in place.

And what happened next, after they had done what they set out to do?

Well, they didn't really know what to do. It could easily have folded at that stage.

Your role was pretty crucial there, wasn't it? You co-ordinated the 'Whole Systems' programme following Eldon Square, then the work on 'Better Government for Older People'. You took responsibility for supporting interagency working, but you weren't constrained by it being any particular piece of work as long as it involved older people. You could be receptive to opportunities as they came up.

It's not high on anybody else's agenda, or if it is then there are objectives and deadlines that undermine it. Anyway, one of the group was interested in house design and thought it crazy that houses are so often designed on the assumption that the occupants will always be fit and healthy; and equally crazy for one lot of people to be ripping out handrails and stairlifts in one set of properties while another lot are putting them into another set of properties. Of course, building regulations have changed since this all began so nowadays new buildings have more requirements for level access, downstairs toilets, and so on.

(That's an example of how effective it can be to operate through top-down designed hierarchical mechanisms that are quite the opposite of self-organization. How to use

formal power structures to lay down and enforce national minimum standards – the things that people usually mean by rules.)

We wondered if estate agents could do more to promote houses that are suitable for older people. But we didn't get any interest from estate agents, and the people who had been fired up to produce the directory weren't really interested in the new direction. (*They no longer shared the same purpose. We can see this as their recognizing that they were no longer part of the same system – and once the new purpose was clear, new people realized that they were now part of it.*

So the meaning and purpose is what enables people to know that they are part of the system – it's what sets the boundaries to the system.

Exactly. Which is why spending time clarifying purpose is time well spent.)

So that was when the focus shifted more towards 'independent living'. Older people wanted more information about what could be done, particularly to their own homes, to make it easier for them to live independently.

Attractors and energy

(*Would you say then that 'living independently in our own homes as we grow older' was an attractor for the system?*

No, definitely not. It's so easy to slip into thinking about an attractor as something that attracts things. And then for this whole language of complexity to become just a way of dressing up the old ways of doing things – attractors just become the vision thing, for example. And the idea of an attractor is too useful to lose like that – it's a chance to get quantitative in a meaningful way, as David Byrne keeps reminding us.[7] I'd use the term attractor to describe a pattern you can observe.

Suppose you plotted the population of a city on three dimensions – living independently, degree of disability and net personal wealth. If you could recognize a pattern in this plot, I'd describe it as an attractor. And if I didn't like the pattern, if it showed that wealthy people stay independent but not poorer people for example, I'd know that I wanted to perturb the system. And I'd know if things had changed by re-plotting the attractor and seeing if it had shifted.

You're getting quite hot under the collar about the theory now. We've talked, too, about passion being important in whole-system work and in the housing group. I believe you, but has it really got anything to do with complex adaptive systems?

Well, complex order arises in dissipative structures – the vortex in the bathtub, the breaking wave, the clock ticking in Conway's Game of Life. What's the source of energy in human systems? Of course we need food and water to sustain individual life, and organizations need a flow of cash. But there's a lot more to it than that. Even the cash is a sort of proxy for people wanting something to happen, whether this is to acquire a private good in the private sector or to achieve a public good in a public service. But in the sort of interorganizational work we were thinking about, things happen because people care and want to make them happen. Once we started to use the word 'passion', people kept using it – it seemed to give them permission to own up to how much they care.)

A real house

So, the group had identified a new purpose, but it was a bit abstract. We had a few meetings but we couldn't see what we could do that would be useful – it felt like going round in circles. That was when we had the idea of getting a real house to adapt to demonstrate independent living, to show people what was possible.

I think what sparked it was talking about how information gets to be useful to people. 'Information' is always top of the list when people talk about how to improve things, but actually there's almost never a dearth of facts. There usually is a handbook somewhere, the problem is that it's not in my hands when I want it. It's about a lack of communication, not a lack of information. Or it's about the information not being the information I want to hear – more an issue of power than facts.

(My guess is that when the housing group made their directory, it was the production that was more useful than the product. What makes a difference are conversations in which people inform themselves and learn about what is important to each other. As they do something together, like producing a handbook, they co-ordinate their behaviours through communication. They learn new connections and learn to trust each other.)

Our first idea was to try to get the house converted by one of those TV crews who are helicoptered in and given 36 hours to complete the work – showing lots of wonderful conversations with the older people talking about how the plans had come about. We decided against that because we were nervous that the house might fall apart after the TV crews left.

And we didn't get the media interest we'd hoped for. I think our mistake was that we didn't follow our principle of 'no elders, no meeting'. If the older people had been handling the media coverage, it might have been a completely different story. But the idea of *doing* something as a group was energizing – exciting to feel that you could transform a house.

(Doing something in the here and now provides a container for conversations – like making the directory was.)

Absolutely. Several new people came and found us at that point. And the council came on board. You see that over and over again now – once older people get enthusiastic about something, there's the possibility to engage the formal organizations, and then it really does become a system issue – and of course the organizations have the resources.

Our system or the system?

(Getting the right people involved is such a critically important aspect of this way of working. The people who can make it happen have to join in – whether that's older people, or the council, or whoever. You know something has changed when people start talking about 'our system' instead of 'the system'.

The danger with the word 'system' is that it seems to encourage some people to think that they can stand outside the system and take on the role of system designer or system engineer.

Yes, even the metaphor of gardener can be one of an outside fixer. I think this is one of the reasons why the whole issue of the quality of public services is so problematic at the moment. Government ministers and departments treat the health service and other public services as somehow 'out there', to be directed and incentivized and named and shamed. Their behaviour, and our behaviour out in the field, would be quite different if we all believed we were all in the same system with the same sense of purpose.

If we saw ourselves as part of the same system, we would be talking together about our aspirations and what we hold ourselves accountable for. But instead we are held to account for targets which are often either laughable or counter-productive because of their unexpected consequences.

You're getting into 'them and us' thinking yourself now. There must be ways to push the boundaries of the system and build a sense of solidarity that includes government, public services and the public.)

What the council wanted

Well, even on a local scale it was crucial to get the council involved. What was in it for them? What was their self-interest?

It was partly that they wanted to establish closer mainstream working between housing and health, and this was a way of demonstrating good faith and building trust by doing something positive together. Partly they were attracted by something that would show the council in good light. And I don't think it would have happened without Mary. She'd been at Eldon Square, in fact she was on the planning group so she must have been interested in working across boundaries as a district nurse. Then after Eldon Square the housing department advertised for somebody to work across health and housing, and Mary got it. She knew who we should deal with, where to send the paper saying 'we'll offer to do this if you do that'. That's what makes it a whole-system thing – that you're working all the time with insiders and with outsiders.

(That's an interesting example of an action that fosters reciprocity. A clear offer and request like that gets co-operation going from enlightened self-interest, win–win, and from there you often discover areas of shared purpose.)

So, you asked them if they had a house that they were having trouble letting that you could convert as a 'show home'?

Which, looking back on it, would never have worked. But the housing department said 'If we're going to do it, we're going to do it for real'. They found a house that people wanted to live in, not one that's hard to let, and that actually needed conversion for somebody with special mobility needs. We went to a meeting – we thought it was another meeting to try to persuade them – and the men in suits came in with plans of the house, and suddenly we had a timetable to hit.

Adapting the house

So the housing group took overall responsibility for the House for Life, and you brought in more elders.

Yes, about a dozen people were keen to join a sort of reference group. They had a series of meetings with expert informants about things like heating, and access, and sensory awareness and the garden. And everybody was so enthusiastic – the experts to share and the elders to learn. They had ten sessions in all, over about nine months.

And was it as easy to agree the recommendations with the council?

Well, the council was worried at the beginning that the elders would want gold-plated taps. They called it the House for Real, to keep this in check. The older people called it the House for Life. I think to begin with the ambiguity helped, for all that we talk about getting purpose clear. It contained the anxiety. But there was no need – the council were amazed at just how reasonable the elders were. They wanted it to be real too. People understood that they were trying to do this together – there was a lot of give and take.

People working in public services so often have the expectation that 'they'll want the earth'. And as a consequence of this mental model, workers have a rule of thumb that keeps telling them 'don't raise expectations'. All of your experience and ours is that if people are involved early and honestly, they are astonishingly realistic.

Simple rules

(There's a lot of scepticism about the idea of 'simple rules', but I'm quite sure that if public sector workers doing consultation exercises have a rule of thumb running round in their head that says 'don't raise expectations', then the pattern of order that arises in the consultation process is going to be very different from one arising from 'be honest about the givens'.

Talk about 'rules' is so easily incorporated in the mental model of designed systems. It's the same as 'whole systems' or 'network' or even 'partnership' – for a while people are intrigued as they recognize that this may be a way of thinking that might allow some space for working in a more organic way. Then in no time 'whole systems' means 'plans for everything', network means 'managed clinical network', and 'partnerships' have to put their energy into designing their organizational structures. I heard a civil servant recently saying that 'four-hour trolley waits' in A&E would make a good 'simple rule'. It might make a desirable system goal, but it's not something that could shape the behaviour of the people whose behaviour produces the waits – patients and the people who work in general practice, A&E, diagnostics, hospital wards and social services. No wonder there is scepticism – and a good thing too.

I think we did have one powerful rule of thumb though – 'no elders, no meeting'. I'm sure the work would have been entirely different if elders had been optional extras.)

All right, back to the house. Weren't there any battles about the recommendations?

The elders wanted a stair-lift and the council found it difficult to convince them that it wouldn't work. In the end the elders gave in and accepted that it had to be a through-the-floor lift. They got the full-length patio doors though – they were adamant that the room needed more light and that you need to be able to see the garden when sitting down. The council hadn't thought it important enough to warrant the extra expense. And the council got a bit panicky when we got in some people to talk about low-maintenance gardens, though by this stage the older people were just interested in what was possible, not trying to put pressure on. In the end, I think the designers began to really understand how important access to the garden is for a disabled person. They went that extra inch by implementing more of the low-maintenance design than they originally agreed to do.

And then the work on the house was done, and you opened to the public. Remember how proud you all were when you showed us round?

Yes, it was a very good feeling. One of the elders was always there to show people round for the whole three weeks it was open. It meant that when older people came round, or their families, they could ask 'somebody like us'. The same thing worked at the Age Concern exhibition and conference later that year. We had a stand about the House for Life which was one of the most visited, mainly I think because it was staffed by older people, not by younger professionals.

What the council got out of it

And what did the council get out of it?

Well, they certainly used the three weeks that the house was open. A team came to make a video. Housing managers brought round their staff to see the house and talk to the older people. I've already mentioned their surprise at how reasonable the elders were, and how positive and useful the process was. I think they really began to understand just what a big difference quite small things can make to people's quality of life – you have to live that, not just hear it.

(*So the house, while it was open, provided a container for all sorts of conversations that would otherwise never have taken place.*)

They got good publicity too – the House for Life was shortlisted for the Roy Griffiths Award in *The Guardian*, wasn't it?

And it was a good experience too. Somebody from social services said, 'Usually when I go out from the office I get torn to shreds'. Now they know it doesn't have to be like that. So we've become something of a resource to the system now – we're doing a 'listening event' to engage elders in the development of the housing strategy. We've got an 'older persons' and carers' reading group' that formed to comment on a draft leaflet about independent living. I think we may get into drafting things now, not just commenting on them.

And the council asked us to contribute to the Best Value Review. The House for Life was held up as an example of working positively with local people. There were lots of building contractors there, and we ended up talking about 'Homes for Life', so we were almost back full circle, picking up on our early interest in designing new homes.

It would be interesting if they got to involving elders in the design process. Wasn't there something about a smart house too?

Yes, that's still going on. The housing department thought the House for Life had gone so well they've asked the group to do something similar about a high-tech house.

What the elders got out of it

So the council got a lot out of this – what about the elders, do you think?

Well, they had a chance to talk about this. There was a research project about 'Housing Choices' who asked if they could interview the group, and they agreed. Some of them liked the purpose, the fact that it was so positive. Some liked the fact that they were learning new things. For some it was contributing, making a difference, being engaged in the world – there are so few ways available to people to influence public services apart from complaining or being consulted. And some of it was social, and that's fine too.

(*Yes, if it's self-organization it has to feed people, not just exhaust their goodwill. Reciprocity again. One of the other groups that formed at Eldon Square was about discharge from hospital, and I remember one man coming to a planning meeting with a bottle of his home-made wine and he said, 'It's one of the things I learned at Eldon Square – you can make a difference and still have fun'.*)

Human systems

I've certainly enjoyed hearing about this again. It really was a great piece of work.

(But is it in any way connected to complex adaptive systems? Haven't we just been describing an example of good practice that could have happened anywhere at any time?

People do have a lifetime's experience of operating in complex human systems. It's just that we don't seem to use it much in our organizational life compared with, say, our families and networks of friends. Thinking of human systems as complex adaptive systems is a way of making this experience explicit. It reminds us that we can trust that we don't need to design and plan and vision and measure and performance manage and motivate everything. It reminds us that people in positions of formal power are often most effective when they identify a sense of meaning and purpose that others identify with, and behave as though they are part of that system. It reminds us that repeated local interactions can produce patterns of order. Things happen. They cause themselves to happen again. They cause something else to happen. Yes, the House for Life might well have happened anyway, even if none of us had ever heard of complex adaptive systems. It wouldn't necessarily have done it in chronological order, though.)

References

1 Harries J, Gordon P, Plampling D *et al.* (1999) *Elephant Problems and Fixes that Fail: the story of a search for new approaches to interagency working.* Whole-Systems Thinking Working Papers Series. King's Fund, London.
2 Adams D (1992) *Mostly Harmless.* Heinemann, London.
3 Better Government for Older People: *House for Life report 1999–2000,* bgopnewcastle @nhcp.freeserve.co.uk.
4 Pratt J, Gordon P and Plampling D (1999) *Working Whole Systems: putting theory into practice in organisations.* King's Fund, London.
5 Weisbord MR and Janoff S (1995) *Future Search: an action guide to finding common ground in organizations and communities.* Berrett-Koehler, San Francisco, CA.
6 Douglas B (1997) It's the elephant they never forget. *Working with Older People.* **July:** 18–22.
7 Byrne D (1998) *Complexity Theory and the Social Sciences.* Routledge, London.

CHAPTER 26

Complex adaptive systems: interesting theory or useful practice? The Piedmont Hospital Bed Control Experiment

Leigh Hamby, Laura Day and Sarah Fraser

This chapter provides an example of a successful quality initiative that has been delivered through techniques other than the traditional improvement methods. It was not approached in the analytical way of gathering baseline data, mapping the process, analysing it, testing and making changes, and monitoring progress with a run chart. Instead, staff were provided with a simple real-time system that enabled them to receive feedback on their personal impact on the system so they could adjust their behaviour to achieve the system's goals. It demonstrates that complexity principles can generate satisfactory solutions as an alternative to traditional re-engineering techniques.

Introduction

I am a physician who practised general surgery in a private community hospital for several years and had left practice with visions of learning how to become a 'change agent'. I was scheduled to start a new job at Piedmont Hospital as 'physician advisor' and wanted to experiment with thinking about healthcare organizations as complex adaptive systems. In general, most were stories that used complexity to explain an outcome retrospectively (stock-market crash, fall of the Berlin Wall, etc.). While the concepts resonated with my own experiences,

I was left wondering if there was really any use to the ideas beyond reconstructing the past. Could they be applied to moving into the future?

After reading everything I could get my hands on about complexity, I decided to actually start a 'project' with the intention of using complexity thinking. I wanted to see if:

- a net improvement in a complex adaptive system (like a hospital) could be accomplished intentionally using ideas from complexity thinking
- it would be easier and 'more fun' for myself and others participating in the change compared to past 'change approaches'
- I could somehow collect the experience when it was over and make some statement about whether complexity was actually useful, rather than merely interesting.

Now that I was hired specifically to give advice for the improvement of patient flow through a hospital, it seemed like a good time to take complexity for a test drive. To start this, I realized that if I wanted results *different* than my prior experience with change, I was going to have to be *different*.

The changes in my own personal behaviour that would be necessary were simple but profound:

- to stop planning the change as much as I usually did in advance
- to stop telling others how I think they should change. Instead I was going to have to listen to them, 'follow their lead' and 'adapt on the fly'
- to stop trying to resolve conflict and 'get everybody on the same page'.

I knew I was going to have to relinquish control of the change process more than I had in the past. This was both frightening and liberating. I will start the story there as it's as good as any other place to start . . .

Context

Piedmont hospital is a 450-bed, acute-care hospital struggling with issues related to diversion. Diversion is used to describe a hospital that is operating near or beyond maximum capacity. This requires patients to be redirected elsewhere because there is no available capacity (beds and/or nursing staff). The amount of time that Piedmont had spent on diversion had continually increased over the preceding one to two years. Concerns were being raised about capacity issues impacting patient, staff and physician satisfaction as well as revenue and reputation that were potentially at stake. While there is pride in being 'so popular that you are too busy', most in leadership at the hospital felt that something should be done. The board of directors had decided to recruit a physician to work with the existing utilization review staff to lower the length of stay and 'work with' practising physicians on improving their efficiency and 'stewardship' of the hospitals resources – namely the hospital bed. Physician advisor was my new title.

My prior experience had taught me to appreciate the importance physicians place on their own autonomy. I also learned that you cannot get a complete clinical picture of patients by reviewing just their chart and laboratory data. One quick peak into a patient's room whose chart appeared ready for discharge was worth a thousand words. Finally, I found myself agonizing about how one could shorten length of stay and movement of patients through the system without pestering physicians. Feeling frustrated, I had caught myself trying to 'control' the change again. I decided to work elsewhere.

Controlling bed access

Bed access was managed by the Bed Control Group, made up of:

- A bed control nurse (a nurse who works a 12-hour shift which changes at 7 a.m. or 7 p.m., seven days a week). Their work, while dispersed throughout the hospital, is to process bed requests from various areas in the hospital and outside the hospital. They communicate to each other via the phone or fax to match the patient needs to an available bed.
- A direct admit nurse (Joanie works Monday to Wednesday and Denise, Thursday and Friday). They control direct access from the physician's office, helping to avoid patients going to the emergency department and waiting for admission.
- The admissions clerk, Christie. She assigns the room number into the hospital's main computer system following input from the above nurses.

However, this process had become so successful that demand had increased and waiting times for bed assignment became the new problem. Only 18% of requests resulted in a bed assignment within one hour of the request and 22% of patients were waiting more than four hours, with the resulting dissatisfaction for both patients and doctors.

In an attempt to try to understand the work processes for a bed control nurse, I invited myself to make rounds with Lori one morning. She is a quiet, serious-minded woman in her late forties. While she was tolerant of my tagging along, she seemed perplexed by my silly questions. Questions like 'Why do we do things that way?' or 'What about . . .'. She was very kind and patient and her answers were usually some variation of 'Because it seems to work' or 'It's the way we have always done it'. Lori's job is to make rounds on the seven to eight medical/ surgical units and discuss with the charge nurses in each area the patients likely to be discharged. She also determines how the unit is doing in terms of staffing, patient issues, upset families, etc. While trying to conduct these rounds, she was constantly (every 60 seconds or so) being interrupted by a phone call on her mobile phone with a bed request. These requests came from the emergency department, transfer out of the intensive care unit (ICU) or patients who needed to be moved to another area of the hospital. During rounds, she had accumulated a significant number of names on her clipboard. After completing rounds, I asked her what she was going to do about all the bed requests she had collected. 'Now,' she said, 'we go see Christie.'

Christie is a twenty-something Southern lady who works in the admissions office. While her education includes some college, she is not a nurse. At first glance, I would have guessed her to be a restaurant hostess rather than the cornerstone for admissions at a large urban hospital. After only a few moments, I discovered that this straight-talking Georgia girl was up to the task.

Christie's job is to take the myriad of bed requests from the bed control nurse, recovery room, outside hospitals, direct admit nurse and internal transfers. She sprinkles in requests from individual patients and physicians, accounts for the specific capabilities of nursing staff and physical characteristics of each area, and produces a room number. Some of the requests are pre-sorted into bed type and priority by the direct admit or bed control nurse. Christie's ability to recall which rooms had been assigned to a patient – the when, where and why – was similar to watching an auctioneer dealing blackjack while talking to a crippled jumbo jet from an air traffic control tower. After several days of observation, I grew to appreciate the complexity of what she did and the skill with how she did it.

Christie suffered from constant phone interruptions, the same as Lori. In fact, many of their phone interruptions came from each other. This was augmented with use of voice-mail and follow-up phone calls about whether they had received their voice-mails from each other. Compounded on top of this was the fact that when patients, doctors or nurses were dissatisfied with the rapidity with which they received their bed assignment, Christie would receive an occasional harsh phone call. Most times, Christie had more patients needing a bed than she had beds to assign. Christie worked in a pressure cooker similar to Wall Street stock traders as seen in popular movies.

I began to think of the label of Bed Control at Piedmont Hospital as a living, breathing ecosystem comprised of Christie, the bed control nurse, the direct admit nurse, and now, despite my reluctance to admit it, me. The ecosystem feeds on patients and beds. The ecosystem helps convert those raw materials into patients healing after discharge from their inpatient bed. The by-products of the system were dirty beds, paper, phone calls and tremendous personal energy expenditure. To remove any one of these elements would disrupt the entire system. Despite its many frustrations, the ecosystem had reached a steady state and survived up until now, using the same methods for several years. However, the intensity and aggravation of living as a member of that ecosystem struck me as not consistent with long-term survival of an individual agent. In thinking about diversion, it seemed this ecosystem was not able to meet the needs of patients and physicians waiting for beds. The question then arises, how could the ecosystem *intentionally evolve* into something seen as better?

Evolution versus transformation

We started with a fundamental question: where was there waste in the system? When I asked 'What has already been done to deal with waste in the system?', the answer I got was 'We bought a bigger trash can!'.

Everyone admitted much of the time on the phone felt like a waste. For example:

'I just sent you the fax about the bed request on Mr Jones. Did you get it?'
'Yes, I got it, and no, I don't have a bed assignment yet.'

Thirty minutes later the phone rings again:

'Bed yet for Mr Jones?'
'Yes, I just left it on your voice-mail while you were calling me.'

Given that approximately 2200 admissions are processed each month, two phone calls per admission seemed like a large opportunity for waste reduction. In fact, one of the bed control nurses (who has since retired) had develop a callous on her ear from using the phone so much!

It was 2 a.m. and I couldn't sleep because of a recurring dream I was having. Christie was working in an air-traffic control tower trying to land a jumbo jet and the phone kept ringing. It hit me in one of those 'night inspirations' that we all have, but rarely can recall or make sense of the next day. Bed control is really very similar to air traffic control. Christie needs incoming arrival information (bed requests) and departing flight information (discharges to free up beds for incoming arrivals). How could we format the incoming arrivals without all of the phone calls and paper waste?

The next morning I described my nightmare to Christie, who immediately grasped the concept. 'What if this could be done electronically so that I could see the bed request [without a phone call]. I could enter the bed assignment to be seen whenever Joanie came back to her desk, instead of voice-mail and fax?' We excitedly called Joanie with the idea and shared it with her. She could think of about 20 different reasons why it wouldn't work, the most important of which seemed to be her concern that Denise would be unwilling to type in the information instead of the fax/two phone call system. We all agreed that there had to be a better way, but what was 'it' going to be?

On the search for 'it', we dismissed the use of email, walkie-talkies, tin cans on a string and a variety of other ideas that just didn't seem to fit. During one of these conversations, I was paged to a number I didn't recognize. I dialled the number and got John, the Vice President of Information Technology (IT) at Piedmont: 'Dr Hamby, I just wanted to welcome you to Piedmont and introduce you to Ms Bees. She will be able to help you with any IT issues that you might have in your new job here.' Sheepishly I told him thanks and hung up. Christie asked, 'Who was that?'

'The IT guy,' I said.

'What is IT?' she asked. I explained about the information technology people who run all of the computers. 'Oh,' she says. 'I wondered why somebody would have the title of "it" guy.' We both paused as we realized the implications of what she had said. She had just said that IT could be the 'it' we were looking for.

'Hey, maybe they could start us a website and tell everybody to put the requests in there.'

'Yeah, right . . .' [nervous laughter].

'Yeah, right. That's it! IT is "it"!'

I called Ms Bees and thanked her for being my official IT connection: 'Do you know anybody who can build websites?'

'Sure, we have a guy named John that does that for us. Here is his number!' John is a youngster (in my eyes) who builds websites for the hospital to be used for marketing, etc. I called him and pitched him this idea. Joanie, the direct admit nurse, would get phone calls from doctors' offices about a patient that required a bed. Joanie would type the information into a website that was viewable to both her and Christie. The website would make an audible 'ding' on Christie's side to let her know that a bed had been requested. Christie would secure the bed and input the room number into the website for it to send an audible 'ding' back to Joanie. The website would sort the requests into a queue for Christie to view by whatever priority Joanie would assign highest to lowest. John said, 'Get Christie and Joanie to come up with the input screen for Joanie and the output screen for Christie.'

I asked, 'By the way, could you start a timer to be associated with every patient, so we know how long patients are waiting?'

'No problem, give me a couple of weeks.'

The next two weeks were filled with dreaming of a website. Joanie and Christie worked together, with me running back and forth, to develop the screen that Joanie would enter information into for a bed request and the screen Christie would view and input a room number. I forwarded these to John and after two weeks he called and said he wanted to show us what he had.

John met me in the hospital lobby and we walked over to the admissions office. He pulled up the website and showed it to Christie and talked through a couple of simulated patients. She loved it. We then went over to direct admit and found Joanie was not there that day, but Denise was. We showed it to Denise, who hadn't heard anything about this up until now: 'I like it, but be sure and get Joanie's input.' The next day, we showed Joanie. She thought it looked pretty good. Joanie and Christie decided to try to use it the next day. For the next several weeks, we excitedly shared different ideas as we thought of them. We would forward the new ideas for improvements to John, who would add them to the system. As their confidence in the technology grew, they began using the application regularly for real patients (*see* Figure 26.1).

I was struck by how easily and readily these people took hold of this change. So much of our lives in organizations is spent agonizing about how hard it is to 'get people to change their behaviour', and yet this seemed so easy. In fact, this was actually fun. It made it exciting to come to work everyday to see what new ideas they would have. An example of how powerful the desire was for this change came one day when John was trying to work on the website while they were using it. He put on the site in big red letters 'website under construction – do not use', but it was used anyway. You couldn't stop them! Even though it crashed several times in a day, they kept reloading the patients and using it. Were these two people unusual? Was there something about this kind of change that made it more fun? Was it me? Was it John?

Upon reflection, what seemed different about this was the people impacted by the changed actually *designed* the change. I simply stayed out of their way and provided resources (John) that made sense to them, and it allowed them the

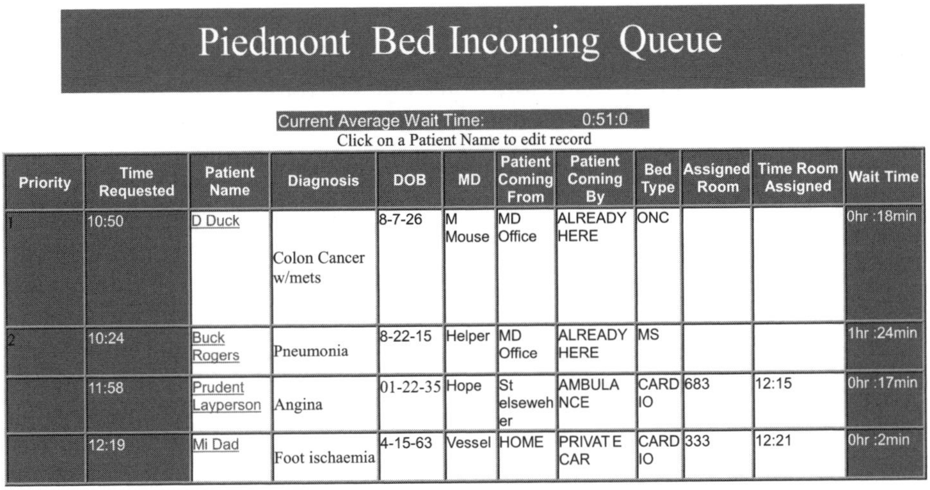

Piedmont Bed Incoming Queue

Priority	**Time Requested**	**Patient Name**	**Diagnosis**	**DOB**	**MD**	**Patient Coming From**	**Patient Coming By**	**Bed Type**	**Assigned Room**	**Time Room Assigned**	**Wait Time**
1	10:50	D Duck	Colon Cancer w/mets	8-7-26	M Mouse	MD Office	ALREADY HERE	ONC			0hr :18min
2	10:24	Buck Rogers	Pneumonia	8-22-15	Helper	MD Office	ALREADY HERE	MS			1hr :24min
	11:58	Prudent Layperson	Angina	01-22-35	Hope	St elseweher	AMBULANCE	CARDIO	683	12:15	0hr :17min
	12:19	Mi Dad	Foot ischaemia	4-15-63	Vessel	HOME	PRIVATE CAR	CARDIO	333	12:21	0hr :2min

Current Average Wait Time: 0:51:0
Click on a Patient Name to edit record

Figure 26.1   Web page screenshot.

freedom to play with the application and improve it. The amount of energy they put into it was unlike anything thing I had seen before. They were animated and constantly thinking of new ideas of how to improve the web application. It does help to have an IT person on your side who enjoys the work too! The group seemed most energized by their making a request for a change and seeing it 'come alive' in such a short turnaround.

Another interesting observation was the relationship between these folks improved as a result of the change. Perhaps the change was successful because of a growing relationship between the four of us. I don't know or care which is which. Members of the group would go to sports events together. The level of respect they held for each other seemed to increase daily.

The impact of the system on the hospital gathered pace rapidly. Over the next year our system had been adopted by the recovery room and emergency department, and the bed control nurses, initially reluctant to embrace the web technology, were using hand-held computers. We were also supplying physicians directly with information on bed waits through a number of channels.

Reflection

Our approach appears to have worked in that the desired improvement in waiting time for a bed to be assigned has been dramatically improved compared with the alternative option of increasing bed capacity (*see* Table 26.1). All this has been achieved without expenditure on additional capacity.

One of the concerns with complex redesign projects is the uncertainty of their impact on the system as a whole and the difficulties of implementing an improvement when most staff feel the only solution is to add capacity. In this study, instead of fighting the organization, we developed a system of feedback that would enable stakeholders to modify their behaviour and work *with* the bed assignment system, rather than to conduct a full redesign project. This minimized the disruption and tension that can be caused by management-led change initiatives whilst improving the workflow for the individuals involved. The reality was that no individual person had knowledge of what the 'right' design would be that could balance a variety of competing imperatives. However, there was a belief that all the staff in the hospital wanted the desired outcome (less time waiting for a bed) and that given adequate feedback about their role in the system they would take personal responsibility to act appropriately, with the group in mind, i.e they had the ability to self-organize around a key goal.

So how did the improvement take place if there were no ordinary management activities like mapping of processes, meetings, discussions about what to change, etc.? One way of explaining the behaviour in the system is that collective intelligence was at work. Davenport defines collective intelligence as

Table 26.1   Benefits of web-based feedback solution vs. adding capacity

	Web feedback to improve utilization of existing 'hidden capacity'	Adding beds to existing capacity
Time to implement	6 weeks	1–2 years
Cost	$	$$$
Change tactic	Social processes and the task worked together	Task-based management intervention
Impact for patients	Improve waiting times through new process. 64% of patients allocated a bed within 1 hour (220% improvement). Approximate two-thirds reduction in numbers waiting over 4 hours	Possibly improve waiting times though still use existing cumbersome processes
Impact for physicians	More continuous knowledge and learning about current system performance. Potentially more 'aggravating' now that connection of doctor to 'hospital system' more explicit	Easier to use more beds
Impact for hospital	Improve staff satisfaction to make existing work process easier. Reduction in paperwork and phone calls	Add more work for existing staff

'insight which is based on collective understanding of work practices'.[1] Szuba builds on this by suggesting it is 'a property of a social structure, initializing when individuals interact, and as a result acquires the ability to solve new or more complex problems'.[2]

To enable collective intelligence there needs to be four key factors:

- *Shared goals* are critical in enabling individuals within a system to use the information they receive to adjust their behaviour in the direction of achieving the desired outcome.[3,4] In this bed assignment initiative the goals were quite clear – to reduce the time patients spent waiting for a bed. It was a simple outcome for which no detailed discussion was planned or took place to agree such a goal.

- *Feedback* needs to be about *individual* performance, so the individual can 'see' their part in the whole and influence their own behaviour for the benefit of the group.[5] Feedback also needs to be as real-time as possible so the physician can make immediate small changes. So performance measures that are listed perhaps monthly that are two to five weeks out of date may provide a measure of performance in the past, but are unlikely to provide individuals within the system the means by which they can 'see' where they fit and adjust their behaviour accordingly. This is the difference between a 'report card' versus an 'instrument panel'.[6,7] The report card method of providing data after the fact may be helpful for measuring performance. However, an instrument panel provides immediate feedback, enabling individuals in the system to react, correct and improve straight away, i.e. the improvement is continuous.
- *Connectivity.* How individuals are connected makes a difference to how both individual and group decisions are made.[8–11] The networks of physicians and staff around Piedmont Hospital create a unique social structure that bears little resemblance to the formal structure and hierarchy of the organization. It is well known that the adoption of good ideas, of good practice, depends on communication through these social structures.[12,13] In this bed assignment work, the focus was on working with these social processes.
- *Dialogue.* The ongoing two-way communication that is an essential ingredient for collective intelligence to emerge.[14,15] There were no formal structures or infrastructure created at Piedmont Hospital to enable dialogue, other than the creation of the web system as an augmentation of the existing telephone bed request process. The physicians and staff used their current networks and developed new ones if appropriate and necessary.

We now have a group of seven to ten people talking regularly (daily) about the web applications and little tweaks from time to time. This entire 'project' never had a strategic plan, a budget, a project manager, one memo or meeting. Instead we have people who know and respect each other, come together on the fly to problem solve and work out issues. In terms of 'job satisfaction', most of them have come up to me and told me how much more fun it has been to work here now compared to two years ago. Diversion hours are down by 50% and the number of patients actually treated has increased by 3%. Members of the group have actually expressed concerns: 'Is the hospital less busy than it used to be? It just doesn't seem to be as hectic around here as it used to be'. The actual data prove otherwise. Periodically we all go out to the ball game together, drink a beer and eat some food.

For me personally, I have found using principles described in complex adaptive systems thinking in an ongoing collaboration very liberating. I don't feel like I need to maintain control of things or people. I have seen more collaboration, energy, excitement and new ideas from a group of people unlike anything I have participated in previously. There is a real sense of transformation.

The most important take-home point for me has been how much this effort has shown me that the work in organizations is really about relationships. Technology and tools are only as good as the relationships they are developed to support. However, the development of those tools and technology can help build better relationships. Each member of the group contributed and the transformation would not have occurred without each of us. To those folks I want to extend my gratitude for letting me play along.

References

1 Davenport E (2000) Social intelligence in the age of networks. *Journal of Information Science.* **26** (3): 145–52.

2 Szuba T (2001) A formal definition of the phenomenon of collective intelligence and its IQ measure. *Future Generation Computer Systems.* **17** (4): 489–500.

3 Castelfranchi C (1998) Modelling social action for AI agents. *Artificial Intelligence.* **103** (1–2): 157–82.

4 Frantz TG (1998) Visioning the future of social systems: evolutionary and discontinuous leap approaches. *Systems Research and Behavioral Science.* **15** (3): 173–82.

5 Kelly K (1994) *Out of Control: the new biology of machines.* Addison-Wesley, Reading, MA.

6 Nelson EC, Batalden PB, Plume SK *et al.* (1995) Report cards or instrument panels: who needs what? *Joint Commission Journal on Quality Improvement.* **21** (4): 155–66.

7 Nugent WC, Schults WC, Plume SK *et al.* (1994) Designing an instrument panel to monitor and improve coronary artery bypass grafting. *Journal of Clinical Outcomes Management.* **1** (2): 57–64.

8 Yang HL (1995) A network model for organizational decision making. *Cybernetics and Systems.* **26** (2): 211–36.

9 Valente TW (1993) Diffusion of innovations and policy decision making. *Journal of Communication.* **43** (1): 30–45.

10 Valente TW (1996) Social network thresholds in the diffusion of innovations. *Social Networks.* **18** (1): 69–89.

11 Valente TW and Davis RL (1999) Accelerating the diffusion of innovations using opinion leaders. *Annals of the American Academy of Political and Social Science.* **566**: 55–67.

12 Rogers EM (1995) Lessons for guidelines from the diffusion of innovations. *Joint Commission Journal on Quality Improvement.* **21** (7): 324–8.

13 NHS Centre for Reviews and Dissemination (1999) Getting evidence into practice. *Effective Health Care.* **5** (1). University of York.

14 Taylor JR (2001) The 'rational' organization reconsidered: an exploration of some of the organizational implications of self-organizing. *Communication Theory.* **11** (2): 137–77.

15 Wright T (1999) Systems thinking and systems practice: working in the fifth dimension. *Systemic Practice and Action Research.* **12** (6): 607–31.

CHAPTER 27

Applying complexity theory to primary healthcare organizations

Paul Thomas

> In this chapter I intend to give some examples of how I have translated complexity and whole-system theories into practice. These examples all allow different perspectives to be considered within an evolving story. Reflecting as a team on these helps to make sense of the overall emerging direction. At the level of an individual practitioner, I struggle to be a *reflective practitioner* using the ideas of *narrative-based primary care* to consider different kinds of evidence when helping a patient to make sense of their multiple problems. At an organizational level, I use the ideas of *organizational learning* to devise multiple feedback loops and multidisciplinary working to allow the whole organization to optimistically move forward. At a systems level, I weave together different research paradigms, set inside a heartbeat of *whole-system participatory action research*.

Introduction – the relevance of complexity theory to practice, to organizations and to research and development in primary care

I like complexity theory because it allows me to believe in common sense. Every gardener knows that different flowers, insects and animals are constantly interacting and affecting each other's growth. Neatly separated rows of flowers and straight lines have always been created artificially. Common sense says that sometimes sun and sometimes rain is needed for good growth, and what grows well one year may fail the next. Keen sensitivity to local conditions is needed to know when to protect from wind and rain, how much to prevent a strongly growing flower from overpowering others and how to use the growth of one thing to enhance the growth of other things. Common sense is what the gardener develops from witnessing the patterns arising from complex interactions of multiple factors.

Yet we academics seem to forget this truth when theorizing about the world. Instead we dream theories about a simple, ordered world where things neither interact nor change. Complexity theory offers an alternative model where individual parts are in constant evolution, and connected within bigger wholes, which themselves are in constant adaptation to other parts and other wholes. So applying complexity theory in practice is the same thing as operating in a way that allows parts and wholes to evolve in synchrony. Complexity theory leads to whole-system theory.

As a general practitioner, I know that people present not with a set of diagnoses but with stories. They expect me to engage with these stories. We (me, the patient or both of us together) identify discrete problems inside these stories that become labelled as 'diagnoses'. These discrete separated diagnoses are extracted from a much richer, more meaningful and connected concept of health. This is what complexity and whole-system theories imply – that multiple diverse factors in people's lives are meaningfully connected. Part of the role of the generalist healer is to bring into view these diverse connections so the person can make sense of their health as a whole and not merely as a list of discrete diseases.

As a developer of primary healthcare, I know that the metaphor of 'carrot and stick' gives no insight to the skill of leading and managing change. 'Carrot and stick' is a metaphor made for donkeys. But a carrot does not have enough calorific value to sustain more than a short journey of the strongest donkey. And the main purpose of a stick is to inflict pain, not to help understand why a journey might be worth taking. Most self-respecting donkeys, I am sure, would prefer a map and understanding of the general direction. Complexity and whole-system theories imply the need to respect the intelligence of everyday people and value their participation. Diverse members of an organization need to take part in defining the overall strategy and through dialogue and ongoing review, both internally and externally, find the paths that make best sense for them as individuals and for the organization(s) as a whole.

As a researcher in primary healthcare, I know that the so-called 'gold standard' of randomized controlled trials has no predictive power when more than a few factors are involved. That is why they need 'laboratory conditions' that control for (that is, prevent) the normal adaptation of one thing to another. As a consequence this method is not able to bring into view the result of complex interactions. Complexity and whole-system theories require us to recognize that research insights do not stand alone, but are windows into bigger, deeper, more connected, richer and more human wholes than any one insight on its own can reveal.

Applying complexity/whole-system theories as a generalist practitioner – working with the ideas of narrative-based primary care

The main role of primary care is to help people to develop new narratives for themselves.

(Launer, 2002[1])

General practice educational literature seems united about the value of the concept of the reflective practitioner. Schon writes: 'I have advocated an epistemology of practice based on the idea of reflection-in-action.'[2] Epistemology seeks to define knowledge and establish its limits.[3] Epistemology asks 'what is the nature of the relationship between the knower (the inquirer) and the known (or knowable)?'[4] To which Schon might reply that the knower and the known cannot be totally separated and to be meaningful, knowledge must be reflected on and acted out in a real-life situation. This is the social constructionist argument that truth is generated through interaction of various factors. Consequently, knowledge is only completely valid in the context of its generation. Or put another way, scientific facts are not as objective and reliable as we are taught to believe – a reflective practitioner must use scientific evidence wisely and be open to multiple interpretations and the value of different kinds of knowledge.

I have nothing here to add to what others have said about the value of reflection-in-action, expect to make a connection with the concept of narrative-based primary care. Launer, in his very accessible book, argues the need to replace the idea of patient-centredness with the idea of being 'story-centred'.[1] He reminds us that when we extract a diagnosis from the enormously complex life story of a patient, we are focusing on one medical part – but the overall health of a patient requires integration of all aspects of their health. It is the meaning in people's stories, the sense they make of them, that connects the parts and the wholes. In complexity theory terms, meaning or sense making are fractal. It is a central part of the generalist role to explore with patients their stories and what sense they make of their multiple problems and overall health.

The theory of complexity and whole systems can be a mental struggle – it can't avoid using long words and several ideas at the same time. The application is a different kind of struggle – it is hard work. It takes time, patience, planning and concentration to be a reflective practitioner. But it does make sense and it is very personally rewarding. These are some of the things I try to do to live it out – that is, to connect with patients' stories and to reflect with them on the meaning of it all:

- Scan the patient's notes before they come in and read my previous notes about what I thought we might do next time, preparing to quickly re-establish connection with their story.

- Try to quickly get out of the way factual things to leave more time for sense making. For example, I go to the waiting room to call the next patient in and as we enter the room I might say something like 'Good news, all your tests are normal', perhaps getting them out of the way to create space for different kinds of conversations when we sit down.
- Ask patients for a list of complaints at the beginning of the consultation; then ask about anything else; then get them to prioritize them before we look at them together. I find that this helps to build a richer picture of their situation and to cut quickly to the most helpful focus.
- Ask patients what sense they themselves make of their complaints, and use personal anecdotes and humour to relate to this.
- Use portfolio learning, a diary and to-do lists to capture my own learning needs.

Applying complexity/whole-system theories in primary care organizations – working with the ideas of organizational learning

Most organizational theorists, as well as most philosophers, mistake the certainty of structures seen in hindsight for the emergent order that frames living forward. Neither group of scholars has come to grips with the fact that their conceptual understandings trail life and are of a different character than is living forward.

(Kierkegaard[5])

The popularization of the concept of the *learning organization* owes much to Peter Senge.[6] He describes the 'fifth discipline' that is needed to be a leader in these organizations as *systems thinking*. Systems thinking means thinking about connections. So systems thinking, like reflective practice, is concerned with considering the connections between various different parts and knowing that what has already happened in the past does not exactly determine what will happen in the future. Senge's other 'disciplines' are personal mastery, mental models, building shared vision and team learning – all important for effective leadership within complex systems. There are many other writers about organizational learning. Huxom describes processes and structures to support whole organizational learning.[7] Argyris and Schön (the same Schön who described reflective practice) describe the need for simultaneous single-, double- and deutero-learning in such organizations.[8] All are worth reading.

Between 1999 and 2003, I was researching the factors in primary care groups and primary care trusts that facilitate innovation and learning. Our team gathered data from four case-study primary care groups and used cross-London surveys and stakeholder workshops to identify what things help people to learn and innovate in the midst of multiple interacting factors. In effect, we were researching how to apply complexity theory in organizations. These are the headline conclusions:

- Understandable corporate and clinical governance, quality leadership and the vision of a learning organization provide a good basis for a primary care group to facilitate learning and innovation.
- Multi-level 'learning spaces' that connect throughout the whole system are needed if innovative thinking in one part of the system is to be built on elsewhere. This approach is unfamiliar in primary care.
- Both clinicians and managers are needed in leadership roles. A facilitative leadership style that encourages participation is needed from both. They must be able to consider the impact of innovation throughout the whole system and not merely in isolated parts.
- The right timing for an initiative is an important determinant of success and established interventions for learning and change need to be adapted to the local context.
- External facilitation is useful when it provides an opportunity for people to make sense of their experience and to agree both long-term vision and short-term steps towards this vision.

These are examples of applying complexity/whole-systems theories. They help create an environment that can make sense of multiple interacting factors. They help identify and meaningfully manage complex interactivity.

Applying complexity/whole-system theories in primary care research and development – working with the idea of whole-system participatory action research

What we observe is not nature itself, but nature exposed to our method of questioning.

(Heisenberg[9])

One unavoidable concept hidden inside complexity theory is that all knowledge is bound by the context of its generation. This is tricky because it challenges the centrality of an objective notion of truth, which underpins much scientific theory. The idea that order emerges from complex interactions has been termed 'social constructionism' – literally, truth is constructed through social interaction. Shotter describes in a very accessible way the role of language in this process.[10] The research paradigm that accepts this understanding of natural processes is termed 'constructivism'. Guba gives an elegant summary of the different epistemological, ontological and methodological meanings in constructivism compared with post-positivism and critical theory.[4] These philosophical discussions are important to the practical application of complexity theory because they help to understand the role that different understandings of science can have.

In this short chapter further elaboration is not desirable, but we have at least to acknowledge that there is more to knowledge than scientific facts and the concepts of absolute objectivity and generalizability are contested. The concept of generalizability needs to be replaced with the more humble concept of utility or transferability – something may be useful or transferable, but we cannot assume this and we need to test it out. So facts, scientific evidence and top-down protocols are useful ways of starting conversations – they are food for thought and opportunities for reflective practice. Different research paradigms, such as qualitative research, quantitative research, action research and literature reviews, make different epistemological assumptions. Particularly in complex situations, a combination of all approaches can crystallize a rich picture.[11]

Between 1998 and 2002, I was director of the West London Research Network (WeLReN). This was set up following the principles of organizational learning, with multiple learning spaces, feedback loops and facilitation at interfaces to help people develop relationships. The data show that this approach was particularly effective at engaging a diversity of people to become involved.[12]

Here are some of the things we did to apply the principles of complexity/whole-system theories:

- Facilitate multidisciplinary research teams to reflect on why they were interested in a research topic, and what difference this would make to their own lives and to the local evolving story of healthcare. We would encourage the groups to refocus the research question to incorporate the interests of other team members. This would frequently result in richer research questions than anyone had thought of at the outset and also lasting friendships across disciplines.
- Encourage, and fund, research of different paradigms, and wherever possible connect research projects of different paradigms (e.g. qualitative and quantitative and action research). This resulted in people becoming more aware of the whole picture of local healthcare rather than merely their own research project. Some researchers became enthusiastic developers and local leaders. It seemed to unleash in some a desire to understand the system as a whole.

Between 1989 and 1995, I was a facilitator for primary care in Liverpool. There I learned that when people participated in the process of reflecting on evidence and the needs of the whole system, energy for change was unleashed and fast progress made. It was as though everyone involved came to understand why their own actions would make a difference to the whole, and from this became motivated to act. Through workshops, feedback and multidisciplinary leadership, we undertook a large number of whole-system projects. For example:

- *Practice nurse employment.* In 1989, I sent a series of bulletins to all GPs in the city asking about their development priorities. I amalgamated these and sent them back to the same people for further prioritization. It was a form of Delphi exercise. Among the many priorities identified, the employment of practice nurses was particularly frequently mentioned. The Family Practitioner Committee (FPC) was also keen on this because the imminent new GP contract would not work without practice nurses. There were at that time only eight practice nurses in a city of 110 practices. We held a conference to explore with people from different sectors how we could together change this situation. Representatives from Liverpool University Departments of Nursing and General Practice, the Local Medical Committee, GPs, nurses and FPC managers attended. We fed back progress to everyone over time. We kept the conversations going in a variety of ways, identifying new practice nurse issues and finding ways of solving them. Within two years there were 110 practice nurses employed (a 14-fold increase) and they all had appropriate job descriptions. We had set up the first UK practice nurse mentor scheme and these mentors had their own dedicated learning set. The university practice nurse course was completely updated and took three times the number of students. Practice nurses attended and led multidisciplinary, geographically based educational meetings. And there was no sense of panic. It all happened like a well-oiled machine and people hardly seemed to notice.
- *Whole-system dialogue and cross-sectoral leadership.* This formula of allowing priorities to emerge through ongoing dialogue that have broad-based grassroots support and enabling cross-sectoral leadership is an application of complexity/whole-system theories. We repeated this approach with many other issues, for example the Occupational Health Project developed in collaboration with trade unions. The GPs were paid nothing and had no contractual obligation to do this sort of work, but one-half of all practices joined in. Patients were interviewed in the waiting rooms by lay health workers and data were fed back to the practitioners. On another occasion, an alliance between the Medical Audit Advisory Group and the Family Health Services Authority Advisor (the FPC became the FHSA before it became part of the health authority) oversaw new contract arrangements for health promotion – every practice in the city was represented at the same event as a multidisciplinary team and each, in small groups, worked out audits of 'quantity, quality and consensus' (different inquiry paradigms) for later

implementation. On another occasion, we brokered a city-wide consensus about how to improve heart disease with high-profile agreements between the health authority, local businesses, the local authority, the universities, the trade unions and voluntary groups. We later facilitated a similar broad consensus about the future of learning in primary care. Each of these resulted from a mechanism that made parts and wholes relevant to each other – mechanisms that helped people to find their useful contribution to the whole healthcare effort.

- *Local multidisciplinary facilitation teams.* Mechanisms that assist formal and informal crossing of established boundaries are needed to harness diverse enthusiasm for change. They permit challenge by different views and trusted relationships that assist whole-system collaboration. The corner shop, the Christmas party, the corridors at conferences, the pub after work all are places where relationships are made across boundaries. We attempted to make this boundary crossing easier by forming four local multidisciplinary facilitation teams to cover over half of the practices in the city. Between 1993 and 1996, five individuals of different disciplines were appointed as teams, each to facilitate development in a cluster of about 20 general practices.[13] They held a series of multidisciplinary educational events within and between practices on their patch, and made formal and informal contacts with different disciplines. A dedicated university course and facilitators from the Medical Audit Advisory Group supported the teams. This was a rich project that revealed both how difficult and how enabling it can be to work with complex interacting agendas. There were multiple successes of broad thinking and collaborative action facilitated by these teams. But it also revealed how difficult it is to develop and maintain collaborative practice with large numbers of people of different disciplines.

All of these examples required dialogue and participation throughout the whole system of concern. Also, people from a diversity of perspectives in this system were involved in reflecting on their own experience, creating a new idea and testing the idea out in practice. I recognize this to be a transferable principle of success that I call *whole-system participatory action research.* By this I mean that perspectives from throughout the system of concern are involved at all stages of the research/development process.[14]

Facilitators of such projects must create pathways to enable this. Large numbers of people with diverse perspectives can be involved by defining a cycle of activity with places that are open for people to enter (pathways), and places that are closed. This provides a heartbeat of opening out to engage large numbers of people with ideas about priorities, and a closing in to focus on the priorities identified, with multidisciplinary coalitions leading the next stage – like carrying the Olympic flame, different people take part at different times but all share a common purpose.

At the next opening out, the 'learning community'[15] reflects on feedback from the previous cycle before reforming ideas in the light of changing contexts. This mechanism allows progress to be made, but also for that progress to be modified in the light of learning along the way. A variety of traditional research projects can find valuable places inside this process, providing increasingly rich insights. I find it takes four or more cycles before people start to see the value of this heartbeat and welcome it. There are not many situations in primary healthcare that have the luxury of going through so many cycles. However, general practice and PCTs are two places where it would be easier than most to institute such long-term cycles of whole-system reflection and action. The new primary care structures therefore offer potential for whole-system operating never before possible.

What primary care organizations can do

In April 2002, all of England adopted the new structure of PCTs. These replace the role of health authorities and community trusts and relate to geographical areas of approximately 250 000 people, served by something like 60 general practices. The PCTs, and their equivalent primary care organizations in Scotland and Wales, will be responsible for research and clinical governance throughout the whole area. About five to eight PCTs will comprise a sector served by a strategic health authority. One PCT in the sector will lead on behalf of the others for learning and one for research. This provides for the first time a shared patch to which those who serve personal lists and those who serve populations (e.g. public health) can both relate. The potential for developing robust connections for services, education and research has never been greater.

It remains to be seen if the optimists are right – that these new organizations will lead a renaissance of generalist practice where diseases are considered in the context of a whole human being, as well as strong public health and social care. Presently there are more pessimists who say that the PCTs will collapse under the strain of having to do too many things with too little capacity at too fast a pace. I believe that ideas arising from complexity and whole-systems thinking potentially offer ways to an optimistic future. It will be through connecting diverse efforts that success will come and complexity/whole-system theories are theories about connections.

There are many things that a PCT could do to enhance complexity/whole system theories:

- *Explore the theories and evaluate their application.* We in the health service are overly used to linear and hierarchical ideas about the world. People find the whole-system idea attractive, but they shy away from the theory and practice. Some of this is understandable – did *you* relate as easily to the paragraphs in this chapter about theory as well as you did to the examples? But without theory and experience there can be no widespread application. So the PCT can agree at board level the intention to make relevant to each other different quality programmes, including research, education, clinical governance and organizational development. They can also explain this to their constituencies. But without people with the understanding and experience to lead it, people who will argue that the messy, iterative process is an essential part, it is likely to remain wishful thinking. PCTs must invest in their staff to understand things at a deeper theoretical level if the words are to translate into practical policy.

- *Include whole-system theory and practice in leadership courses.* PCTs will need to commission courses to develop their leaders. They can insist that courses include whole-system ideas. The idea of the leader as a knight in shining armour needs to be replaced by the idea of the leader as a sense maker within complex adaptive systems. Places such as the Open University that have been teaching this for years could supply distance learning courses and local organizations can facilitate local learning sets for the students, thereby bringing together high-level theory with high-level local knowledge and local networking for leaders.

- *Promote models that show connections.* A directory of local services could be written to show how different organizations connect. A diagram can show how the meetings of an organization connect, and how decisions go from one to another and are then fed back to all.

- *Develop cycles of inquiry and pathways between different PCT functions.* All practitioners could be asked through email what are priority themes for development and these themes could be adopted by a variety of PCT functions for the subsequent year, including research, audit and organizational development. Care pathway research, interface audits and multidisciplinary audits could help understand the whole system. Cross-committee representation can aid synchronous working. Whole-system events can assist complex integration of effort. Practitioners could be encouraged to develop part-time involvement in activities that serve local PCT interests, so that informal networks and personal development happen at the same time.

- *Synchronize research and development policy across a sector.* The Research PCT and Teaching PCT within a strategic health authority could devise shared strategy for whole-system research, organizational development, clinical governance and learning. Their facilitating teams and administrators could perhaps share office space and databases. Pathways could be created to allow medical, nursing and management students from local universities to engage in PCT/general practice audit and research. A book could be written to describe the whole sector as a case study of health service delivery – this could be a reference for students and practitioners to better understand the whole system. 'Research and development practices' could be developed rather than separate research practices and teaching practices. Better connections between their different accreditation schemes could be made.

Conclusion

Complexity theory challenges PCTs to take a lead with the theory and practice of joined-up thinking. But their overwhelming agenda may doom them to fail. The challenge goes beyond PCTs to challenge academic and organizational development bodies to develop strategies that help everyone to work for the system as a whole. Universities need better ways of resourcing participatory approaches to research. Hospitals and specialists need better ways to help patients understand their multiple problems. Politicians need better models of community participation and empowerment. We all need to develop a better balance between long-term sustainability, that requires complexity thinking, and short-term projects, that can often get away with simple, traditional, linear understandings of the world.

References

1   Launer J (2002) *Narrative-based Primary Care: a practical guide*. Radcliffe Medical Press, Oxford.
2   Schön DA (1983) *The Reflective Practitioner*. Maurice Temple Smith Ltd, London.
3   Bullock A and Trombley S (1999) *The New Fontana Dictionary of Modern Thought* (3e). Harper Collins, Glasgow.
4   Guba E (1990) *The Paradigm Dialog*. Sage, Newbury Park, CA.
5   Weick KE (1999) That's moving: theories that matter. *Journal of Management Inquiry*. 8 (2): 134–42.
6   Senge P (1993) *The Fifth Discipline*. Century Hutchinson, London.
7   Huxom C (1996) *Creating Collaborative Advantage*. Sage, London.
8   Argyris C and Schön DA (1978) *Organisational Learning*. Addison-Wesley, Reading, MA.
9   Capra F (1997) *The Web of Life*. Flamingo, London.
10 Shotter J (2000) *Conversational Realities: constructing life through language*. Sage, London.
11 Janesick VJ (2000) The choreography of qualitative research design. In: Denzin N and Lincoln Y (eds) *Handbook of Qualitative Research* (2e), pp. 379–99. Sage, Thousand Oaks, CA.
12 Thomas P and While A (2001) Increasing research capacity and changing the culture of primary care: the experience of the West London Research Network (WeLReN). *Journal of Interprofessional Care*. 15 (2): 133–9.

13 Thomas P and Graver LD (1997) The Liverpool intervention to promote teamwork in general practice: an action research approach. In: Pearson P and Spencer J (eds) *Promoting Teamwork in Primary Care: a research-based approach*. Arnold, London.

14 Whyte WF (1991) *Participatory Action Research*. Sage, New York.

15 Wenger E (2000) Communities of practice and social learning systems. *Organization*. 7 (2): 225–46.

CHAPTER 28

Using complexity science in community health promotion: novel perspectives and a tool for change

Vivian S Rambihar

This chapter describes how insights from chaos and complexity theory were used as tools for change in a number of projects involving community heart health promotion over the past decade. The approach was used to initiate change and explain causation within a framework of evidence adjusted to context. These projects were amongst the first of their kind to translate complexity theory into practice.

Key points
- Chaos and complexity insights can be used as an organizing, management and leadership science in health promotion projects.
- The traditional hierarchical command and control is replaced with the concepts of autonomy, adaptation, creativity, self-organization and distributive structure.
- Fractals are used to describe disease patterns and as a model for identity and diversity.
- Four health promotion projects are described with an emphasis on cardiovascular health.
- Heart disease was seen as an emergent property of non-linear dynamic interactions of intrinsic and extrinsic factors.

Introduction

Individuals and populations interact within complex frameworks of social, economic and healthcare systems that shape their health and well-being.[1,2] Chaos and complexity theory offers us insights into the unpredictable but boundable future that emerges from these interactions.

The term *chaos* is used interchangeably with *complexity* in this chapter, to mean all ideas arising from chaos theory, and includes order and disorder intertwined. As the only term available at the onset of this project in 1990, *chaos* was used and referenced in the ensuing publications, presentations and books referred to in this chapter. In time, *chaos* has become more associated with disorder and the newer term *complexity* with order or emergence. The term *complexity* is used in this chapter, consistent with the usage in this book as 'the qualitative study of non-linear systems, drawing upon the metaphors that chaos theory offers'.

As a community cardiologist, I have been involved with prevention of heart disease for over 20 years with particular interest in health promotion to the sizeable South Asian community in Toronto and elsewhere. I had been aware for some time that the organization of prevention programmes used an outdated model that saw scientific evidence and recommendations disseminated through rigid structures to achieve desired and predictable outcomes. There was little feedback and adaptation to local needs and unique circumstances. Health promotion related more to the available resources and quality of the healthcare professionals who offer expert advice. Cultural sensitivity about alternative methods of learning and achieving change were not explored and training and policy implementation did not reflect local context. Risk analysis data used to guide prevention were not representative of the population's experience, but directly transferred from other populations without considering context. The impact of subtleties, nuances and small inputs was not recognized or explored. In summary, the trajectory of intended health promotion was considered predictable and predetermined.

By the early 1980s, I had recognized that health promotion was not reaching the people who needed it most with sufficient impact. The focus was on behaviour rather than interaction, and both content and context appeared external and foreign to the targeted population. Barriers relating to knowledge, insight and confidence prevailed and the needs of the providers seemed to be served more than of the population in need. The older models of causation used for teaching and prevention were at odds with the experience in the community of surprise, variability, uncertainty and a web of causation. Exposure to newer ideas on interactive and patient-centred learning at McMaster University Medical School alerted me to alternative perspectives. By 1988, after reading James Gleick's *Chaos: making a new science* and other chaos material, I recognized that chaos provided a scientific basis for the introduction of novel ideas and practice.[1-4]

This chapter describes a decade-long experience with chaos and complexity applied to healthcare across a number of programmes, with a focus on preventative heart care. The South Asian component of these programmes will be emphasized in this chapter, since it illustrates the ideas better.

The context of heart disease in South Asians

South Asians worldwide have higher rates of heart and vascular disease than expected from the usual risk factors.[4-7] Migration to western countries and urbanization expose all communities to an adverse lifestyle and environment for which they may not be adapted. South Asians seem to be more sensitive to this, developing obesity, adverse lipid profiles, high blood pressure, prediabetes and diabetes, with consequent high rates of heart and blood vessel disease.[4-7] Clustering of risk factors and elevated levels of emerging risk factors such as homocysteine and Lp(a), which amplify risk (a non-linear response), are found in migrant South Asians.[4,6] Also, an intense tradition and culture among South Asians encourages a high-fat, refined carbohydrate diet; little physical exercise (especially among women); high stress levels from migration, assimilation and acculturation; and for some, the acceptance of a somewhat fatalistic approach to health. Strong cultural, religious and community influences maintain resistance to the erosion of heritage and tradition.

Recognition of biological, social and other non-linear interactions and greater degree of emergence of heart disease in this community should guide newer and more effective prevention strategies. With limited research data in this population, treatment and prevention should be adjusted according to context and, guided by evidence used in context – a chaos-based approach.[2-4]

Applying complexity theory to community healthcare projects

Numerous complex adaptive systems interact to shape the health of individuals and populations. These co-evolve with each other and with the environment in a constant dance of change,[4,8] reshaping themselves and the surrounding world. Such systems are intertwined in society and culture, improving or diminishing health in both subtle and overt ways. Highly visible examples are the fast food industry, cigarette lobby, alcohol promotion, fitness groups, sports clubs and community activities, and various systems involving culture, custom and tradition.

To reflect the complex characteristics of the community, health promotion systems were developed that were non-hierarchical, emphasizing distributive structure, with self-organization, flexibility, a small number of simple rules and adaptation.[1-4] No formal organization was established. Community leaders, religious leaders, teachers, healthcare professionals and anyone else interested were invited to take health promotion messages and resources to their communities at various levels. A network of individuals and organizations informally shared ideas, which were allowed to evolve and self-organize without formal structure. The few rules used were:

- promote heart health using existing resources
- adapt to local needs
- use innovative and creative ideas
- create and use new resources where necessary.

The organizational emphasis was on diversity, creativity and autonomy. Uncertainty and unknowability were accepted and surprise anticipated, with improvisation and innovation encouraged. Ownership of the process was shared, to offer everyone the opportunity to influence change. The project was multilayered with flexible, variable, autonomous or shared involvement.

A chaos-based or evidence-based in context approach was used to transfer evidence to the individuals and subgroups to guide prevention.[2,4,9,10] The validity of evidence-based practice and decision making was considered dependents on the nature, source and strength of evidence, and the degree of fit when extrapolating to individuals or subgroups not represented or different from the group studied. For instance, the heart risk of South Asians is underestimated in the commonly used risk tables derived from the Framingham study, which did not include South Asians. In the context of absence of South Asian-specific risk analysis data, and the recognition of higher rates of premature heart and blood vessel disease, more aggressive prevention and treatment targets were used for South Asians at risk and for other individuals or subgroups whose risks were considered underestimated. A modification of the Stacey practice diagram, which maps the degree of certainty and validity of practice on a background of complexity, establishes this use of evidence in context as chaos and complexity based.[9]

Causation and determinants of heart disease were explained from a non-linear dynamics perspective, with 'strange' predictability but expected surprise and some uncertainty, rationalizing the experiences observed in the community and guiding prevention practice. The impact of nuances, subtleties and small changes was emphasized, especially in communication. The novel ideas of fractals, chaos and complexity were introduced and found to be useful, not only in the organization of health and in understanding the complex dynamics of health and society, but also as a tool for change. Print and video images of simple fractals were shown and described in relation to nature, using examples of tree branches, ocean waves and waterfalls to illustrate self-similarity and irregular, dynamic, stable patterns. Metaphors of sand piles and the last straw breaking the camel's back were used to illustrate self-criticality in plaque rupture in heart attacks, and this analogy was extended to social, economic and political systems. Images of networks, ecosystems, global health and the butterfly effect were used to illustrate sensitive dependence, interconnectedness and webs of causation.

Understanding heart disease in the South Asian community using complexity theory

As a very diverse, migrant community in transition with strong culture, tradition and heritage resistant to change, the South Asian community has developed strong interconnections, structures and functions characteristic of complex adaptive systems and should benefit from a chaos and complexity approach to the organization of health promotion.

The high rates of heart disease observed across the wide diversity of South Asian communities were considered an emergent property, related to a sensitivity or susceptibility to westernization and migration, with implications for different strategies for prevention.[1,4] The distribution of the South Asian population and thus of high rates of coronary artery disease in South Asians in self-similar, but slightly different patterns worldwide were seen as fractal with consequent need for a fractally distributed targeted health promotion. For example, South Asians in the US, despite high rates of coronary artery disease, may be denied necessary targeted health promotion, being included for statistical purposes in the lower risk category of Asian and Pacific Islanders, rather than seen as fractal elements with unique needs within the larger community. Fractals also became a model for the ever-changing belonging and identity that define individuals and subpopulations, and their diversity within diversity, which generates inhomogeneity and determines individual needs.[1,2,4]

Complexity-based community health projects

Four projects within the programme are described that have taken place over the past two decades:

- Annual Valentine's Day heart health event
- South Asian Heart: preventing heart disease
- South Asian Heart Month
- Diversity and health.

Annual Valentine's Day heart health event

This type of event was completely different from community health events at the time, which consisted mostly of formal lectures on predetermined topics, fixed audiovisual aids, with interaction limited to few questions at the end and essentially little active participant involvement. Attendance at those events was usually poor, retention of information little, and continued involvement and interest absent.

An interactive, agenda-less, shared learning experience open to everyone was used to focus on heart health promotion on Valentine's Day. The format changed in response to feedback. Nutritionists and fitness, nursing and medical personnel facilitated audience-driven discussion after a brief update. This evolved into a two-hour drop-in event with topics changing every 15 minutes. Participants joined in the fitness sessions, viewed the displays and enjoyed heart-healthy snacks. They were invited to take these ideas to their communities, forming a network with influence beyond the time and place of the event.

This annual event raised awareness of heart health in the wider community in an interactive and participative way. People attending felt ownership of this process and were encouraged to do similar events in their spheres of influence in widening circles. Feedback was extremely positive and the event has continued on demand for 20 years so far, validating the methodology responding to need.

Imagery and metaphors from chaos and complexity captured the imagination of participants, conveying more vividly and realistically the dynamics of healthcare. Complexity science became a tool for change for individuals and the community and was used to explain the unpredictability and surprise observed in everyday living. Using complexity science in this fashion for organization, and to explain how and why things happen at a personal and meta-level, rejuvenated excitement and interest in heart health.

South Asian Heart: preventing heart disease

This ten-year project, first started in 1990, responded to a need in this community for targeted health promotion to reduce high rates of heart disease reported. Ideas on health promotion were planted in the community with few and simple rules, and resources made available. Local health promotion activities were allowed to self-organize around simple concepts and desired outcomes, seeking to tap into the benefit of 'order for free', and flexibility and improvisation were encouraged. Established guidelines were adapted to offer earlier and more aggressive prevention, while awaiting research data.

Innovation and improvisation were encouraged in changing the aspects of culture, customs and tradition that increased heart risk, reaching deep into the community at multiple levels. This entailed tapping into community links and strengths, through not only structures but methods of function. In addition to seeking health promotion through established structures and organizations like places of worship, schools and health seminars, health messages were sent by word of mouth to families and friends attending social and other functions, and at shopping plazas and businesses, and cultural and other events not traditionally associated with health promotion. Network connections and random contacts amplified information transfer and the spread of ideas through what is now recognized as the power of linkages, the 'small world' phenomenon and information cascades in complex systems.[11-14]

The complexity-based aspects of this project were similar to those for the other projects described. Community events, including a South Asian Heart Health Fair, were open-ended and participant driven with interactive discussions. Panel discussions featured an interdisciplinary team responding to questions rather than lecturing. Innovation at the fair included South Asian songs for heart and linkage of heart health information to South Asian interests such as cricket. Women and children, who traditionally did not attend such events, were specially invited and involved. Snacks provided were heart-healthy and participants were challenged to improvise similarly and share ideas widely for an improved South Asian cuisine. A later initiative used internet technology to create self-organizing networks for sharing information across the diaspora worldwide, similar to its usage in health promotion reported by Munnecke and Wood,[15] and also used random and network connections to amplify benefit.[11-14]

South Asian Heart Month: from 2002

This more recent project is experimental, further testing the use of complexity ideas in health promotion and in a novel method of healthcare organization without borders.

A 'Make May South Asian Heart Month and every day South Asian Heart Day' campaign arose out of the South Asian Heart Project. This was linked to the proclamation in 2001 of May as South Asian Heritage Month in Ontario. Rather than seek proclamation of a South Asian Heart Month, this idea was planted and circulated to test interest. If such a proposal was thought to be useful, there would be spontaneous self-organization across the community worldwide to make it happen. No specific events would be planned centrally, but any initiatives emerging would be supported and resources provided, such as brochures, patient-oriented books, websites, etc. A Fractal Heart Foundation was established in 2003 to intensify these efforts.

In this experiment in healthcare organization, no strategic plan was devised, just simple ideas left to self-organize. This was much like planting idea viruses or cultural memes, anticipating 'tipping points'[16] in the emergence of new behaviour and function, using the 'order for free' available to complex systems. Selected Heritage Month events were used as a launching pad for these ideas, which should spread in the networks of weak and strong links and random contacts, essential for spread of ideas. The internet was used to invite network dissemination of these simple rules and concepts, described in simple brochures made freely available.

Innovative ideas are required to overcome strong, ingrained habits resistant to change, and the idea that health and social activities are separate. 'Two Minute Heart', proposing a two-minute discussion on heart health at all Heritage Month events, and at all South Asian social and cultural events is a small initiative hoping to achieve this. Another initiative invites everyone to provide heart-healthy choices for friends and guests at social functions, anticipating a spontaneous self-organization towards improved nutrition across the community. Organizations are also invited to show that it is possible to overcome the difficulties related to traditional catering, pre-set menus and resistance to change, in providing heart-healthy choices at their events, illustrating leadership by example.

Diversity and health

Complexity science was used as the organizing methodology for this two-year project, which included monthly, agenda-less, participant-directed, interactive meetings on diversity and health and quarterly special events with invited speakers. Initially designed open-ended, it was ended after two years since the stated objectives were achieved, the discussion was becoming repetitive and the facilitators were assigned other priorities in the midst of a hospital amalgamation. Whether or not it would have been self-sustaining beyond this period is uncertain. This project changed attitudes on diversity, and specifically ethnicity, and created an environment where ethnicity and race could be discussed openly for the first time. Diversity and health issues became an accepted part of healthcare discussions. The format was interactive and the agenda, direction and outcome allowed to self-organize. Health professionals, patients and members of the public participated equally, guided by a facilitator. Discussions and interest continued beyond the time and space of the meetings, extending in fractal-like patterns of overlapping dynamic networks. Emergent ideas were transferred to community and clinical practice.

An ever-changing, non-hierarchical, interdisciplinary, complex dynamic group interaction emerged. Information was disseminated and education provided in a shared learning, rather than a teaching, environment. Participants spontaneously assumed leadership, ownership and responsibility for the process and outcomes. Changed thinking influenced clinical practice and community events, leading to further research, publications and lobbying for change.

Topics discussed varied from women and health, native people's health, the homeless, traditional healing, diet across cultures, smoking and young women, ethics, support systems, the impact of culture, customs and belief systems on health, to global issues and individual responsibility as well as the utility and validity of diversity in health research and discussion. There was improvisation in exploring these topics, such as patient narratives and a slide-show of homeless people set to mood-enhancing music. The importance of nuance, subtlety and small changes in influencing outcomes, especially in communication between patients or the public and healthcare personnel, was emphasized.

The concepts of fractals, chaos and complexity were used in the organization of health, in understanding the complex dynamics of health and society, and as a tool for change.

Conclusion

Four projects within a complexity-based health programme have been described, illustrating the use of complexity science in healthcare organization. Common features of these projects were distributive structure, emphasis on interactions and interrelationships, creation of networks, the use of improvisation, open-ended discussion, agenda-less meetings directed by participants, diversity of opinions, autonomy, self-organization and emergence from few and simple rules. Interdisciplinary dialogue developed and networks with strong and weak ties and random contacts were established. Complexity science was also used as a powerful tool for change and a lever to amplify small inputs. Uncertainty, unknowability and the unexpected were accepted and anticipated, leading to learning methods to deal with inevitable surprise. A chaos and complexity perspective was used to explain causation of heart disease and the 'strange predictability', surprise and uncertainty observed. Evidence was adjusted according to context to guide prevention in a chaos-based or evidence-based in context approach.[2,4,9,10]

This project is the first we know of to use chaos and complexity in health.[1-4,9] It ventured into unknown territory, first recognizing the relevance of chaos and complexity to medicine, health and nursing, then using the ensuing novel ideas for leadership, management, organization and as a tool for change. The experience shows that complexity science could be used in healthcare organization and should be explored in the pursuit of innovation and improvement of health and healthcare. Recent developments in complex systems related thinking, such as the power of networks, random and network connections, the small world phenomenon,[11–14] the internet,[15] idea viruses, cultural memes, tipping points[16] and information cascades,[12] hold promise for even much greater benefit from the use of complexity science in health promotion and healthcare organization.

Acknowledgements

The author thanks Dr D Jagdeo, J Wilson, Y Vali, L LeBlanc, D LeBlanc, C Caryer, E Howes, R Bodrug, and the many others involved for their enthusiastic support and tremendous courage to venture into the unknown territory of chaos and complexity in its early days, to dare to think differently that chaos and complexity can be used to make a difference and can be applied to health, and to make it work. The author also thanks Vanessa Rambihar for manuscript preparation and The Scarborough Hospital for providing the staff, facilities and support, without which this project would not have been possible.

References

1 Rambihar V (1996, 2000) *CHAOS 2000 From Cos to Cosmos: making a new medicine for a new millennium.* Vashna Publications, Toronto.

2 Rambihar V (2000) *A New Chaos-based Medicine Beyond 2000: the response to evidence.* Vashna Publications, Toronto.

3 Rambihar V, Wilson J, Vali Y et al. (1999) Chaos 2000: a new science for nursing for the new millennium. *Complexity and Chaos in Nursing Journal.* 4: 35–8.

4 Rambihar V (1996) *South Asian Heart: Preventing Heart Disease. From the heart to the edge of the diaspora, from the heart to the edge of chaos.* Vashna Publications, Toronto.

5 McKeigue, Miller, Marmot et al. (1989) Coronary artery disease in South Asians overseas: a review. *Journal of Clinical Epidemiology.* 142: 597–609.

6 Anand S, Yusuf S, Vuksan V et al. (2000) Differences in risk factors, atherosclerosis, and cardiovascular disease between ethnic groups in Canada: the Study of Health Assessment and Risk in Ethnic Groups. *Lancet.* 356: 279–84.

7 Bhopal R (2002) Epidemic of cardiovascular disease in South Asians: prevention must start in childhood [editorial]. *BMJ.* 324: 625–6.

8 McDaniel R and Driebe D (2001) Complexity science and health care management. *Advances in Health Care Management.* 2: 11–36.

9 Rambihar V (2003) *Discovering Chaos and Complexity in Medicine, Health, and Everything Else.* Vashna Publications, Toronto.

10 Rambihar V (2000) Science, evidence and the use of the word scientific [letter]. *Lancet.* 355: 1730.

11 Watts D (1999) *Small Worlds: the dynamics of networks between order and randomness.* Princeton University Press, Princeton, NJ.
12 Watts D (2003) *Six Degrees: the science of a connected age.* WW Norton and Company, New York.
13 Barabási A-L (2002) *Linked: the new science of networks.* Perseus Publishing, Cambridge, MA.
14 Buchanan M (2002) *Nexus: small worlds and the groundbreaking science of networks.* WW Norton and Company, New York.
15 Munnecke T and Wood H (1995) *Creating an Epidemic of Health with the Internet.* Available at www.vvaleo.org/papers/EOHInternet.htm.
16 Gladwell M (2000) *The Tipping Point: how little things can make a big difference.* Little, Brown, New York.

Epilogue:
being vaguely right rather
than precisely wrong

Organizational theory is an area hedged with constraints, intermediate positions, arguments, and counter arguments characterized by the common perception that organizations are linear, reductionist and deterministic systems over which there is political and managerial control. Experience suggests that this may be wishful thinking.

Complexity theory certainly offers useful models and metaphors that resonate with the way that practitioners and healthcare managers see the world. And we should take note when disparate disciplines converge to similar themes. Some commentators herald a revolutionary science that offers 'new perceptions of reality with profound implications for science, philosophy, healthcare, education, business, politics and everyday life. An overarching account of how processes work'. However, others see it merely as 'the emperor's new clothes – merely articulating good sense' or 'a compendium of misapplied metaphors for the credulous healthcare manager on an inadequate budget'. Perhaps it is all just a harmless articulation of homely values emphasizing that we should all be nice to each other? Only time will tell. But in the meanwhile, what can we hold on to? What sense can I make of it all?

When I first started general practice over 20 years ago, it was with the confidence of a medical scientist. With the application of science to medicine, the essential truth of the world could be discovered and consolidated. My healthcare interventions were to be directed by explicit guidelines derived from rigorous enquiry. The age of certainty had arrived in healthcare.

Ten years later, disappointment. Attempts at applying a rational framework to an inherently irrational process was falling short of expectation. Decisions were being made on the basis of the very confounding factors that the randomized controlled trial of medical science sought to avoid. I became a healthcare engineer (engineer: Latin *ingenium* – clever at contriving), using the scientific map but with a degree a pragmatism, empirical observation and intuition. The shift was from the pursuit of truth to honesty, seeking results that were good enough, not optimum.

Ten years again, I have put away my engineering toolbox. I have become a healthcare bricoleur (bricolage: French – the art of making do), using whatever practical tools and materials are at hand supported by a theoretical rag bag – an assortment of models and metaphors tucked away on the principle that something may come in handy some time, and approaching each problem by framing and reframing it in a way that is dependent on context and local perspective. My resources may be less well suited to the project in hand but they are all I have. Perhaps this book is just a bricoleur's rag bag.

If nothing else, complexity theory alerts us to the fact that there are no quick policy fixes or any easy way to integrate analytical techniques to participatory processes. Over 60 years ago, the economist Keynes suggested that 'we need to invent wisdom for a new age and that in the meantime, we must appear unorthodox, troublesome and dangerous'. The science of complexity may or may not be this new wisdom that we seek. If it only sensitizes us to the interplay of patterns that perpetually transforms our systems against all attempts to the contrary, it may just help us to do things a little better. What is irrefutable is that the dominance of linear orthodoxy has been challenged.

Appendix 1:
Some complexity metaphors

The following metaphors can be found in the organizational literature. However, they have been developed in biological, chemical and physical systems and should be interpreted with caution when applied to human organizations.

Auto-catalytic sets
Catalysis is an action that speeds up a process. Auto-catalytic sets are systems in which one element catalyses the interaction of others, which in turn catalyses the original element. For example, A catalyses B, B catalyses C, C catalyses D and D catalyses A. Auto-catalytic interaction creates order and can describe how organizations and networks emerge. Networks come together by identifying niches for themselves which would not normally have been planned.[1]

Auto-poesis
The concept of auto-poesis[2] was derived from cellular biology. Auto-poetic mechanisms serve to enhance the stability of systems through self-referential feedback loops. Such systems have no task, goal or purpose other than maintaining their own identity. The notion of auto-poesis is useful in understanding the nature of single cells but there is disagreement as to whether it can be applied to other living systems.

Dissipative structures
A fundamental principle of physics and economics is that systems tend towards equilibrium. Yet reality and experience show that a system working away from equilibrium will thrive and be more innovative. A dissipative framework was described by Prigogine[3] from observations of chemical/physical systems. The classical model was the phenomenon of convection and the behaviour of a fluid as heat is progressively applied to its base. Energy (or information) is imported from the environment, moving the system through a range of attractors. Bifurcation points occur with spontaneous self-organization that cannot be predicted from the nature of the component behaviour. The system may disintegrate into instability, expelling energy, or leap to a new level of order that

requires more energy (or information) to sustain it. Dissipative structure theory differs from chaos in that a dissipative system has an internal capacity to change spontaneously.

Fitness landscape

The concept of fitness landscape was first introduced by Wright in 1931.[4] It represents a two-dimensional possibility space showing the locations of the global maximum (highest peak) of fitness and the global minimum (lowest value). Systems are seen as evolving across a landscape of peaks and valleys. The peak represents a fit and adaptive position whereas the valley represents a low level of fitness or maladaption. Evolution is a process where the aim is to move out of the valleys to the highest peak in a landscape that is continually changing.

From a biological perspective, natural selection keeps evolution moving towards peaks but with periodic disasters into unknown valleys along the way. From a complexity perspective, the emphasis is on co-evolution with, rather than adaptation to a changing environment.

References

1   Kauffman S (1995) *At Home in the Universe: the search for the laws of self-organization and complexity*. Oxford Univesity Press, New York.
2   Maturana H and Varela F (1980) *Autopoesis and Cognition: the realization of the living*. Reidel, Dordrecht.
3   Prigogine I (1997) *The End of Certainty: time chaos and the new laws of nature*. The Free Press, New York.
4   Wright S (1931) Evolution in mendelian populations. *Genetics*. **16:** 97–159.

Appendix 2:
Cynefin domains

Kurtz and Snowden[1] suggest a four-domain model to support organizational decision support and strategy. The focus is on how people in organizations perceive and make sense of situations in order to make decisions, and also on the types of component connections most prevalent in each domain.

Knowledge is seen both as a flow and a concrete entity. It improves decision making and creates the conditions for innovation. The channels through which knowledge flows are as important as knowledge itself.

This model emphasizes the importance of boundaries in sense making and has been used successfully in a number of organizational contexts. It is designed to allow shared understanding to emerge through multiple discourses of the decision-making group.

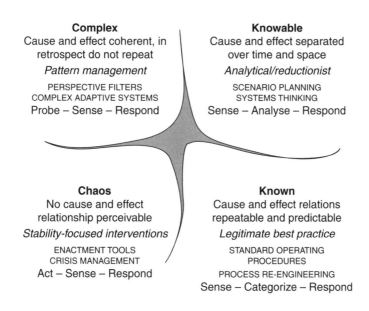

Figure A2.1 The Cynefin model domains (reproduced with permission).

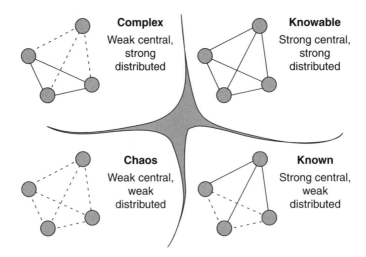

Figure A2.2   The Cynefin model connection strengths for each domain (reproduced with permission).

Reference

1   Kurtz C and Snowden D (2003) The new dynamics of strategy: sense making in a complex world. *IBM Systems Journal*. **Fall**.

Glossary of complexity terms

Adaptability
The extent to which a system can change in response to environmental changes.

Agents
The name given to the elements that interact in a complex system.

Attractor
An area of state space in which all trajectories in its vicinity are drawn.

Bifurcation
The point in which there is an abrupt change in behaviour of a dynamic system when one of the parameters reaches a critical value.

Capability
The facility of individuals and their organizations to generate new knowledge and continuously improve performance by using feedback.

Cellular automata
Programs for generating patterns on a computer according to rules specified by the programmer. They are precisely defined but have dynamic quality that leads to features of complexity that can be studied.

Chaos
The behaviour of a system that appears random but when studied in a particular way, ordered features and patterns are discernible. These chaotic patterns form the signature of non-linear behaviour that arises from recursive feedback among a system's components, i.e. the output of one stage feeds back into the input of the next.

Co-evolution
When agents change they change their environment and the agents are in turn changed in a reiterative process. Agents cannot be separated from each other or their environment.

Complex system
A system that is interconnected such that change in one agent changes the context for all other agents.

Complexity theory
The study of how elements interact within a non-linear network.

Deterministic system
A system that is predictable at any time if its initial conditions and describing equations are known.

Dynamic system
A system in which the state of its variables changes with time and is dependent on what has gone before.

Edge of chaos
A region of non-linear system that is associated with rapid self-organization and optimal adaptation. Connections are neither too loose and extensive nor too tight and limited. Also known as self-organized criticality.

Efficiency
From a biological perspective, a measure of the energy expenditure needed to change in response to changes in the environment. From an organizational perspective, obtaining the most out of limited resources, either by achieving a given output from the minimum possible input or producing the maximum possible from a fixed resource.

Emergence
Patterns emerge from the interaction of system agents that cannot always be predicted and which informs the behaviour of the agents within the system and the behaviour of the system itself. For example, a termite hill has a maze of interconnecting passages and spaces. Yet there is no grand plan – the hill just emerges as a result of the termites following a few simple local rules.

Fractal
A system that has detailed structure that repeats itself at many scales. This is a feature of chaotic systems.

Iteration
A process in which the solution of an equation is fed back into the original equation as a new initial condition.

Linear system
A system in which the relationship between input and output varies in a constant fashion.

Nested systems
Complex systems are nested within other systems and many systems are systems of smaller systems. For example, the health centre within the primary care organization within the health authority within the NHS.

Phase space
The area of space that contains the range of values that can be found for a particular system.

Random behaviour
Behaviour that can never be predicted but can only be described by statistics such as mean and standard deviation.

Recursive feedback
The output of one stage of a system feeds back into the input of the next. (*See* iteration.)

Reductionist
An approach to understanding a system by breaking it down into its component parts. The behaviour of the whole can be inferred from its parts.

Self-organization
A process whereby a dynamic system reorganizes its structure so that it can more effectively cope with environmental demands through the process of emergence and feedback.

Self-organized criticality
See edge of chaos.

System
A collection of components that communicate with one another to produce an output which transcends the output of the components standing alone.

Trajectory
The path of travel of a system in phase space with time.

Useful resources

- www.complexityprimarycare.org
  The spiritual home of this book.

- www.trojanmice.com/
  The home site of book contributor Peter Fryer. Clear, pragmatic information about complexity and its application to organizations.

- www.calresco.org/applicat.htm#med
  A wide range of links to many areas of complexity.

- www.healthcomplexity.net
  A health group based at the University of Exeter.

- www.complexity-society.com/
  The Complexity Society provides a focal point for people in the UK interested in complexity.

- www.plexusinstitute.org
  An American organization designed to foster the use of complexity science in improving the health of private and public organizations. Good links and discussions.

- www.lse.ac.uk/lse/complex/
  The home page of the London School of Economics Complexity Group Network.

- www.herts.ac.uk/business/centres.cmc
  The Complexity and Management Centre – an important UK centre for the application of complexity.

- www.societyforchaostheory.org
  A society with the emphasis on the psychological perspective.

- www.santafe.edu
  The Santa Fé Institute – the spiritual home of chaos theory.

Index

abstraction, simplifying 175–6
accountability
  Humberside TEC 292, 293
  and social capital 252
action, Miller's hierarchy 233, 234
adaptability 207, 353
  designing for 211–13
administrators 118
admissions clerk (Christie) 313, 314, 315–16
adult learning 230, 231
affordability 133
agent-based computer simulation 160, 161,
   162
  combined with whole-system working
    163–4
  practical example 168–9
agent-based working 130, 159–70
  practical example 164–9
  theoretical basis 161–4
agents (elements of complex systems) 27,
   353
  behaviour of individual 26–7
altruism 250
analytical method 8
  destructive effects 28
andragogy (adult learning) 230, 231
anxiety, and performance 234–6
appointments
  same-day 148, 152
  waiting times in general practice 56, 145,
   148
appointment systems
  general practice 145, 148
  QSD/QPID approach 55–6, 145–8
appraisal
  Humberside TEC 295
  in self-directed learning 231
appropriateness 132
artefacts
  cultural 107
  symbolic 176–9

arts
  performing 130, 181–8
  visual 130, 171–9
assumptions, cultural 108
attractors 19, 20, 32, 353
  chaotic or strange 18, 19
  health systems 19, 32
  housing project for elderly 303–4
  periodic 17
  point 17
  working with 122–4
audit 133
  clinical 61, 63, 192
auto-catalytic sets 349
autonomy, in learning 231
auto-poesis 349

Baddely, Alan 258
Bandura, A 228, 256
Beacon and Old Hill estate project 279–87
  background 279–80
  complexity perspective 283–6
  process 281–3
behaviourism 258
benefits, in economic evaluations 209,
   211
Bible, English 257
bifurcation 17, 353
Biggs 3P model of learning and teaching
   235
Bohm, David 184
boids 72, 161
boundaries
  complex systems 27
  critical care services 219
  facilitating relationships across 330
  setting 122, 123, 165
bounded rationality 45, 135
brain metaphor 85
Bristol Royal Infirmary 108
buddying, in general practice 194, 195

budgets, removal of   295–6
butterfly effect   27

café, centrally sited   294
capability   228, 353
  basic human   228, 229
  education for   227–40
  improving individual   62
capital   246
  see also social capital
cardiovascular disease   249
CATWOE framework   51–2
causality, in SD diagrams   145, 146
celebration of success   65
cellular automata   353
change
  critical care services   223
  cultural   108–11
  first-order   108
  organizational *see* organizational change
  second-order   108
chaos   15–16, 353
  community health promotion and   336–7,
    343–4
  edge of *see* edge of chaos
  non-linearity and   16–18
chaos theory   2, 13–21
  insights and metaphors   31–6
chaotic state   34
clinical discretion   98, 99
clinical effectiveness   192
clinical governance   189, 191–204
  complexity insights   198–203
  components   192–3
  defined   192
  leads   193–4
  primary care
    implementation   192, 193–5
    routine challenges   195–8
clinicians *see* healthcare professionals
co-evolution   198, 219, 353
  clinical governance   200–1, 202–3
  community regeneration project
    285
  in partnership development   207
  teamworking   211–13
cognitive learning theories   258
cognitive mapping   52–4
cognitive systems, complex   25
collaborative interventions   98, 101
collective intelligence   318–20

Commission for Healthcare Audit and
    Inspection (CHAI)   252
Commission for Health Improvement
    (CHI)   192
communities
  building local   252
  methods of interacting with   251–2, 253
  patient   260, 262
  regeneration of deprived   275, 279–87
  see also Beacon and Old Hill estate project;
    networks
communities of practice   110, 242, 255–63
  healthcare and   259–60
  health informatics   260–2
  learning theories and   258–9
  live vs hypothetical   262
  PCT learning network   197
  structural elements   242
community health councils   252
community health promotion   276, 335–45
  applying complexity theory   337–9
  complexity-based projects   339–43
  context   337
competence   228, 233–4
  Miller's pyramid   233, 234
competition
  integration with co-operation   97–8
  in partnership development   207
complacency   65
complex adaptive systems   25
  basic characteristics   27–8
  boundaries   27
  clinical governance   197, 200
  computer modelling   161–2
  critical care   218–19
  elements *see* agents
  emergence and self-organization   28–30
  House for Life project   301–2, 309
  NHS   98–101, 219
  organizational change and   72–3
  personal perspectives   275–7
  Piedmont Hospital Bed Control Experiment
    311–21
  principles for managing   121, 122
  reductionist approach   28
complex cognitive systems   25
complexity   24
  approaches   25
  ordinary and emergent   125
  vs chaos   336
  zone of *see* edge of chaos

complexity engineering   40–1
  application   121, 122
complexity metaphors   10, 11, 349–50
  applied to organizations   30–6
  from chaos theory   31–6
  from other disciplines   30
complexity model   9–10
complexity perspectives
  allocation of healthcare resources   136–9
  clinical governance   198–203
  community regeneration project   283–6
  critical care   218–24
  doctor–nurse skill mix   211–14
  education   234–8
  healthcare provision   189–90
  leadership and change   119–27
  organizational culture   110–14
  organizations   30–6, 81–2, 88–9
  partnerships   265–73
  performing arts   182–3
  running an organization   289–98
complexity science   1–2, 72
  paradigm   9–11
complexity theory   23–37, 354
  applications in practice   275–7
  chaos and   2, 13–21
  insights from   198–9
  usefulness   347–8
complex responsive processes (of relating)
      25, 40, 73–8
  organizational change and   74–8
  theory   73–4
  vs systems view   74
complex social systems   25
complex systems   24, 25, 354
  adaptive see complex adaptive systems
  simple   25
  stable, chaotic and edge of chaos states
      33–6
  vs complicated networks   24
complicated networks   24
Comprehensive Critical Care (2000)   218, 219
computer modelling   160
  complex adaptive systems   161–2
confidence, building   293, 294
connectivity   29
  building   294, 330
  diagrams   332
  working with   320
constructivism   328
constructivist view of learning   229, 258–9

continuing professional development (CPD)
      60, 64, 233
  primary care   197, 202–3
  see also education; learning
continuity of care   149–50
co-operation
  integration with competition   97–8
  in partnership development   207
co-ordination
  in partnership development   207
  teamwork   209–11
Coronary Heart Disease (CHD), National
      Service Framework (NSF)   195–6
cost–benefit analysis, doctor–nurse skill
      mix   209–11
council, local   304, 305–6, 307–8
creative arts see performing arts; visual arts
creative skills, rediscovering   183–4
crime   280, 281, 283–4
critical care
  changes made   223
  as complex adaptive system   218–19
  Modernisation Agency programme see under
      Modernisation Agency
  networks   219
  recommendations   218, 219
critical system thinking   47
cultural strategy, defining   108
culture   106
  metaphor, organizations   85
  organizational see organizational culture
curriculum   232
  development   232
  emergence   197
  product and process   232, 233
cybernetics   44, 48
Cynefin domains   351–2

decision making
  in healthcare organizations   129–30
  resource allocation see resource allocation
      decision-making
  spectrum of frameworks   135–6
de-codification   185
depression   250
deterministic system   8, 15, 354
dialogue   29, 123
  agent-based working and   159–70
  hospital bed control project   320
  visual   175–9
  whole-system   329–30

direction pointing   122, 123
discovery interview   222
dissipative structures   349–50
diversion   312–13, 320
diversity and health project   342–3
Dobson, Frank   6
doctors
   clinical discretion   98, 99
   day of reflection   173–5
   erosion of leadership role   124
   hegemony   113, 114
   skill mix see skill mix, doctor–nurse
dog-waste bins   285–6
domination, organizations as instruments
      85
duality, new   198–9
Durkheim, Emil   249
dynamic systems   2, 9, 354

economic evaluation
   doctor–nurse skill mix   209–11
   limitations   210–11
   resource allocation   134
ecosystem metaphor   10, 11
   NHS   99, 100
   Piedmont Hospital Bed Control   314–15
edge of chaos (self-organized criticality)   29,
      198, 220, 354
   applied to organizations   33–6
   clinical governance and   199, 200,
      201–2
   doctor–nurse skill mix and   211, 212
   learning and   236, 238
   NHS operation   101
   organizational culture and   112–13
   resource allocation decisions and   132,
      136, 138–9
   Stacey diagram see Stacey diagram
   state   34–6
   surfer's wave analogy   35
education
   community regeneration project   282
   healthcare professionals   190, 227–40
      aims and methods   237–8
      competence, performance and action
         233–4
      complexity insights   234–8
      curriculum development   232, 233
   to increase social capital   251
   instrumentalist view   232
   PCT learning networks   197, 202–3

progressivist view   232
   see also continuing professional
      development; learning; teaching
effectiveness   133
efficacy   132
efficiency
   as attractor   32
   defined   206–7, 354
   designing for   209–11
   economic evaluation   209–10
   edge of chaos state   34
   resource decision making   133
elderly
   caring for   250
   House for Life project   276, 299–309
Eldon Square   300–1, 302, 305, 308
Elias, N   73
email   251
emergence   28–9, 219, 354
   community regeneration project   285
   education curriculum   197
   in healthcare organizations   129–30
   heart disease in South Asians   339
   management strategy   198–9
   partnerships   267–8, 272
   performing arts to facilitate   181–8
   resource decision-making   137–9
   visual arts to facilitate   171–9
emergency care networks   165
emergency care system see urgent care system
empowerment   65, 285–6
energy   303–4
environments
   building local   252
   community regeneration project   282
epistemology   325
equity   32, 133
evidence-based medicine   63
exercises   186
expert patients   251, 260

facilitators   173, 182
feedback   10, 29
   critical care programme   220–2
   hospital bed control project   318, 320
   Humberside TEC   294–5
   narrative   222
   negative (damping/stable)   27
   positive (amplifying/unstable)   27
   recursive see recursive (reiterative)
      feedback

'Feeling Comfortable with Feeling
    Uncomfortable' programme   292–4
Fillingham, David   102
A First-class service: quality in the new NHS   64
fitness landscape   350
five degrees of separation   247
Fordism   87
formal channels (rules)   110–11
    dissonance created by   113, 114
    interplay with informal rules   112–13, 120
formal organizational structures   111
Forrester, Jay   48
Foucault, M   125
foundation trusts   252
Fractal Heart Foundation   342
fractals   18, 354
    in community health promotion   338–9
    in organizations   32
    in performing arts   183, 185
Frome Medical Practice, patient access
    study   148–52, 155–7

games   186
garbage can model   34, 135
gender   107
general practice
    clinical governance *see under* primary care
    managerial problems   144
    patient access   130, 143–57
        Frome study   148–52, 155–7
        problems   144–5
        QSD/QPID approach   55–6, 145–8
Giddens, A   97
goals
    healthcare professionals   208
    learning   231, 232
    shared   319
goodwill   250
governance   189
    clinical *see* clinical governance
government, NHS leadership and   125–6
governmentality   125
Griffin, D   74, 75, 77–8
Griffiths Inquiry (1983)   96
group visits   251

Hadridge, Phil   199
hard systems   44, 46
    methods   46, 47–9
    role   57
    thinking   39–40, 87

health
    community-based promotion *see* community
        health promotion
    community regeneration and   282
    social capital and   249–50
healthcare
    communities of practice and   259–60
    post-normal   98–101
    resource decision-making *see* resource
        allocation decision-making
healthcare organization(s)
    allocating limited resources   131–42
    applying creative arts to development
        184–5
    building social capital   251–2, 253
    facilitating emergence   129–30
    vs commercial/industrial sector   94
    see also healthcare system; primary care
        trusts
healthcare professionals (clinicians)
    computer modelling   160
    day of reflection   173–5
    education   190, 227–40
    individual and collective goals   208
    skill mix   189, 205–15
    see also doctors; nurses
healthcare system
    complexity perspectives   81–2
    culture   106–7
    leadership objectives   118
    management aims   118
    policy development   95–101
    see also National Health Service
health informatics community   260–2
The Health of the Nation (1998)   27
health visitors   152, 281–2
heart attack   250
heart disease in South Asians   276, 336
    community health promotion   337–9
    complexity-based community projects
        339–43
    complexity-based understanding   339
    context   337
historical context   27, 33
holistic partnerships   266, 267
    ideal vision   268, 269
    problems   269–70
hospital bed availability project   276, 311–21
hospital drug purchasing system   52
House for Life project   276, 299–309
housing quality   280, 282

human activity systems (HAS)   44
human potential, belief in   65
Humberside Training and Enterprise Council
    (TEC)   289–98
    building on complexity model   292–7
    results of complexity approach   297
    reversing into complexity   290–1
    successor organizations   297–8
hybrid system problems   144
    QPID approach   145–8
hybrid systems   45

ID *see* influence diagram
image theatre   185–6
impartiality   8
improvisation   186, 187
incremental models, resource decision-making
    135
influence diagram (ID)   55, 145
    Frome patient access study   148–9, 157
    QPID approach   145–7
informal channels (rules)   110–11
    dissonance with formal rules   113
    interplay with formal rules   112–13, 120
information
    politics of control   257–8
    sharing   256, 260–2
information technology (IT)
    hospital bed control   316–18
    networks   251, 260–2, 341
initial conditions   18
    organizations   33
    recognition of importance   212
intelligence, collective   318–20
interdependency   29
internet   251, 260, 341, 342
iteration   354

jargon, simplifying   175–6

Kennedy Report (2001)   108
knowledge
    explicit   4, 5
    figurative   199
    mobility   65
    operational   199
    as power   257–8
    tacit   4, 5, 65
knowledge management   4
Kolb, David   221, 229, 230
Kuhn, Thomas   7

leaders
    covert and overt   126
    qualities   124–5
    role   124
leadership   81, 117–27
    complexity insights   119–22
    in complex systems   113–14
    courses   332
    cross-sectoral   329–30
    definitions   118, 119, 124
    to facilitate learning   327
    holding style   296–7
    in NHS   124–6
        government and   125–6
        transactional nature   113–14, 119
    objectives   118
    traditional theories   118–19
    transactional   113, 119, 121
    transformational   113–14, 120–2
Leadership Centre, NHS   119, 124
learning
    3P model   235
    about learning   61–2, 63, 67
    adult   230, 231
    complexity insights   235–6
    cycle   229–30
    deep   229, 230
    double-loop   61, 63, 66–7
    generative   220, 221
    levels   61–4
    lifelong   64, 231
    national quality framework and   64
    non-linear   236–7
    problem-based   63, 238
    reasons for developing effective   60–1
    role of reflection   221
    self-directed   231
    single-loop   61, 63, 66–7
    social and situated theories   259
    surface   230
    team   62, 67
    theories   229–31, 258–9
    transformative   238
    see also education; teaching
learning network, primary care trust   197,
    202–3
learning organizations   41, 60–4, 87–8, 326
    cultural values   64–6
    key features   62
lectures, formal   238
Le Grand, L   88

lifelong learning 64, 231
linearity–non-linearity balance 198–9
linear system 8, 355
Lipsky, M 112
list size adjustment 152
local rules 26–7
logical positivism 7
loops
  Frome patient access study 149–51
  goal-seeking 146
  in QPID 145–6, 147
  in QSD 55–6
  reinforcing 146, 149–51
Lyapunov exponent 15

machine metaphors 10, 85
  NHS 96, 100
management 117–18
  aims 118
  complex adaptive systems 121, 122
  complexity approach in practice 289–98
  general practice, problems 144
  hard systems approaches 47–9
  NHS approach 96
  rational/emergent approaches (new
     duality) 198–9
  soft systems approaches 50–6
  theory, classical 39, 86–7
managerial systems, nature 45
managers 118
  computer modelling 160
  day of reflection 173–5
  leadership role 124
mapping
  cognitive 52–4
  process 220–1, 223
  urgent care system 166–8
marginal analysis 211
market approach, NHS organization 96–7,
  100
Maslow's hierarchy of needs 88
mathematical methods, system modelling 46,
  47–8
meaning, in here and now 76
media 304
memory 29, 258
mental models 26–7, 160
  updating 62
mentoring 251
meta-learning (learning about learning)
  61–2, 63, 67

metaphors 6–7
  complexity see complexity metaphors
  consolidation within paradigms 7
  organizations 85
  visual 174
meta-theory 48
Miligram, Stanley 247
Miller's pyramid 233, 234
minor illness 150, 152
mistakes
  learning from 293
  tolerance 65
models 3–6
  complexity 9–10
  consolidation within paradigms 7
  external and internal consistency 5
  extrinsic 4, 5
  tacit 4, 5
Modernisation Agency 145, 189
  approaches to change 98, 102
  Critical Care Programme 217–25
    feedback methods 220–2
    results 223, 224
    using complexity insights 220
  on leadership 124
modernization agenda, NHS 98
multidimensional phase space 31–2, 214
multiplicity, partnerships 270–1, 272

narrative (storytelling) 5–6, 186
  -based primary care 325–6
  communities of practice model 259–60
  feedback 222
National Health Service (NHS)
  clinical governance see clinical governance
  as complex adaptive system 98–101, 219
  doctor–nurse skill mix 189, 205–15
  leadership see under leadership
  organizational culture 107–14
    changing 108–10
    complexity approach 113–14
    defining a strategy 108
    reductionist approach 107–8
  organizational framework 81, 93–103
    complexity approach 95, 98–101
    historical context 95–8
  resource decision-making 132–40
National Institute for Clinical Excellence
  (NICE), decision-making framework
  139
National Performance Framework 64

National Service Frameworks (NSFs),
    introduction 195–6, 201
nested systems 27, 355
networks 241
    complex *see* complex systems
    complicated 24
    see also communities; *specific types of*
        networks
The New NHS: modern, dependable (1997) 97
NHS *see* National Health Service
NHS Modernisation Agency *see* Modernisation
    Agency
The NHS Plan (2000) 71, 102, 144–5,
    228
    Modernisation Agency 217–18
    skill mix development 208, 214
Nightingale, Florence 39–40
non-linearity 2, 9, 14–15
    chaos and 16–18
    community regeneration project 284–5
    complex systems 27
    educational systems 234–5
    linearity balance 198–9
    trajectory with time 19
non-linear learning 236–7
nurses
    controlling bed access 313–14
    practice 152, 329
    role expansion 206
    skill mix *see* skill mix, doctor–nurse

occupation 107
O'Neill, Anora 252
open-access systems 145
openness 65
open systems thinking 62
operational research (OR) 44
Oregon experiment 134, 250
organism metaphor 85
organization(s)
    complexity perspectives 30–6, 81–2,
        88–9
    formal and informal channels 110–11
    metaphorical interpretations 85
    running, along complexity lines 275,
        289–98
    spectrum of thinking about 39–41
    systems approach 43–58, 87
    Weber's classification 86
    see also healthcare organization(s);
        management

organizational change 69–79
    complexity approach 72–3
    complex responsive processes of relating
        and 73–8
    dominant systems view 71–2, 74
    garbage can model 34
    leadership and 117–27
organizational culture 81, 105–15
    changing 108–11
    complexity perspective 110–14
    integrated or differentiated 107
    learning organizations 64–6
    reductionist perspective 106–10
    three-layered framework 107–8
organizational learning 41, 59–68, 87–8
    primary care organizations 326–7
organizational theory 83–91
    complexity approach 88–9
    healthcare 93–103
    historical perspective 86–8
    limitations of current 86
    traditional 84–5
    traditional vs complexity perspectives
        89
Ouchi's model 95, 97
outcomes, in economic evaluations 209,
    211
outward looking 66

paradigm(s) 7
    modern or normal science 7–8
    post-normal or complexity science 9–11
    shift 7
participation 256
partnership development model 207–8
partnerships 242, 265–73
    emergence 267–8, 272
    holistic view *see* holistic partnerships
    multiplicity 270–1, 272
    relationality 268–70, 272
patient(s)
    access in general practice *see under* general
        practice
    communities 260, 262
    expert 251, 260
patient-centred healthcare 95, 98
    limitations 99, 101
patient–healthcare professional unit 99
performance, health professionals 233–4
    assessment 234
    complexity insights 234–6

performance management   98
performance measures (targets)
  adverse effects   99, 101–2
  Humberside TEC   295
  real-time   320
  social capital and   252
  systems view   71–2
performing arts   130, 181–8
  development of healthcare organization
      184–5
  expressing complexity   182–3
  image theatre   185–6
  rediscovering creative skills   183–4
periodic behaviour   15
phase space   19, 20, 355
  multidimensional   31–2, 214
physicians see doctors
Piedmont Hospital Bed Control Experiment
      276, 311–21
  context   312–13
  evolution vs transformation   315–18
  initial bed control procedure   313–15
  reflection   318–21
plan-do-study-act (PDSA) cycle   88, 221
planning, future   75–6
play   183–4
Plsek, P   31, 72, 121, 123
pluralist systems   46, 47
policy makers, recognition of complexity
      125–6
political system metaphor   85
positivist systems   46, 47
'possibility space'   18
post-modernism   8–9
post-modern perspective, resource
      decision-making   135–6
post-normal healthcare   98–101
post-normal science see complexity science
poverty   279–80
power   84, 85
  to commit   294
  constraints on change   74–5
  decision-making and   137, 138
  formal/informal organizational
      channels   111, 112
  knowledge as   257–8
  skill mix change and   212
  systems approach and   45
  transformational leaders   120
power-law scaling   35
practice nurses   152, 329

predictability
  formal/informal organizational
      channels   111, 112
  non-linear systems   18
  skill mix development and   208, 214
primary care
  applying complexity theory   276,
      323–4
  clinical governance   192
    complexity insights   198–203
    embeddedness   194
    implementation   193–5
  communities of practice model   259–60
  doctor–nurse skill mix   209, 210–11
  narrative-based   325–6
  organizational learning   326–7
  research and development   327–31,
      332–3
  subcultures   32, 213
  see also general practice
primary care trusts (PCTs)
  enhancing complexity/whole system
      theories   331–3
  introducing National Service Frameworks
      195–6
  learning network   197
principles, shared   29
priority-setting   134
problem-based learning   63, 238
process mapping   220–1, 223
profit   32
psychic prison metaphor   85
purchaser–provider split   97
purpose, importance of   302–3
Putnam, Robert   247–8

qualitative politicized influence diagrams
    (QPID)   47, 55–6, 130, 144
  hybrid system problems   145–8
  patient access in general practice   148–53,
      155–7
qualitative system dynamics (QSD)   46–7,
    55–6
quasi-market framework   97, 100, 122
queuing theory   48

random behaviour   15, 355
rationality   135
  bounded   45, 135
  management strategy   198–9
rationing, healthcare   130, 131–42

receptionists
  clinical   151
  skills loops   150–1
receptive context   198
  clinical governance   200–2
  community regeneration project   283–4
reciprocity, House for Life project   305, 308
recodification   185
recursive (reiterative) feedback   10, 355
  chaos theory and   16–17
  in complex systems   27
redesign, service   98, 99–101
reductionist   8, 355
  approach to complex systems   28
  approach to NHS policy   98
  approach to organizational culture
      106–10
  redundancy, built-in   294
reflection   221, 231
  day of   173–5
reflective practitioner   325–6
reflective space, creating   179
reification   256
relationality, partnerships   268–70, 272
relational practice   184–5
research and development, primary care
      327–31, 332–3
resource allocation decision-making   130,
      131–42
  approaches   133–5
  complexity insights   136–9
  emergence   137–9
  explicit and rational   134
  implicit   134
  open and transparent   134
  public systems   132–3
  spectrum of frameworks   135–6
resource providing   122, 123
responsibility, taking   292, 293, 294
Rogers, E   123
rule-based relationships   162
rules
  local   26–7
  simple see simple rules
  of thumb   122, 167
  see also formal channels; informal channels
run-chart   221
Ryle's 'ghost in the machine'   258, 260

sanctions   248
satisficing behaviour   45, 135

scale invariance   35
Schön, DA   99, 221, 325
science
  classical (modern; normal)
    challenge of post-modernism   8–9
    paradigm   1, 7–8
  post-normal see complexity science
self-directed learning   231
self-organization   28, 29–30, 198, 355
  clinical governance   200–1, 202–3
  community health promotion   340–2
  localized, community regeneration
      285–6
  professional teams   211
self-organized criticality see edge of chaos
Senge, Peter   326
separation, five degrees   247
service redesign   98, 99–101
Shaw, P   187
simple rules   72
  classification   122, 123
  in complexity theory   31, 32
  facilitating emergent decision-making
      138
  housing design project for elderly   306–7
  working with   122–4
skill mix, doctor–nurse   189, 205–15
  designing for adaptability   211–13
  designing for efficiency   209–11
  model for analysing   207–8
  need for differences   213–14
  shift from individual to collective goals
      and   208
small-step change methodology   221
social and situated theories of learning
      259
social capital   241–2
  complex systems and   249
  defined   247
  developing concept   247–9
  influence on health   249–50
  interventions to increase   251–2
  measures   248
social constructionism   328
social networks   241, 245–54
  social capital and   249
social norms   248
social systems, complex   25
social workers   152
society   246
socio-economic class   107

soft system methodology (SSM)   47, 50–2
soft systems   44, 46
   methods   46–7, 50–6
   role   57
   thinking   40, 87
South Asian community, heart disease *see*
   heart disease in South Asians
South Asian Heart Month   341–2
South Asian Heart project   340–1
specialization   107
stable state   33
Stacey, RD   72–3, 112, 182
   complex responsive processes of relating
      73–4, 78
Stacey diagram   35–6, 198
   anxiety and performance   235–6
   clinical governance   200, 201–2
   decision making   136
stakeholders
   interactions, in decision making   137,
      138–9
   role in cultural change   109
storytelling *see* narrative
strategic options development and analysis
      (SODA)   47, 52–4
street-level bureaucracy   112
stress   173–4
subcultures
   hegemony   113
   NHS   107
   primary care organizations   32, 213
success, celebrating   65
suicide   249, 250
supertanker metaphor   6
Sure Start scheme   251
symbolic artefacts   176–9
symbols   5
system(s)   44, 355
   characterization   45–7
   complex adaptive *see* complex systems
   perspectives on whole   241–2
   taxonomy of methods   46–7
   view of organizational change   71–2, 74
system dynamics (SD)   48–9, 145
   see also qualitative politicized influence
      diagrams; qualitative system
      dynamics
system engineering   44
system response   44
systems theory   39–40, 43–58, 87
systems thinking   326

targets *see* performance measures
Taylorism   86–7
teaching
   3P model   235
   classical model   232
   complexity insights   235–6
   progressivist view   232
   tools and techniques   237–8
   see also education; learning
team(s)
   characteristics of agile   212
   learning   62, 67
   local multidisciplinary facilitation   330
   multidisciplinary governance   194, 195
teamworking
   co-evolution   211–13
   co-ordinated   209–11
   improving   70, 77
   shift to   208
telephone
   time wasted on   314, 315
   triage   151
tension   182
thinking and learning skills programme   293
thrombolytic therapy   123
trajectory   355
triage, telephone   151
trust   65
   community regeneration project   284
   enabling cultural change   109
   Humberside TEC   292
   organizations with high and low   109–10
   in partnerships   266–7
   social capital and   248, 252
Tyndale, William   257

unemployment   280
unlearning   63–4
urgent care system
   agent-based working example   164–9
   exploring   166
   making a difference   168–9
   mapping exercise   166–8
   meaning and purpose   165
   setting boundaries   165

Valentine's Day heart health event   340
values
   cultural   107
   transformational leaders   120
vandalism   281, 283–4

vision
    organizational   62, 120
    team, importance of shared   212
visual arts   130, 171–9
    creating reflective space   179
    pausing for day of reflection   173–5
    using visual dialogue   175–9
volunteering   251

waiting lists
    complexity perspective   10, 20, 101
    dysfunctional effects of targets   113
    supertanker metaphor   6
waiting times
    dysfunctional effects of targets   113, 119
    general practice appointments   56, 145,
        148
    hospital bed assignment   313, 318, 319
walk-in centres, NHS   211, 213
Watson, John   258

websites
    hospital bed control   316–18
    useful   357
Weltanschauung   52
Wenger, E   256
West London Research Network (WeLReN)
    328
whole-system participatory action research
    330–1
whole-system working   161, 162–3
    combined with agent-based simulation
        163–4
    partnerships   271
    practical example   299–309
'wicked problems'   45
Winter and Emergency Services Team
    (WEST)   165
Working for Patients (1989)   96–7

zone of complexity see edge of chaos